The Responsibilities of Power, 1900-1929

SOURCES IN AMERICAN HISTORY

GENERAL EDITOR: *George H. Knoles*

Professor of History and Director of
the Institute of American History,
Stanford University

The Responsibilities of Power
1900-1929

Edited by George Harmon Knoles

Stanford University

The Free Press, New York

Collier-Macmillan Limited, London

Foreword

Historians in the United States are inclined in their writing about the American past to select certain movements or events to indicate dramatic or radical departures in the direction which the course of history takes. This tendency reflects an apocalyptic approach to the periodization of history in which the scholar sees earth-shaking consequences in wars; constitutional conventions; treaties; specific elections; new inventions and techniques; and, on occasions, novel ideas. We talk of the Jeffersonian, the Jacksonian, and the Rooseveltian revolutions. Or we write books about "the new United States," or we pose theses arguing that such and such years or decades mark great watersheds dividing periods of history one from another. Perhaps this sort of thing has merit when as scholars we turn to teaching, for education and learning owe much to the functional organization of factual material. One should, however, recognize that there are dangers in overdramatizing events and movements we employ as teaching devices. History is not like the flow of a river with straight stretches and sharp bends; quiet, slow-flowing sections and rushing rapids, dikes and waterfalls. As Lionel Trilling once observed, "a culture is not a flow . . . the form of its existence is struggle, or at least a debate—it is nothing if not a dialectic."

In the essay and selections that follow I have tried not to overstress the uniqueness of the period, 1900-1929; indeed, one of the reasons for having one volume cover this range of years instead of devoting two books to the period—one covering the years, 1900-1920 and one confined to the 1920's—was to stress the continuities rather than the discontinuities inherent in the thirty-year span of time. One will note, however, that some of the documents chosen for inclusion were written by men who sensed that the United States after 1900 had radically shifted direction and was headed into unknown and untried paths some of which were surely fraught with danger.

It is to be hoped that the student in using this book will gain a closer insight into some of the issues and problems that confronted the generations of men and women who came to maturity in these thirty years. Some of the questions bubbling to the surface in the ferment of those years achieved solutions of one kind or another in the period or after; some continue to plague us as a people and as individuals.

Stanford University   GEORGE HARMON KNOLES

Contents

The Responsibilities of Power, 1900-1929

Introduction

Bʀᴏᴏᴋs ᴀᴅᴀᴍs (1848-1927) sʜᴏʀᴛʟʏ ᴀꜰᴛᴇʀ ᴛʜᴇ
Spanish-American War (1898) noted that the war
represented "one of those memorable revolutions wherein
civilizations pass from an old to a new condition of equilibrium."
The "forces of energy and wealth," he observed, were shifting
from England to the United States, and the United States "must
assume the responsibilities and perform the tasks which have
within human memory fallen to England. . . ." Adams, along
with American historians generally, probably overstated the case
for a radical shift in direction resulting from the war because the
continuities in our history are stronger and more persistent than
the discontinuities. He did, however, sense the challenge which
faced the country as it entered the new century. Destiny, Adams
asserted, had decreed that the United States should achieve
supremacy in the affairs of the world; "but supremacy has always
entailed its sacrifices as well as its triumphs, and fortune has
seldom smiled on those who, besides being energetic and industrious, have not been armed, organized, and bold."

Adams was one among many Americans during the opening
years of the present century who recognized that a new United
States was in the making and that a reorganization of society
might be necessary in order to bring forms into harmony with
realities. The nation, Adams warned, should shake off the craven
fear of becoming great—"timidity never yet averted disaster . . .
safety comes from an intelligent appreciation of situations as
they arise. . . ." This kind of self-conscious soul-searching produced an active public debate among statesmen, politicians,
journalists, and others as they sought to define the national purpose and elaborate national goals. Titles such as *The Old Order*

Changeth, The New Democracy, and *The Promise of American Life* suggest the mood of the quest.

Such a search seemed eminently fitting. Dramatic changes had occurred during the half century preceding 1900. Expansion across the plains and beyond the Rocky Mountains completed the occupation of the continent. Economic growth, despite a Civil War and two severe depressions, transformed the country from an agricultural-commercial society to a dynamic industrial nation. Millions of Americans deserted their rural homes to join other millions of immigrants from Europe to swell the urban population in cities across the land. Not since the days of President Monroe had Americans been as conscious of the world beyond the seas; acquisition of an empire and a sphere of influence followed in the wake of the Spanish-American War. For the first time in its history the nation faced unfamiliar colonial problems. The new territories—the Philippines in the Far East, the Hawaiian and other Pacific islands, and Cuba and Puerto Rico in the Caribbean—challenged the statesmanship as well as the diplomatic skill of American leadership.

Intellectual controversy accompanied these changes; ideas jostled one another in the active give and take of argument. Liberals and progressives attacked conservative laissez-faire doctrines and espoused interventionist principles. The atmosphere seemed charged with the electric enthusiasm of those who stood ready to devote their energies to the reordering of American society. "The wealth exists to pay for democracy," one of the young publicists cried. "Our dreams are not idle. We are not a poor people who need to fill our minds with gorgeous and impossible visions. . . . We can enter upon social works to transform our sooty life into something more worthy of our dignity."

American Colonialism

The United States had come into being partly as a result of a failure of British leadership to accommodate economic and political institutions to the requirements of a growing empire. The United States' initial experience as a colonial power involved the organization of a continental domain contiguous to its expanding borders and scantily occupied by human beings. As part of the spoils of victory following the Spanish-American War the United States took possession of the Philippine Islands and the island of Puerto Rico and assumed a protectorate over Cuba. Responsibility for these former Spanish colonies immersed the United States in problems for which its earlier history afforded no clear directives. The new territories were not contiguous to the United States; they lay overseas—in the case of the Philippines 6,000 miles from California. Instead of vacant or sparsely settled lands, the recent acquisitions already supported substantial populations speaking languages unfamiliar and in some cases unknown to the conquerors. Moreover, the new areas had little or no knowledge or tradition of self-government. The new domains for the most part lay in the tropics and were not objects of heavy immigration from mainland America. Assuming the white man's burden, therefore, meant that the United States undertook to direct the destinies of about 10 million people of differing races, languages, cultures, and levels of achievement devoid of any attachment to or appreciation for Anglo-Saxon principles of self-government. But the age was an ebullient one, and the United States did not lack leaders who were willing and anxious to try their hands at governing an empire.

In the case of Cuba, the anti-imperialists, not an inconsiderable body, succeeded in pushing through a self-denying ordinance as a concomitant to the declaration of a state of war with Spain. The Teller amendment (1898) to the war resolution adopted by the Congress declared that the United States had "no disposition or intention to exercise sovereignty, jurisdiction or control over Cuba except for its pacification." The Cubans were to enjoy the privileges of independence and self-government. Following the war the United States established a military government to bridge the gap between defunct Spanish control and independent Cuban administration. Cuban authorities who had drawn a constitution modeled after that of her liberators reluctantly accepted the status of an American protectorate the terms of which were spelled out in the Platt amendment (1901) and regularized in a treaty between the United States and Cuba (1903).

In the ensuing years the economic life of the new nation improved, and trade between the United States and Cuba increased rapidly while Americans heavily invested in Cuban sugar, tobacco, mines, railroad, and other public utilities. The United

States intervened on a number of occasions in Cuba to maintain political and economic stability. Eventually, for a variety of reasons including a realization that policy might be pursued by less obvious and distasteful means than military intervention, the United States terminated the protectorate in 1934 by formally abrogating the Platt amendment.

The island of Puerto Rico, not subject to the Teller amendment, was more closely tied to the United States. Following a brief interlude of military government, Congress under the Foraker Act (1900) made Puerto Rico an unincorporated territory of the United States and gave its people a government with a Puerto Rican elected House of Representatives, an Executive Council named by the President of the United States to serve as an upper chamber of the legislature, and a Governor General appointed by the American President. Congress during the Wilson administration conferred American citizenship upon the Puerto Ricans and granted increased measures of self-government. Improvements in levels of living followed upon the establishment of political stability. Yet Puerto Rico remained a problem child for several decades. Only in more recent years have massive efforts been made to improve the economy and conditions of living.

The United States converted the Caribbean into a sphere of influence and exerted its power in a number of instances to preserve its pre-eminent position there. The construction of the Panama Canal and the need to protect this vital link between the two coasts of the United States imparted a strategic importance to an area already of considerable economic and political significance to the United States. Diplomacy, military and naval force, and economic and political pressure were all used to advance American interests in this region.

The Philippine Islands presented an even greater challenge to American ingenuity, for no thought had been given to the Philippines as a possible colony of the United States prior to 1898. Here were 7,000 tropical islands lying more than 6,000 miles west of San Francisco with 7 million people speaking 87 languages and displaying the whole range of cultural development from primitive savagery to sophisticated European civilization. The seizure of the archipelago came almost as an afterthought (see Ray Ginger, ed., *The Nationalizing of Ameri-*

can Life, 1877-1900 in this series); but once decided upon, it became necessary to organize a colony.

The United States inherited a bloody and protracted war for independence when it acquired the Philippines. The Filipino patriots early in 1899 had declared their independence, established a republican form of government patterned after the United States, and elected a president in the expectation that the United States would recognize their government as the sovereign power in the Philippines. Instead the Americans branded the movement an insurrection and proceeded to crush it. On July 4, 1902, President Roosevelt proclaimed the end of the war for Philippine independence.

In the meantime, the United States had already commenced to organize a civil government for the islands. President McKinley announced basic American policy in January, 1899: "The Philippines are ours, not to exploit, but to develop, to civilize, to educate, to train in the science of self-government. This is the path of duty which we must follow or be recreant to a mighty trust committed to us." He sent a commission in April 1900, headed by the capable administrator William Howard Taft, which organized a civil government. Congress in 1902 passed an Organic Act giving the Filipinos a constitution and making the Philippines an unincorporated territory of the United States.

Following pacification considerable progress was made toward improving the economy, sanitation and health, communications, and the education of the people. Taft succeeded in negotiating a settlement with the Roman Catholic Church for the acquisition and redistribution of 400,000 acres of land owned by religious bodies. Moreover, sufficient steps were taken in the direction of self-government so that Congress authorized the establishment of an elective legislative assembly which held its first meeting in 1907. Its opening provided an occasion to summarize and weigh the results of American tutelage [1].*

Both of the American political parties were committed to independence for the Philippines; disagreement arose principally over the question of when the islanders were ready to assume autonomy. Additional measures of self-government were granted during the Wilson administration, but the Republican adminis-

---

*Numerals within square brackets denote the number of the selection cited in this book.

trations of the 1920's proceeded slowly and cautiously. Despite the hesitancy of the government to move faster, pressure mounted within the United States in support of independence. Particularly vocal were those who found the competition of Filipino producers of sugar, fats, and fibers in the American market distasteful. Responding to some of these pressures which grew more insistent during the depression and reflecting the long-time concern of the Democratic Party in Philippine independence, the New Deal in 1934 initiated a program leading toward full autonomy for the islands by 1946. World War II intervened to complicate the situation, but on July 4, 1946, the transfer of sovereignty was effected.

An unheralded although significant shift in the character of American foreign relations occurred during and following World War I. In the first two decades of the twentieth century colonial problems were primarily political in nature, and political solutions were uppermost in the minds of those charged with the responsibility of administering an empire. That the United States succeeded in organizing self-government in its colonies and granting them self-determination reflects a basic idealist strain in the American character as well as a strong commitment of the American people to the idea of the mission of America. After 1920 colonial problems were primarily economic in nature, and as such they became more subtle and less obvious—at least less obvious to the home folks. As a consequence Americans in general no longer thought of themselves as a colonial power and found it difficult to understand the cries from around the world to mount a crusade against American imperialism. Today colonialism and imperialism are dirty words, and we tend to shy away from suggestions that we may still be engaged in exercising control over other peoples. But, no such hesitancy hampered leaders like Henry Cabot Lodge, Theodore Roosevelt, Elihu Root, and William Howard Taft at the opening of the present century. They felt something of the same sentiment voiced by one of their contemporaries, Albert J. Beveridge: "It is a glorious history our God has bestowed upon His chosen people. . . . We cannot fly from our world duties; it is ours to execute the purposes of a fate that has driven us to be greater than our small intentions. We cannot retreat from any soil where Providence has unfurled our banner."

Economic and Social Change

American agriculture in the two decades after 1900 enjoyed a golden age. Domestic and foreign markets expanded in response to the general prosperity of the country and to the insatiable demands of World War I for food and fibers. Farm produce, valued at $4.7 billions in 1899, reached $19.3 billion in 1920. Despite farm prosperity, however, the proportion of rural to urban dwellers dropped markedly; in 1900 over 60 per cent of the population lived in the country, but by 1920 less than half of the American people—48.8 per cent—lived in rural areas.

Even more startling developments occurred in industry. Wage earners almost doubled in number while wages increased five times and the value of output grew sixfold. Meanwhile the size, power, and scope of business organizations expanded so rapidly that it frightened the public into demands for controls. Consolidation of enterprises on a national scale, underway at an increased pace since the 1870's, reached a peak in the early years of the twentieth century. The organization of the United States Steel Company in 1901 with a capitalization of $1 billion symbolized the climax of this early period of business growth.

Among the more significant consequences of economic development was an increase in wealth. New sources of power applied to machines supplied by advances in technology produced an increased flow of goods and services. The national wealth of the country, which in 1900 was about $88.5 billion, by 1917 had leaped to $351.7 billion. The national income was by no means distributed equally among the nation's families, for while the poor probably were not growing poorer, the rich certainly were growing richer. The first years of the century, unlike the last decade of the nineteenth century, were a period of rising prosperity and, perhaps more important, of rising expectations. Reflecting some of the latter, conditions of living and working slowly improved as reformers and unions exerted pressure upon governments and employers.

Important demographic changes also occurred during the first two decades of the twentieth century including a substantial increase of the population—nearly 30 million; a decline in the rate of population growth; a quickening of Negro migration northward; an enlarged influx of immigrants; and a continuation of internal mobility. The westward movement of population persisted as a long-term trend despite the announcement in the 1890's that the frontier as a region ceased to exist. On the other hand industry, rather than agriculture, after 1910 became the determining factor in the internal migration of our population. The ethnographic complexion of the nation increased in complexity as millions of new immigrants poured into the country— an average of 1 million a year during the first 15 years of the twentieth century. By 1920 close to 14 million foreign-born, nearly 12 million Europeans, lived in the United States. The huge influx of newcomers revived latent nativist tendencies among the older groups who supported movements to curtail unrestricted entry into the United States.

Urbanization, another long-term trend, continued at an accelerated pace in response to industrialization and the expansion of commerce. Urban population grew by 38.8 per cent between 1900 and 1910 and 28.8 per cent between 1910 and 1920. Two fifths of the new city dwellers were immigrants, a little less than a third came from rural America in response to the lure of the city, while one fifth were new births; less than 10 per cent became urbanites as a result of annexation of fringe areas. Urbanization was a phenomenon affecting all sections of the country, although the greatest concentrations were north of the Ohio River and east of the Mississippi River. Cities generally were unprepared to meet the new influx; feverish growth produced festering slums—dirty, insanitary, poorly ventilated, inadequately served by government and public utilities. Cities were not a new phenomenon in America; but they exerted a powerful fascination as well as attraction for the nineteenth- and twentieth-century Americans who flocked to them by the millions. Deserting their more prosaic and cramped rural surroundings for the bright lights and opportunities of urban centers they brought with them codes of morality and standards of ethics imbued in them by a still vigorous evangelical protestantism. The newcomers were both enchanted and shocked at what they saw—the city sinister contended against the city of light in their thinking. It is not suprising, therefore, that authors penned such books as Lincoln Steffens' *The Shame of the Cities* (1904) on the one hand and Frederic C. Howe's *The City: The Hope of Democracy* (1905) on the other. Urban reformers sprang to the barricades to end some of the more blatant practices of the existing power structure, then referred to as "the system"—defined by Webster as "The combination of a political machine with big financial or industrial interests for the purpose of corruptly influencing a government."

The Revolt Against Formalism

Changes such as these in American life engendered a ferment that affected all levels of society. The confusions and complexities of living in an atmosphere of uncertainty evoked a varied response. Woodrow Wilson complained in 1897 that it was no longer easy to be human; "haste, anxiety, preoccupation, the need to specialize and make machines of ourselves have transformed the once simple world. . . ." Others sought to escape into one retreat or another. The more typical response of the intellectuals was to subject society to a critical analysis, define problems, propose solutions, then act, using government or private agencies to direct change into more socially desirable channels.

The poet Edwin Markham had startled his contemporaries with "The Man with the Hoe" [2]. In those few lines he described, warned, and prophesied. Markham implied that laissez-faire principles had been tried and found wanting. A new approach to man's life in society was needed. Markham, of course, did not produce the temper of the times, he reflected it. The twentieth century was to be a century of hope; the age was dynamic, vital. A new ordering of society was evolving, and new ways of thinking were needed to cope with the rich currents of life flowing through the nation. William James refashioned some older principles into a philosophy he called pragmatism [3]. Ideas for James did not exist for men to discover; men created ideas out of the struggles of life and put them to work in the market place, in the forum, and in the temple. Those ideas that worked were true regardless of age, logical consistency, or class support. John Dewey (1859-1952) further elaborated James' philosophy and insisted that thought divorced from action was sterile; ideas were tools to be used to refashion the world into a better place in which to live.

Social scientists too abandoned the traditional formulas in

which their subjects had been held and struck out on new paths. Economics for Thorstein Veblen (1857-1929) was an inquiry into how people actually organized the production and distribution of goods. Political Science became a study not of the universal laws lying behind and above government but of political processes occurring in everyday life. Sociology and anthropology became sciences of human behavior rather than organized searches for the basic and fundamental laws of society [4]. Historians touched by the new spirit argued, as did James Harvey Robinson (1863-1926), that history should be systematically exploited, not for enjoyment or entertainment, but to facilitate social reform. Even religion responded to the new forces. Clergymen and theologians joined in revitalizing Christianity and redirected it toward social as well as individual salvation [5]. The social gospel movement in American Protestantism (similar expressions were found in certain Catholic and Jewish circles) preached that the historic Protestant churches had failed their trust and that henceforth they should either reform the world or surrender to it.

Literature mirrored the novel tendencies of the day; authors influenced by realism and naturalism trained their penetrating eyes upon society and subjected it to critical analyses. Frank Norris, Stephen Crane, Theodore Dreiser, Jack London, Upton Sinclair, and others explored some of the problems of modern life including the farmer battling against the impersonal business structure, the lonely girl in the city enmeshed in the toils of others' greed, the worker exploring the potentialities of socialism as a way out of society's impasse, the individual pushed and pulled by external and internal forces over which he had no control. Literature and the other arts could be progressive and liberal too. Vachel Lindsay (1879-1931), mystic poet who dreamed of a reanimated America, suggested the mood:*

> I am unjust, but I can strive for justice.
> My life's unkind, but I can vote for kindness.
> I, the unloving, say life should be lovely.
> I, that am blind, cry out against my blindness.
>
> Man is a curious brute—he pets his fancies—
> Fighting mankind, to win sweet luxury.

---

*Vachel Lindsay, "Why I Voted the Socialist Ticket" [1913], in *Collected Poems* (New York: The Macmillan Company, 1925), pp. 301-02.

So he will be, tho' law be clear as crystal,
Tho' all men plan to live in harmony.

Come let us vote against our human nature,
Crying to God in all the polling places
To heal our everlasting sinfulness
And make us sages with transfigured faces.

A group of young painters, dubbed the Eight, also caught the spirit; revolting against the pretty academic art of the salons, they began to paint the America they saw round about them, with all of its ugliness as well as its beauty. This was the path of reality.

The Progressive Movement

The reform movement bubbling up during the first decade and a half of the twentieth century manifested itself in a variety of ways. Reformers waged a war against political bosses who allegedly thwarted the people's will; others carried the attack against monopolies in business; and humanitarians mounted crusades against a host of presumed ills resulting from dislocations engendered by rapid and haphazard industrialization. Several streams having their origin in the nineteenth century merged in the twentieth century and issued forth as the Progressive movement. Agrarian, socialist, temperance, women's rights, antimonopoly, urban renewal, antipoverty, social gospel, child protection, political reform, and pacifist advocates all added strength to the impulse to reshape the nation. A group of journalists, nicknamed "Muckrakers" by Theodore Roosevelt, found the public receptive to stories exposing the ills and evils besetting society. Herbert Croly (1869-1930), the publicist and first editor of *The New Republic* (the very name of this weekly magazine has symbolic significance), in a widely read book expounded progressive principles. *The Promise of American Life* (New York: The Macmillan Company, 1909) summarized the movement's objectives. "The . . . American," Croly wrote, "conceives the better future which awaits himself and other men in America as fundamentally a future in which economic prosperity will be still more abundant and still more accessible than it has yet been either here or abroad."

To realize the promise meant hard work and struggle, for ob-

stacles stood in the way. A strong moralistic and evangelical
mood characterized the reformers as they faced the presumed
enemies of society. Croly noted that the redemption of the national promise, "like all sacred causes," must "be propagated by
the Word and by the right arm of the Word, which is the
sword." The delegates to the Progressive Party Convention of
1912 sang "We stand at Armageddon and we battle for the Lord"
as they nominated Theodore Roosevelt for the presidency on a
reform platform. The progressive newspaper editor William
Allen White sought to arouse his readers to action with words
drawn from the Old Testament prophet Isaiah: " 'Arise, shine; for
thy light is come, and the glory of the Lord is risen upon thee.'
It is but dawn in the new day of spiritual awakening."

The reformers, convinced that government at all levels had
fallen into the hands of corrupt politicians dominated by equally
corrupt business leaders, sought to cure the ills of democracy
with more democracy. Acting on the theory that the voice of the
people was the voice of God, they extended the suffrage to
women; took from state legislatures the right to elect United
States Senators and gave it to the voters of the respective states;
and introduced the direct primary, the secret ballot, the initiative, the referendum, and the recall into a number of states and
agencies of local government. They advanced a variety of proposals aimed at reforming the government of American cities—
reputedly the worst governed in the world. They placed restraints upon monopolies in business and sponsored legislation
regulating economic enterprise in a host of ways with the object
of protecting the workers and the consuming public from some
of the more rapacious practices of businessmen. They inaugurated programs to conserve the nation's resources, natural and
human. They fought for improved housing; better sanitary facilities; cleaner air, water, and milk supplies; and increased recrea-
tional space in urban centers. They carried on campaigns to
protect children and women workers in industry. They secured
legislation against organized prostitution. They succeeded in
outlawing the manufacture, transportation, and sale of alcoholic
beverages.

The Progressive movement represented a reawakening of
American idealism. American self-consciousness concerning its
opportunities and responsibilities achieved a new intensity. It

reached its climax in World War I, when Americans set upon a great crusade to save the world for democracy. The movement suffered a partial eclipse after 1918; yet many of our current attitudes toward political and social issues reach back to the 1900's and 1910's.

The Politics of Progressivism

The presidential campaign of 1900 brought the two adversaries of the 1896 battle, Republican William McKinley and Democrat William Jennings Bryan, together for a rematch. The Republicans chose the youthful and popular Theodore Roosevelt (1858-1919), the hero of San Juan Hill, as McKinley's running mate. The Republicans won the election, but McKinley was assassinated not long after his second inaugural, bringing TR to the White House. Roosevelt, despite his great popularity, had to win the confidence of Republican leadership. Proceeding cautiously, especially in domestic affairs, TR gained control of the party and succeeded in winning the election of 1904 handily. A believer in strong executive leadership, Roosevelt unceremoniously brushed aside the stodgy traditions and formalities of half a century that held the presidency in a tight grip and embarked upon a vigorous administration of the powers of government. He interfered in the anthracite coal strike on the side of labor; he used a big stick on business, breaking monopolies and endorsing regulatory legislation; he expanded and publicized measures aimed at conserving the nation's natural resources. In foreign affairs he initiated the digging of the Panama Canal; completed the organization of government for the Philippines; converted the Caribbean into an American lake by intervening in the affairs of Latin American neighbors and elaborating and extending the Monroe Doctrine; and finally, sensing that Europe was entering into a period of decline, he believed that the United States should accept the opportunity to lead the world to its next stage of development. Roosevelt played the role of peacemaker following the Russo-Japanese war; he sent the navy's battle fleet around the world to exhibit American power abroad; and he helped head off a European war by sending a delegation to the Algeciras Conference (1906) to deal with the Moroccan crisis, earning the Nobel Peace Prize for his efforts.

Roosevelt put the stamp of his personality upon the period 1901-1909. He restored the presidency to its original position as one of the three coordinate branches of government. Moreover, he strengthened the federal arm at a time when great aggregations of organized capital threatened the integrity of the national government. Perhaps of equal importance, he advanced the stature of the nation in the council chambers of the world and challenged his fellow citizens to accept the opportunities and responsibilities of greatness.

The Rough Rider picked his friend and associate William Howard Taft (1857-1930) as his successor. Taft, with TR's endorsement, won the election of 1908 against Bryan. The amiable and portly Taft tried to continue Roosevelt's policies during his administration of the presidency, but it was his misfortune not to have the same colorful personality as his predecessor. In the end he alienated large segments of the electorate, including the progressive wing of his own party as a result of measures he fostered, administrative decisions he made, and party leaders whom he consulted. When Roosevelt arrived home from his African and European tour he turned against his old friend, assumed leadership of the progressives in the party, and fought with Taft in the Republican National Convention of 1912 for control of the party. The administration forces won; thereupon Roosevelt broke with his organization and accepted the nomination of the Progressive Republican Party.

Perhaps Roosevelt sensed the drift of sentiment toward progressive reform among the electorate following his return to the United States. At any rate, as early as August of 1910, he enunciated his views in an address at Osawatomie, Kansas [6]. Henceforth, the "New Nationalism" became the rallying cry of the progressives. The Progressive Republicans at their 1912 convention elaborated and spelled out the details of the new nationalism. In "A Contract with the People" the party pledged itself to support the direct election of United States Senators (accomplished in the 17th Amendment to the Constitution ratified May 31, 1913), nationwide preferential primary elections for Presidential candidates (to remove nominations from party bosses and party conventions), extensions of the initiative, referendum, and the recall; woman suffrage (accomplished in the 19th Amendment to the Constitution, ratified August 26, 1920);

the recall of judicial decisions; prohibition of child labor; mini-mum wages for women workers; tariff revision; and strict regulation of business enterprise.

Meanwhile the Democratic Party, long under Bryan's leader-ship, seeing that the Republicans were headed for internecine warfare, cast about for someone who might provide the party a safe and sane liberal leadership. Woodrow Wilson, former col-lege professor and President of Princeton University, had in 1910 resigned his post and entered politics in New Jersey. There he campaigned on a liberal platform, won the governorship of the state, beat the political bosses "to a frazzle," and chalked up a modest record of progressive reform. After a prolonged struggle in the national convention the Democrats nominated the ex-college professor for the presidency.

In the campaign Wilson and Roosevelt fought for the votes of the liberals and progressives. Roosevelt had a program; Wilson developed one. Wilson, in harmony with his generation, felt the dynamic thrust of a rapidly changing America. He too faced the paradox of progress and poverty stated so sharply by Henry George. Wilson found a solution to the problem in freedom. America was no longer free because monopolists and political bosses had gained control of the nation. We needed a "new freedom," said Wilson, a freedom that would release the vital energies of all our people [7]. In the New Nationalism Roosevelt, sensing that America's problems were no longer solely local and regional but national in scope, stressed the nation, a kind of twentieth-century Hamiltonianism; in the New Freedom, Wilson, perceiving the threats to human integrity posed by the great impersonal institutions of modern society, emphasized the indi-vidual—a type of twentieth-century Jeffersonianism. Each re-flected a strain of political thought to be found throughout American history; the two met in a confrontation during the presidential campaign of 1912.

Wilson won the election of 1912, and following his inaugura-tion (cast in an evangelical mood of dedication), his adminis-tration chalked up a remarkable record of reform legislation. This included the first major downward revision of the tariff in decades, the creation of the Federal Reserve Banking system with its provisions for a sound flexible currency, additional means for the supervision and regulation of business, and a further strengthening of the tradition of responsible presidential leadership. In foreign affairs the Wilson administraion adopted what one of his biographers called "missionary diplomacy." In essence this envisioned the slow and ofttimes painful process of helping our neighbors remake their governments, and perhaps economies, in the American image. "My passion," said the President, "is for the submerged eighty-five per cent of the republic [of Mexico] who are now struggling for liberty." "My ideal," he said, "is an orderly and righteous government in Mexico; I am going to teach Latin American governments to elect good men."

There was a certain ambivalence in the reception accorded Wilson's New Freedom—as there was indeed in the President himself and in his analysis and prescription. Some of the younger intellectuals, for example, chafed at a plan of action so obviously couched in the rhetoric of the eighteenth and nineteenth centuries. They sensed a negative quality in Wilson's formulas and program which disturbed them. They envisaged a more positive, less doctrinaire approach to the problems of the twentieth century than that which evolved under Wilson's leadership [8]. The electorate, despite these misgivings, returned Wilson to the White House in the elections of 1916 when he campaigned against Charles Evans Hughes and a Republican party still smarting from the wounds suffered in the mtramural fight of 1912. The eruption of World War I precluded any normal working out of the New Freedom or any fair appraisal of it. In the end, it lost momentum and the President's interest in domestic reform flagged, occupied as he came to be with international problems and the means to perpetuate peace.

World War I and the United States

When war broke out in Europe in the late summer of 1914 President Wilson immediately proclaimed American neutrality. Neutrality proved difficult to maintain in face of the efforts of the belligerents to gain American assistance or to deny that assistance to the enemy. Moreover, many Americans found it impossible to preserve a spirit of impartiality. For a number of reasons there was a steady reinforcement of sentiment favoring England and France (the principal partners among the Allied powers) against Germany and her allies (usually known as the Central Powers).

Early in the war the British with control of the seas blockaded Germany and tried to prevent neutral ships from trading with her. The United States, the largest of the neutral shippers, ran afoul of the British regulations, which produced embarrassing incidents. Germany, threatened with economic strangulation, struck back with the submarine. Use of the submarine violated American sensibilities because U-boat commanders, owing to the nature of their vessels, had to strike quickly and in secret to avoid being destroyed; this meant the loss not only of property but of human lives, sometimes American lives. President Wilson repeatedly and with increasing vehemence protested against violations of American neutral rights and especially he protested against Germany's use of the submarine. Eventually this issue brought the United States into the struggle.

The President realized that probably the only way for the United States to escape involvement in the war was to end it before the nation became engulfed in the conflict. Consequently he bent every effort to get the belligerents to sit down at the conference table and arrange a truce, or better yet, a peace. To this end he repeatedly offered the good offices of the United States to the warring nations and attempted to get them to state the conditions under which they would agree to stop the carnage. The President also outlined American objectives in the crisis [9].

Meanwhile, Wilson squeaked through the presidential election of 1916. Ensconced again in the White House, he renewed his efforts to end the war while at the same time bolstering America's capabilities for waging war. The months between his reelection and American entry into the conflict were painful ones for the President. Wilson concluded that the Allies would probably win the war if the United States joined them. He faced the alternative of a German victory with a questionable peace or an Allied victory and a durable peace brought about and supported by American power. This would mean that the United States would help write the peace treaty. If the United States was present at the negotiations, he concluded, some hope of a just and durable peace could be offered the peoples of the world in return for their incalculable sacrifices of blood and treasure upon the altar of Mars. But to insure the American presence at a peace conference, the United States would perforce have to become one of the warring parties.

Causes aplenty existed for going to war. In fact, following American refusal to budge from its claimed right of trading with the belligerents and its denial of Germany's right to use submarines against merchant ships, it was only a matter of time before the two powers collided. When Germany launched its all-out submarine campaign early in 1917 the United States and Germany entered into a state of warfare. All that remained was legally to recognize that such had happened. On April 2, 1917, the President went to the Congress in a solemn mood and asked for a declaration of a state of war [10]. The Senate (April 4) passed a war resolution 82 to 6; the House concurred (April 6) 373 to 50.

The nation mobilized its men and resources for waging war in the ensuing months. The task was a stupendous one, for the American people hitherto had had little experience in national regimentation. Haltingly, and with some fumbling, the country was transformed. A kind of wartime socialism emerged with unheard-of powers concentrated in the President's hands. "It is not an army we must train for war, it is a nation," said the President. Men, money, the economy, and opinion were all mobilized to fight in a European war across 3,000 miles of ocean.

The first troops arrived in France in June 1917; by October American troops entered the battle zones. Early in 1918 Germany launched what proved to be its final big offensive calculated to win the war before American might could be made effective. The turning point of the fighting occurred June-July 1918 as the German thrust failed to break the lines along the western front and as the Allies and the United States mounted a crushing counteroffensive. An American army of 1.2 million men led the assault that ended on November 11, 1918, when Germany signed an armistice based on the "Fourteen Points," Wilson's statement of American war aims presented before an enthusiastic Congress January 8, 1918.

American participation in the war cost us 48,900 battle deaths; 2,900 missing in action; 4,400 prisoners; 56,900 dead from disease, and 6,500 dead from other causes. The total direct cost in dollars amounted to $21.85 billion; our government loaned an additional $1.4 billion to our associates. No one can estimate the cost in spiritual resources and in freedom. President Wilson took the lead in converting the war into a crusade—a holy war—for democracy and a peaceful future. This was a war to make the world safe for democracy, a war to end war. As such it became like a great morality play in which the real actors were not simply men but the forces of good ranged against the forces of evil in a life and death struggle. It is not surprising that the American people generously backed the war and on occasions developed a spirit of intolerance toward dissenters.

Despite the nature and character of the emotional support engendered for the war, no such unanimity as was achieved in the Spanish-American War or in World War II emerged in 1917-18. Opponents of the war could be found among Christian pacifists, Midwest Progressives, Socialists, conscientious objectors, and some liberal intellectuals [11]. The American tradition of freedom of speech suffered a partial eclipse during the crusade. The government and the public brought heavy pressure to bear upon dissenters, and hundreds of persons were jailed including Eugene V. Debs, the leading Socialist in the country. The problem of freedom of speech in wartime eventually came to the courts for adjudication [12].

Peacemaking

The horrendous blood bath should have bought a peaceful world; the war-weary peoples of the earth hopefully looked to their leaders to achieve something more than a cessation of hostilities. President Wilson had already decided to assume personal direction of the Paris Peace Conference, and toward that end he sailed for France in December 1918. His hand had been seriously compromised by his party's failure to capture both houses of Congress in the mid-term elections of 1918; disappointed but not daunted, Wilson pursued his intention to play a decisive role at the conference. The victors refused to permit the vanquished to participate in the discussions; they were presented with a document to sign or else suffer a resumption of the war. Wilson faced, therefore, not a hostile foe, but, as matters turned out, a hostile group of victors. He envisaged an honorable peace among equals without indemnities and without punishing terms imposed upon the losers. The settlement was to be crowned with a League of Nations empowered to maintain an orderly world based upon the principles of self-determination of all peoples, self-government, free trade, and equal access to natural resources. His associates, however, lacking some of Wilson's foresight and bound by a collection of secret treaties that looked to a revision of the map of the world in complete disregard of the self-determination principle, forced the President to compromise on a number of issues. Moreover, in order to secure any reasonable settlement and an agreement on the League, Wilson had to give in on the matter of indemnities— France especially wanted either treaty guarantees in case of renewed German aggression or a crushing indemnity and restrictions on Germany's war-making capabilities. After six months of wrangling the conference produced a treaty which the German representatives signed June 28, 1919.

Americans took an avid interest in the negotiations and probably would have ratified the treaty had it been presented to the electorate in the summer or fall of 1919. In the United States, however, the task of ratification of treaties is assigned by the Constitution to the Senate of the United States rather than to the voters. The Senate, after the elections of 1918, had passed into the hands of the opposition party led by some of Wilson's implacable enemies. Senator Henry Cabot Lodge (1850-1924) of Massachusetts and Senator William E. Borah of Idaho led those who had determined to defeat the President on the issue of the treaty including its provisions for a League of Nations. Even before the President formally presented the document to the Senate for its consideration, the battle lines began to form. As early as February 1919, Senator Borah went before the Senate to denounce the settlement and particularly the League of Nations [13]. Following months of debate in and out of Congress, a debate in which the President carried the issue to the people, the Senate agreed to ratify the treaty with certain reservations safeguarding American security and freedom of action. The President refused to agree to the reservations, and eventually the Senate voted not to ratify the document. Had Wilson been less adamant in his opposition to compromise and had he been willing to accept the reservations and to negotiate their ac-

ceptance by the other powers, it is possible that the Senate might
have ratified the treaty, thus bringing the United States into the
League of Nations. The President can be faulted for his stubborn
refusal to agree to some modification of his handiwork; he must
share some of the blame for the failure of the treaty to clear the
Senate. We can only speculate concerning what might have occurred had the United States shouldered some of the burdens of
shaping an international peace-keeping organization during the
1920's and 1930's. The outcome could hardly have been worse
than the reality.

Meanwhile, Wilson's health had been impaired following a collapse while stumping the country in support of the League. He
lived, a broken man, until 1924. The President's party went down
to defeat in the presidential election of 1920. With the President's
collapse went the hopes for a peaceful world.

The New Conservatism

The Republicans nominated Senator Warren G. Harding
(1865-1923) of Ohio, a conservative stand-patter, for the presidency in 1920. For his running mate they nominated Calvin
Coolidge (1872-1933), at the time governor of Massachusetts.
A Democratic party, demoralized by the Treaty imbroglio, nominated James M. Cox (1870-1957) of Ohio, who had kept free of
the League fight, and Franklin D. Roosevelt (1882-1945). The
campaign, a quiet one, turned on a number of issues, the chief
of which was that elusive something which Harding called
"normalcy." The country seemingly had tired of reform and the
high moral ferver of the war years. The electorate gave the Republican Harding over 16 million, the Democrat Cox 9 million,
and the Sociailst Debs 900,000 votes.

Demobilization of the armed services and liquidation of the
wartime agencies commenced in the later months of the Wilson
administration, continued with great rapidity under President
Harding until little more than the experience remained from the
war-born excursions into federal control of the economy.

Despite an intense, short-lived postwar depression in 1920-21,
the United States generally enjoyed very prosperous times during
the 1920's. Basic to this well-being was the steady growth of the
gross national product. The expansion of machine industry fed

by new industries such as the manufacture of automobiles, radios, and plastics; the widespread application of science and technology to every phase of industry, agriculture, and business; and the utilization of two new sources of power—electricity and the internal combustion engine—to the production and exchange of goods, all contributed to the growth of prosperity [14].

A number of observers sought to account for the new prosperity. Several attributed the phenomenon to American business and its leadership and to the relationship of business to government. Business achieved a status in American culture unknown in other periods and in other countries. The businessman, a publicist remarked, is now the "dictator of our destinies," ousting the "statesman, the priest, the philosopher, as the creator of standards of ethics and behavior and becoming the final authority on the conduct of American society." Some observers were concerned with what they believed to be a deterioration of traditional American values such as industriousness, frugality, and concern for the well-being of others. America, they warned, might be gaining the riches of the whole world but losing its soul in the morass of materialism.

The reaction against progressivism which occurred during the 1920's began as soon as the war was over. An early manifestation of the new conservatism appeared in the "Big Red Scare." Rumors of a widespread plot against the United States led by the forces of international communism spread across the land. A number of bombs aimed at prominent public figures were thought by jittery Americans to be the opening moves of the impending communist revolution. Groups of Americans struck back and in the process a number of presumed radicals were rounded up and their headquarters sacked or destroyed. Some lost their lives as sacrifices to American intolerance.

Meanwhile, under the Republican administrations of the 1920's government regulation, so highly regarded by the progressives, declined. In response to the new mood, Congress raised the tariff and lowered taxes. The government relaxed its enforcement of the antitrust laws and promoted the formation of trade associations. Presidents vetoed measures aiding agriculture and signed bills granting subsidies to selected enterprises. The courts opposed regulation of business and helped erect legal defenses of private property [15]. Spokesmen for rugged individualism reminded the public that the American traditions of independence, self-reliance, and laissez faire were more trustworthy guides to individual and social well-being than government regulation and ownership. Organized labor during the 1920's, under heavy pressure from business leadership supported by government and beset by an energy-sapping prosperity, found the going tough. Union membership, interest, and participation declined and labor achieved no significant gains during the decade [16].

Agriculture, along with coal mining, textiles, and shipbuilding failed to bounce back after the 1920-21 depression. Several factors operated to keep farm income out of balance. For one thing, following the war the belligerents went back to raising much of their own produce at the same time turning to older sources of supply in the world market. Then too our own domestic market failed to absorb the generous surpluses produced by our war-stimulated agriculture—changes in diet partly induced by wartime controls and partly inspired by new styles emphasizing youth and slimness had a bearish effect on commodity prices. Also, the lack of any form of organization similiar to labor unions or trade associations to control production and manipulate prices handicapped agriculture. Lulled into a false sense of security during boom times farmers had extended their holdings, purchased new equipment and homes, and demanded and received a host of new services from government including hard-surface roads and schools. Fixed charges in the form of interest and taxes took a heavy toll when prices skidded as they did. While the cost of goods farmers bought steadily climbed, receipts for farm goods fell behind.

Agrarian discontent flared as farmers and their leaders searched for solutions to the farm problem. Older farm organizations revived and new ones appeared. A Farmer-Labor party emerged and campaigned unsuccessfully in the presidential contest of 1924. Gradually a new tactic gained favor. In the old days when the rural population of the country exceeded the urban, farm leadership talked of ways of restoring the republic to the people and clearing the obstacles to democratic government. But when farmers became a minority segment of the population, as they did after the war, more and more they began to use the tactics of organized pressure groups to wring concessions from government. The Farm Bloc, organized in 1921 by 14

Republican and 12 Democratic Senators of the West and South who joined forces to support measures favorable to agriculture and to oppose unfavorable legislation regardless of party sponsorship, pioneered the new approach. Success in a number of instances revealed the potentialities of the method.

The major effort at farm relief involved schemes to achieve parity between farm and industrial prices; leaders sought to win acceptance of the notion that agriculture was a special national interest that deserved special treatment such as certain industries enjoyed under the tariff laws. But businessmen and politicians, despite their support of tariff protection for industry, branded similar treatment for agriculture as un-American and socialistic. Consequently such measures as the McNary-Haugen Bill designed to establish one price for farm produce sold overseas and another price—higher—for the domestic market met a stern rebuke—President Coolidge twice vetoed the measure and President Hoover indicated his hostility to similar plans. President Hoover's administration established a Federal Farm Board to regulate marketing through cooperatives and stabilization corporations, but by the time the agencies were operative the Great Depression engulfed the nation and prices continued their disastrous decline while output increased.

By the close of the 1920's despite the general aura of prosperity, labor and agriculture were dissatisfied with the way the national wealth was distributed under the leadership of the Republican party. It is no wonder that the New Deal enjoyed widespread support during the 1930's from these segments of the society.

Politics During the Golden Twenties

President Harding, following the exposure of scandals touching his administration, died suddenly in August 1923, Calvin Coolidge succeeding to the presidency. In the election of 1924 he easily won over his opponent, John W. Davis (1873-1955) of West Virginia, who had been nominated for the presidency by a strife-torn and badly divided Democratic party. Coolidge's second administration was even more propitious than his first. Peace and prosperity reigned and the President did nothing to jeopardize either. Coolidge, extravagantly popular with the beneficiaries of the new prosperity, doubtless could have had another term. He chose, however, not to run in 1928. His party nominated Herbert Hoover (1874-1964), a California business-man who had forsaken his profession to become Food Administrator under Wilson and Secretary of Commerce under Harding and Coolidge. The Democrats, although not wholly recovered from the intraparty warfare plaguing the party since 1920, nominated Alfred E. Smith (1873-1944), four-time Governor of New York and wildly popular with the urban masses. Smith, handicapped in an America not yet ready to tolerate widespread divergencies from the norm—he was Catholic, anti-Prohibitionist, urban, and of recent immigrant stock—ran a good race. The electorate was in no mood for a change, and prosperity more than anything else probably elected Hoover.

During the years of Republican ascendancy and before the panic of 1929 a number of political problems agitated the public. One of the more persistent was what to do about benefits for veterans. Veterans' organizations grew in numbers and influence following the war, and they sought to justify their existence by bringing pressure upon Congress for more government financial aid to veterans. Presidents Harding, Coolidge, Hoover, and Roosevelt vetoed bonus measures coming to their desks. The matter of enforcement of the laws against the manufacture, sale, or transportation of intoxicating beverages authorized by the 18th Amendment to the Constitution also provided ample cause for political debate. The amendment represented the climax of almost a hundred years of work to outlaw alcohol. Great enthusiasm attended its ratification. Although the consumption of alcohol declined sharply, and although governments made heroic efforts to enforce the laws, the public became increasingly dissatisfied with the experiment. Prohibition was repealed in 1933 with New Deal support. Immigration restrictionists, long active in the United States and aided in the 1920's by the isolationist, nativist, nationalist temper of the times, succeeded in their efforts to staunch the flow of newcomers into the country [17]. The new measures severely restricted the numbers coming from Southern and Southeastern Europe and denied admission to Asiatics.

After the war, with Republican control of the White House and the Congress, the United States returned to the tradition of protection. The tariff legislation of the 1920's, culminating with the Hawley-Smoot Tariff Act of 1930, pushed the schedules to the highest peacetime rates in American history. The Hawley-Smoot Act contained overtones of isolationism and resurgent nationalism; it was designed to give American producers a monopoly of the domestic market regardless of the consequences abroad. In the realm of foreign affairs, it evoked retaliation; made it difficult if not impossible for foreign governments to repay their war debts to the United States; stifled world trade; and in general promoted economic nationalism.

Other political issues of the day such as regulation of transportation, water power and its control, and the control of public utilities produced divisions of opinion reminiscent of the Progressive era. In general, Republican Congresses and administrations took sides sympathetic to business management.

Foreign Affairs

Neither the American people nor their government thought that imperialism was a major attribute of their foreign policy during the postwar decade. As long as the United States did not exercise direct political control over foreign people its policies could not be called colonial. We hardly regarded our tutelage of the Philippines and our supervision of Caribbean states as manifestations of imperiaism; after all we had promised the Philippines its independence as soon as its people learned how to maintain good and stable government, and we intervened in the Caribbean to guarantee peace and orderly development there.

On the other hand the years during and after the war witnessed a tremendous expansion of our economic interest abroad. Our foreign trade had grown steadily since 1900; it had doubled between 1900 and 1914, it doubled again during the war, and by 1929 it was four and a half times its 1900 volume. A shift too in the character of the trade had occurred reflecting changes in our economy; in 1900 about two thirds of our exports were farm products while by 1930 two thirds were manufactured goods. In the latter year about 10 per cent of American production entered into foreign trade. Our industrial plant had become dependent upon foreign markets—markets in which to sell surplus goods, markets in which to purchase needed raw materials, and markets for the investment of our surplus capital. At the same time the

United States shifted from the staus of a debtor to a creditor nation. Our aid in financing World War I was the major cause of this alteration; by 1918 Europe owed $8.5 billion to the United States. During the 1920's private and public investments abroad mushroomed, so that by 1930 the world owed the United States and its citizens $27 billion.

Curiously, our people failed to recognize that these commitments bound the destinies of the United States to those of Europe, Latin America, and Asia with a myriad of ties from which there was no simple escape. The spirit of isolationism grew almost in proportion to the growth of our overseas economic interests; Americans seemingly were more concerned with recovering the past than laying hold of the future. We wanted no part of the League of Nations nor any other organization or alliance designed to keep the peace. Our government beat a strategic retreat from advanced positions taken in Asia, Europe, and Latin America at the turn of the century. At the Washington Conference (1921-22) the United States initiated efforts to scale down naval armaments (efforts that were continued throughout the decade) and helped produce two pacts (Four Power and Nine Power) involving nations with interests in the Pacific and in Eastern Asia. In the first, the signatories agreed to respect each other's rights and possessions in the Far East and pledged themselves to settle their controversies peaceably. The Four Power Pact thus exempted the United States from the sole responsibility of enforcing peace and stability in the Pacific. The Nine Power Pact guaranteed Chinese sovereignty and independence as well as the territorial and administrative integrity of China; the signatories also agreed to the Open Door principle in China. Again the United States sought assistance of others to back its peculiar interests in the Far East.

In Latin America the United States began during the 1920's to develop what later President Roosevelt called the Good Neighbor Policy. The United States sought to convert the Monroe Doctrine, an exclusively nationalist policy, into a multilateral doctrine. The steps taken by Presidents Coolidge and Hoover in this direction represented a tacit recognition that our traditional policies could be better pursued by simpler and more agreeable means than interventions and demonstrations of American military and naval power.

The maintenance of peace seemed to American leadership to be a prerequisite to continued American prosperity. The United States, therefore, "committed itself to a peace policy in order to maintain the delicate arrangements of trade, to continue the supply of raw materials to her factories, to keep open the markets for the sale of American wares, and to provide a free flow of interest payments to New York." So, although the United States refused to join the peace-keeping machinery it helped establish—the League of Nations and the World Court—it attempted by other means to maintain the status quo. The Four and Nine Power Pacts were expressions of this policy, as was the assistance our government gave to the problem of German reparations. The peace movement during the decade reached its greatest intensity in 1928 when the United States joined other governments in signing the Paris Peace Pact [18].

Society and Cultural Expression

The population of the United States grew rapidly during the 1920's—the largest increase in American history up to that time. This growth, achieved despite a drastic curtailment in immigration, was one of the marks of American well-being. Spatial as well as social mobility continued. The West (and Florida) experienced the greatest percentage gains in the population, although Michigan, New Jersey, North Carolina, and New York posted substantial percentage increases reflecting the continued industrial and commercial growth of the country. A significant demographic phenomenon was the war-induced large-scale migration of Negroes to the industrial centers of the North. By 1920 almost 2.5 million of the 11.8 million Negroes lived in the Northeast and North Central States.

Some evidence suggests that social gradations were becoming more sharply differentiated and more rigid; yet the general increase in, and widespread diffusion of, wealth opened the way for the mass media of communications to exert a subtle nationalizing and conforming function on society.

One of the more picturesque features of social life during the period, one giving the twenties its nickname of "The Jazz Age," was the climax of the revolution in manners and morals initiated earlier in the century. The younger generation—flaming youth—

completed the overthrow of Victorian codes of morality and
established a freer and more realistic posture toward human relationships than that held by their parents and grandparents. One
of the more significant outcomes of the rebellion was the further
emancipation of women from traditional restrictions that hedged
them about in a protective shell. As one author described it,
"The Lady Vanishes" and "The Woman Takes Over."

Two generations of intellectuals, one coming to maturity before and one after the war, joined to review the nation's past and
current cultural achievements and responsibilities. The older of
the two probed the limitations and failures of a cultural tradition—the genteel tradition—that reached its apogee in the
Progressive era.

> My heart rebels against my generation,
> That talks of freedom and is slave to riches,
> And toiling 'neath each day's ignoble burden,
> Boasts of tomorrow.*

wrote the philosopher-poet, George Santayana (1863-1952), expressing the mood of revolt. "The most hopeful thing of intellectual promise in America today is the contempt of the younger
people for their elders; they are restless, uneasy, disaffected. . . .
it is a genuine and moving attempt to create a way of life free
from the bondage of an authority that has lost all meaning. . ."
observed Harold E. Stearns, another of the rebels.

The younger generation, unwilling to share what Van Wyck
Brooks called "the pessimistic determinism" of his generation,
accepted the challenge to restructure American culture and to
refashion it according to new principles and to the newly acquired knowledge of human nature and human relationships.
Convinced that it was a mistake to pour new wine into old
bottles, the younger generation of artists experimented with new
forms of expression in the search for more appropriate means to
voice their convictions and judgments about the life surrounding
them. Painters and sculptors tested nonrepresentationalism; com-
posers abandoned the classical rules of music composition;
dramatists made innovations in stage design, tried new dialogue
sequences, novel characterizations, different manipulations of

---

*From George Santayana, *Poems* (New York: Scribner, 1923). Used by
permission.

space and movement, and brought abstractions and symbolism into the theater; novelists worked at using the discontinuous stream of consciousness technique; and poets explored the possibilities of symbolism and imagery. Since they linked the old forms to a dying or dead past, the new forms needed to be newly inspired and newly devised. [19].

Another distinguishing mark of the cultural expression of the period was the debate consciously and unconsciously carried on between the defenders of "our business civilization" and those who severely berated American middle-class culture for its shortcomings and its utter failure to furnish the foundations for a new moral order grounded in the new science. The dramatist Eugene O'Neill (1888-1953) stated it succinctly, if ungrammatically, as he dug for the roots of the current spiritual sickness resulting from "the death of an Old God and the failure of science and materialism to give any satisfactory new one for surviving religious instinct to find a meaning for life in, and to comfort its fear of death with." Science, too, engaged in rebellion and reconstruction; the critics mined the scientists' laboratories for new knowledge to destroy traditional, outworn beliefs as well as to provide the means for rebuilding an intelligible morality that transcended the limitations of middle-class culture.

Severe and searching criticism of American society and culture did not, in most cases, signify an intention to abandon the United States to the philistines. Rather, the critics wanted to purify the culture of its dross, to free the nation from the bonds that held it in thralldom, to help shape the future. Surely, a young intellectual of the period testified, "the America of our natural affections rather than the present one of enforced dull standardization may some day snap the shackles of those who today keep it in a spiritual prison."

The Panic of 1929

The panic of 1929 burst the bubble of American optimism and shattered the dream of a New Day when, as Herbert Hoover phrased it in 1928, "poverty will be banished from this nation." American prosperity during the golden twenties had been spotty and economic problems of a serious nature persisted throughout the decade. But these somehow were ignored in the golden glow that surrounded the nation. Frederick Lewis Allen in 1930 noted that "Under the impact of the shock of the panic, a multitude of ills which hitherto had passed unnoticed or had been off-set by stock market optimism began to beset the body economic, as poisons seep through the human system when a vital organ has ceased to function normally."

An unhealthy diversion of money and credit into speculation especially in the stock market was one of "the multitude of ills" besetting the economy and one which ultimately sparked the explosion. The stock exchange in a competitive market economy serves as a kind of barometer for business. The speculative fever reached its peak during 1928 and 1929. Government made efforts to curb speculation through the machinery of the Federal Reserve Board. Despite these efforts of the Board and despite certain storm signals and the warnings of a few cautious observers, the speculators who by 1928 included a substantial segment of the population went their merry way. The market reached its ultimate glittering heights early in September 1929. Then on October 23 a severe wave of selling hit Wall Street. The following day, "Black Thursday," 12.8 million shares traded hands, and the gigantic structure built largely on speculative credit toppled like a house of cards. On October 29 a perfect Niagara of sales occurred—over 16.4 million shares were exchanged; the Stock Exchange closed its doors for the weekend. Panic conditions prevailed until the middle of November; prices of stocks reached their lowest point in 1929 on November 13. The market value of stocks listed on the New York Exchange on October 1, 1929, stood at $87 billion; one month later this figure had skidded to $55 billion, and by March 1, 1933 the sum shrank to $19 billion [20].

The stock market crash rang down the curtain on the New Day. A deep and cruel depression followed the panic; it did not bottom out until March 1933. Hardly a person in America escaped the influence of the big bull market and its collapse. Americans soon found themselves in a different world calling for adjustments in ideas, habits, and values. (See Clarke A. Chambers, *The New Deal at Home and Abroad, 1929-1945,* in this series.) How much of the old could they or should they take into the altered world of the 1930's and the 1940's? The question was not academic.

The Responsibilities of Power

Self-consciousness concerning America's role in the family of nations and in civilization has a tradition that reaches back into the seventeenth century. What America is, what it might be, and what it ought to be are questions which have provoked the thoughtful in each generation in our history. As American power has grown, so have American responsibilities and these responsibilities have had an inward as well as an outward reach. During certain epochs of history a general agreement among a large proportion of the population as to national goals seems to prevail, whereas in other periods dissatisfaction and frustration appear endemic. In all probability a more accurate view would reveal a constant tension between critics and defenders of the status quo.

The thirty years beginning in 1900 generated a very lively discussion concerning the national purpose and the means to achieve it. The progressives sensed the serious contradiction between progress and poverty and searched for the means to improve the material conditions of life for all as well as to upgrade the quality of living in America. World War I interrupted the struggle and diverted the nation's energies into a foreign war. Although the 1920's witnessed a falling away from the goals established by the progressives the dialogue continued between those who wanted a breather from the high emotional demands of the reform movement and of the crusade to make the world safe for democracy and those who recognized that the tasks of keeping forms consonant with realities admits of no relaxation of effort [20].

1

America's Colonial Experiment
William Howard Taft's Special Report on the Philippines

William Howard Taft (1857-1930) and Elihu Root (1854-1937) were the chief architects of early American policy in the Philippines. Root, as Secretary of War from 1899 to 1904 and Secretary of State from 1905 to 1909, penned the first instructions given to American representatives in the Philippines. Taft headed the second Philippine Commission, which, beginning in September 1900, took over all legislative authority and continued the work initiated by the Army of establishing civil government on the municipal and provincial levels. On July 4, 1901, the Army transferred all executive power to Taft, whom President Roosevelt had appointed as civil governor of the islands, a post he held until 1904, when he became Secretary of War of the United States. During his tenure of the latter office, Taft continued to give a great deal of attention to American colonial problems. President Roosevelt sent him to Manila in 1907 to attend the opening of the first elected Philippine Legislative Assembly. Portions of his special report to the President presented after his return to Washington are reprinted below. For a general discussion of American colonialism see Julius W. Pratt, *America's Colonial Experiment: How the United States Gained, Governed, and in Part Gave Away a Colonial Empire* (New York: Prentice-Hall, Inc., 1951). Garrel A. Grunder and William E. Livezey in their *The Philippines and the United States* (Norman: University of Oklahoma Press, 1951) cover the relationships of the two nations during the half century after 1898. The standard biography of Taft is Henry F. Pringle's *The Life and Times of William Howard Taft, A Biography* (New York: Farrar and Rinehart Company, 1939). One might also consult with profit *Howard K. Beale's *Theodore Roosevelt and the Rise of America to World Power* (Baltimore: Johns Hopkins Press, 1956). In reading this selection note

---

William Howard Taft, *Special Report of Wm. H. Taft, Secretary of War, to the President on the Philippines, January 23, 1908.* Senate Document 200, 60 Cong., 1 sess., pp. 5-8, 14-15, 23-34, 40-42, 67-68, 71-79.

*Editor's note: An asterisk preceding an author's name in the headnotes in this book indicates that the cited volume is available in a paperback edition.

(1) how President Roosevelt characterized American action in the Philippines; (2) what elements of policy Secretary Taft emphasized in his report; (3) who, in Secretary Taft's judgment, should decide the issue of Philippine independence; (4) what steps were taken to activate American policy in the islands; (5) how Taft contrasted the political education of the Filipinos under Spain and the United States; (6) what role education was expected to play in implementing American designs and what steps were taken to improve the extent and quality of education in the islands; (7) by what means practical political education was to be advanced; (8) what Taft had to say about civil rights and their protection; (9) what his views were concerning current and future business conditions in the Philippines; (10) his judgment regarding the political future of the islands; (11) Taft's defense of American policy; and (12) the tone and mood of the report as a whole.

To the Senate and House of Representatives:

I transmit herewith the report of Secretary Taft upon his recent trip to the Philippines. I heartily concur in the recommendations he makes, and I call especial attention to the admirable work of Governor Smith and his associates. It is a subject for just national gratification that such a report as this can be made. No great civilized power has ever managed with such wisdom and disinterestedness the affairs of a people committed by the accident of war to its hands. If we had followed the advice of the misguided persons who wished us to turn the islands loose and let them suffer whatever fate might befall them, they would have already passed through a period of complete and bloody chaos, and would now undoubtedly be the possession of some other power which there is every reason to believe would not have done as we have done; that is, would not have striven to teach them how to govern themselves or to have developed them, as we have developed them, primarily in their own interests. Save only our attitude toward Cuba, I question whether there is a brighter page in the annals of international dealing between the strong and the weak than the page which tells of our doings in the Philippines. I call especial attention to the admirably clear showing made by Secretary Taft of the fact that it would have been equally ruinous if we had yielded to the desires of those who wished us to go faster in the direction of giving the Filipinos self-government, and if we had followed the policy advocated by others, who desired us simply to rule the islands without any thought at all of fitting them for self-government. The islanders have made real advances in a hopeful direction, and they have opened well with the new Philippine Assembly; they have yet a long way to travel before they will be fit for complete self-government, and for deciding, as it will then be their duty to do, whether this self-government shall be accompanied by complete independence. It will probably be a generation, it may even be longer, before this point is reached; but it is most gratifying that such substantial progress toward this as a goal has already been accomplished. We desire that it be reached at as early a date as possible for the sake of the Filipinos and for our own sake. But improperly to endeavor to hurry the time will probably mean that the goal will not be attained at all.

THEODORE ROOSEVELT

The White House
January 27, 1908

SPECIAL REPORT OF THE SECRETARY OF WAR

War Department
Washington, D. C., January 23, 1908

Mr. President:

By your direction I have just visited the Philippine Islands. I sailed from Seattle September 13, last; reached Manila October 15; remained in the Islands until November 9, when I returned to the United States via Trans-Siberian Railway, reaching New York December 20. The occasion for my visit was the opening of the Philippine Assembly. The members of the Assembly were elected in July last, in accordance with the organic act of Congress, by the eligible voters of the Christian provinces of the Islands, divided into 80 districts. The Assembly becomes a branch of the legislature of the Islands coordinate with the Philippine Commission. This makes a decided change in the amount of real power which the Philippine electorate is to exercise in the control of the Islands. If justified by substantial improvement in the political conditions in the Islands, it is a monument of progress.

It is more than nine years since the battle of Manila Bay and the subsequent surrender of Manila by the Spaniards to the American forces. It is more than eight years since the exchange of ratifications of the treaty of Paris, by which the Philippine Islands passed under the sovereignty and became the property of the United States. It is more than seven years since President McKinley, by written instructions to Mr. Root, Secretary of War, committed the government of the Philippine Islands to the central control of the Philippine Commission, subject to the supervision of the Secretary of War. It is more than six years since the complete installation of a quasi civil government in the Islands, with a civil governor as excutive and the Commission as a legislature, all by authority of the President as Commander in Chief of the Army and Navy. It is more than five years since the steps taken by President McKinley and yourself in establishing and maintaining a quasi civil government in the Islands were completely ratified and confirmed by the Congress in an organic act which, in effect, continued the existing government, but gave it needed powers as a really civil government that the President under constitutional limitations was unable to confer. The installation of the Assembly seems to be, therefore, an appropriate time for a precise statement of the national policy toward the people of the Philippines adopted by Mr. McKinley, continued by you, and confirmed by Congress, for an historical summary of the conditions political, social, and material, existing in the Islands when the United States became responsible for their government, and for a review of the results of governmental measures taken to improve the conditions of law and order, the political and intellectual capacity of the people, and their sanitary and material welfare.

The policy of the United States toward the Philippines is, of course, ultimately for Congress to determine, and it is difficult to see how one Congress could bind another Congress, should the second conclude to change the policy declared by the first. But we may properly assume that after one Congress has announced a policy upon the faith of which a whole people has for some years acted and counted, good conscience would restrain subsequent Congresses from lightly changing it. For four years Congress in silence permitted Mr. McKinley and yourself, as Commanders in Chief of the Army, to adopt and carry out a policy in the Philippines, and then expressly ratified everything which you had done, and confirmed and made part of the statute certain instructions which Mr. McKinley issued for the guidance of the Philippine Commission in making civil government in the Islands. Not only this, but Congress closely followed, in the so-called organic act, your recommendations as to provisions for a future change in the Philippine government. The national policy may, therefore, be found in the course pursued and declarations made by the Chief Executives in Congressional messages and other state papers which have met the approval of Congress.

Shortly stated, the national policy is to govern the Philippine Islands for the benefit and welfare and uplifting of the people of the Islands and gradually to extend to them, as they shall show themselves fit to exercise it, a greater and greater measure of popular self-government. One of the corollaries to this proposition is that the United States in its government of the Islands will use every effort to increase the capacity of the Filipinos to exercise political power, both by general education of the densely ignorant masses and by actual practice, in partial self-government, of those whose political capacity is such that practice can benefit it without too great injury to the efficiency of government. What should be emphasized in the statement of our national policy is that we wish to prepare the Filipinos for *popular* self-government. This is plain from Mr. McKinley's letter of instructions and all of his utterances. It was not at all within his purpose or that of the Congress which made his lettter part of the law of the land that we were merely to await the organization of a Philippine oligarchy or aristocracy competent to administer government and then turn the Islands over to it. On the contrary, it is plain, from all of Mr. McKinley's utterances and your own, in interpretation of our national purpose, that we are the trustees and guardians of the whole Filipino people, and peculiarly of the ignorant masses, and that our trust is not discharged until those masses are given education sufficient to know their civil rights and maintain them against a more powerful class and safely to exercise the political franchise. This is important, in view of the claim, to which I shall hereafter refer, made by certain Filipino advocates of immediate independence under the auspices of the Boston anti-imperialists, that a satisfactory independent Philippine government could be established under a governing class of 10 per cent and a serving and obedient class of 90 per cent.

Another logical deduction from the main proposition is that when the Filipino people as a whole show themselves reasonably fit to conduct a popular self-government, maintaining law and order and offering equal protection of the laws and civil rights to rich and poor, and desire complete independence of the United States, they shall be given it. The standard set, of course, is not that of perfection or such a governmental capacity as that of an Anglo-Saxon people, but it certainly ought to be one of such popular political capacity that complete independence in its exercise will result in progress rather than retrogression to chaos or tyranny. It should be noted, too, that the tribunal to decide whether the proper political capacity exists to justify independence is Congress and not the Philippine electorate. Aspiration for independence may well be one of the elements in the make-up of a people to show their capacity for it, but there are other qualifications quite as indispensable. The judgment of a people as to their own political capacity is not an unerring guide.

The national Philippine policy contemplates a gradual extension of popular control, i.e., by steps. This was the plan indicated in Mr. McKinley's instructions. This was the method indicated in your recommendation that a popular assembly be made part of the legislature. This was evidently the view of Congress in adopting your recommendation, for the title of the act is "For the temporary government of the Philippine Islands" and is significant of a purpose or policy that the government then being established was not in permanent form, but that changes in it from time to time would be necessary. . . .

Promise of Extension of Self-Government

President McKinley announced as his policy that the Philippine Islands would be taken over by the American Government to be governed for the benefit of the Filipinos, and that as they developed fitness for partial self-government it should be gradually extended to them. In order to enforce and give evidence of this purpose, he appointed a Commission in 1899, known from its chairman, Hon. J. G. Schurman, as the "Schurman Commission," to visit the Philippine Islands and extend local self-government as rapidly as possible. The Commission was able only to investigate conditions and to report that in its judgment the Filipinos were not fit for self-government. It was able to be present at the organization of municipal government in a few towns which had been captured by the Americans, but it practically was able to do no constructive work, in view of the conditions of war that existed while it was there. It returned to the United States and made its report.

In February of 1900 a new Commission was appointed by President McKinley, who gave it much more ample powers than its predecessor, for the purpose of organizing civil government in the wake of war as rapidly as conditions would permit. The powers conferred were set forth in a letter of instructions delivered by President McKinley to Mr. Root, Secretary of War, for his guidance and that of the Commission in respect of the policy to be pursued in the Philippines. The Commission arrived in June, 1900. The Commission was not authorized to assume any authority until the 1st of September and spent its time from June until September, 1900, in making investigations. It then took over the power and duty of enacting legislation to make a government for that part of the Islands in which war had ceased to exist and to make appropriations from funds raised by taxation for civil purposes. The preparation and enactment of a municipal and a provincial code for the organization and maintenance of municipalities and provinces in the Islands occupied much of the attention of the Commission during the remainder of the year 1900.

For the three or four months prior to the Presidential election in November, 1900, it was impossible to proceed with the actual organization of civil government. The insurgents were assured that the Administration of Mr. McKinley would be defeated and that his defeat would be immediately followed by a separation of the Islands from the United States. Everything hung on the election. The re-election of Mr. McKinley was a great blow to the insurrectos. . . .

Present Condition

Peace prevails throughout the Islands to-day in a greater degree than ever in the history of the Islands, either under Spanish or American rule, and agriculture is nowhere now impeded by the fear on the part of the farmer of the incursion of predatory bands. Under the policy already stated, inaugurated by the instructions of President McKinley to Secretary Root, in reference to the establishment of a temporary government in the Philippines, a community consisting of 7,000,000 people, inhabiting 300 different islands, many of whom were in open rebellion against the Government of the United States for four years, with all the disturbances following from robber and predatory bands which broke out from time to time, due to local causes, has been brought to a state of profound peace and tranquillity in which the people as a whole are loyally supporting the government in the maintenance of order. This is the first and possibly the most important accomplishment of the United States in the Philippines.

The Political Capacity and Intellectual Development of the Filipinos

Very little practical political education was given by the Spaniards to the Filipinos. Substantially all the important executive offices in the Islands were assigned to Spaniards, and the whole government was bureaucratic. The provincial and municipal authorities were appointed and popular elections were unknown. The administration of the municipalities was largely under the supervision and direction of the Spanish priest of the parish. No responsibility for government, however local or unimportant, was thrust upon Filipinos in such a way as to give them political experience, nor were the examples of fidelity to public interest sufficiently numerous in the officeholders to create a proper standard of public duty. The greatest difficulty that we have had to contend with in vesting Filipinos with official power in municipalities is to instill in them the idea that an office is not solely for private emolument.

There was an educated class among the Filipinos under the Spanish régime. The University of St. Thomas, founded by the Dominican Order early in the seventeenth century, has furnished an academic education to many graduates. The same order, as well as the Jesuits and the Augustinians, maintained secondary and primary schools for the well-to-do. Quite a number of Filipinos were educated in Spain or France. As compared with the youth and young men of school and college age in the Islands, the number, however, was very small. These men were educated either as lawyers, physicians, pharmacists, or priests. In politics their knowledge was wholly theoretical. They imbibed liberal ideas from the spread of republican doctrines in Spain, and the repressive policy of the Spanish Government, of course, operated only to encourage them. They were patriotic, and soon conceived of the Philippines as a nation. Rizal, a leader of Philippine thought, a poet, and a political writer, did not favor independence, for he believed his people not yet fitted, but he sought reform in the Spanish government of the Philippines and some popular voice in it.

As the protest against Spanish domination grew, the aspiration for complete independence took possession of many, and in the insurrections which followed there were many patriots moved by as high ideals as those which have led to revolutions in any country. Their conceptions of liberty, of independence, of government were wholly ideal, however. When in the course of events they came to actual government they were unable to realize their conceptions, and only a one-man power or an oligarchy with class privilege, and no real civil rights for the so-called serving or obedient class, followed. They needed as much education in practical civil liberty as their more ignorant fellow-countrymen in reading, writing, and arithmetic.

The efforts of the American Government to teach the ignorant their civil rights and to uplift them to self-governing capacity finds only a languid sympathy from many of the "ilustrados." From them comes the only objection to teaching English to the common people, lest they lose their national character; as if it were necessary to keep the people confined to 16 barbarous dialects in order that they should be distinctly Filipino. The real motive for the objection, whether conscious or not, is in the desire of the upper class to maintain the relation of the ruling class to the serving and obedient class.

The educated Filipino has an attractive personality. His mind is quick, his sense of humor fine, his artistic sense acute and active; he has a poetic imagination; he is courteous in the highest degree; he is brave; he is generous; his mind has been given by his education a touch of the scholastic logicism; he is a musician; he is oratorical by nature.

The educated Filipino is an aristocrat by Spanish association. He prefers that his children should not be educated at the public schools, and this accounts for the large private schools which the religious orders and at least one Filipino association are able to maintain. In arguing that the Philippines are entirely fit for self-government now, a committee of educated Filipinos once filed with the civil governor a written brief in which it was set forth that the number of "ilustrados" in the Islands was double that of the offices—central, provincial, and municipal—and therefore the country afforded two "shifts" of persons competent to run the government. This, it was said, made clear the possibility of a good government if independence was granted. The ignorance of the remainder of the people, admitted to be dense, made no difference. I cite this to show of how little importance an intelligent public opinion or an educated constituency is regarded in the community and government which many of the educated Filipinos look forward to as a result of independence. I do not say that there are not notable exceptions to this among leading Filipinos, but such persons are usually found among those who are not so impatient to lose American guidance in the government. Indeed, I am gratified to hear that the first bill which passed the Assembly was an appropriation of a million pesos for barrio schools. On the whole, however, there is reason for believing that were the government of the Islands now turned over to the class which likes to call itself the natural ruling class, the movement initiated by the present government to educate the ignorant classes would ultimately lose its force. The candor with which some of the representatives of the independista movement have spoken of the advantage for governmental purposes of having 80 per cent of the people in a serving or obedient class indicates this.

No one denies that 80 per cent of the Filipino people are densely ignorant. They are in a state of Christian tutelage. They are childlike and simple, with no language but a local Malay dialect spoken in a few provinces; they are separate from the world's progress. The whole tendency under the Spaniards was to keep them ignorant and innocent. The Spanish public school system was chiefly on paper. They were for a long time subject completely to the control of the Spanish friar, who was parish priest and who generally did not encourage the learning of

Spanish or great acquaintance with the world at large. The world owes to the Spanish friar the Christianization of the Filipino race. It is the only Malay or oriental race that is Christian. The friars beat back the wave of Mohammedanism and spread their religion through all the Islands. They taught the people the arts of agriculture, but they believed it best to keep them in a state of innocent ignorance. They did not encourage the coming into the Filipino local communities of Spaniards. They feared the influence of world knowledge. They controlled the people and preached to them in their own dialects. They lived and died among them.

The friars left the people a Christian people—that is, a people with Western ideals. They looked toward Rome, and Europe, and America. They were not like the Mohammedan or the Buddhist, who despise Western civilization as inferior. They were in a state of tutelage, ripe to receive modern Western conceptions as they should be educated to understand them. This is the reason why I believe that the whole Christian Filipino people are capable by training and experience of becoming a self-governing people. But for the present they are ignorant and in the condition of children. So, when the revulsion from the Spanish domination came, as it did, the native priest or the neighboring "ilustrado" or "cacique" led them into the insurrection. They are a brave people and make good soldiers if properly led. They learn easily, and the most striking fact in our whole experience in the Philippines is the eagerness with which the common Filipino agricultural laborer sends his children to school to learn English.

There is no real difference between the educated and ignorant Filipinos that can not be overcome by the education of one generation. They are a capable people in the sense that they can be given a normal intellectual development by the same kind of education that is given in our own common school system. Now they have not intelligence enough to exercise the political franchise with safety to themselves or their country; but I do not see why a common school education in English, with industrial teaching added, may not make the children of these people capable of forming an intelligent public opinion needed to sustain a popular government if, at the same time that the oncoming generations are being educated in schools, primary and industrial, those who are intelligent are being given a political education by actually exercising the power of the franchise and actually taking part in the government.

As will be seen hereafter, the Philippine government has not funds enough to educate in primary and industrial schools all the present generation of school age, and unless some other source of funds than governmental revenues is found it will take longer than a generation to complete the primary and industrial education of the common people. Until that is done, we ought not to lift our guiding hand from the helm of the ship of state of the Philippine Islands. With these general remarks as to the present unfitness of the Filipino people for popular self-government and their capacity for future development so that they may, by proper education, general and political, become a self-governing people, I come to the methods pursued by the Philippine government in furnishing to the Filipinos the necessary education. I shall consider the subject under two heads:

1. Education in schools for the youth of school age.

2. Practical political education by the extension, step by step, of political control to an eligible class.

First: Education in Schools

Reference has already been made to the fact of the very great ignorance and illiteracy that prevails among the Filipino people. It is not too much to say that knowledge of Spanish is a fairly good indication whether an individual can be said to be educated. Statistics show that but 7 per cent of the people of the Islands speak Spanish; all the others speak in the varying dialects, which among the civilized people number some 16. The Philippine people should be educated sufficiently to have a common medium of communication, and every man, woman, and child should have the benefit of the primary education in that common medium. Reading, writing, and arithmetic are necessary to enable the rural laborer and the small hemp, cocoanut, or tobacco farmer to make contracts for the sale of his products and to know what price he should receive for that which he has to sell. With this knowledge, too, he will soon be able to know his own rights and to resist the absolute control which is now frequently exercised over him by the local cacique.

The necessity for a common school system was emphasized in the instructions of President McKinley to Secretary Root, and those responsible for the government of the Islands have been earnest and active in seeking to establish one. The language selected for the schools is English. It is selected because it is the language of business in the Orient, because it is the language of free institutions, and because it is the language which the Filipino children who do not know Spanish are able more easily to learn than they are to learn Spanish, and it is the language of the present sovereign of the Islands. The education in English began with the soldiers of the American Army, one of whom was detailed from each company to teach schools in the villages which had become peaceful. When the Commission assumed authority it sent to the United States for 1,000 American teachers, and after the arrival of these pioneers in the Islands, a system of primary schools was inaugurated together with normal schools.

Public educational work in the Islands is performed under the bureau of education, with the central office located in Manila, having 37 divisions, each in charge of a division superintendent, embracing in all 379 school districts each in charge of a supervising teacher. The total number of schools in operation during the past year was: Primary schools, 3,435; intermediate schools, 162; arts and trades schools, 32; agricultural schools, 5; domestic-science schools, 17, and provincial high schools, 36, making a total of 3,687 and an increase from the previous year as follows: 327 primary schools, 70 intermediate schools, 15 arts and trades schools, 3 agricultural schools, and 9 domestic-science schools. There are engaged in the teaching of these schools at present 717 permanent American teachers and 109 temporary appointees, and all of these are paid out of the central treasury. In addition to these there are what are known as Filipino insular teachers, numbering 455, who are paid out of the central treasury. In addition to these there are 5,656 municipal Filipino teachers, all of whom speak and teach English and who are paid out of the treasuries of the municipalities.

The 6,000 Filipino teachers who are now teaching English have received their English education from our normal schools or our American teachers. Their number is growing, and they represent and are the most valuable educational asset we have acquired in working out our school system. The average annual

salary of the Filipino insular teacher is 533.2 pesos a year, while
that of municipal teachers is 210.36 pesos. The Filipino insular
teachers are drawn from graduates of normal schools and also
from the students sent by the government and at the expense of
the government to the United States to be educated there. Forty-
six of these students have recently returned from the United
States and have been appointed as insular teachers at salaries
ranging from 840 to 960 pesos per annum. The average paid to
the American teacher is about $1,200 per annum. The total en-
rollment for the year, inclusive of the Moro Province—the schools
in which are conducted under a separate system—was 479,978.
This was in the month of March at the close of the school year,
when the enrollment reached its highest point. The average
enrollment total by months was 346,245, of whom 62 per cent
were boys and 38 per cent were girls. The average daily attendance was 269,000, or a percentage of attendance of about 85
per cent. The highest percentage of attendance was 94, in the city
of Manila. The lowest percentage in some of the provinces was 78.
The attendance and enrollment in schools begins in August, which
is the beginning of the school year, and ends in March. As August
is one of the wet months, the attendance begins at the lowest
figure and increases gradually into the dry season until its highest
point at the close of the school year in March.

The central government this year for school purposes and
construction of schools has appropriated 3,500,000 pesos. The
maintenance of primary schools is imposed by law upon the
municipalities, and involves a further expenditure of nearly a
million and a half pesos. In order to relieve distress incident to
agricultural depression, it was found necessary to suspend the
land tax, a part of the proceeds of which by mandatory provision
of law was appropriated to the support of municipal schools.
The central government in the first year appropriated a sufficient
sum from the internal revenue to meet the deficit caused by the
failure to impose the land tax, but in the present year it was only
able to appropriate 50 per cent of the amount which would have
been raised by the land tax, and next year no such appropriation
will be made, and it will be left optional with the province
whether the land tax shall be imposed or not.

The great difficulty in the matter of education in the Islands is
the lack of funds to make it as extended as it should be. The

suspension of the land tax is subjecting the educational system to a crisis, but the revival of agriculture in many parts of the Islands leads to the hope that the crisis may be successfully passed. It would be entirely possible to expend for the sole benefit of the Philippine people, without the least waste, upward of two or three millions of dollars annually in addition to all that the government of the Philippine Islands—central, municipal, and provincial—can afford to devote to this object. We are not able to educate as they should be educated more than a half of the youth of school age in the Islands. The government, while contributing to the maintenance of high schools in each province, is devoting its chief attention to the spread of primary education, and in connection with primary education, and, at its close in the intermediate schools, to industrial education. Primary and industrial education carried on until the child is 14 or 15 years old is thought to be the best means of developing the Filipino people into a self-sustaining and self-governing people, and the present government has done all that it has been possible to do in developing and maintaining a proper system for this purpose. The tendency toward the development of industrial education the world over has created such a demand for industrial teachers as to make it impossible for the Philippine government to secure as many as are needed for the purpose in the Islands, and in order to have these industrial teachers it must take the time to educate them as such, just as it did the Filipino primary teachers in English.

There are now in the Islands, including art and trade schools, agricultural schools, and domestic-science schools, at least one industrial school to every province, and it is the purpose to increase this number as rapidly as resources and opportunity will permit. Under the influence of the traditions of the Spanish régime, when manual labor seems to have been regarded as an evidence of servitude, it was at first impossible to secure pupils for the great manual training school in Manila. Boys preferred to be "escribientes" or clerks and gentlemen rather than to learn to win a livelihood by the skill of their hands, but this has been rapidly overcome. In the insular school of arts and trades in Manila, where the plant and equipment is quite satisfactory, instruction is now given some 350 pupils in English, arithmetic, geography, mechanical drawing, woodworking (bench work, carving, turning, and cabinet making), ironworking (bench work, filing, blacksmithing, and iron machine work), and finishing, including painting and varishing, to which will be added next year boat building and wheelwrighting. At the present time there are on the waiting list some 200 pupils who seek admission but for whom no places are available. A large insular agricultural school is to be established in Manila for giving instruction in practical agriculture, and the money, 100,000 pesos, necessary for the building and construction has already been appropriated.

The influence of the primary instruction in English is shown throughout the Islands by the fact that to-day more people throughout the Islands, outside of Manila and the large cities, speak English than speak Spanish. A noticeable result of the government's activity in the establishment of English schools has been the added zeal in teaching English in private educational establishments. A Filipino school managed and taught only by Filipinos, called "Liceo," has some 1,500 pupils in Manila, and English is regularly taught as part of the curriculum of that school; the Dominican order of friars, which is primarily an educational order, has schools in and about Manila with upward of 2,000 students, and English is now made a very important part of the curriculum of those schools. The Jesuits also have two very large schools in Manila, embracing some 1,000 or 1,500 pupils drawn from all parts of the Islands, in which English is made an important branch of the study. There is considerable competition in this matter and there seems now to be a united effort to spread the knowledge of English in accordance with the government's policy. At times, as already intimated, a discordant note is heard in the suggestion that the American Government is seeking to deprive the Filipino of his native language. As his native language is really 15 or 16 different dialects, this does not seem a great deprivation. It is possible that some effort will be made to include in the primary instruction the reading and writing of the local dialect in the local schools. No objection can be made to this unless it shall interfere with the instruction in English, which it is hoped it may not do.

Should Congress be anxious to facilitate and hurry on the work of redeeming the Philippine Islands and making the Filipino people a self-governing community, it could take no more effective step than a permanent appropriation of two or three millions of dollars for ten or fifteen years to the primary and industrial education of the Filipino people, making it conditional on the continued appropriation by the Philippine government of the same amount to educational purposes which it has devoted and is now devoting annually to that purpose. The influence of the educational system introduced has not only been direct in the spread of education among the younger of the present generation, but it has also been an indirect means of convincing the Filipino people at large of the beneficent purpose of the American Government in its remaining in the Philippine Islands and of the sincerity of its efforts in the interest of their people.

Filipino Cadets at West Point

Section 36 of the act of Congress, approved February 2, 1901, referring to Philippine Scouts, provides that

When, in the opinion of the President, natives of the Philippine Islands shall, by their services and character, show fitness for command, the President is authorized to make provisional appointments to the grades of second and first lieutenants from such natives, who, when so appointed, shall have the pay and allowances to be fixed by the Secretary of War, not exceeding those of corresponding grades of the Regular Army.

As it is thought that better results will be obtained if a few young Filipinos, especially selected, be appointed to the United States Military Academy with a view to their being commissioned officers of scouts upon graduation, I strongly recommend that Congress, by appropriate legislation, authorize the appointment of seven young Filipinos, or one for about every million of inhabitants of those Islands, as cadets at the Military Academy at West Point. This action on the part of Congress would, in my judgment, tend to further increase the zeal and efficiency of a body of troops which has always rendered faithful and satisfactory services.

Second: Practical Political Education

There is no doubt that the exercise of political power is the best possible political education and ought to be granted whenever the pupil has intelligence enough to perceive his own interest even in a rude practical way, or when other competent electors are sufficiently in the majority to avoid the injury likely to be done by a government of ignorance and inexperience. The Philippine government concluded that the only persons in the Philippines who had intelligence enough to make their exercise of political power useful to them as an education and safe as a governmental experiment where those who spoke and wrote English or Spanish, or who paid $7.50 a year taxes, or whose capacity had been recognized in Spanish times by their appointment as municipal officials. Adult males who came within these classes, it was thought, ought to begin their political education by assuming political responsibility, and so they were made electors in municipal, provincial, and assembly elections, and embraced, as near as it can be estimated, about 12 to 15 per cent of the adult male population. Of course, as the common school education spreads, the electorate will increase.

Let us now examine the political education which has been given in practice to these eligible electors and the results.

Municipalities and Provinces

By the municipal code the old municipalities under the Spanish régime, which resembled the townships of the West and the towns of New England, were authorized to reorganize under the American Government. They consisted generally of the población, or the most centrally located and most populous settlement, with a number of barrios or outlying wards or villages, all within the municipality and under its control. The provisions of the code did not differ materially from those of similar codes in the United States, except that wherever possible and practicable the unobjectionable customs of the country were recognized and acquiesced in formally in the law. The towns were divided into classes and the salaries of the officials were limited accordingly. The provincial code provided for the organization of governments in the provinces which had been recognized as provinces under the Spanish régime. Under the original provisions of that code the government of the province—

legislative and executive—was under a provincial board, consisting of a governor and treasurer and a supervisor of roads and buildings. Other appointed officers were provided, as the prosecuting attorney and the secretary of the province, who did not sit on the provincial board. The governor was originally elected by the councilmen of all the towns of the province assembled in convention, they themselves having previously been elected by the people. The treasurer and supervisor were each selected and appointed under the rules adopted in accordance with the merit system provided in a civil-service law, which was among the first passed by the Commission.

One of the early difficulties in the maintenance of an efficient government in the provinces was the poverty of the provinces and the lack of taxable resources to support any kind of a government at all. It was soon found that the provincial supervisor, who, it was hoped, might be an American engineer, was too expensive a burden for the province to carry. For a time the district superintendent of education of the province was made the third member of the provincial board instead of the supervisor, whose office was abolished. This, however, did not work well, because the time of the superintendent was needed for his educational duties. Subsequently, therefore, it was thought wise to provide a third member of the board, who served with but little compensation and who was elected as the governor was elected. The system of electing the governor by convention of councilmen of all the towns of the province was changed, so that now the governor and the third member of the board are elected by direct popular vote, while the treasurer is still appointed. It will be seen that, in this way, the government of the towns is comletely autonomous, subject only to visitation and disciplinary action of the governor of the province and of the governor-general on appeal. The provincial government now, though not originally, is completely autonomous in the sense that a majority of the board which governs the province are elected by the people. The duties of the provincial treasurer are burdensome, complex, and important to such a degree as to make it impossible thus far to find Filipinos who have been able to master the duties of the office and to give satisfaction therein, although there are quite a number of Filipino assistant treasurers and subordinates in the office of treasurer who give reasonable ground to expect that the American treasurers may be in a reasonable time supplanted by Filipino treasurers.

The question now arises what has been shown in the government of these municipalities and of the provinces in respect to the capacity of the Filipinos for complete self-government in local matters? It is undoubtedly true that the municipalities would be much more efficient had the policy been pursued of appointing Americans to the important offices in the municipalities, but there would have been two great objections to this course, one that the municipal government would not have attracted the sympathetic attention of the people as the present municipalities have—and we would thus have lost a valuable element in making such government a success—and the other that the educational effect upon the people in training them for self-government would have been much less.

When I say that the development of municipal government in the Philippines has been satisfactory, I am far from saying that it has been without serious defects. All I mean is that considering the twofold object in view—first governmental, second educational—the result thus far with all its shortcomings shows progress toward both ends and vindicates the course taken.

Up to the time of our occupation, the government had represented to the Filipino an entity entirely distinct from himself with which he had little sympathy and which was engaged in an attempt to obtain as much money as possible from him in the form of taxes. He had been taught to regard an office as the private property of the person holding it and in respect to which ordinary practice justified the holder in making as much profit from it as he could. The idea that a public office is a public trust had not been implanted in the Filipino mind by experience, and the conception that an officer who fails in his duty by embezzlement or otherwise was violating an obligation that he owed to each individual member of the public, he found it difficult to grasp. He was apt to regard the robbing of the government by one of its officers as an affair in which he had little or no interest and in which, not infrequently, his sympathies were against the government. As a consequence, the chief sense of restraint felt by municipal officials in handling public funds comes from a fear of inspection by the central government and its prosecution. The fear of condemnation by the public opinion of the local community has a much less deterrent force, even if the official is to seek reelection. The sense of responsibility for the government they control and whose officers they elect is brought home to the people of a municipality with slowness and difficulty. This is the political education that is going on in the Filipino municipalities. We are making progress, but we must be patient, for it is not the task of a day to eradicate traditions and ideas that had their origin in a system of government under which this people lived for centuries.

Hence when we find that there is still a considerable percentage of Filipino municipal officers who have to be removed and prosecuted for embezzlement, we must not be discouraged. Early in the American occupation we had to prosecute sixteen or seventeen American provincial treasurers for defalcations in public funds. It was bitterly humiliating for the dominant race to furnish such an example, when we were assuming to teach the Filipinos the art of self-government. The American embezzlers were all promptly sent to Bilibid Penitentiary for long terms. This had an excellent effect upon both Americans and Filipinos in the Islands. The defalcations were due to a lack of good material available for these positions in the Islands. To-day the American provincial treasurers are of the highest order of public servants and are a credit to the American name. Their example has been of the utmost benefit in the training of Filipino municipal and provincial officials.

Another difficulty arising from a similar cause that we have had to meet and overcome has been the disposition of municipal councils to vote all of the available funds for the payment of their own salaries and leave nothing for the improvement or repair of roads, the construction of buildings, or the payment of school-teachers, and this although the law may, by mandatory provision, have set aside certain definite shares of the public funds for such purposes. These evils have had to be remedied by placing the funds in the hands of the provincial treasurer so as to secure the payment of the amount required by law to be devoted to educational purposes and by imposing upon the discretion of common councils to vote salaries from their funds a limitation that the total of salaries shall not exceed a certain percentage of the total funds in control of the town. . . .

Civil Rights

Before discussing the provision for the national assembly and its influences, educational and otherwise, I must refer to the effort of President McKinley to extend to the Filipinos the guaranties of life, liberty, and property, secured by the Federal Constitution to those within Federal jurisdiction. The guaranties assured in the instructions of Mr. McKinley included all those of the Federal Constitution except the right to bear arms and to trial by jury.

The right to bear arms is one that can not safely yet be extended to the people of the Philippines, because there are among those people men given to violence, who with the use of arms would at once resort to ladronism as a means of livelihood. The temptation would be too great and ought not to be encouraged. Nor are the people fit for the introduction of a jury system. Not yet has any considerable part of the community become sufficiently imbued with the sense of responsibility for the government and with its identification with the government. This responsibility and identification are necessary before jurors can sit impartially between society and the prisoner at the bar. Without it they are certain always to release the prisoner and to sympathize with him in the prosecution against him. The fair treatment of the prisoner is sufficiently secured in a country never having had a jury trial by the absolute right of appeal from the decision of a single judge to the decision of seven judges, with a writ of error thence to the Supreme Court of the United States. It may be that in the future it will seem wise gradually to provide for a jury in various classes of cases, but at present it would be premature.

The civil rights conferred by Mr. McKinley's instructions were expressly confirmed by the organic act of July 1, 1902. It has been the purpose of the Philippine government to make the extension of these rights a real thing and a benefit for the poorer Filipino, and progress is being made in this direction. The great obstacle to it arises from the ignorance of the people themselves as to what their rights are and their lack of knowledge as to how those rights may be asserted.

The work of impressing a knowledge of these things upon the people goes, however, rapidly on, and with the education in

English of a new generation and their succession to the electorate, we can be certain that the spread of education as to popular rights and the means of maintaining them will be wider and wider, until we can have a whole community who know their rights, and knowing, dare maintain them.

Charges have been made that the existing Philippine government has not properly preserved these guaranties of civil rights. It is true that the Commission has, in effect, suspended these guaranties in a condition equivalent to one of war in some of the provinces, and has been sustained in so doing by the supreme court of the Islands and of the United States. It is also true that during a condition equivalent to war the Commission provided that no one should advocate independence, even by peaceable means, because agents of insurrection were inciting actual violence under the guise of such peaceable propaganda. With the coming of peace, the statute ceased to have effect. To-day, however, the writ of habeas corpus runs without obstruction. The liberty of the press and of free speech is real. There is no censorship of the press and no more limitation upon its editors than there is in the city of Washington. The publication of criminal libel or seditious language calculated and intended to cause public riot and disturbance is punishable in Manila and the Philippines as it is in many of the States of the Union. This freedom of discussion and this opportunity to criticise the government, educate the people in a political way and enable them more intelligently to exercise their political rights.

The National Assembly

In recommending to Congress the provision for a national assembly contained in the organic act of the Philippine government, Secretary Root and the Commission were moved by the hope and belief that the promise in the act, conditioned, as its fulfillment was, on the existence of peace in the Islands, would stimulate activity on the part of all Filipinos having political ambition to bring about tranquillity. In this respect, as already pointed out, the result has abundantly vindicated their judgment. They were further moved by the conviction that this step toward greater popular self-government would strengthen the hands of the Government by securing from the people readier acquiescence in, and greater obedience to, measures which their representatives had joined in passing, than when they were the decrees of an alien government. They further believed that by means of the assembly much more exact and practical knowledge of the needs of the country would be brought to the law-making power than in any other way. Finally, they thought that the inauguration of such an assembly would be a most important step in the main plan or policy of educating Filipinos in the science and practice of popular representative government. They were aware of the possible danger that this was a step too far in advance. They did not deny that on the part of a number elected there would be a strong inclination to obstruct the smooth working of existing government on lines of political and material progress. They anticipated the probability that in the first assembly elected the majority would be in favor of immediate independence; but in spite of all this they were clear in their forecast that the responsibilities of power would have both a sobering and educational effect that would lead ultimately to conservatism of action and to strengthening the existing government. . . .

General Business Conditions

Of course, the depression in certain business branches of agriculture, like sugar, tobacco and rice, due to lack of markets for the first two, and to a lack of draft animals in the production of sugar and rice has had a direct effect upon the business of the islands of a depressing character. Gradually, however, business has grown better. In spite of adverse conditions the importations of rice have decreased from $12,000,000 gold to $3,500,000 gold, and, while the imports as a whole have increased not to their highest previous figure, they have been maintained within four and a half millions of their highest mark, and, as already said, the exports are higher than ever in the history of the islands, the balance of trade in their favor for the last fiscal year being about five millions, exclusive of gold and silver and government and railway free entries.

I found in the islands a disposition on the part of both American and Philippine business men and of the leaders of all parties in the Philippine Assembly to make a united effort to improve business and general conditions.

Business Future of Philippines

I do not hesitate to prophesy that during the next twenty-five years a development will take place in the agriculture and other business of the Philippine Islands, which will be as remarkable in its benefits to the United States and the Philippine Islands as was the development of Alaska during the last ten or fifteen years. Hope of this is not what has actuated the government in pursuing the policy that it has pursued in the development of the islands, but this is as inevitable a result as if it had been directly sought, and perhaps the absence of selfishness in the development of the islands is a greater assurance of profitable return than if business exploitation by the United States had been the chief and sole motive. The growth in the production of hemp and other fiber products, in cocoanuts, in rubber and many other tropical crops and in peculiar manufactures of the islands may be looked forward to with certainty.

Gold Standard Currency

One of the great benefits conferred upon the islands by the American Government has been the introduction of the gold standard. This has doubtless prevented the larger profits which were made in the old days by the purchasers of hemp and other agricultural products in the islands, who sold again in European and American markets, because under the system then prevailing, they bought in silver and sold in gold, and by watching the markets they were able to add very much to the legitimate profit of the middlemen by what constituted a system of gambling in exchanges. The same features characterized the banking in the islands. Now, however, with the gold standard the gambling feature in business is very largely eliminated. The coinage is satisfactory to the people, the silver certificates circulate well and are popular, and there seems to be no ground for complaint of the currency.

Need of Capital—Agricultural Bank

One of the crying needs of the Philippines is capital, and this whether it be for the development of railroads, wagon roads, manufactures, or in the promotion of agriculture. The usurious interest which has to be paid by the farmers is so high as to leave very little for his profit and maintenance and ever since we entered the islands the cry for an agricultural bank which would lend money for a reasonable interest, say, 10 per cent, has been urged upon the Commission. Last year Congress authorized the government to guarantee the interest at 4 per cent on a certain amount of capital invested in such a bank, but up to this time no one has embraced the opportunity thus offered to undertake the conduct and operation of a bank although negotiations are pending looking to such a result. It is now proposed that the government shall undertake this instead of a private individual. . . .

Mines and Mining

There has been a good deal of prospecting in the islands and gold and copper have been found in paying quantities in the mountains of northern Luzon, the provinces of Benguet and Bontoc and Lepanto, as well as in the Camarines in southeastern Luzon, and in Masbate, an island lying directly south of Luzon; but great complaint is made, and properly made, of the limitations upon the mining law which prevent the location by one person of more than one claim on a lode or vein. Mining is such a speculative matter at any rate, and the capital that one puts into it is so generally lost that it would seem that, in a country like the Philippines where development ought to be had, there should be liberal inducements for the investment of capital for such a purpose. Secretary Worcester of the interior department has frequently recommended that this limitation of the law be repealed. The Commission joins in this recommendation and I cordially concur.

While I do not favor large land holdings, I also concur in the recommendation of the secretary of the interior and the Commission that the prohibition upon corporations holding more than 2,500 acres of land be also stricken out. It certainly might well be increased to 10,000 acres if any limitation is to be imposed at all.

U.S. Coastwise Trading Laws

It is proposed by some to put in force the coastwise trading laws in respect to the navigation between the United States and the islands. I think this a very short-sighted policy. To-day the trade between the United States and the islands, export and import, is about 17 per cent of the total. The proportion of the total export trade from the Philippines to the United States is growing and is certain to grow more rapidly in the future, especially if proper legislation is adopted in respect to sugar and tobacco. Now a coastwise trading law will exclude altogether the use of foreign bottoms between the ports of the United States and the ports of the Philippine Islands, and will confine that commerce to United States vessels. There is very grave doubt whether there are enough United States vessels to carry on this trade as it is, and even if there were they could not carry on the trade without a very great increase in freight rates over what they now are. The minute that these rates are advanced, while the rates to other countries remain the same, the trade between the islands and the United States will cease to be. There will be no trade for the vessels of the United States to carry, no one will have been benefited in the United States, and the only person who will reap advantage is the foreign exporter to whom the Philippine business house will naturally turn for exchange of products. The only method possible by which the United States vessels can be given the Philippine trade is by voting a reasonable subsidy for United States vessels engaged in that trade. Any other prohibitive or exclusive provision of law will be merely cutting off the nose to spite the face of the interest which attempts it. I feel certain that when the question of applying the coastwise trading laws to the business between the United States and the islands is fully investigated, even those representing the shipping interests that need and ought to have much encouragement will conclude that the coastwise trading laws applied to the American Philippine trade would merely destroy the trade without benefiting the shipping interests.

In the criticisms upon the Government's Philippine policy to

be found in the columns of the newspapers that favor immediate
separation, it has been frequently said that the coastwise trading
laws of the United States apply as between islands of the Philippines. The truth is that the restrictions upon shipping between
ports in the Philippine Islands are what the Legislature of the
islands imposes, and Congress has made no provision of limitation in respect to them. The coastwise regulations in force
within the Archipelago are as liberal as possible. . . .

Political Future of the Islands

There are in the Philippines many who wish that the government shall declare a definite policy in respect to the islands so
that they may know what that policy is. I do not see how any
more definite policy can be declared than was declared by
President McKinley in his instructions to Secretary Root for
the guidance of the Philippine Commission, which was incorporated into law by the organic act of the Philippine government,
adopted July 1, 1902. That policy is declared to be the extension
of self-government to the Philippine Islands by gradual steps
from time to time as the people of the islands shall show themselves fit to receive the additional responsibility, and that policy
has been consistently adhered to in the last seven years now
succeeding the establishment of civil government.

Having taken some part and sharing in the responsibility for
that government, of course my views of the results are likely to
be colored by my interest in having the policy regarded as
successful, but eliminating as far as is possible the personal bias,
I believe it to be true that the conditions in the islands to-day
vindicate and justify that policy. It necessarily involves in its
ultimate conclusion as the steps toward self-government become
greater and greater the ultimate independence of the islands,
although of course if both the United States and the islands were
to conclude after complete self-government were possible that
it would be mutually beneficial to continue a governmental
relation between them like that between England and Australia,
there would be nothing inconsistent with the present policy in
such a result.

Any attempt to fix the time in which complete self-government
may be conferred upon the Filipinos in their own interest, is I

think most unwise. The key of the whole policy outlined by President McKinley and adopted by Congress was that of the education of the masses of the people and the leading them out of the dense ignorance in which they are now, with a view to enabling them intelligently to exercise the force of public opinion without which a popular self-government is impossible.

It seems to me reasonable to say that such a condition can not be reached until at least one generation shall have been subjected to the process of primary and industrial education, and that when it is considered that the people are divided into groups speaking from ten to fifteen different dialects, and that they must acquire a common medium of communication, and that one of the civilized languages, it is not unreasonable to extend the necessary period beyond a generation. By that time English will be the language of the islands and we can be reasonably certain that a great majority of those living there will not only speak and read and write English, but will be affected by the knowledge of free institutions, and will be able to understand their rights as members of the community and to seek to enforce them against the pernicious system of caciquism and local bossism, which I have attempted in this report to describe.

But it is said that a great majority of the people desire immediate independence. I am not prepared to say that if the real wish of the majority of all the people, men, women, and children, educated and uneducated, were to be obtained, there would not be a very large majority in favor of immediate independence. It would not, however, be an intelligent judgment based on a knowledge of what independence means, of what its responsibilities are or of what popular government in its essence is. But the mere fact that a majority of all the people are in favor of immediate independence is not a reason why that should be granted, if we assume at all the correctness of the statement, which impartial observers can not but fail to acquiesce in, to wit: that the Filipinos are not now fit for self-government.

The policy of the United States is not to establish an oligarchy, but a popular self-government in the Philippines. The electorate to which it has been thought wise to extend partial self-government embraces only about 15 or 20 per cent of the adult male population, because it has been generally conceded by Filipinos and Americans alike that those not included within the electorate are wholly unable to exercise political responsibility. Now, those persons who demanded and were given a hearing before the delegation of Congressmen and Senators that visited the islands in 1905, to urge immediate independence contended that the islands are fit for self-government because there are from 7 to 10 per cent of intelligent people who are constituted by nature a ruling class, while there are 90 per cent that are a servile and obedient class, and that the presence of the two classes together argues a well balanced government. Such a proposition thus avowed reveals what is known otherwise to be the fact that many of those most emphatic and urgent in seeking independence in the islands have no thought of a popular government at all. They are in favor of a close government in which they, the leaders of a particular class, shall exercise control of the rest of the people. Their views are thus wholly at variance with the policy of the United States in the islands.

The presence of the Americans in the islands is essential to the due development of the lower classes and the preservation of their rights. If the American government can only remain in the islands long enough to educate the entire people, to give them a language which enables them to come into contact with modern civilization, and to extend to them from time to time additional political rights so that by the exercise of them they shall learn the use and responsibilities necessary to their proper exercise, independence can be granted with entire safety to the people. I have an abiding conviction that the Filipino people are capable of being taught self-government in the process of their development, that in carrying out this policy they will be improved physically and mentally, and that, as they acquire more rights, their power to exercise moral restraints upon themselves will be strengthened and improved. Meantime they will be able to see, and the American public will come to see the enormous material benefit to both arising from the maintenance of some sort of a bond between the two countries which shall preserve their mutually beneficial business relations.

No one can have studied the East without having been made aware that in the development of China, Japan and all Asia, are to be presented the most important political questions for the next century, and that in the pursuit of trade between the Occident and the Orient the having such an outpost as the Philippines, making the United States an Asiatic power for the time, will be of immense benefit to its merchants and its trade. While I have always refrained from making this the chief reason for the retention of the Philippines, because the real reason lies in the obligation of the United States to make this people fit for self-government and then to turn the government over to them, I don't think it improper, in order to secure support for the policy, to state such additional reason. The severe criticism to which the policy of the Government in the Philippines has been subjected by English Colonial statesmen and students, should not hinder our pursuit of it in the slightest. It is of course opposed to the policy usually pursued in the English government in dealing with native races, because in common with other colonial powers, most of England's colonial statesmen have assumed that the safest course was to keep the native peoples ignorant and quiet, and that any education which might furnish a motive for agitation was an interference with the true and proper course of government. Our policy is an experiment, it is true, and it assumes the risk of agitation and sedition which may arise from the overeducation of ambitious politicians or misdirected patriots, in order that the whole body of the people may acquire sufficient intelligence ultimately to exercise governmental control themselves.

Thus far the policy of the Philippines has worked. It has been attacked on the ground that we have gone too fast, that we have given the natives too much power. The meeting of the assembly and the conservative tone of that body thus far disclosed, makes for our view rather than that of our opponents, but had the result been entirely different with the assembly, and had there been a violent outbreak at first in its deliberations and attempts at obstruction, I should not have been in the least discouraged, because ultimately I should have had confidence that the assembly would learn how foolish such exhibitions were and how little good they accomplished for the members of the assembly or the people whom they represented. The fact that this natural tendency was restrained is an indication of the general conservatism of the Filipino people.

Though bearing the name of immediate independistas, the members of the controlling party of the assembly are far from being in favor of a policy which those words strictly construed would mean. Moreover, the recent election held, since the Assembly was organized, in which fifteen progresista and fifteen nationalista governors were elected, is an indication that the nationalist feeling is by no means so overwhelming as was at first reported when the returns from the election of the assembly were published in the press.

The fact that Filipinos are given an opportunity now to take part in the forming of the governmental policies in the islands, will I hope satisfy many of them that the United States is in earnest in attempting to educate them to self-government, will so occupy their ambitions and minds as to make the contention for immediate independence more of an ideal than of a real issue, will make more permanent and lasting the present satisfactory conditions as to peace and tranquillity in the islands, and will turn their attention toward the development of the prosperity of the islands by improvement of its material conditions and the uplifting of the people by their education, sanitation and general instruction in their political, social and material responsibilities.

There has been in the United States in the last year a recurring disposition on the part of many of the press and many public men to speak of the Philippine policy as if foredoomed to failure, and the condition of the islands as a most deplorable one. No one who knew the islands in 1900, and who has visited them during the present year and especially during the meeting of the assembly can honestly and fairly share such views. To one actually responsible in any degree for the present conditions by reason of taking part in the government of those islands, the changes made and the progress made under the circumstances are most gratifying.

Cost of the Present Government of the Islands

The most astounding and unfair statements have appeared in the press from time to time and have been uttered by men of political prominence who should know better, in respect to the cost to the United States of the Philippine Islands. The question of the cost of the islands to the United States as affecting its future policy can not of course include the cost of a war into which the United States was forced against its will, and which whether it ought to have been carried on or not, was carried on and was finished more than five years ago. The only question of cost that is relevant to the present discussion is the cost to the United States of the maintenance of the present Philippine government, including in that the cost of the maintenance of that part of the army of the United States which is in the Philippine Islands. Nor is it fair to include the entire cost of the army of the United States in the Philippine Islands for the reason that even if we did not have the Philippines, we should certainly retain the present size of our standing army which hardly exceeds 60,000 effective men, a very small army for 80,000,000 people. Moreover, it is worthy of note that the greatest increase in the Army of recent years has been in that branch of the service—to wit, the coast artillery—which has not been used in the Philippines for some years.

The only additional cost therefore that the maintenance of the army can be said to entail upon the United States is the additional cost of maintaining 12,000 soldiers in the islands over what it would be to maintain the same number of soldiers in the United States. This has been figured out and roughly stated amounts to about $250 a man or $3,000,000, together with the maintenance of 4,000 Philippine Scouts at a cost of $500 a man, or in all $2,000,000, which makes a total annual expenditure of $5,000,000. The United States at present contributes something, perhaps $200,000, to the expense of the coast survey of the islands. With this exception, there is not one cent expended from the treasury of the United States for the maintenance of the government in the islands. The additional cost of the 12,000 men in the islands, figured above at $250 a man, includes the cost of transportation and the additional cost of food supplies and other matters.

There is an item of cost, which perhaps may be charged to the Philippine Islands. I refer to the expense of fortifying the bay of Manila, the port of Iloilo and the port of Cebu, so that in holding the islands the United States shall not be subject to sudden and capricious attack by any ambitious power. This may reach a total of ten millions. But it is hardly fair to charge this to the Philippine policy; for almost everyone concedes the necessity of maintaining and fortifying coaling stations in the Orient whether we have the Philippines or not.

The question is, therefore, whether, in order to avoid the expenditure of $5,000,000 a year, the United States should pursue the humiliating policy of scuttle, should run away from an obligation which it has assumed to make the Philippines a permanently self-governing community, and should miss an opportunity at the same time of building up a profitable trade and securing a position in the Orient that can not but be of the utmost advantage in obtaining and maintaining its proper proportion of Asiatic and Pacific trade.

From time to time there has been quite severe criticism of the present Philippine government on the ground that it is such an expensive government as to be burdensome to the people. The facts are that the taxes which fall upon the common people are much less than they ever were under the Spanish régime. The taxes which fall upon the wealthy are considerably more, because as a matter of fact the Spanish system of taxation was largely devised for the purpose of avoiding taxation of the wealth of the islands. I have not at hand and am not able to insert in this report the figures and statistics which demonstrate this fact. They are now being prepared in Manila, and I hope at some future date to submit them for your consideration. Not only is the comparison to be instituted with the conditions existing under the Spanish régime, but also with the taxation of other dependencies. The data with respect to these are difficult to get and frequently liable greatly to mislead when the conditions of each particular colony are not fully understood and stated. But my information is derived from Governor Smith and Mr. Forbes that the cost per capita of the government of the Philippines will compare most favorably with that of colonial governments presenting substantially similar conditions.

The reports from the governor-general, the heads of departments and of bureaus have not reached Washington. I was able before I left the islands to read informal drafts of some of them and much of the information as to the last year's operations I have derived from them. I shall submit the reports immediately upon their arrival.

Recommendations

I therefore recommend:

First. That legislation be adopted by Congress admitting the products of the Philippine Islands to the markets of the United States, with such reasonable limitations as may remove fear of interference with the tobacco and sugar interests in the United States;

Second. That the present restrictions be removed as to the acquisition of mining claims and the holding of lands by corporations in the Philippines;

Third. That further legislation be passed authorizing the Philippine government, if it chooses, to open and condurt an agricultural bank, with a capital not exceeding $2,000,000; and

Fourth. That the coastwise laws of the United States be made permanently inapplicable to the trade between the ports of the islands and the ports of the United States.

Sincerely, yours,   WM. H. TAFT
The President

2

A Poem Catches the Mood of the Times
Edwin Markham's "The Man with the Hoe"

Edwin Markham (1852-1940) quickly earned fame and fortune with the publication of "The Man With the Hoe." First published in the *San Francisco Examiner*, January 15, 1899, the poem caught the imagination of a generation of progressive reformers who believed that human nature could be changed for the better by altering the social environment in which men and women lived and reared their children. Henry George in *Progress and Poverty* (1879) had called attention to one of the more patent contradictions of modern times: "Where population is densest, wealth greatest, and the machinery of production and exchange most highly developed—we find the deepest poverty, the sharpest struggle for existence, and the most enforced idleness." Why should this be true? Could man do nothing to help himself, or must he drift along hoping that natural forces would somehow, in the long run, right the wrongs induced by technological advance? In these few lines Markham reflected the sharp concern of those who sensed, as he put it, "the slow but awful degradation of man through endless, hopeless and joyless labor" imposed upon the worker by the industrial changes of the past several decades. For an uncritical impressionistic biography of the poet see William L. Stidger, *Edwin Markham* (New York: The Abingdon Press, 1933). One might also consult Louis Filler's brief biography of Markham in the *Dictionary of American Biography*, XXII (Supplement Two), pp. 428-30, and Mark Sullivan's *Our Times. The United States, 1900-1925* (New York: Charles Scribner's Sons, 1926-1935), II, pp. 236-253. *Samuel P. Hays's *The Response to Industrialism, 1885-1914* (Chicago: University of Chicago Press, 1957) is an excellent introduction to the subject of the impact of industrialism upon the nation. One might with profit also see Robert W. Schneider's impressive study, *Five Novelists of the Progressive Era* (New York: Columbia University Press, 1965). In reading the poem note (1) the symbolism implied in the use of the man with the hoe; (2) what direction—up from the animal or down from the divine—man has been moving; (3) what or

Edwin Markham, *The Man With the Hoe and Other Poems* (New York: Doubleday and McClure Company, 1899), pp. 15-18.

who in the poet's view was responsible for the workers' plight; (4) what warning or prophesy is contained in the lines; (5) what form the poet uses; and (6) what effect the cadence employed has upon the auditor when the lines are read aloud.

Written After Seeing Millet's World-Famous Painting

God made man in His own image,
in the image of God made He him.—Genesis

Bowed by the weight of centuries he leans
Upon his hoe and gazes on the ground,
The emptiness of ages in his face,
And on his back the burden of the world.
Who made him dead to rapture and despair,
A thing that grieves not and that never hopes,
Stolid and stunned, a brother to the ox?
Who loosened and let down this brutal jaw?
Whose was the hand that slanted back this brow?
Whose breath blew out the light within this brain?
Is this the Thing the Lord God made and gave
To have dominion over sea and land;
To trace the stars and search the heavens for power;
To feel the passion of Eternity?
Is this the Dream He dreamed who shaped the suns
And pillared the blue firmament with light?
Down all the stretch of Hell to its last gulf
There is no shape more terrible than this—
More tongued with censure of the world's blind greed—
More filled with signs and portents for the soul—
More fraught with menace to the universe.

What gulfs between him and the seraphim!
Slave of the wheel of labor, what to him
Are Plato and the swing of Pleiades?
What the long reaches of the peaks of song,
The rift of dawn, the reddening of the rose?
Through this dread shape the suffering ages look;
Time's tragedy is in that aching stoop;
Through this dread shape humanity betrayed,
Plundered, profaned and disinherited,
Cries protest to the Judges of the World,
A protest that is also prophecy.

O masters, lords and rulers in all lands,
Is this the handiwork you give to God,
This monstrous thing distorted and soul-quenched?

How will you ever straighten up this shape;
Touch it again with immortality;
Give back the upward looking and the light;
Rebuild in it the music and the dream;
Make right the immemorial infamies,
Perfidious wrongs, immedicable woes?

O masters, lords and rulers in all lands,
How will the Future reckon with this Man?
How answer his brute question in that hour
When whirlwinds of rebellion shake the world?
How will it be with kingdoms and with kings—
With those who shaped him to the thing he is—
When this dumb Terror shall reply to God,
After the silence of the centuries?

3

The Revolt Against Formalism in Philosophy

William James's "The Present Dilemma in Philosophy"

William James (1842-1910) was one of those intellectuals at the turn of the century who expressed the liberal, experimental, evolutionary temper of the age. A new world was coming into being; new energies clamored for release. Old systems of thought no longer served the busy, rapidly changing society of the twentieth century. Logic, abstraction, deduction from first principles were unsuited to the demands of the complex, living currents of life; a new approach to philosophy was needed. James sensed the inadequacies of the familiar formulas and hoped to provide a philosophy in tune with the times. Adopting the name *pragmatism*, James developed a philosophy which affirmed that "the meaning of ideas is to be sought in their practical consequences, that thought is a guide to action, and that truth is to be tested by the practical results of belief." In a world that was constantly changing, truth too was evolving. The best intellectual biography of James is Ralph Barton Perry's *The Thought and Character of William James*, 2 vols. (Boston: Little, Brown and Company, 1935). °Morton G. White's *Social Thought in America: The Revolt Against Formalism* (New York: The Viking Press, 1949) is indispensable to one beginning the study of the ideas of the Progressive period. More formal in its approach is Edward C. Moore, *American Pragmatism: Peirce, James and Dewey* (New York: Columbia University Press, 1961). David W. Noble's *The Paradox of Progressive Thought* (Minneapolis: University of Minnesota Press, 1958) raises some important issues concerning progressivism as he deals with a variety of exponents of the revolt against formalism. In the lecture reprinted here James indicates some of the reasons for his dissatisfaction with the older approaches to philosophy; other lectures in the same collection provide an elaboration of what he meant by pragmatism. In reading the selection note (1) what he implied by the phrase *the present dilemma in philosophy;* (2) what he meant by saying that for the individual, philosophy was one's "dumb sense of what life honestly and deeply

William James, *Pragmatism. A New Name for Some Old Ways of Thinking, Popular Lectures on Philosophy* (New York: Longmans, Green and Company, 1907), pp. 3-40.

means"; (3) how he divided philosophical thought into two camps
and his justification for doing so; (4) what dissatisfied James with
each of these alternative camps and what he liked about each; (5) how
he pictured the inadequacies of the older, formal approaches to philosophy; and (6) in what direction his own solution to the dilemma
of philosophy was taking.

IN THE PREFACE TO THAT ADMIRABLE COLLECTION OF
essays of his called "Heretics," Mr. Chesterton
[Gilbert K. (1874-1936), English essayist] writes these words:
"There are some people—and I am one of them—who think that
the most practical and important thing about a man is still his
view of the universe. We think that for a landlady considering a
lodger it is important to know his income, but still more important to know his philosophy. We think that for a general
about to fight an enemy it is important to know the enemy's
numbers, but still more important to know the enemy's philosophy. We think the question is not whether the theory of the
cosmos affects matters, but whether in the long run anything
else affects them."

I think with Mr. Chesterton in this matter. I know that you,
ladies and gentlemen, have a philosophy, each and all of you,
and that the most interesting and important thing about you is
the way in which it determines the perspective in your several
worlds. You know the same of me. And yet I confess to a certain
tremor at the audacity of the enterprise which I am about to
begin. For the philosophy which is so important in each of us
is not a technical matter; it is our more or less dumb sense of
what life honestly and deeply means. It is only partly got from
books; it is our individual way of just seeing and feeling the
total push and pressure of the cosmos. I have no right to
assume that many of you are students of the cosmos in the
classroom sense, yet here I stand desirous of interesting you in
a philosophy which to no small extent has to be technically
treated. I wish to fill you with sympathy with a contemporaneous
tendency in which I profoundy believe, and yet I have to talk
like a professor to you who are not students. Whatever universe
a professor believes in must at any rate be a universe that lends
itself to lengthy discourse. A universe definable in two sentences

is something for which the professorial intellect has no use. No faith in anything of that cheap kind! I have heard friends and colleagues try to popularize philosophy in this very hall, but they soon grew dry, and then technical, and the results were only partially encouraging. So my enterprise is a bold one. The founder of pragmatism himself [Charles Sanders Peirce (1839-1914)] recently gave a course of lectures at the Lowell Institute with that very word in its title—flashes of brilliant light relieved against Cimmerian darkness! None of us, I fancy, understood *all* that he said—yet here I stand, making a very similar venture.

I risk it because the very lectures I speak of *drew*—they brought good audiences. There is, it must be confessed, a curious fascination in hearing deep things talked about, even though neither we nor the disputants understand them. We get the problematic thrill, we feel the presence of the vastness. Let a controversy begin in a smoking-room anywhere, about free-will or God's omniscience, or good and evil, and see how every one in the place pricks up his ears. Philosophy's results concern us all most vitally, and philosophy's queerest arguments tickle agreeably our sense of subtlety and ingenuity.

Believing in philosophy myself devoutly, and believing also that a kind of new dawn is breaking upon us philosophers, I feel impelled, *per fas aut nefas* [by hook or by crook], to try to impart to you some news of the situation.

Philosophy is at once the most sublime and the most trivial of human pursuits. It works in the minutest crannies and it opens out the widest vistas. It "bakes no bread," as has been said, but it can inspire our souls with courage; and repugnant as its manners, its doubting and challenging, its quibbling and dialectics, often are to common people, no one of us can get along without the far-flashing beams of light it sends over the world's perspectives. These illuminations at least, and the contrast-effects of darkness and mystery that accompany them, give to what it says an interest that is much more than professional.

The history of philosophy is to a great extent that of a certain clash of human temperaments. Undignified as such a treatment may seem to some of my colleagues, I shall have to take account of this clash and explain a good many of the divergencies of philosophers by it. Of whatever temperament a professional philosopher is, he tries, when philosophizing, to sink the fact of his temperament. Temperament is no conventionally recognized reason, so he urges impersonal reasons only for his conclusions. Yet his temperament really gives him a stronger bias than any of his more strictly objective premises. It loads the evidence for him one way or the other, making for a more sentimental or a more hard-hearted view of the universe, just as this fact or that principle would. He *trusts* his temperament. Wanting a universe that suits it, he believes in any representation of the universe that does suit it. He feels men of opposite temper to be out of key with the world's character, and in his heart considers them incompetent and "not in it," in the philosophic business, even though they may far excel him in dialectical ability.

Yet in the forum he can make no claim, on the bare ground of his temperament, to superior discernment or authority. There arises thus a certain insincerity in our philosophic discussions: the potentest of all our premises is never mentioned. I am sure it would contribute to clearness if in these lectures we should break this rule and mention it, and I accordingly feel free to do so.

Of course I am talking here of very positively marked men, men of radical idiosyncrasy, who have set their stamp and likeness on philosophy and figure in its history. Plato, Locke, Hegel, Spencer, are such temperamental thinkers. Most of us have, of course, no very definite intellectual temperament, we are a mixture of opposite ingredients, each one present very moderately. We hardly know our own preferences in abstract matters; some of us are easily talked out of them, and end by following the fashion or taking up with the beliefs of the most impressive philosopher in our neighborhood, whoever he may be. But the one thing that has *counted* so far in philosophy is that a man should *see* things, see them straight in his own peculiar way, and be dissatisfied with any opposite way of seeing them. There is no reason to suppose that this strong temperamental vision is from now onward to count no longer in the history of man's beliefs.

Now the particular difference of temperament that I have in mind in making these remarks is one that has counted in literature, art, government, and manners as well as in philosophy. In manners we find formalists and free-and-easy persons. In government, authoritarians and anarchists. In literature, purists or academicals, and realists. In art, classics and romantics. You recognize these contrasts as familiar; well, in philosophy we have a very similar contrast expressed in the pair of terms "rationalist" and "empiricist," "empiricist" meaning your lover of facts in all their crude variety, "rationalist" meaning your devotee to abstract and eternal principles. No one can live an hour without both facts and principles, so it is a difference rather of emphasis; yet it breeds antipathies of the most pungent character between those who lay the emphasis differently; and we shall find it extraordinarily convenient to express a certain contrast in men's ways of taking their universe, by talking of the "empiricist" and of the "rationalist" temper. These terms make the contrast simple and massive.

More simple and massive than are usually the men of whom the terms are predicated. For every sort of permutation and combination is possible in human nature; and if I now proceed to define more fully what I have in mind when I speak of rationalists and empiricists, by adding to each of those titles some secondary qualifying characteristics, I beg of you to regard my conduct as to a certain extent arbitrary. I select types of combination that nature offers very frequently, but by no means uniformly, and I select them solely for their convenience in helping me to my ulterior purpose of characterizing pragmatism. Historically we find the terms "intellectualism" and "sensationalism" used as synonyms of "rationalism" and "empiricism." Well, nature seems to combine most frequently with intellectualism an idealistic and optimistic tendency. Empiricists on the other hand are not uncommonly materialistic, and their optimism is apt to be decidedly conditional and tremulous. Rationalism is always monistic. It starts from wholes and universals, and makes much of the unity of things. Empiricism starts from the parts, and makes of the whole a collection—is not averse therefore to calling itself pluralistic. Rationalism usually considers itself more religious than empiricism, but there is much to say about this claim, so I merely mention it. It is a true claim when the individual rationalist is what is called a man of feeling, and when the individual empiricist prides himself on being hard-headed. In that case the rationalist will usually also be in favor of what is called free-will, and the empiricist will be a fatalist—I use the terms most popularly current. The rationalist finally will be of dogmatic temper in his affirmations, while the empiricist may be more sceptical and open to discussion.

I will write these traits down in two columns. I think you will practically recognize the two types of mental make-up that I mean if I head the columns by the titles "tender-minded" and "tough-minded" respectively.

THE TENDER-MINDED	THE TOUGH-MINDED
Rationalistic (going by "principles")	Empiricist (going by "facts")
Intellectualistic	Sensationalistic
Idealistic	Materialistic
Optimistic	Pessimistic
Religious	Irreligious
Free-willist	Fatalistic
Monistic	Pluralistic
Dogmatical	Sceptical

Pray postpone for a moment the question whether the two contrasted mixtures which I have written down are each inwardly coherent and self-consistent or not—I shall very soon have a good deal to say on that point. It suffices for our immediate purpose that tender-minded and tough-minded people, characterized as I have written them down, do both exist. Each of you probably knows some well-marked example of each type, and you know what each example thinks of the example on the other side of the line. They have a low opinion of each other. Their antagonism, whenever as individuals their temperaments have been intense, has formed in all ages a part of the philosophic atmosphere of the time. It forms a part of the philosophic atmosphere today. The tough think of the tender as sentimentalists and soft-heads. The tender feel the tough to be unrefined, callous, or brutal. Their mutual reaction is very much like that that takes place when Bostonian tourists mingle with a population like that of Cripple Creek. Each type believes the other to be inferior to itself; but disdain in the one case is mingled with amusement, in the other it has a dash of fear.

Now, as I have already insisted, few of us are tender-foot Bostonians pure and simple, and few are typical Rocky Mountain toughs, in philosophy. Most of us have a hankering for the good things on both sides of the line. Facts are good, of course—give us lots of facts. Principles are good—give us plenty of principles.

The world is indubitably one if you look at it in one way, but as indubitably is it many, if you look at it in another. It is both one and many—let us adopt a sort of pluralistic monism. Everything of course is necessarily determined, and yet of course our wills are free: a sort of free-will determinism is the true philosophy. The evil of the parts is undeniable, but the whole can't be evil: so practical pessimism may be combined with metaphysical optimism. And so forth—your ordinary philosophic layman never being a radical, never straightening out his system, but living vaguely in one plausible compartment of it or another to suit the temptations of successive hours.

But some of us are more than mere laymen in philosophy. We are worthy of the name of amateur athletes, and are vexed by too much inconsistency and vacillation in our creed. We cannot preserve a good intellectual conscience so long as we keep mixing incompatibles from opposite sides of the line.

And now I come to the first positively important point which I wish to make. Never were as many men of a decidedly empiricist proclivity in existence as there are at the present day. Our children, one may say, are almost born scientific. But our esteem for facts has not neutralized in us all religiousness. It is itself almost religious. Our scientific temper is devout. Now take a man of this type, and let him be also a philosophic amateur, unwilling to mix a hodge-podge system after the fashion of a common layman, and what does he find his situation to be, in this blessed year of our Lord 1906? He wants facts; he wants science; but he also wants a religion. And being an amateur and not an independent originator in philosophy he naturally looks for guidance to the experts and professionals whom he finds already in the field. A very large number of you here present, possibly a majority of you, are amateurs of just this sort.

Now what kinds of philosophy do you find actually offered to meet your need? You find an empirical philosophy that is not religious enough, and a religious philosophy that is not empirical enough for your purpose. If you look to the quarter where facts are most considered you find the whole tough-minded program in operation, and the "conflict between science and religion" in full blast. Either it is that Rocky Mountain tough of a Haeckel [Ernst Heinrich Haeckel (1834-1919), German biologist and philosopher] with his materialistic monism, his ether-god and his jest at your God as a "gaseous vertebrate"; or it is Spencer [Herbert Spencer (1820-1903), English philosopher] treating the world's history as a redistribution of matter and motion solely, and bowing religion politely out at the front door:—she may indeed continue to exist, but she must never show her face inside the temple.

For a hundred and fifty years past the progress of science has seemed to mean the enlargement of the material universe and the diminution of man's importance. The result is what one may call the growth of naturalistic or positivistic feeling. Man is no lawgiver to nature, he is an absorber. She it is who stands firm; he it is who must accommodate himself. Let him record truth, inhuman though it be, and submit to it! The romantic spontaneity and courage are gone, the vision is materialistic and depressing. Ideals appear as inert by-products of physiology; what is higher is explained by what is lower and treated forever as a case of "nothing but"—nothing but something else of a quite inferior sort. You get, in short, a materialistic universe, in which only the tough-minded find themselves congenially at home.

If now, on the other hand, you turn to the religious quarter for consolation, and take counsel of the tender-minded philosophies, what do you find?

Religious philosophy in our day and generation is, among us English-reading people, of two main types. One of these is more radical and aggressive, the other has more the air of fighting a slow retreat. By the more radical wing of religious philosophy I mean the so-called transcendental idealism of the Anglo-Hegelian school, the philosophy of such men as Green, the Cairds, Bosanquet, and Royce [Thomas Hill Green (1836-1882), English philosopher; Edward (1855-1908) and John Caird (1820-1898), Scotch metaphysicians; Bernard Bosanquet (1848-1923), English philosopher; Josiah Royce (1855-1916), American philosopher and one of James's colleagues at Harvard]. This philosophy has greatly influenced the more studious members of our protestant ministry. It is pantheistic and undoubtedly it has already blunted the edge of the traditional theism in protestantism at large.

That theism remains, however. It is the lineal descendant, through one stage of concession after another, of the dogmatic scholastic theism still taught rigorously in the seminaries of the catholic church. For a long time it used to be called among us the philosophy of the Scottish school. It is what I meant by the philosophy that has the air of fighting a slow retreat. Between the encroachments of the hegelians and other philosophers of the "Absolute," on the one hand, and those of the scientific evolutionists and agnostics, on the other, the men that give us this kind of a philosophy, James Martineau [(1805-1900), English Unitarian clergyman and philosopher], Professor Bowne, Professor [George Trumbull] Ladd [(1842-1921), American psychologist and theologian] and others, must feel themselves rather tightly squeezed. Fair-minded and candid as you like, this philosophy is not radical in temper. It is eclectic, a thing of compromises, that seeks a *modus vivendi* above all things. It accepts the facts of Darwinism, the facts of cerebral physiology, but it does nothing active or enthusiastic with them. It lacks the victorious and aggressive note. It lacks *prestige* in consequence; whereas absolutism has a certain *prestige* due to the more radical style of it.

These two systems are what you have to choose between if you turn to the tender-minded school. And if you are the lovers of facts I have supposed you to be, you find the trail of the serpent of rationalism, of intellectualism, over everything that lies on that side of the line. You escape indeed the materialism that goes with the reigning empiricism; but you pay for your escape by losing contact with the concrete parts of life. The more absolutistic philosophers dwell on so high a level of abstraction that they never even try to come down. The absolute mind which they offer us, the mind that makes our universe by thinking it, might, for aught they show us to the contrary, have made any one of a million other universes just as well as this. You can deduce no single actual particular from the notion of it. It is compatible with any state of things whatever being true here below. And the theistic God is almost as sterile a principle. You have to go to the world which he has created to get any inkling of his actual character: he is the kind of god that has once for all made that kind of a world. The God of the theistic writers lives on as purely abstract heights as does the Absolute. Absolutism has a certain sweep and dash about it, while the usual theism is more insipid, but both are equally remote and vacuous. What *you* want is a philosophy that will not only exercise your powers of intellectual abstraction, but that will make some positive connexion with this actual world of finite human lives.

You want a system that will combine both things, the scientific loyalty to facts and willingness to take account of them, the spirit of adaptation and accommodation, in short, but also the old confidence in human values and the resultant spontaneity, whether of the religious or of the romantic type. And this is then your dilemma: you find the two parts of your *quaesitum* [object of your search] hopelessly separated. You find empiricism with inhumanism and irreligion; or else you find a rationalistic philosophy that indeed may call itself religious, but that keeps out of all definite touch with concrete facts and joys and sorrows.

I am not sure how many of you live close enough to philosophy to realize fully what I mean by this last reproach, so I will dwell a little longer on that unreality in all rationalistic systems by which your serious believer in facts is so apt to feel repelled.

I wish that I had saved the first couple of pages of a thesis which a student handed me a year or two ago. They illustrated my point so clearly that I am sorry I can not read them to you now. This young man, who was a graduate of some Western college, began by saying that he had always taken for granted that when you entered a philosophic classroom you had to open relations with a universe entirely distinct from the one you left behind you in the street. The two were supposed, he said, to have so little to do with each other, that you could not possibly occupy your mind with them at the same time. The world of concrete personal experiences to which the street belongs is multitudinous beyond imagination, tangled, muddy, painful and perplexed. The world to which your philosophy-professor introduces you is simple, clean and noble. The contradictions of real life are absent from it. Its architecture is classic. Principles of reason trace its outlines, logical necessities cement its parts. Purity and dignity are what it most expresses. It is a kind of marble temple shining on a hill.

In point of fact it is far less an account of this actual world than a clear addition built upon it, a classic sanctuary in which the rationalist fancy may take refuge from the intolerably confused and gothic character which mere facts present. It is no *explanation* of our concrete universe, it is another thing altogether, a substitute for it, a remedy, a way of escape.

Its temperament, if I may use the world temperament here, is utterly alien to the temperament of existence in the concrete. *Refinement* is what characterizes our intellectualist philosophies. They exquisitely satisfy that craving for a refined object of contemplation which is so powerful an appetite of the mind. But I ask you in all seriousness to look abroad on this colossal universe of concrete facts, on their awful bewilderments, their surprises and cruelties, on the wildness which they show, and then to tell me whether "refined" is the one inevitable descriptive adjective that springs to your lips.

Refinement has its place in things, true enough. But a philosophy that breathes out nothing but refinement will never satisfy the empiricist temper of mind. It will seem rather a monument of artificiality. So we find men of science preferring to turn their backs on metaphysics as on something altogether cloistered and spectral, and practical men shaking philosophy's dust off their feet and following the call of the wild.

Truly there is something a little ghastly in the satisfaction with which a pure but unreal system will fill a rationalist mind. Leibnitz [(1646-1716)] was a rationalist mind, with infinitely more interest in facts than most rationalist minds can show. Yet if you wish for superficiality incarnate, you have only to read that charmingly written "Théodicée" of his, in which he sought to justify the ways of God to man, and to prove that the world we live in is the best of possible worlds. Let me quote a speci·men of what I mean.

Among other obstacles to his optimistic philosophy, it falls to Leibnitz to consider the number of the eternally damned. That it is infinitely greater, in our human case, than that of those saved, he assumes as a premise from the theologians, and then proceeds to argue in this way. Even then, he says:

"The evil will appear as almost nothing in comparison with the good, if we once consider the real magnitude of the City of God. Coelius Secundus Curio has written a little book, 'De Amplitudine Regni Coelestis,' which was reprinted not long ago. But he failed to compass the extent of the kingdom of the heavens. The ancients had small ideas of the works of God. . . .

It seemed to them that only our earth had inhabitants, and even
the notion of our antipodes gave them pause. The rest of the
world for them consisted of some shining globes and a few
crystalline spheres. But to-day, whatever be the limits that we
may grant or refuse to the Universe we must recognize in it
a countless number of globes, as big as ours or bigger, which
have just as much right as it has to support rational inhabitants,
tho it does not follow that these need all be men. Our earth
is only one among the six principal satellites of our sun. As all
the fixed stars are suns, one sees how small a place among visible
things our earth takes up, since it is only a satellite of one among
them. Now all these suns *may* be inhabited by none but happy
creatures; and nothing obliges us to believe that the number of
damned persons is very great; for *a very few instances and
samples suffice for the utility which good draws from evil.*
Moreover, since there is no reason to suppose that there are
stars everywhere, may there not be a great space beyond the
region of the stars? And this immense space, surrounding all
this region . . . may be replete with happiness and glory. . . .
What now becomes of the consideration of our Earth and of its
denizens? Does it not dwindle to something incomparably less
than a physical point, since our Earth is but a point compared
with the distance of the fixed stars. Thus the part of the Universe
which we know, being almost lost in nothingness compared with
that which is unknown to us, but which we are yet obliged to
admit; and all the evils that we know lying in this almost-nothing;
it follows that the evils may be almost-nothing in comparison
with the goods that the Universe contains."

Leibnitz continues elsewhere:

"There is a kind of justice which aims neither at the amendment of the criminal, nor at furnishing an example to others,
nor at the reparation of the injury. This justice is founded in
pure fitness, which finds a certain satisfaction in the expiation
of a wicked deed. The Socinians and Hobbes objected to this
punitive justice . . . which God has reserved for himself at
many junctures. . . . It is always founded in the fitness of things,
and satisfies not only the offended party, but all wise lookers-on,
even as beautiful music or a fine piece of architecture satisfies
a well-constituted mind. It is thus that the torments of the
damned continue, even tho they serve no longer to turn any one

away from sin, and that the rewards of the blest continue, even tho they confirm no one in good ways. The damned draw to themselves ever new penalties by their continuing sins, and the blest attract ever fresh joys by their unceasing progress in good. Both facts are founded on the principle of fitness . . . for God has made all things harmonious in perfection as I have already said."

Leibnitz's feeble grasp of reality is too obvious to need comment from me. It is evident that no realistic image of the experience of a damned soul had ever approached the portals of his mind. Nor had it occurred to him that the smaller is the number of "samples" of the genus "lost-soul" whom God throws as a sop to the eternal fitness, the more unequitably grounded is the glory of the blest. What he gives us is a cold literary exercise, whose cheerful substance even hell-fire does not warm.

And do not tell me that to show the shallowness of rationalist philosophizing I have had to go back to a shallow wigpated age. The optimism of present-day rationalism sounds just as shallow to the fact-loving mind. The actual universe is a thing wide open, but rationalism makes systems, and systems must be closed. For men in practical life perfection is something far off and still in process of achievement. This for rationalism is but the illusion of the finite and relative: the absolute ground of things is a perfection eternally complete.

I find a fine example of revolt against the airy and shallow optimism of current religious philosophy in a publication of that valiant anarchistic writer Morrison I. Swift. Mr. Swift's anarchism goes a little farther than mine does, but I confess that I sympathize a good deal, and some of you, I know, will sympathize heartily with his dissatisfaction with the idealistic optimisms now in vogue. He begins his pamphlet on "Human Submission" with a series of city reporter's items from newspapers (suicides, deaths from starvation, and the like) as specimens of our civilized regime. For instance:

"After trudging through the snow from one end of the city to the other in the vain hope of securing employment, and with his wife and six children without food and ordered to leave their home in an upper east-side tenement-house because of non-payment of rent, John Corcoran, a clerk, today ended his life by drinking carbolic acid. Corcoran lost his position three weeks ago through illness, and during the period of idleness his scanty savings disappeared. Yesterday he obtained work with a gang of city snow-shovelers, but he was too weak from illness, and was forced to quit after an hour's trial with the shovel. Then the weary task of looking for employment was again resumed. Thoroughly discouraged, Corcoran returned to his home last night to find his wife and children without food and the notice of dispossession on the door. On the following morning he drank the poison.

"The records of many more such cases lie before me (Mr. Swift goes on); an encyclopedia might easily be filled with their kind. These few I cite as an interpretation of the Universe. 'We are aware of the presence of God in his world,' says a writer in a recent English review. [The very presence of ill in the temporal order is the condition of the perfection of the eternal order, writes Professor Royce (*The World and the Individual,* II, p. 385)].* 'The Absolute is the richer for every discord and for all the diversity which it embraces,' says F. H. Bradley (*Appearance and Reality,* p. 204). He means that these slain men make the universe richer, and that is philosophy. But while Professors Royce and Bradley and a whole host of guileless thoroughfed thinkers are unveiling Reality and the Absolute and explaining away evil and pain, this is the condition of the only beings known to us anywhere in the universe with a developed consciousness of what the universe is. What these people experience *is* Reality. It gives us an absolute phase of the universe. It is the personal experience of those best qualified in our circle of knowledge to *have* experience, to tell us *what is.* Now what does *thinking about* the experience of these persons come to, compared to directly and personally feeling it as they feel it? The philosophers are dealing in shades, while those who live and feel know truth. And the mind of mankind—not yet the mind of philosophers and of the proprietary class—but of the great mass of the silently thinking men and feeling men, is coming to this view. They are judging the universe as they have hitherto permitted the hierophants of religion and learning to judge *them.* . . .

"This Cleveland workingman, killing his children and himself

---

*William James's interpolation.

[another of the cited cases]* is one of the elemental stupendous facts of this modern world and of this universe. It cannot be glozed over or minimized away by all the treatises on God, and Love, and Being, helplessly existing in their monumental vacuity. This is one of the simple irreducible elements of this world's life, after millions of years of opportunity and twenty centuries of Christ. It is in the mental world what atoms or sub-atoms are in the physical, primary, indestructible. And what it blazons to man is the imposture of all philosophy which does not see in such events the consummate factor of all conscious experience. These facts invincibly prove religion a nullity. Man will not give religion two thousand centuries or twenty centuries more to try itself and waste human time. Its time is up; its probation is ended; its own record ends it. Mankind has not aeons and eternities to spare for trying out discredited systems."†

Such is the reaction of an empiricist mind upon the rationalist bill of fare. It is an absolute "No, I thank you." "Religion," says Mr. Swift, "is like a sleep-walker to whom actual things are blank." And such, tho possibly less tensely charged with feeling, is the verdict of every seriously inquiring amateur in philosophy to-day who turns to the philosophy-professors for the where-withal to satisfy the fulness of his nature's needs. Empiricist writers give him a materialism, rationalists give him something religious, but to that religion "actual things are blank." He becomes thus the judge of us philosophers. Tender or tough, he finds us wanting. None of us may treat his verdicts disdainfully, for after all, his is the typically perfect mind, the mind the sum of whose demands is greatest, the mind whose criticisms and dissatisfactions are fatal in the long run.

It is at this point that my own solution begins to appear. I offer the oddly-named thing pragmatism as a philosophy that can satisfy both kinds of demand. It can remain religious like the rationalisms, but at the same time, like the empiricism, it can preserve the richest intimacy with facts. I hope I may be able to leave many of you with as favorable an opinion of it as I preserve myself. Yet, as I am near the end of my hour, I will not introduce pragmatism bodily now. I will begin with it

---

*William James's interpolation.

†Morrison I. Swift, *Human Submission*, Part Second, Philadlephia Liberty Press, 1905, pp. 4-10.

on the stroke of the clock next time. I prefer at the present moment to return a little on what I have said.

If any of you here are professional philosophers, and some of you I know to be such, you will doubtless have felt my discourse so far to have been crude in an unpardonable, nay, in an almost incredible degree. Tender-minded and tough-minded, what a barbaric disjunction! And, in general, when philosophy is all compacted of delicate intellectualities and subtleties and scrupulosities, and when every possible sort of combination and transition obtains within its bounds, what a brutal caricature and reduction of highest things to the lowest possible expression is it to represent its field of conflict as a sort of rough-and-tumble fight between two hostile temperaments! What a childishly external view! And again, how stupid it is to treat the abstractness of rationalist systems as a crime, and to damn them because they offer themselves as sanctuaries and places of escape, rather than as prolongations of the world of facts. Are not all our theories just remedies and places of escape? And, if philosophy is to be religious, how can she be anything else than a place of escape from the crassness of reality's surface? What better thing can she do than raise us out of our animal senses and show us another and a nobler home for our minds in that great framework of ideal principles subtending all reality, which the intellect divines? How can principles and general views ever be anything but abstract outlines? Was Cologne cathedral built without an architect's plan on paper? Is refinement in itself an abomination? Is concrete rudeness the only thing that's true?

Believe me, I feel the full force of the indictment. The picture I have given is indeed monstrously over-simplified and rude. But like all abstractions, it will prove to have its use. If philosophers can treat the life of the universe abstractly, they must not complain of an abstract treatment of the life of philosophy itself. In point of fact the picture I have given is, however coarse and sketchy, literally true. Temperaments with their cravings and refusals do determine men in their philosophies, and always will. The details of systems may be reasoned out piecemeal, and when the student is working at a system, he may often forget the forest for the single tree. But when the labor is accomplished, the mind always performs its big summarizing act, and the system forthwith stands over against one like a living thing, with that strange simple note of individuality which haunts our memory, like the wraith of the man, when a friend or enemy of ours is dead.

Not only Walt Whitman could write "who touches this book touches a man." The books of all the great philosophers are like so many men. Our sense of an essential personal flavor in each one of them, typical but indescribable, is the finest fruit of our own accomplished philosophic education. What the system pretends to be is a picture of the great universe of God. What it is—and oh so flagrantly!—is the revelation of how intensely odd the personal flavor of some fellow creature is. Once reduced to these terms (and all our philosophies get reduced to them in minds made critical by learning) our commerce with the systems reverts to the informal, to the instinctive human reaction of satisfaction or dislike. We grow as peremptory in our rejection or admission, as when a person presents himself as a candidate for our favor; our verdicts are couched in as simple adjectives of praise or dispraise. We measure the total character of the universe as we feel it, against the flavor of the philosophy proffered us, and one word is enough.

"Statt der lebendigen Natur," we say, "da Gott die Menschen schuf hinein"—that nebulous concoction, that wooden, that straight-laced thing, that crabbed artificiality, that musty schoolroom product, that sick man's dream! Away with it. Away with all of them! Impossible! Impossible!*

Our work over the details of his system is indeed what gives us our resultant impression of the philosopher, but it is on the resultant impression itself that we react. Expertness in philosophy is measured by the definiteness of our summarizing reactions, by the immediate perceptive epithet with which the expert hits such complex objects off. But great expertness is not necessary for the epithet to come. Few people have definitely articulated philosophies of their own. But almost every one has his own

---

*EDITOR'S NOTE: From Faust's opening monologue in Goethe's *Faust*. Faust had complained about his failure through book learning to experience the fullness and richness of life. A rough and free translation of James's quotation along with the two succeeding lines of the poem might read: "Instead of living in the natural world provided by God for man, I have accepted an existence surrounded by the bones of beasts amidst the smoke and mould of fleshless dead."

peculiar sense of a certain total character in the universe, and of the inadequacy fully to match it of the peculiar systems that he knows. They don't just cover *his* world. One will be too dapper, another too pedantic, a third too much of a job-lot of opinions, a fourth too morbid, and a fifth too artificial, or what not. At any rate he and we know off-hand that such philosophies are out of plumb and out of key and out of "whack," and have no business to speak up in the universe's name. Plato, Locke, Spinoza, Mill, Caird, Hegel—I prudently avoid names nearer home!—I am sure that to many of you, my hearers, these names are little more than reminders of as many curious personal ways of falling short. It would be an obvious absurdity if such ways of taking the universe were actually true.

We philosophers have to reckon with such feelings on your part. In the last resort, I repeat, it will be by them that all our philosophies shall ultimately be judged. The finally victorious way of looking at things will be the most completely *impressive* way to the normal run of minds.

One word more—namely about philosophies necessarily being abstract outlines. There are outlines and outlines, outlines of buildings that are *fat*, conceived in the cube by their planner, and outlines of buildings invented flat on paper, with the aid of ruler and compass. These remain skinny and emaciated even when set up in stone and mortar, and the outline already suggests that result. An outline in itself is meagre, truly, but it does not necessarily suggest a meagre thing. It is the essential meagreness of *what is suggested* by the usual rationalistic philosophies that moves empiricists to their gesture of rejection. The case of Herbert Spencer's system is much to the point here. Rationalists feel his fearful array of insufficiencies. His dry schoolmaster temperament, the hurdy-gurdy monotony of him, his preference for cheap make-shifts in argument, his lack of education even in mechanical principles, and in general the vagueness of all his fundamental ideas, his whole system wooden, as if knocked together out of cracked hemlock boards—and yet the half of England wants to bury him in Westminster Abbey.

Why? Why does Spencer call out so much reverence in spite of his weakness in rationalistic eyes? Why should so many educated men who feel that weakness, you and I perhaps, wish to see him in the Abbey notwithstanding?

Simply because we feel his heart to be *in the right place* philosophically. His principles may be all skin and bone, but at any rate his books try to mould themselves upon the particular shape of this particular world's carcass. The noise of facts resounds through all his chapters, the citations of fact never cease, he emphasizes facts, turns his face towards their quarter; and that is enough. It means the right *kind* of thing for the empiricist mind.

The pragmatistic philosophy of which I hope to begin talking in my next lecture preserves as cordial a relation with facts, and, unlike Spencer's philosophy, it neither begins nor ends by turning positive religious constructions out of doors—it treats them cordially as well.

I hope I may lead you to find it just the mediating way of thinking that you require.

4

A New Look at Poverty in the United States
Robert Hunter's "Poverty"

Robert Hunter (1874-1942) took an A.B. degree at Indiana University in 1896. Deeply touched by conditions suffered by the workers during the depression following the panic of 1893, he dedicated his life to social reform. He visited England in the summer of 1899 and resided for a time at Toynbee Hall, the pioneer settlement house in London. Returning to Chicago he lived at Hull House from 1899 until 1902, publishing in 1901 a memorable report on "Tenement Conditions in Chicago." In 1902 he went to New York and became active in the movement to improve child labor conditions. Following a trip to Europe in 1903, where he met a number of labor leaders, social workers, socialists, and revolutionists, he published *Poverty*, one of the first studies of its kind resting upon statistical evidence. Admittedly the data were inadequate, but Hunter's book was widely hailed as a pioneering sociological study of America's poor. Hunter helped inaugurate a new attitude toward poverty and pauperism, at the same time emphasizing the social as distinct from the individual causes of poverty in modern American society. The broader setting for Hunter's work can be sought in *Eric F. Goldman's *Rendezvous with Destiny: A History of Modern American Reform* (New York: Alfred A. Knopf, 1952) and in *Richard Hofstadter's *The Age of Reform: From Bryan to F.D.R.* (New York: Alfred A. Knopf, 1955). An unusually significant and relevant study is Robert Bremner's *From the Depths: The Discovery of Poverty in the United States* (New York: New York University Press, 1956). In reading this selection note (1) the author's definition of poverty; (2) how he distinguishes poverty from pauperism; (3) what he considered necessary for maintaining the physical efficiency of a worker; (4) his estimate of those in poverty in the United States in 1904; (5) his characterization of the status of statistical information in the country; (6) what methods he used to measure the extent of poverty in America; (7) what he saw as the causes of poverty; and (8) what solutions he advanced.

---

*Robert Hunter, *Poverty* (New York: The Macmillan Company, 1904), pp. 1-65.

WILLIAM DEAN HOWELLS SAID TO ME RECENTLY, after I had told him of a visit to Tolstoy: "It is wonderful what Tolstoy has done. He could do no more. For a nobleman, with the most aristocratic ancestry, to refuse to be supported in idleness, to insist upon working with his own hands, and to share as much as possible the hardship and toil of a peasant class, which, but recently, was a slave class, is the greatest thing he could do. But it is impossible for him to share their poverty, for poverty is not the lack of things; it is the fear and the dread of want. That fear Tolstoy could not know." These remarks of Mr. Howells brought to mind the wonderful words of Thomas Carlyle: "It is not to die, or even to die of hunger, that makes a man wretched; many men have died; all men must die. . . . But it is to live miserable we know not why; to work sore and yet gain nothing; to be heart-worn, weary, yet isolated, unrelated, girt in with a cold, universal Laissez-faire." To live miserable we know not why, to have the dread of hunger, to work sore and yet gain nothing—this is the essence of poverty.

There are many people in the world who believe that the provisions of charity are in the present day so generous and varied that no one need suffer; but, even if this were true, it would not materially lessen the sorrow of the poor. To thousands and thousands of working-men the dread of public pauperism is the agony of their lives. The mass of working-men on the brink of poverty hate charity. Not only their words convey a knowledge of this fact, but their actions, when in distress, make it absolutely undeniable. When the poor face the necessity of becoming paupers, when they must apply for charity if they are to live at all, many desert their families and enter the ranks of vagrancy; others drink themselves insensible; some go insane; and still others commit suicide. Recently a man who had been unable to find work and in despair committed suicide, left a note to his wife, saying: "I have gone forever; there is one less in the world to feed. Good-by. God help you to care for Tony; don't put her away." This is the fear and dread of pauperism; "don't put Tony away" is the last thought of the man whose misery caused him to take his own life.

These are the terrible alternatives which the working people in poverty accept in preference to pauperism, and yet it is a curious fact, which psychology alone explains, that the very men who will suffer almost anything rather than become paupers are often the very ones who never care to be anything else when once they have become dependent upon alms. When a family once become dependent, the mental agony which they formerly had disappears. Paupers are not, as a rule, unhappy. They are not ashamed; they are not keen to become independent; they are not bitter or discontented. They have passed over the line which separates poverty from pauperism.

This distinction between the poor and paupers may be seen everywhere. There are in all large cities in America and abroad, streets and courts and alleys where a class of people live who have lost all self-respect and ambition, who rarely, if ever, work, who are aimless and drifting, who like drink, who have no thought for their children, and who live more or less contentedly on rubbish and alms. Such districts are certain portions of Whitechapel and Spitalsfield, etc., in London, Kitrof Rynock in Moscow, parts of Armour Avenue in Chicago, Rat Hollow in Cincinnati, and parts of Cherry Hill and the Minettas in New York City, and so on in all cities everywhere. The lowest level of humanity is reached in these districts. In our American cities Negroes, Whites, Chinese, Mexicans, Half-breeds, Americans, Irish, and others are indiscriminately housed together in the same tenements and even in the same rooms. The blind, the crippled, the consumptive, the aged—the ragged ends of life; the babies, the children, the half-starved, under-clad beginnings in life, all huddled together, waiting, drifting. This is pauperism. There is no mental agony here; they do not work sore; there is no dread; they live miserably, but they do not care.

In the same cities and, indeed, everywhere, there are great districts of people who are up before dawn, who wash, dress, and eat breakfast, kiss wives and children, and hurry away to work or to seek work. The world rests upon their shoulders; it moves by their muscle; everything would stop if, for any reason, they should decide not to go into the fields and factories and mines. But the world is so organized that they gain enough to live upon only when they work; should they cease, they are in destitution and hunger. The more fortunate of the laborers are but a few weeks from actual distress when the machines are stopped. Upon the unskilled masses want is constantly pressing. As soon as employment ceases, suffering stares them in the face. They are the actual producers of wealth, who have no home nor any bit of soil which they may call their own. They are the millions who possess no tools and can work only by permission of another. In the main, they live miserably, they know not why. They work sore, yet gain nothing. They know the meaning of hunger and the dread of want. They love their wives and children. They try to retain their self-respect. They have some ambition. They give to neighbors in need, yet they are themselves the actual children of poverty.

It is with this latter class that this chapter deals. For the purpose of making the distinction perfectly clear between these two social classes—for it is an important distinction to make—definitions are necessary. A pauper is one who depends upon public or private charity for sustenance. A man may be in utter destitution and may even die of starvation, but he may not be called a pauper unless he applies for and receives charitable relief. Paupers must be included among those in poverty, but poverty is a much broader term than pauperism. Many, many thousand families, who are in no sense paupers, are in poverty. Those who are in poverty may be able to get a bare sustenance, but they are not able to obtain *those necessaries which will permit them to maintain a state of physical efficiency.* They are the large class in any industrial nation who are on the verge of distress. Only the most miserable of them are starving or dependent upon charity, but all of them are receiving too little of the common necessities to keep themselves at their best, physically. It would be difficult to over-estimate the importance of sufficient food, adequate clothing, and a sanitary home to those men, women, and children who must depend at all times upon their labor power and their physical efficiency, to produce an income sufficient to maintain themselves in working order. There is a fundamental here. If they must work to live, they must have those necessities which will enable them to work. The necessities for maintaining physical efficiency are very different from those essential to mere living. A Hottentot, a Lazzarone, or a vagrant may live well enough on little or nothing, because he does not spend himself. The modern workman demands a far higher standard of living in order to keep pace with intense

industrial life. Physical efficiency, not mere existence, is to him
vital. His necessities are necessities! It is a terrible word, for
"Necessity's sharp pinch" is like that of a steel vise. There is no
give to it. Necessity is like flint or granite. It is irresistible. It
cannot be shuffled with nor altered. If physical efficiency is an
absolute and vital necessity to the workman, so to him are
certain necessities for maintaining that physical efficiency. The
fundamental thing in all this is that every workman who is
expected by society to remain independent of public relief and
capable of self-support must be guaranteed, in so far as that is
possible, an opportunity for obtaining those necessaries essential
to physical efficiency. Such a standard is the basis of almost
everything; for, unless men can retain their physical efficiency,
they must degenerate. To continue in poverty for any long period
means in the end the loss of the power of doing work, and to
be unable to work means in the end pauperism. A standard of
physical efficiency is, of course, purely a materialistic standard;
it does not include mental efficiency except as that is involved
in physical well-being. It does not mean the maintenance of
national efficiency. To live up to the standard, or, in other words,
to be above the poverty line, means no more than to have a
sanitary dwelling and sufficient food and clothing to keep the
body in working order. It is precisely the same standard that a
man would demand for his horses or slaves. Treating man merely
as the "repository of a certain sort of labor power," it makes
possible the utilization of that power to the fullest extent. No
one will fail to realize how low such a standard is. It does not
necessarily include any of the intellectual, aesthetic, moral, or
social necessities; it is a purely physical standard, dividing
those in poverty from those who may be said to be out of it.

The necessaries for maintaining physical efficiency are not
difficult to determine. Professor Alfred Marshall says: "The
necessaries for the efficiency of an ordinary agricultural or of
an unskilled town laborer and his family, in England, in this
generation, may be said to consist of a well-drained dwelling
with several rooms, warm clothing, with some changes of under-
clothing, pure water, a plentiful supply of cereal food, with a
moderate allowance of meat and milk, and a little tea, etc.,
some education, and some recreation, and lastly, sufficient freedom for his wife from other work to enable her to perform

properly her maternal and her household duties. If in any district unskilled labor is deprived of any of these things, its efficiency will suffer in the same way as that of a horse that is not properly tended, or a steam engine that has an inadequate supply of coals." This standard is a reasonable one. A sanitary dwelling, a sufficient supply of food and clothing, all having to do with physical well-being, is the very minimum which the laboring classes can demand. Anything less means the ruin of that very physical power which alone suffices to keep them from dependence upon public relief. It resolves itself into the necessity for "fair wages" and regular employment. Such a standard has been established naturally by every one in his treatment of animals; no one would think of supplying less to any man or beast for whom he was personally responsible. Serfs and slaves were always given at least enough to keep them physically well. But present-day society has ignored the wisdom of this fair provision. Carlyle, even in his day, protested against this modern injustice of not making proper provision for the physical well-being of the working-classes. "Why, the four-footed worker," he exclaims, "has already got all that this two-handed one is clamoring for! How often must I remind you? There is not a horse in England able and willing to work, but has due food and lodging; and goes about sleek-coated, satisfied in heart. And you say, it is impossible. Brothers, I answer, if for you it be impossible, what is to become of you? It is impossible for us to believe it to be impossible. The human brain, looking at these sleek English horses, refuses to believe in such impossibility for English men." To repeat again, poverty means the lack of "due food and lodging" and clothing.

In England the economists and students of poverty have determined that in ordinary times from fifteen to eighteen shillings a week would enable an agricultural laborer to obtain for himself and family the necessaries of life, and about thirty shillings a week would enable a city workman to obtain the same necessaries. Mr. B. S. Rountree, in his study of the poverty of York, England, fixed a standard of twenty-one shillings eight pence a week as a necessary one for a family of ordinary size. Anything less than this amount would not enable a family to live without certain deprivations which would in time impair their physical efficiency. With this sum, as a weekly income, the family could with care keep themselves above the poverty line. But Mr. Rountree says: "A family, living upon the scale allowed for in this estimate, must never spend a penny on railway fare or omnibus. They must never go into the country unless they walk. They must never purchase a half-penny newspaper or spend a penny to buy a ticket for a popular concert. They must write no letters to absent children, for they cannot afford to pay the postage. They must never contribute anything to their church or chapel, or give any help to a neighbour which costs them money. They cannot save, nor can they join sick club or Trade Union, because they cannot pay the necessary subscription. The children must have no pocket money for dolls, marbles, or sweets. The father must smoke no tobacco and must drink no beer. The mother must never buy any pretty clothes for herself or for her children, the character of the family wardrobe as for the family diet being governed by the regulation, 'Nothing must be bought but that which is absolutely necessary for the maintenance of physical health, and what is bought must be of the plainest and most economical description.' Should a child fall ill, it must be attended by the parish doctor; should it die, it must be buried by the parish. Finally, the wage-earner must never be absent from his work for a single day."

It would seem imperative that every nation should know the number of people in its dominions who, although using their best efforts, are failing to obtain sufficient necessaries for maintaining physical efficiency. How many people in this country are in poverty? Is the number yearly growing larger? Are there each year more and more of the unskilled classes, pursuing hopelessly the elusive phantom of self-support and independence? Are they, as in a dream, working faster only the more swiftly to move backward? Are there each year more and more hungry children, and more and more fathers whose utmost effort may not bring into the home as much energy in food as it takes out in industry? These are not fanciful questions, nor are they sentimental ones. I have not the slightest doubt that there are in the United States ten million persons in precisely these conditions of poverty, but I am largely guessing and there may be as many as fifteen or twenty million! But ought we not to know? If poverty were due to purely individual causes, it would perhaps be fair to deny the moral necessity of national inquiries at periodic intervals into the condition of all the people and especially of the poor. But no one knowing the many active social causes of individual poverty and misery could deny this necessity in a democracy of professedly Christian people. To neglect even to inquire into our national distress is to be guilty of the grossest moral insensitiveness. There are many who would demand not only inquiries, but remedies. A few men, such as Morris, Ruskin, and Emerson, hold up constantly the ideal of the great nation as the one wherein there may be no rich, but wherein there must be "as many as possible full-breathed, bright-eyed, and happy-hearted human creatures." And all great men have universally deplored that nation wherein "wealth accumulates and men decay." They are, of course, right; but until society manifests some desire to know the extent of the misery in which men decay—not until then may we hope for anything more than a petty individual dealing with a question mainly social.

During the entire last century many of the best minds were engaged in the study of social and economic questions. At the beginning of this new century we are still asking "riddles about the starving." After many years of most elaborate investigations, printed in thousands of volumes issued by federal and state governments, we are almost as far from any definite knowledge concerning the extent of poverty as we have ever been. The United States spends more money than any other nation in the world upon statistical investigations, and yet we know less about the poverty of the people than almost any other great nation of the Western world. An immense sum is expended yearly in taking the census and in maintaining the many bureaus in Washington to investigate the conditions of commerce, of labor, of agriculture, of railways, etc. Almost every state has local bureaus existing for the same purpose. After the existence of these bureaus for a period of from twenty to thirty years, no one can tell, or give anything like a fair estimate of, the number of people existing in the community unable to obtain a living wage or its equivalent; or, in other words, unable to obtain the necessaries for maintaining physical efficiency. We cannot now, in any very satisfactory way, tell the number of unemployed, the number of unskilled workers or their wages; we do not know the number of underfed children, or even, and this seems most absurd of all, the number of persons dependent upon the public

for support. We do not know the number of men killed by accidents in industry, or injured by dangerous trades. There are
immense volumes of wage statistics containing averages so
general, and confusing so skilfully all the different classes of
labor, that it is next to impossible to make anything specific
out of the material. Almost each new publication warns any one
from trusting or basing any arguments upon material previously
gathered and published. The extent of poverty in the United
States is absolutely unknown. Mr. Carroll D. Wright, who of
all persons should be able to throw some light on this subject,
is unable to quote any statistics whatever when writing on the
subject of poverty in his book. His chapter on poverty is in itself
a restatement of well-known generalizations of questionable usefulness, and based largely upon the investigations and statements
of Professor Amos G. Warner, who, largely as a result of private
inquiry, produced an invaluable book upon "American Charities."
With no figures whatever to bear out his statement, Mr. Wright
takes occasion to speak of the assertion that the "rich are growing
richer and the poor poorer" as "false in its premises and misleading in its influence." It is unnecessary to say that we might
choose to take Mr. Wright's statement or choose to take his
opponent's statement. It is largely a matter of temperament
which side one takes in the matter, for in either case we have
no facts to support our position.

It is difficult without certain fundamental facts, if it is not
indeed impossible, to make any worth-while estimate of poverty.
This is proved most clearly by two examples—one in England
and the other in Germany. A few years ago England did not
know the extent of her own poverty. Economists and writers
gave opinions of all kinds. Some said conditions were "bad,"
others said such statements were misleading; and here they were,
tilting at each other, backward and forward, in the most pon-
derous and serious way until Mr. Booth, a business man, undertook to get at the facts. No one, not even the most radical economist, would have dared to have estimated the poverty of London
as extending to 30 per cent of the people. The extent of poverty
—the number underfed, underclothed, and in insanitary houses—
was greater than could reasonably have been estimated. Another
illustration may be taken from Germany. A few years ago no

one in that country knew the number of accidents which occurred yearly in industry. There were various estimates. It was generally thought that there might be thirty or forty thousand injuries per year due to machinery. Mr. John Graham Brooks says: "The first investigation showed three times this number; when the investigation became more complete, six times the number." This shows how impossible it is, without carefully collected data, to make anything like a correct estimate of existing social conditions. In both of these cases the facts proved the actual conditions to be far worse than any one had dared to estimate them. We are at present in precisely this state of ignorance, in the United States, as to accidents, unemployment, pauperism, wages, the number of unskilled, the number of underfed school schildren, etc., and, therefore, ignorant of the extent of poverty. We do not know whether poverty is gaining or losing ground. We are uncertain whether or not the causes of poverty are more active now than they were in the past. We cannot be sure that we have less poverty than any other country. In the two above-mentioned instances, the conditions abroad proved to be far worse than the highest estimates. Whether this will be true of the United States also must, of course, remain unknown until careful inquiries are made.

Although there are no facts treating of the extent of poverty, there are a great many books filled with descriptions and discussions and riddles. Charles B. Spahr, Walter A. Wyckoff, Mrs. John Van Vorst and Miss Marie Van Vorst, I. K. Friedman, and A. M. Simons have given us some idea of the conditions among the poorest class of laborers in various industrial centres over the country. Jacob A. Riis, Ernest Poole, and Mrs. Lillian Betts have given us most sympathetic descriptions of poverty among the people of the tenements. Flynt and others have given us impressionistic stories of tramps, vagrants, and mendicants. They bring before our very eyes, through books and magazines, stories of needless deaths from insanitary conditions, of long hours of work, of low pay, of overcrowded sweatshops, of child labor, of street waifs, of vile tenements, of the hungry and the wretched.

All these books and articles are extremely valuable and useful, but if anything is to be done about the matter, we should begin as soon as possible to know the extent of these conditions and the causes which bring such terribly serious misery and wretchedness into the world. Some few attempts of real importance have been made to ascertain more detailed facts concerning the living and working conditions of the people, but they also are insufficient. The "Hull House Maps and Papers," Robert A. Wood's "The City Wilderness" and "The Americans in Process," and Dr. Peter Robert's "The Anthracite Coal Communities" are the most important contributions. The investigations of the Bureau of Labor into the conditions of the Italian laborers in Chicago and of the negroes in various cities are all efforts in the right direction, but that is about all that can be said of them. While men in Germany and England have been making exhaustive studies of the poverty and social misery in those countries, and have aroused the people to the grave necessity of social reform, the United States has made almost no progress in obtaining exact knowledge of the condition of the working-classes.

As has been said, it was not until Mr. Charles Booth published in 1891 the results of his exhaustive inquiries that the actual conditions of poverty in London became known. About 1,300,000 people, or about 30 per cent of the entire population of London, were found to be unable to obtain the necessaries for a sound livelihood. They were in a state of poverty, living in conditions, if not of actual misery, at any rate bordering upon it. In many districts considerably more than half of the population were either in distress or on the verge of distress. When these results were made public, the more conservative economists gave it as their opinion that the conditions in London were, of course, exceptional and that it would be unsafe to make any generalizations for the whole of England on the basis of Mr. Booth's figures for London. About ten years later, Mr. B. S. Rountree, incited by the work of Mr. Booth, undertook a similar inquiry in his native town, York, a small provincial city in most ways typical of the smaller towns of England. In a large volume in which the results are published, it is shown that the poverty in York was only slightly less extensive than that of London. In the summary Mr. Rountree compares the conditions in London with those in York. His comments are as follows: "The proportions arrived at for the total population living in poverty in London and York respectively were as under:

	%
London	30.7
York	27.84

"The proportion of the population living in poverty in York may be regarded as practically the same as in London, especially when we remember that Mr. Booth's information was gathered in 1887-1892, a period of only *average* trade prosperity, whilst the York figures were collected in 1899, when trade was unusually prosperous."

He continues: "We have been accustomed to look upon the poverty in London as exceptional, but when the result of careful investigation shows that the proportion of poverty in London is practically equalled in what may be regarded as a typical provincial town, we are faced by the startling probability that from 25 to 30 per cent of the town populations of the United Kingdom are living in poverty." The invaluable work of these two men, done at their own expense, has had the effect of making the poverty of England understood, and that is the beginning of any reform.

It is, of course, deplorable that we have not made even a beginning in finding out the extent of poverty in America. As has been said, we have no facts which will enable us to make an exact comparison of our conditions with those abroad. There are, however, certain fragments of information which may make us question the prevalent notion that all is well, and that "comparatively speaking," as an economist said to me recently, "we have no poverty." There is a general spirit of optimism, which is not unlike that which existed in England previous to the work of Mr. Booth and Mr. Rountree. It is an optimism which results from ignorance or from the lack of any real concern. Such facts as we have are not sufficient to enable us to make any conclusive estimate, and they are used only for the purpose of serving as indications of the extent of poverty in this country.

These fragments of information, indicative of a widespread poverty, fall under the following heads: Pauperism, the general distress, the number of evictions, the pauper burials; the overcrowding and insanitation due to improper housing; the death rate from tuberculosis; the amount of unemployment; and the number of accidents in certain trades. By means of such data as we have concerning these conditions, a partial, but of course a most imperfect, comparison can be made between the poverty of England and that of the United States.

In the face of widespread poverty there have not been for over half a century in England so few paupers, either actually or proportionately, as there are now. The population of England has increased from about 18,000,000 persons in 1851 to 29,000,000 in 1889. During this period the number of paupers actually fell off. It is said that London "has lost in pauper population fifteen times as fast as she has gained in general population." The total number of paupers in the United States in the year 1891 was about 3,000,000 according to the estimates of Professor Richard T. Ely and of Mr. Charles D. Kellogg, then secretary of the Charity Organization Society of New York City. The census figures are too incomplete to be relied upon, but the returns from the almshouses show that the number of paupers increased almost as fast as population during the decade from 1880 to 1890. In Hartford, Connecticut, the number of paupers increased about 50 per cent during the same decade. An increase not less great took place in many other cities of the country. It is questionable whether the same increase occurred in the last decade. In two or three states a more economical administration of the poor-law funds, during the last decade, has diminished the number of persons dependent upon outdoor relief, although in several states the number of paupers has increased. But the figures of most of the states are too incomplete to permit of an exact statement concerning the increase or decrease of pauperism. Only by means of an estimate, such as Professor Ely made in 1891, can we gain any idea of the number of dependent persons. Taking a similar basis to the one used by him, there is every indication that not less than 4,000,000 persons are now dependent upon the public for relief. What relation, if any, pauperism bears to the poverty of this country has not been determined. The amount of pauperism in any community depends so much upon the way in which the poor law is administered that any comparison of the pauperism in various cities, states, or countries would yield no trustworthy data concerning the extent of poverty.

The general distress, as shown by the demands made upon *both* public and private charities, is a better test of the extent of poverty than that furnished by the numbers dependent upon the poor funds of the state alone. Mr. Jacob A. Riis, a few years ago, used some figures which showed that about one-third of the people of New York City were dependent upon charity at some time during the eight years previous to 1890. The report of the United Hebrew Charities for 1901 shows very similar conditions existing among the Jewish population of New York. But even more astonishing than all other facts we have are those furnished by the State Board of Charities. In 1897 the Board endeavored to collect figures of the number of persons assisted by both public and private charities. It was of course impossible to prevent duplications or to get returns from hundreds of the more personal sources of relief-giving, but it was a creditable and most useful piece of public work. Three years later the work was curtailed by decision of the Court of Appeals, and consequently the more complete figures are only available for the three years 1897, 1898, and 1899. I quote the following figures from a letter by Robert W. Hebberd, secretary of the State Board:

Year	State Institutions	Hospitals	Dispensaries	Outdoor Relief In Homes	Outdoor Relief Homeless	Total
1897	7720	98,960	1,451,713	266,431	288,380	2,113,204
1898	8272	106,835	1,052,177	364,814	368,101	1,900,199
1899	8161	114,199	932,072	395,632	338,863	1,788,927

These figures unquestionably contain many duplications. How many, it is impossible to say. It would not be reasonable to believe that 29 per cent of the people of New York found it necessary in the year 1897, or 24 per cent in 1899, to apply for relief. And yet it should be said that these figures of the State Board do not include the relief given by the many small clubs, circles, committees, and Trade Unions; nor is the relief given by many benevolent individuals recorded. There must, of course, be many thousand cases of distress receiving relief regularly and solely from these personal or private sources. But even though the figures do not include all persons in distress, it is reasonable to suppose that there are a large number of duplications and that they make the totals considerably larger than they should be.

Excluding half the number of persons relieved by the dispensaries (in order to make some arbitrary allowance for duplications), even then the number of persons relieved would indicate that the poverty of New York State is enormous. In actual figures as reduced, the persons in distress in 1897 number 1,387,348, or about 19 per cent of the people of New York, and in 1899 they number 1,322,891, or about 18 per cent.

It is possible to compare with these figures those for Boston just published by the city's official statistician. During the year 1903 over 136,000 persons were aided by the *public* authorities alone, or, estimating the present population at 606,600, more than 20 per cent of the entire population. It is estimated that 336,000 persons were aided in *private* hospitals, dispensaries, asylums, etc.; and these are, of course, not included, except by duplications, in the above figures, and the mere fact that such an estimate is made would indicate that the official figures do not measure the full extent of the distress. If the figures are correct as published, the persons in New York State in distress in 1897, and in Boston in 1903, would equal proportionately the number of those in poverty in London.

The amount of actual distress in the community may be measured also by two additional sets of data. The number of evictions in any community is a fairly good measure of the minimum distress. In the year 1903, 60,463 families in the borough of Manhattan were evicted from their homes. This is about 14 per cent of the total number of families in the borough. As another indication, the number of pauper burials should be cited. Every one familiar with the poor knows how desperately they struggle to give a decent burial to their dead. A poor person will resort to almost any means in order to prevent a member of his or her family having a pauper burial, or, as they say, "lying in a pauper's grave." Even the poorest people have friends, politicians or others, who save them, if possible, from this last disgrace. And yet one in every ten persons who die in New York is buried at public expense in Potter's Field. This is, without question, the lowest limit of misery. If observation counts for anything, I should say that the number of pauper burials certainly does not represent half of the actual distress in any community.

The results stated concisely are as follows:

1903   20 per cent of the people of Boston in distress.
1897   19 per cent of the people of New York State in distress.
1899   18 per cent of the people of New York State in distress.
1903   14 per cent of the families of Manhattan evicted.
Every
year   10 per cent (about) of those who die in Manhattan have
       pauper burials.

On the basis of these figures it would seem fair to estimate
that certainly not less than 14 per cent of the people, in prosperous times (1903), and probably not less than 20 per cent in bad
times (1897), are in distress. The estimate is a conservative one,
for despite all the imperfections which may be found in the data,
and there are many, any allowance for the persons who are given
aid by sources not reporting to the State Board, or for those
persons not aided by the authorities of Boston, or for those persons who, although in great distress, are not evicted, must
counterbalance the duplications or errors which may exist in the
figures either of distress or evictions.

These figures, furthermore, represent only the distress which
manifests itself. There is no question but that only a part of
those in poverty, in any community, apply for charity. I think
any one living in a Settlement will support me in saying that
many families who are obviously poor—that is, underfed, underclothed, or badly housed—never ask for aid or suffer the social
disgrace of eviction. Of course, no one could estimate the proportion of those who are evicted or of those who ask assistance
to the total number in poverty; for whatever opinion one may
have formed is based, not on actual knowledge, gained by inquiry, but on impressions, gained through friendly intercourse.
My own opinion is that probably not over half of those in
poverty ever apply for charity, and certainly not more than that
proportion are evicted from their homes. However, I should not
wish an opinion of this sort to be used in estimating, from the
figures of distress, etc., the number of those in poverty. And yet
from the facts of distress, as given, and from opinions formed,
both as a charity agent and as a Settlement worker, I should not
be at all surprised if the number of those in poverty in New
York, as well as in other large cities and industrial centres, rarely
fell below 25 per cent of all the people.

Without now making any further efforts to estimate the extent, we will continue with the various indications of poverty. The amount of unemployment is an excellent test. Here again our figures are too imperfect to enable us to compare them satisfactorily with those of England. The causes of unemployment, however, appear to be more active here than in that country. Of course, the most serious interruptions to regular employment are industrial depressions, at which times great masses of men are thrown out of employment for long periods. Depressions, however, occur periodically in all industrial countries with much the same regularity. The other industrial causes of unemployment vary considerably in the different nations. The reorganization of industry into trusts, causing many thousands of men to lose temporarily their employment; the introduction of new machinery, having the same effect; the speeding up of the machines, which exhausts and displaces workmen at an early age; excessive hours in many trades and a too plentiful supply of labor in many industrial centres, obtained by artificially stimulated immigration, are all causes of unemployment which seem more active in this country than abroad. Even the contract and sweating systems are more developed in this country. Englishmen visiting our industrial centres are amazed at the rapidity of the changes in industrial methods, from the changing of machines to the entire reorganization of an industry. Thousands of men are thrown out of employment whenever these changes occur. However beneficial to society these revolutions in industrial methods are, they are unquestionably active causes of widespread unemployment or of irregular employment. Mr. Jack London, writing in the *Atlantic Monthly* on "The Scab," refers to the United States as a scab nation, and to the working-men of this country as scab workmen, because the workers in this country work more intensely, longer hours, and more cheaply than those of other great industrial nations. In other words, we are underbidding the other nations by a lower standard of work, and underselling them as a result, not of fair, but of scab methods. Without question, the causes, which produce on the one hand long hours and overemployment, result on the other hand in short periods of work, underemployment, or unemployment.

The figures of unemployment, although very imperfect, show that the evil is widespread, even in times of prosperity. The census of 1890 shows that 3,523,730, or 15.1 per cent of all the workers over ten years of age, engaged in gainful occupations, were unemployed a part of the time during that year. These figures are, however, criticised by the census of 1900 as incomplete. In the last census the number found to be unemployed at some time during the year was 6,468,964, or 22.3 per cent of all the workers over ten years of age, engaged in gainful occupations. Thirty-nine per cent of the male workers unemployed, or 2,069,546 persons, were idle from four to six months of the year. These figures are for the country as a whole, and for all industries, including agriculture. In manufacturing alone the unemployment rose to 27.2 per cent of all of the workers. In the industrial states of the East and North the percentage of unemployment is larger than for the country as a whole. The Massachusetts census for 1895 showed that 8339 workmen were unemployed continuously during that year, and that 252,456 persons were irregularly employed. This means that over 27 per cent of all persons covered by the inquiry were idle some portion of the year. That this is not exceptional is shown by the Massachusetts census for 1885. At that time over 29 per cent of the workmen were irregularly employed. In other words, the annual wages of more than one workman in every four suffered considerable decrease by reason of a period of enforced idleness, extending in some cases over several months. In the industrial towns, such as Haverhill, New Bedford, and Fall River, the irregularity of employment was even greater. In these towns from 39 to 62 per cent of the workmen were idle during some part of the year. Still another investigation, made in 1897 in Massachusetts, showed that there were 100,000 workers in certain factories in that state who found employment when the factories were most active, but who were unemployed when the factories were least active. This fluctuation of the number of employed means that about 30 per cent of the maximum number employed in the busiest season are rendered idle during the slack seasons. This uncertainty of employment is not peculiar to Massachusetts. In every industrial community, the same insecurity of livelihood, due to irregular employment, exists. It has been said that during the anthracite coal strike of 1902 the entire supply of mined coal was exhausted, but the excess of laborers in that district is so great that within a short time after the strike was settled a report was sent out on reliable authority that "intermittent labor is again the lot of anthracite employees. The collieries do not average more than two-thirds time."

Men employed in navigation on the Great Lakes are particularly subject to seasonal demands for their labor. During the three months, January, February, and March, one-third of all the workmen are unemployed. In the clothing trades of New York City it is very much the same. During the first seven months of the year 1903 there were never less than one-fifth of the men unemployed, and at times between one-third and one-fourth of all the workmen were without employment. In other words, during this time, from 20 to 30 per cent of the working people were in enforced idleness. The workers in these seasonal trades are compelled to have regularly recurring periods of poverty. The long seasons of idleness mean in many cases serious distress to large numbers of workmen and their families.

With the exception of 1885 and 1895 none of the years for which figures have been quoted are to be considered as years of industrial depression. In these times of industrial crises, the number of unemployed men, who with their families are in poverty, reaches a point where the whole nation is moved to pity. In these times the lodging-houses of our cities are overcrowded with idle men. The vagrant class increases to large proportions, and the despair and wretchedness of the workless people cause the ruin of thousands. There is a very large increase in the number imprisoned for vagrancy, petty crimes, and drunkenness. "Modern life," Mr. John Hobson has said, "has no more tragical figure than the gaunt, hungry laborer wandering about the crowded centres of industry and wealth, begging in vain for permission to share in that industry, and to contribute to that wealth; asking in return, not the comforts and luxuries of civilized life, but the rough food and shelter for himself and family, which would be practically secured to him in the rudest form of savage society."

One is apt to forget the tragedies which result from unemployment. Not only are the better classes of labor pulled down to the very verge of poverty by irregular employment, but the poorer classes of unskilled labor are carried during a season of unemployment into conditions of actual poverty. The great mass of laborers must in all cases exercise economy, frugality, and good common sense in order to obtain for themselves those things necessary to maintain a standard of living which we proudly boast is American. For the lower classes of labor, the maintenance of an American standard, even under the most favorable conditions, is hardly possible, and by a period of unemployment, extending from one to three months in the year, their annual wage is invariably changed from a living one to a poverty one. That this happens, not only during industrial depressions, but at certain seasons every year, is, I think, without question. There is a fierce competition going on, especially in our cities, among various classes of immigrants for work requiring no special skill. At best, this labor market is always oversupplied, unemployment is greatest and wages are always at the lowest level. In consequence, there is a sort of devastation, due to constantly recurring poverty, which sadly afflicts this class of common laborers and their families.

There are very few figures regarding the unemployment among unskilled workers; but an investigation into the condition of the Italians in Chicago makes one realize that it is far more extensive among the unskilled than among the skilled workers. The figures given above concern the unemployment of all classes of labor. The federal reports of this inquiry show that "of the 2663 employed in remunerative occupations, 1517, or 56.97 per cent, were unemployed some part of the year. . . . and the average time unemployed for these 1517 persons was therefore over seven months." Two hundred and thirty-two persons were idle eight months of the year; 310 persons nine months; 161 ten months; 68 eleven months during the year. When it is realized that the average earnings, for all classes of work engaged in by the Italians, amounted to less than $6 a week, it is easy to realize the poverty and suffering which result from unemployment. The Italians, for a time, try to do the heavy and intense work required of them here on the same poor diet which supplied their needs in Italy, and superstitiously hang small salt bags about their children's necks to drive away the devil of malnutrition and starvation. Nothing could show the misery resulting from unemployment and underfeeding more clearly than the physical condition of the Italians in this country.

It is doubtful if one is warranted in considering the above conditions to be the same among the unskilled laborers of other foreign colonies. It may, however, be nearer the average for similar classes of laboring men than we imagine. The figures of the last federal census indicate this to be true. It states that 44.3 per cent of the unskilled workers were unemployed some part of the year. Common observation also lends its support to this conclusion. Everywhere—in the anthracite coal district, in South Chicago, and in many other industrial communities of Illinois, Pennsylvania, New York, and Massachusetts—there are among unskilled laborers indications of extreme poverty. The Irish of "Archy Road," the Poles and Hungarians of the Stock Yards district, the Italians of New York and Chicago, and the Jews of the east side of New York, differ considerably in ability; but from all appearances it seems that very nearly the same amount of poverty exists among all those workers, of whatever nationality, whose labor is unskilled and irregular. The temperance and intelligence of the Jews save them from the worst miseries. The unskilled and unorganized Irish laborers, who have been unable to obtain city jobs by political influence, are, I dare say, as wretchedly poor as any other class of immigrants. It would, of course, be unwise to carry this comparison of the conditions among the unskilled workers of various nationalities too far. It is necessarily based largely upon observation, and that is always more or less limited and imperfect. But it is safe to conclude that employment is much more irregular among all classes of unskilled workers than among the workers in the skilled and organized trades. As the wages of unskilled workmen, as will be shown later, are in general only sufficient to keep them above the poverty line while they are at work, unemployment means for these classes underfeeding, insufficient clothing, and uncertain tenure of home. It is hardly too much to assume that in the larger industrial states, in ordinary times, 30 per cent of the unskilled workers are in poverty some part of the year as a result of unemployment. This, of course, is only one of many causes of poverty. Sickness and injuries are perhaps not less important, either as indications of poverty or as causes.

The indications of poverty which lie in the figures of accidents, diseases, and casualties, resulting from industrial employments, are very significant, although the figures are most incomplete. It has been determined that nine out of every ten working-class families in Europe require charitable aid after injuries due to some industrial accident. Probably not so large a proportion in this country would, under the same circumstances, find it necessary to apply for charitable relief; but in nearly all cases where the breadwinner suffers permanent injury, or is suddenly killed, the family must receive assistance of some sort, until other members of the family are able to assume the responsibility of its support. Mr. John Graham Brooks, in his recent book, "The Social Unrest," has called attention to "that frightful list of stricken laborers that are now thrown back upon themselves or their families with recompense so uncertain and niggardly as to shock the most primitive sense of social justice."

Unfortunately, the facts regarding these industrial causes of poverty are so incomplete as to make it impossible to estimate the amount of distress resulting from them. Such facts as we have apply only to the industries of mining and railroading. The following table, taken from the reports of the Interstate Commerce Commission, will fully illustrate how terribly dangerous is the work of a railway employee:

Railroad Accidents in the United States

Year	EMPLOYEES		PASSENGERS		OTHER PERSONS		TOTAL	
	Killed	Injured	Killed	Injured	Killed	Injured	Killed	Injured
1897	1,693	27,667	222	2,795	4,522	6,269	6,437	36,731
1898	1,958	31,761	221	2,945	4,680	6,176	6,859	40,882
1899	2,210	34,923	239	3,442	4,674	6,255	7,123	44,620
1900	2,550	39,643	249	4,128	5,066	6,549	7,865	50,320
1901	2,675	41,142	282	4,988	5,498	7,209	8,455	53,339
1902	2,969	50,524	345	6,683	5,274	7,455	8,588	64,662

These figures are frightful. In 1901 one out of every 399 employees was killed and one out of every 26 was injured. The trainmen, such as engineers, firemen, conductors, etc., are the greatest sufferers. One was killed for every 137 employed, and one was injured for every 11 employed. It is difficult to believe that such slaughter is permitted to go on year after year. It would seem as if the owners of the railroads would make the safety of their workmen their first obligation; but, strange as it is, they resist powerfully every attempt made to have them adopt safety appliances. The energetic efforts of the Interstate Commerce Commission have been but partially successful in compelling the railroads to put on such appliances as are necessary in order to diminish the number of accidents and fatalities. Up to the present the Commission has not been successful in compelling the railroads to introduce the Block System, which would greatly diminish the number killed and injured. The railroads consider this system an "unwarranted luxury," just as a few years ago they considered the automatic coupler an "unwarranted luxury." Such increased expenses for the safety of the employees reduce profits, and with that only in view the railroads either forget, or have no concern for, the families whose breadwinners are lost or injured by this criminal policy of preferring murder to decreased dividends. The following are chosen merely as examples of the injuries:

Back wrenched	workman, age 24
Leg cut off	workman, age 19
Foot crushed	workman, age 25
Foot and hip injured	workman, age 35
Foot cut off	workman, age 27

These injuries to railway workmen are more serious than at first appears, for very few of the men who are injured are over thirty-five, and most of them are in the twenties. This period—between twenty and thirty-five—is the most important period of a workman's life. It is the time when he is of utmost value to his family, since the children are still too young to take up the support of the family.

The responsibility of the railroads for poverty resulting from injuries or casualties is of three kinds at least. First: In many cases they overwork their employees. Dr. Samuel McCune Lindsay says: "Emergencies frequently occur due to accidents or condition of weather when men may be required to work continuously from twenty to thirty hours, and, in exceptional cases, men have been continuously at work in train service for thirty-six hours." Second: Many railroad systems have resisted and violated the law compelling them to put on automatic couplers, and they are now fighting the introduction of the

Block System, both of which improvements are designed to prevent accidents and injuries. Third: In case of accidents, "company" physicians and lawyers hasten immediately to the place of the accident, and, if possible, pursuade the workmen to sign contracts by which they agree, for some small immediate compensation, to release the company from any further liability. I have known many, many cases where workmen have, for a few dollars, signed away their rights to sue when their injuries have been as serious as the loss of a leg or arm. In the seventeen years ending June 30, 1902, 103,320 persons were killed and 587,028 injured by the railway industry.

The returns of those killed and injured in the mining districts are less complete than the ones given for the railroads. Dr. Peter Roberts, who has for several years studied with great care the industrial and social conditions of the anthracite regions, states that in certain sections of that commmunity the non-fatal injuries are more serious now than they were in past decades. He says that "nearly half the employees have no provision for either the incapacitated through accident or for the maintenance of widows and orphans when death befalls those who provide for them in this hazardous calling. Many operators display generosity worthy of emulation; others manifest criminal indifference to the sufferings of employees and their families because of accident. . . . To leave these men to the mercy of overbearing operators in case of injury and death is unworthy of the civilization of the century in which we live." It is impossible to say how much of the existing poverty is caused by accidents, injuries, and sickness, due to industrial processes and conditions; but such facts as we have would indicate that these poverty-producing causes are more active in the United States than in any other great industrial nation.

These various indications of poverty might be followed by many less significant ones. The earlier age at which men are incapacitated in this country is but one of the more important. An inquiry made several years ago in New Jersey showed that workmen began to decline between the ages of thirty-five and forty-five, although in many cases they were not completely incapacitated until twenty years later. Dr. Roberts shows that the average age of the deceased in the anthracite district was

24 for the female and 24.8 for the male, although the average
for the country as a whole was 35.2 years. But there are too
many of such minor indications to be worthy of detailed examination. In lieu of definite, accurate figures concerning the
extent of poverty, such figures as we have of distress, of insanitary housing conditions, of overcrowding, of deaths from tuberculosis, of unemployment and of accidents, indicate that the
poverty in certain portions of this country is hardly less extensive
than that of certain parts of England.

From a different point of view—from figures of the ownership
of wealth in this country—another indication of poverty may be
considered. Wealth and poverty seem to be inevitably associated
with each other. In the report of the Royal Commission on
Labor, presented to the Houses of Parliament in 1894, the following sentences, succeeding an account of the poverty and
wretchedness existing in English towns, show the relation which
these two things—poverty and wealth—bear toward each other.
"It is impossible to refrain from connecting this deplorable condition of the working class with the fact that two-thirds of the
annual product of the community is absorbed by one-fourth of
its members, and that the annual tribute of rents, royalties, and
dividends levied upon the industry of the nation amounts to
nearly 500,000,000 sterling." Here again our figures are deplorably deficient when compared with English ones. There is a
general impression that we have a widespread diffusion of
property ownership. It is, of course, natural that, with great
tracts of land opened within the last century to millions of
individuals, there should be an extent of individual ownership
of farms in this country far greater than that existing elsewhere.
But nevertheless, Mr. George K. Holmes, a cautious and conservative investigator, shows, on the basis of the census figures
for 1890, that over 34 per cent of our farmers are renters and
an additional 18.6 per cent have their farms mortgaged. All
together there are over 52 per cent of the farmers in this country
who have only a partial ownership of their farms, or who are
propertyless.

The number of persons owning farms is an indication of the
ownership of property in the rural districts only; while the figures
concerning the ownership of homes give us an indication of the

number of persons in cities, towns, and agricultural districts, having no property interests. The census figures for 1900 show that 8,365,739, or considerably over half of the families in the United States, do not own the homes in which they live. In the cities the ownership of homes is much less common than in the smaller towns. Illustrations of this fact are seen in the following percentages of homes hired in various cities:

	%
Boston	81.1
Chicago	74.9
Cincinnati	79.1
Fall River	82.
Holyoke	80.6
New York (Manhattan)	94.1
Philadelphia	77.9

The percentages show that of all the persons living in these cities a very large proportion do not own the homes in which they live. Probably no wage-earners in Manhattan own their homes, and in several other large cities probably 99 per cent of the wage-earners are propertyless. The significant thing in this lack of ownership lies in the fact that a very large majority, probably 90 per cent, of the workmen in the cities and industrial communities, are propertyless, and, furthermore, are involved in a weekly indebtedness for rent of from one-fifth to two-fifths of their earnings, regardless of whether they have work or not.

The estimates of wealth and of the distribution of wealth, made by Mr. Holmes, are less reliable than the aforegoing figures of ownership, but they indicate, nevertheless, that there exists in this country "an enormous culture bed for poverty." The entire wealth of the country was estimated by the census of 1890 at $65,000,000,000. Mr. Holmes concludes, on the basis of his inquiries, that three-tenths of one per cent of the families in this country own one-fifth of this wealth, that is to say, 20 per cent of the wealth of the country. Nine per cent of the families in the country own 71 per cent of the total wealth.

Mr. Charles B. Spahr has estimated, with most painstaking care, the distribution of incomes in the United States. The results of his inquiries are very effectively set forth in the following tables and diagrams:

The United States 1890

Estates	Number	Aggregate Wealth	Average Wealth
The Wealthy Classes			
$50,000 and over	125,000	$33,000,000,000	$264,000
The Well-to-do Classes			
$50,000 to $5,000	1,375,000	23,000,000,000	16,000
The Middle Classes			
$5,000 to $500	5,500,000	8,200,000,000	1,500
The Poorer Classes			
under $500	5,500,000	800,000,000	150
TOTAL	12,500,000	$65,000,000,000	$5,200

From this table Mr. Spahr concludes that less than half of the
families in the United States are propertyless; nevertheless,
seven-eighths of the families hold but one-eighth of the national
wealth, *while but one per cent of the families hold more than
the remaining ninety-nine per cent.*

Another table, based upon Mr. Spahr's inquiry, and accompanied by a diagram, is taken from Mr. John Graham Brooks'
"The Social Unrest."

Distribution of Wealth in the United States

Class	Families	Per Cent	Average Wealth	Aggregate Wealth	Per Cent
Rich	125,000	1.0	$263,040	$32,880,000,000	54.8
Middle	1,362,500	10.9	14,180	19,320,000,000	32.2
Poor	4,762,500	38.1	1,639	7,800,000,000	13.0
Very Poor	6,250,000	50.0			
TOTAL	12,500,000	100.0	$4,800	$60,000,000,000	100.0

Mr. Brooks says regarding this latter table: "I do not personally believe that trustworthy statistical sources exist that
enable one to make tables of this character that are more than
mere guesses at the fact. Yet if it were known what the possessions of the one hundred and twenty-six thousand richest
families in the United States are, the result would be all that
any agitator need ask." How many liberties have been taken
with Mr. Spahr's figures in order to construct this latter table I
do not know; it can be said, however, that while neither his
figures nor those of Mr. Holmes have escaped criticism, the
critics have not, thus far, been able to make out a case against

DIAGRAMS SHOWING, BY PERCENTAGES, THE POPULATION AND
WEALTH DISTRIBUTION IN THE UNITED STATES

Fig. 1

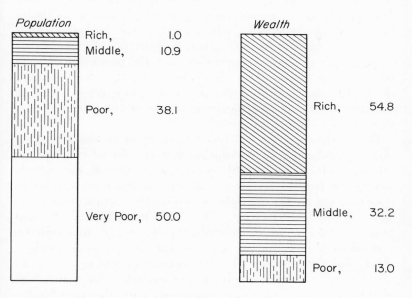

them which necessitates any material alteration either of the
handling of the data, or of the conclusions finally drawn. Without
committing ourselves implicitly to them, we must acknowledge
that they indicate an inequality of wealth distribution which
should have before now received exhaustive investigation by our
official statisticians.

A propertyless person is one without any economic reserve
power. He is in no position to ward off the sufferings which
must frequently come to most persons depending wholly upon
their ability to labor and upon the demand, in the community,
for their services. In an industrial crisis, for instance, a person
without any property which he may convert, if necessary, into
the means of sustenance, is unable to keep off distress until
economic conditions revive sufficiently to require his labor. His
family must suffer in case of his being unemployed or incapacitated or killed, unless there should be some one else in the family
able to take his place as breadwinner. The loss of profits or

earnings from property is a serious loss to thousands of families more or less dependent upon incomes from that source; but the classes who possess no property, not even a home from which they may not be evicted, must of necessity pursue that precarious livelihood which depends solely upon health and strength and upon economic conditions, which may, or may not, at any time, require the services of the worker. Security of livelihood in the present state of society comes only with the possession of property; and the large masses of people, whom this short summary of wealth distribution indicates to be propertyless, have no assurance whatever that they may not be at any time, if indeed they are not already, in poverty.

Before summarizing the facts dwelt upon in the aforegoing pages as indicative of widespread poverty, let us consider one other important method of measuring its extent; namely, the number of persons, so far as that can be determined, who are not receiving an income sufficient to enable them to maintain a state of physical efficiency. There are many, many thousand families who receive an income adequate enough to supply the necessities of physical life, but who, for one reason or another— drink, ignorance, sickness, extravagance, misfortune, or weakness—do not manage to obtain the essentials for maintaining physical efficiency. There are also many, many thousand families who receive wages so inadequate that no care in spending, however wise it may be, will make them suffice for the family needs. If every penny were spent judiciously, the income would not be sufficient to provide enough of the necessaries to maintain in efficient working order the various members of the family. Such wages are neither "fair" nor "living" wages: they are poverty wages.

It is obvious enough that it is impossible to determine a sum which may be called a "fair" or "living" wage, and which will apply with equal justice to the various parts of the country. There are at least two reasons for this. First, the prices of commodities differ greatly in so large and varied a country. The cost of necessaries is much lower in the South than in the North, and lower in Boston than in New York, and lower in Fort Wayne than in Chicago. When the cost of living in rural and urban districts is compared, it will be found that rents are perhaps responsible for the most considerable difference, and the prices of food and fuel also vary. This variation in the cost of living renders any fixed estimate of a necessary wage for the whole country practically valueless. There is a second element which is sometimes suggested as important when making estimates of the necessary cost of living. If it were indeed an important element, it would make any computation of a necessary income in this country almost impossible. The foreign peoples represented among our working classes are said to require various standards of living. The Jews, for instance, seem to thrive in the most insanitary tenements, despite poor food and insufficient clothing. The Italians and Hungarians seem to do as well as the Irish on a much more limited diet. The Jews, who are most saving and economical in their ways of living, do unquestionably manage to live better on a smaller income than many other races; and in so far as this is true of any race, that race, of course, will be able to live better than another which is less wise in its economies. The same thing is true of different families. But the income of any family must increase with the increase of physical expenditure. And for all races the increase of physical expenditure in the industrial life of America, over what they were formerly required to make in their native countries, is the principal reason for an increased standard of living, and consequently for an increased income. The element of the exhaustion of the physical energies by work must enter into all calculations concerning a required income. It is therefore very doubtful if the Italian and other of the recent immigrants will be able to do as much hard, sustained, and intense work as the American or the Americanized Irishman or German, without a meat diet or, at least, without a much more ample vegetarian diet than that which the Italian, for instance, has been in the habit of having in the milder climate of Italy, doing a lighter and easier and a less sustained kind of work. It is well known that immigrants are at first very easily exhausted in trying to keep pace with the intense, ceaseless rush of the American methods of work. Nowhere abroad is seen the same intense working activity which is customary in the United States.

The breathless and exhausting pace required in the workshops of this country is not seen in the workshops of Europe. For instance, the Jew in the Russian Ghettos runs a sewing machine as one would expect a human being to run a machine, intermittently, with brief periods of rest; not as a sweated, starving creature in New York or Chicago runs one, never easing the twisted spine, never rising to fill the half-closed lungs. In Russia a man runs a machine in competition with other men, and not in competition with the tireless, bodiless, and soulless power of steam or electricity. The Italian, in a sunny climate, in the vine-yards and olive fields, needs little more to fit him for his work than a limited vegetarian diet, a small supply of clothes, and an indifferent house. But the Italian, the Jew, or the Hungarian will need good food, warm clothing, and a sanitary tenement, if he is to be paced by the the swiftest workman, and rushed by a machine, which must be tended and cannot be stopped to permit a full breath or a moment's rest until the day's labor is done. The present industrial life "takes it out of a man," as the saying is, and it must be put back into a man, or the human machine depreciates and degenerates. It is hardly to be doubted that nearly all men, exhausting themselves at the same rate, require very much the same necessities to keep them in working order. For these reasons I do not consider that there should be different wage standards established for the different nationalities, although, unquestionably, the standards for the varying parts of the country should vary in relation to the varying cost of commodities, etc.

Without regard to these apparent differences in the standards of living required by different races and the varying costs of commodities, there are, nevertheless, a number of opinions concerning the necessary income for a family of average size. It was shown by the Massachusetts Bureau of Statistics that it takes $754 a year for a family of five persons to live on. John Mitchell has said that a minimum wage of $600 a year is necessary in the anthracite district for a worker with a family of ordinary size. The New York Bureau of Labor considers that $10 a week or $520 a year is inadequate for city workmen. A prominent official of one of the largest charities in New York City thinks that $2 a day, or about $624 a year, is necessary for a family of five in that city. Granting that these estimates are above the amount necessary to supply only the strictest necessities for useful, efficient living, they are, nevertheless, the opinions of well-informed persons as to a fair wage. It is unnecessary to say that, if any one of these estimates were taken as the standard necessary wage, an enormous number of working people, practically all of the unskilled and a considerable percentage of the skilled, would fall under the poverty line. However desirable and however socially valuable an income of $754 a year for each family would be, it is unquestionably too high for a fair estimate of the minimum necessary one. While $624 a year is probably not too much for New York City, in view of the excessive rents (consuming in some cases 40 per cent of the income) and other almost inevitable expenses such as car fare, etc., it is, nevertheless, an estimate which could not apply, with equal fairness, to all of the industrial states of the North. When one gets below these figures, however, every dollar cut off may mean depriving a family of a necessity of life, in times of health even, and unquestionably in times of sickness. But to estimate in the most conservative way possible, let us take more or less arbitrarily $460 a year as essential to defray the expenses of an average family—a father, a mother, and three children—in the cities and industrial communities of the New England states, of New York, Pennsylvania, Indiana, Ohio, and Illinois. In the cities the amount ought to be placed higher and in the smaller towns the estimate would naturally be lower, but on the whole the average seems a fair one. In the South about $300 a year would probably cover the cost of like necessaries. This estimate of $300 for a family of average size in the South, and of $460 for a family of average size in the industrial states of the North, would approach very nearly a fair standard for the poverty line; that is to say, if any working-class family should be unable to obtain this wage, they would in all likelihood be unable to obtain the necessaries for maintaining physical efficiency.

Even if all were agreed upon these amounts, as fair estimates of necessary yearly wages in the North and South, there is still an obstacle in the way of measuring the extent of poverty by this method. This obstacle consists in the inadequacy of our wage statistics. It is hardly to be doubted that the mass of unskilled workers in the North receive less than $460 a year, or that the same class of laborers in the South receive less than $300. But, unfortunately, that cannot be proved by any statistics obtainable. There are, however, some figures which show that a very large number of workmen are unable to obtain for themselves and families an average income equal to these standards.

Testimony was given before the Industrial Commission showing that the 150,000 track hands, working on the railroads of the United States, received wages ranging from 47½ cents a day, in the South, to $1.25 a day in the North. About half of these men are not employed in the winter, so that their yearly wages are further reduced by a period of idleness. But, leaving that out of account, the sum received in the South would amount to less than $150 a year, and the yearly wage in the North would amount to less than $375. The same witness testified that these wages were also paid to the carmen and shopmen in the North and South. There were 200,000 men employed in these latter trades. Before the same Commission testimony was given concerning the wages of the street-car employees. For these workers the wages ranged from $320 a year to $460. Mr. Elsas, of the Georgia cotton mills, confessed that the average wage paid his employees was $234 a year. Even men were given only from 75 to 90 cents a day for twelve hours' work. Dr. Peter Roberts says that the average yearly wage in the anthracite district is less than $500, and that about 60 per cent of the workers do not receive $450. According to the United States census for 1900, 11 per cent of the male workers over sixteen years of age, employed in the New England cotton mills, received a rate of pay amounting to less than $6 per week, or, in other words, about $300 a year. This is the most they could have earned if they had worked every day in the year, which of course they were not able to do. In the Middle states nearly one-third of all the workers are receiving a rate of wages less than $6 per week, that is to say again, less than $300 a year; and in the Southern states 59 per cent are receiving less than this amount. This, it must be remembered, is what the census terms the rate of pay, and will only be received if employment is continuous throughout the year. An inquiry made in Massachusetts showed that the average number of months during which the cotton operatives in Fall River were employed was 9.38. If this proportion would apply to the above operatives, whose wages were investigated by the United States Census, their wages would be reduced nearly one-fourth; in other words, their wages would fall to about $225 a year. . . . It is unfortunate that we are unable to determine the total number of workmen in the country who do not receive the minimum wage of $460 in the North and $300 in the South, because in this way, if the standards were fair ones, we should be able to obtain a very accurate idea of the extent of poverty.

While the above figures are altogether too inadequate to permit us to base upon them any estimate as to the extent of poverty, it seems reasonable to assume that the wages of the unskilled laborers in this country rarely rise above the poverty line. A certain percentage are doubtless able to maintain a state of physical efficiency while they have work, but when unemployment comes, and their wages cease, a great mass of the unskilled workers find themselves almost immediately in poverty, if not indeed in actual distress.

It can be assumed, therefore, fairly, I think, that the problem of poverty in this country is in ordinary times confined to a certain percentage of the unskilled laborers who have employment, to most unskilled laborers without employment, and to many unemployed skilled workers. In addition to these workers in poverty, there are those who are weak, infirm, unfortunate, the widows, the families of the sick or the injured, and those who are too incompetent, drunken, or vicious, etc., to be reliable workmen. These are, in the main, the classes of persons in poverty in this country.

It is safe to say that a large number of workers, the mass of unskilled and some skilled workmen with their families, fall beneath the poverty line at least three times during their lives— during childhood, in the prime of life, and at old age. Mr. Rountree, as a result of his inquiries in York, has made the following diagram which illustrates this fact:

Fig. 2

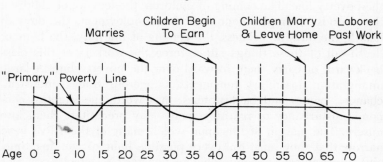

The ordinary increase of family numbers, and the increase or decrease in the family of the capacity for earning, forces the ordinary working-class family above and beneath this line at certain periods, despite their will. Some families may always remain beneath the line by reason of individual or social causes. The curve may at any moment drop to the bottom by reason of unemployment, infirmity, sickness, exhaustion, or accident. There are many observations of fundamental social importance that might be made upon the significance of this diagram. The things of real significance are, however, that the laborer in childhood, when he most needs upbuilding, is in poverty; the wife, when she is bearing children—a time when she most needs good food and relief from want and worries—is in poverty; the aged, when they should be in peace and comfort, are in poverty. The reason for this is that the wages of the ordinary unskilled workman are sufficient to support him and his wife, and perhaps one or two children. As more children arrive, the income gradually becomes less and less adequate to meet their needs. The family drops below the poverty line. They are unable to get sufficient necessaries. They drop lower and lower as the children grow and larger supplies of food and clothing and more house-room are needed. Then as the children begin to earn, the family rises out of poverty again, but it remains above the poverty line only until the children leave home or marry, or for some other reason may not continue to aid in the support of the family. At about this time the father's earnings are likely to drop off through age or infirmity, and again the parents are in poverty. In this way laborers of the poorest class pass backward and forward over the poverty line. The coming of children, the leaving of children, the periods of employment and of unemployment, the days of health, the days of sickness, the coming of infirmity, the hour of death—all of these things either force the workers of this class backward, or carry them forward over the poverty line. A large immigration, insanitary tenements, dangerous trades, industrial changes, panics and bankruptcies—in a word, the slightest economic disturbance or rearrangement—may precipitate them into misery. The margin of life upon which many of them live is so narrow that they must toil every possible hour of working time, and the slightest economic change registers its effect upon this class of workers.

Any one going carefully through the figures which have been given will agree that poverty is widespread in this country. While it is possible that New York State has more poverty than other states, it is doubtful if its poverty is much greater proportionately than that of most of the industrial states. Twelve years ago I made what was practically a personal canvass of the poor in a small town of Indiana. There were no tenements, but the river banks were lined with small cabins and shanties, inhabited by the poorest and most miserable people I have almost ever seen. About the mills and factories were other wretched little communities of working people. All together the distress extended to but slightly less than 14 per cent of the population, and the poverty extended to not less than 20 per cent of the people. I cannot say how typical this town is of other Indiana towns, but I have always been under the impression that conditions were rather better there than in other towns of the same size. In Chicago the conditions of poverty are certainly worse, if anything, than in the smaller towns, and that is also true of the poverty of New York City. On the whole, it seems to me that the most conservative estimate that can fairly be made of the distress existing in the industrial states is 14 per cent of the total population; while in all probability no less than 20 per cent of the people in these states, in ordinarily prosperous years, are in poverty. This brings us to the conclusion that one-fifth, or 6,600,000 persons in the states of New York, Massachusetts, Connecticut, New Jersey, Pennsylvania, Ohio, Illinois, Indiana, and Michigan are in poverty. Taking half of this percentage and applying it to the other states, many of which have important industrial communities, as, for instance, Wisconsin, Colorado, California, Rhode Island, etc., the conclusion is that not less than 10,000,000 persons in the United States are in poverty. This includes, of course, the 4,000,000 persons who are estimated to be dependent upon some form of public relief. While the estimate is unquestionably a conservative one, it may be thought that, although the percentage, as applied to the industrial states, is fair, half of that percentage, as applied to the states largely agricultural, is too high. I think, however, that the figures concerning the number of farms rented and mortgaged would warrant the use of this percentage, if, indeed, there were not many other facts to warrant an assumption of that amount of poverty. Professor C. S. Walker said in 1897, in a discussion before the American Economic Association, "By using all available statistics, it becomes evident again and again that, deducting rent and interest, the American farmer receives less for his exertions than does the laborer in the factory or the hired man on his farm." However, there can be no question but that the estimate is within the mark. The fact that over 2,000,000 male wage earners in the United States were unemployed from four to six months during the year 1900 would alone warrant the estimate that 10,000,000 persons are in poverty.

The conclusion that about 10,000,000 persons in the United States are in poverty is, of course, largely based upon the figures of distress and of unemployment which have been given; and it would be warranted, were there no other indications of widespread poverty. However, many indications lend themselves to the support of this conclusion. A very large proportion of the working classes are propertyless; a very large mass of people, not only in our largest cities, but in all industrial communities as well, live in most insanitary conditions; there is a high death-rate from tuberculosis in most of our states; a large proportion of the unskilled workers receive, even when employed, wages insufficient to obtain the necessaries for maintaining physical efficiency; from all indications, the number injured and killed in dangerous trades is enormous; and, lastly, there is uncertainty of employment for all classes of workers. About 30 per cent of the workers in the industrial states are employed only a part of each year, and, in consequence, suffer a serious decrease in their yearly wages, which, in the case of the unskilled, at least, means to suffer poverty. Nevertheless, the estimate that somewhat over 10,000,000 persons in this country are in poverty does not indicate that our poverty is as great proportionately as that of England. But it should be said that a careful examination would, in all probability, disclose a greater poverty than the estimate indicates.

These figures of poverty have the weakness of all estimates. But even if it were possible to prove that the estimate herein given, of the extent of poverty, is in error, the fact for which I contend is not disproved. Poverty is already widespread in this new country, and knowing this to be true, it seems the height of folly that the nation should disregard so absolutely this enormous problem of misery that not even an inquiry is made as to its extent or as to the causes which add to its volume. Many people give as a reason for this apathy of the fortunate classes that poverty is irremedial. Did not the Lord say, "The poor always ye have with you"? But those who say this fail to distinguish between the poor, who are poor because of their own folly and vice, and the poor who are poor as a result of social wrongs. The sins of men should bring their own punishment, and the poverty which punishes the vicious and the sinful is good and necessary. Social or industrial institutions that save men from the painful consequences of vice or folly are not productive of the greatest good. There is unquestionably a poverty which men deserve, and by such poverty men are perhaps taught needful lessons. It would be unwise to legislate out of existence, even were it possible to do so, that poverty which penalizes the voluntarily idle and vicious. In other words, there are individual causes of poverty which should be eradicated by the individual himself, with such help as his family, the teachers, and the preachers may give him. For him society may be able to do little or nothing. The poor which are always to be with us, are, it seems to me, in poverty of their own making.

But as surely as this is true, there are also the poor which we must not have always with us. The poor of this latter class are, it seems to me, the mass of the poor; they are bred of miserable and unjust social conditions, which punish the good and the pure, the faithful and industrious, the slothful and vicious, all alike. We may not, by going into the homes of the poor, be able to determine which ones are in poverty because of individual causes, or which are in poverty because of social wrongs; but we can see, by looking about us, that men are brought into misery by the action of social and economic forces. And the wrongful action of such social and economic forces is a preventable thing. For instance, to mention but a few, the factories, the mines, the workshops, and the railroads must be forced to cease killing the father or the boy or girl whose wages alone suffice to keep the family from poverty; or, if the workers must be injured and killed, then the family must at least be fairly compensated, in so far as that be possible. Tenements may be made sanitary by the action of the community, and thereby much of this breeding of wretched souls and ruined bodies stopped.

A broader education may be provided for the masses, so that the street child may be saved from idleness, crime, and vagrancy, and the working child saved from ruinous labor. Immigration may be regulated constructively rather than negatively, if not, for a time, restricted to narrower limits. Employment may be made less irregular and fairer wages assured. These are, of course, but a few of the many things which can be done to make less unjust and miserable the conditions in which about 10,000,-000 of our people live.

Among the many inexplicable things in life there is probably nothing more out of reason than our disregard for preventive measures and our apparent willingness to provide almshouses, prisons, asylums, hospitals, homes, etc., for the victims of our neglect. Poverty is a culture bed for criminals, paupers, vagrants, and for such diseases as inebriety, insanity, and imbecility; and yet we endlessly go on in our unconcern, or in our blindness, heedless of its sources, believing all the time that we are merciful in administering to its unfortunate results. Those in poverty are fighting a losing struggle, because of unnecessary burdens which we might lift from their shoulders; but not until they go to pieces and become drunken, vagrant, criminal, diseased, and suppliant, do we consider mercy necessary. But in that day reclamation is almost impossible, the degeneracy of the adults infects the children, and the foulest of our social miseries is thus perpetuated from generation to generation. From the millions struggling with poverty come the millions who have lost all self-respect and ambition, who hardly, if ever, work, who are aimless and drifting, who like drink, who have no thought for their children, and who live contentedly on rubbish and alms. But a short time before many of them were of that great, splendid mass of producers upon which the material welfare of the nation rests. They were in poverty, but they were self-respecting; they were hard-pressed, but they were ambitious, determined, and hard-working. They were also underfed, underclothed, and miserably housed—the fear and dread of want possessed them, they worked sore, but gained nothing, they were isolated, heart-worn, and weary.

5

A Socially Conscious Protestantism
Presents Its Views

Social Creed of
The Federal Council of Churches of Christ in America

Post-Civil War alterations in the social and intellectual climate forced a reconsideration of prevailing religious attitudes and views. Protestant clergymen, especially in the burgeoning industrial and commercial centers, noted that they were not attracting the workingmen and their families to their churches on Sunday mornings. Increasingly too, they wondered what position the churches should take on the pressing social issues of the day—the warfare between capital and labor, the concentration of control and sharp practices in business, woman and child labor, slums, prostitution, poverty, the liquor traffic, bossism in politics, and race relations. Should the churches ignore these problems or should they join other agencies in helping to reconstruct American society in keeping with progressive principles? Religious leaders who thought that organized religion had an obligation to pioneer in the work of social regeneration developed the essentials of the social gospel by 1900. Stressing the fatherhood of God and the brotherhood of man, these prophets called upon their fellow Americans to forsake the fleshpots of the world and to dedicate themselves to social as well as individual salvation. They found inspiration in the teachings of Jesus of Nazareth, particularly the Sermon on the Mount. The task of the churches, one of the spokesmen of the movement declared, was not "a matter of getting individuals to heaven, but of transforming the life of earth into the harmony of heaven." The General Conference of the Methodist Episcopal Church at its Baltimore meeting in May, 1908, adopted a social creed. The Federal Council of the Churches of Christ in America, organized in 1908 with support from thirty-three Protestant sects representing 17 million communicants, endorsed a social creed. On December 9, 1912, the Council adopted an enlarged and revised statement, "The Social Creed of the Churches." C. Howard

---

The Federal Council of the Churches of Christ in America, *Christian Unity at Work . . . Quadrennial Session at Chicago, Illinois, 1912* (New York: The Federal Council of the Churches of Christ in America, 1913), pp. 182-83.

129]

Hopkins's *The Rise of the Social Gospel in American Protestantism, 1865-1915* (New Haven: Yale University Press, 1940) is the standard history of the movement. The student might also consult Henry F. May's excellent study, *The Protestant Churches and Industrial America* (New York: Harper and Brothers, 1949). For related expressions within Catholicism see *Aaron I. Abell's *American Catholicism and Social Action: A Search for Social Justice, 1865-1950* (Garden City: Hanover House, 1960). No comparable study for the Jewish congregations has yet appeared; one might, however, consult Nathan Glazer's *American Judaism* (Chicago: University of Chicago Press, 1957). In reading this selection note (1) what recommendations supported family integrity; (2) what specific ills the creed attacked; (3) what humanitarian objectives the Council sought to promote; (4) what social security provisions the Council advocated; (5) what position the Council took relating to employer-employee relations; (6) the emphasis placed upon purely religious considerations; (7) what similarities and dissimilarities can be found with Markham's poem "The Man with the Hoe."

The Federal Council of the Churches of Christ in America stands:

For equal rights and complete justice for all men in all stations of life.

For the protection of the family, by the single standard of purity, uniform divorce laws, proper regulation of marriage, and proper housing.

For the fullest possible development for every child, especially by the provision of proper education and recreation.

For the abolition of child-labor.

For such regulation of the conditions of toil for women as shall safeguard the physical and moral health of the community.

For the abatement and prevention of poverty.

For the protection of the individual and society from the social, economic, and moral waste of the liquor traffic.

For the conservation of health.

For the protection of the worker from dangerous machinery, occupational disease, injuries, and mortality.

For the right of all men to the opportunity for self-maintenance, for safeguarding this right against encroachments of every kind, and for the protection of workers from the hardships of enforced unemployment.

For suitable provision for the old age of the workers, and for those incapacitated by injury.

For the right of employees and employers alike to organize; and for adequate means of conciliation and arbitration in industrial disputes.

For a release from employment one day in seven.

For the gradual and reasonable reduction of the hours of labor to the lowest practicable point, and for that degree of leisure for all which is a condition of the highest human life.

For a living wage as a minimum in every industry, and for the highest wage that each industry can afford.

For a new emphasis on the application of Christian principles to the acquisition and use of property, and for the most equitable division of the product of industry that can ultimately be devised.

6

Nationalizing Reform

Theodore Roosevelt's "The New Nationalism"—
Speech Delivered at Osawatomie, Kansas, August 31, 1910

Theodore Roosevelt (1858-1919) was a patriot and a nationalist. He was also a reformer who saw in progressive principles an opportunity to strengthen the nation. One of the by-products of modern business and industrial enterprise was a divisive clash of interests between capital and labor which he thought endangered the well-being of all. The safety as well as the progress of the country lay, he was convinced, in doing justice to both sides—the country needed a square deal. As the youngest man to hold the office of President, Roosevelt brought a youthful enthusiasm unique in the history of the presidency to Washington. He had a deep appreciation of power yet he did not fear it; he was convinced that the federal government should be used as an agency of social control. The President had a duty, he observed, "to do anything that the needs of the Nation demanded unless such action was forbidden by the Constitution or the laws." Following nearly two terms as President (1901-1909), Roosevelt became increasingly restive during the administration of William Howard Taft (1909-1913), whom he had picked as his successor. Taft, he believed, had surrendered to the conservatives. After hunting for big game in Africa and a triumphal tour of European capitals Roosevelt returned to the United States and plunged into the fight against Taft then being waged by the insurgent Republicans. In his speech before the Grand Army of the Republic (an organization of former Civil War soldiers of the Union Army) at Osawatomie, August 31, 1910, reprinted below, TR opened a campaign to recapture the leadership of the Republican party preparatory to the presidential contest of 1912. Henry F. Pringle's Pulitzer-prize-winning °*Theodore Roosevelt: A Biography* (New York: Harcourt, Brace & Co., 1931) remains, despite some limitations, the best one-volume life of the Rough Rider. °George E. Mowry's *The Era of Theodore Roosevelt, 1900-1912* (New York: Harper and Row, 1958) is a masterful

---

Theodore Roosevelt, *The New Nationalism* (New York: The Outlook Company, 1911), pp. 3-33.

treatment of a large and complex subject. *John M. Blum's *The Republican Roosevelt* (Cambridge: Harvard University Press, 1954) deals primarily with TR's relationships with his party. In reading the following selection note (1) how TR used the past to serve his own purpose; (2) what he saw as the major issue facing the American people in 1910; (3) what obstacle stood in the way of a realization of the promise of American life; (4) to what traditions in the American value system he appealed for support; (5) what program of action he advocated; (6) his definition of a conservative; (7) his justification for increased governmental controls; (8) how he defined the New Nationalism; and (9) the style and form of his address.

We come here to-day to commemorate one of the epoch-making events of the long struggle for the rights of man—the long struggle for the uplift of humanity. Our country—this great republic—means nothing unless it means the triumph of a real democracy, the triumph of popular government, and, in the long run, of an economic system under which each man shall be guaranteed the opportunity to show the best that there is in him. That is why the history of American is now the central feature of the history of the world; for the world has set its face hopefully toward our democracy; and, O my fellow citizens, each one of you carries on your shoulders not only the burden of doing well for the sake of your own country, but the burden of doing well and of seeing that this nation does well for the sake of mankind.

There have been two great crises in our country's history: first, when it was formed, and then, again, when it was perpetuated; and, in the second of these great crises—in the time of stress and strain which culminated in the Civil War, on the outcome of which depended the justification of what had been done earlier, you men of the Grand Army, you men who fought through the Civil War, not only did you justify your generation, not only did you render life worth living for our generation, but you justified the wisdom of Washington and Washington's colleagues. If this republic had been founded by them only to be split asunder into fragments when the strain came, then the judgment of the world would have been that Washington's work was not worth doing. It was you who crowned Washington's work, as you carried to achievement the high purpose of Abraham Lincoln.

Now, with this second period of our history the name of John Brown will be forever associated; and Kansas was the theater upon which the first act of the second of our great national life dramas was played. It was the result of the struggle in Kansas which determined that our country should be in deed as well as in name devoted to both union and freedom; that the great experiment of democratic government on a national scale should succeed and not fail. In name we had the Declaration of Independence in 1776; but we gave the lie by our acts to the words of the Declaration of Independence until 1865; and words count for nothing except in so far as they represent acts. This is true everywhere; but, O my friends, it should be truest of all in political life. A broken promise is bad enough in private life. It is worse in the field of politics. No man is worth his salt in public life who makes on the stump a pledge which he does not keep after election; and, if he makes such a pledge and does not keep it, hunt him out of public life. I care for the great deeds of the past chiefly as spurs to drive us onward in the present. I speak of the men of the past partly that they may be honored by our praise of them, but more that they may serve as examples for the future.

It was a heroic struggle; and, as is inevitable with all such struggles, it had also a dark and terrible side. Very much was done of good, and much also of evil; and, as was inevitable in such a period of revolution, often the same man did both good and evil. For our great good fortune as a nation, we, the people of the United States as a whole, can now afford to forget the evil, or, at least, to remember it without bitterness, and to fix our eyes with pride only on the good that was accomplished. Even in ordinary times there are very few of us who do not see the problems of life as through a glass, darkly; and when the glass is clouded by the murk of furious popular passion, the vision of the best and the bravest is dimmed. Looking back, we are all of us now able to do justice to the valor and the disinterestedness and the love of the right, as to each it was given to see the right, shown both by the men of the North and the men of the South in that contest which was finally decided by the attitude of the West. We can admire the heroic valor, the sincerity, the self-devotion shown alike by the men who wore the blue and the men who wore the gray; and our sadness that such men should have had to fight one another is tempered by the glad knowledge that ever hereafter their descendants shall be found fighting side by side, struggling in peace as well as in war for the uplift of their common country, all alike resolute to raise to the highest pitch of honor and usefulness the nation to which they all belong. As for the veterans of the Grand Army of the Republic, they deserve honor and recognition such as is paid to no other citizens of the republic; for to them the reublic owes its all; for to them it owes its very existence. It is because of what you and your comrades did in the dark years that we of to-day walk, each of us, head erect, and proud that we belong, not to one of a dozen little squabbling contemptible commonwealths, but to the mightiest nation upon which the sun shines.

I do not speak of this struggle of the past merely from the historic standpoint. Our interest is primarily in the application to-day of the lessons taught by the contest of half a century ago. It is of little use for us to pay lip loyalty to the mighty men of the past unless we sincerely endeavor to apply to the problems of the present precisely the qualities which in other crises enabled the men of that day to meet those crises. It is half melancholy and half amusing to see the way in which well-meaning people gather to do honor to the men who, in company with John Brown, and under the lead of Abraham Lincoln, faced and solved the great problems of the nineteenth century, while, at the same time, these same good people nervously shrink from, or frantically denounce, those who are trying to meet the problems of the twentieth century in the spirit which was accountable for the successful solution of the problems of Lincoln's time.

Of that generation of men to whom we owe so much, the man to whom we owe most is, of course, Lincoln. Part of our debt to him is because he forecast our present struggle and saw the way out. He said:

I hold that while man exists it is his duty to improve not only his own condition, but to assist in ameliorating mankind.

And again:

Labor is prior to, and independent of, capital. Capital is only the fruit of labor, and could never have existed if labor had not first existed. Labor is the superior of capital, and deserves much the higher consideration.

If that remark was original with me, I should be even more strongly denounced as a communist agitator than I shall be anyhow. It is Lincoln's. I am only quoting it; and that is one side; that is the side the capitalist should hear. Now, let the workingman hear his side.

Capital has its rights, which are as worthy of protection as any other rights. . . . Nor should this lead to a war upon the owners of property. Property is the fruit of labor; . . . property is desirable; is a positive good in the world.

And then comes a thoroughly Lincolnlike sentence:

Let not him who is houseless pull down the house of another, but let him work diligently and build one for himself, thus by example assuring that his own shall be safe from violence when built.

It seems to me that, in these words, Lincoln took substantially the attitude that we ought to take; he showed the proper sense of proportion in his relative estimates of capital and labor, of human rights and property rights. Above all, in this speech, as in many others, he taught a lesson in wise kindliness and charity; an indispensable lesson to us of to-day. But this wise kindliness and charity never weakened his arm or numbed his heart. We cannot afford weakly to blind ourselves to the actual conflict which faces us to-day. The issue is joined, and we must fight or fail.

In every wise struggle for human betterment one of the main objects, and often the only object, has been to achieve in large measure equality of opportunity. In the struggle for this great end, nations rise from barbarism to civilization, and through it people press forward from one stage of enlightenment to the next. One of the chief factors in progress is the destruction of special privilege. The essence of any struggle for healthy liberty has always been, and must always be, to take from some one man or class of men the right to enjoy power, or wealth, or position, or immunity, which has not been earned by service to his or their fellows. That is what you fought for in the Civil War, and that is what we strive for now.

At many stages in the advance of humanity, this conflict between the men who possess more than they have earned and the men who have earned more than they possess is the central condition of progress. In our day it appears as the struggle of free men to gain and hold the right of self-government as against the special interests, who twist the methods of free government into machinery for defeating the popular will. At every stage, and under all circumstances, the essence of the struggle is to equalize opportunity, destroy privilege, and give to the life and citizenship of every individual the highest possible value both to himself and to the commonwealth. That is nothing new. All I ask in civil life is what you fought for in the Civil War. I ask that civil life be carried on according to the spirit in which the army was carried on. You never get perfect justice, but the effort in handling the army was to bring to the front the men who could do the job. Nobody grudged promotion to Grant, or Sherman, or Thomas, or Sheridan, because they earned it. The only complaint was when a man got promotion which he did not earn.

Practical equality of opportunity for all citizens, when we achieve it, will have two great results. First, every man will have a fair chance to make of himself all that in him lies; to reach the highest point to which his capacities, unassisted by special privilege of his own and unhampered by the special privilege of others, can carry him, and to get for himself and his family substantially what he has earned. Second, equality of opportunity means that the commonwealth will get from every citizen the highest service of which he is capable. No man who carries the burden of the special privileges of another can give to the commonwealth that service to which it is fairly entitled.

I stand for the square deal. But when I say that I am for the square deal, I mean not merely that I stand for fair play under the present rules of the game, but that I stand for having those rules changed so as to work for a more substantial equality of opportunity and of reward for equally good service. One word of warning, which, I think, is hardly necessary in Kansas. When I say I want a square deal for the poor man, I do not mean that I want a square deal for the man who remains poor because he has not got the energy to work for himself. If a man who has had a chance will not make good, then he has got to quit. And you men of the Grand Army, you want justice for the brave man who fought, and punishment for the coward who shirked his work. Is not that so?

Now, this means that our government, national and state, must be freed from the sinister influence or control of special interests. Exactly as the special interests of cotton and slavery threatened our political integrity before the Civil War, so now the great special business interests too often control and corrupt the men and methods of government for their own profit. We must drive the special interests out of politics. That is one of our tasks to-day. Every special interest is entitled to justice—full, fair, and complete—and, now, mind you, if there were any attempt by mob violence to plunder and work harm to the special interest, whatever it may be, that I most dislike, and the wealthy man, whomsoever he may be, for whom I have the greatest contempt, I would fight for him, and you would if you were worth your salt. He should have justice. For every special interest is entitled to justice, but not one is entitled to a vote in Congress, to a voice on the bench, or to representation in any public office. The Constitution guarantees protection to property, and we must make that promise good. But it does not give the right of suffrage to any corporation.

The true friend of property, the true conservative, is he who insists that property shall be the servant and not the master of the commonwealth; who insists that the creature of man's making shall be the servant and not the master of the man who made it. The citizens of the United States must effectively control the mighty commercial forces which they have themselves called into being.

There can be no effective control of corporations while their political activity remains. To put an end to it will be neither a short nor an easy task, but it can be done.

We must have complete and effective publicity of corporate affairs, so that the people may know beyond peradventure whether the corporations obey the law and whether their management entitles them to the confidence of the public. It is necessary that laws should be passed to prohibit the use of corporate funds directly or indirectly for political purposes; it is still more necessary that such laws should be thoroughly enforced. Corporate expenditures for political purposes, and especially such expenditures by public service corporations, have supplied one of the principal sources of corruption in our political affairs.

It has become entirely clear that we must have government supervision of the capitalization, not only of public service corporations, including, particularly, railways, but of all corporations doing an interstate business. I do not wish to see the nation forced into the ownership of the railways if it can possibly be avoided, and the only alternative is thoroughgoing and effective regulation, which shall be based on a full knowledge of all the facts, including a physical valuation of property. This physical valuation is not needed, or, at least, is very rarely needed, for fixing rates; but it is needed as the basis of honest capitalization.

We have come to recognize that franchises should never be granted except for a limited time, and never without proper provision for compensation to the public. It is my personal belief that the same kind and degree of control and supervision which should be exercised over public service corporations should be extended also to combinations which control necessaries of life, such as meat, oil, and coal, or which deal in them on an important scale. I have no doubt that the ordinary man who has control of them is much like ourselves. I have no doubt he would like to do well, but I want to have enough supervision to help him realize that desire to do well.

I believe that the officers, and, especially, the directors, of corporations should be held personally responsible when any corporation breaks the law.

Combinations in industry are the result of an imperative economic law which cannot be repealed by political legislation. The effort at prohibiting all combination has substantially failed. The way out lies, not in attempting to prevent such combinations, but in completely controlling them in the interest of the public welfare. For that purpose the Federal Bureau of Corporations is an agency of first importance. Its powers, and, therefore, its efficiency, as well as that of the Interstate Commerce Commission, should be largely increased. We have a right to expect from the Bureau of Corporations and from the Interstate Commerce Commission a very high grade of public service. We should be as sure of the proper conduct of the interstate railways and the proper management of interstate business as we are now sure of the conduct and management of the national banks, and we should have as effective supervision in one case as in the other. The Hepburn Act, and the amendment to the Act in the shape in which it finally passed Congress at the last session, represent a long step in advance, and we must go yet further.

There is a widespread belief among our people that, under the methods of making tariffs which have hitherto obtained, the special interests are too influential. Probably this is true of both the big special interests and the little special interests. These methods have put a premuim on selfishness, and, naturally, the selfish big interests have gotten more than their smaller, though equally selfish, brothers. The duty of Congress is to provide a method by which the interest of the whole people shall be all that receives consideration. To this end there must be an expert tariff commission, wholly removed from the possibility of political pressure or of improper business influence. Such a commission can find the real difference between cost of production, which is mainly the difference of labor cost here and abroad. As fast as its recommendations are made, I believe in revising one schedule at a time. A general revision of the tariff almost inevitably leads to log-rolling and the subordination of the general public interest to local and special interests.

The absence of effective state, and, especially, national, restraint upon unfair money getting has tended to create a small class of enormously wealthy and economically powerful men, whose chief object is to hold and increase their power. The prime need is to change the conditions which enable these men to accumulate power which it is not for the general welfare that they should hold or exercise. We grudge no man a fortune which represents his own power and sagacity, when exercised with entire regard to the welfare of his fellows. Again, comrades over there, take the lesson from your own experience. Not only did you not grudge, but you gloried in the promotion of the great generals who gained their promotion by leading the army to victory. So it is with us. We grudge no man a fortune in civil life if it is honorably obtained and well used. It is not even enough that it should have been gained without doing damage to the community. We should permit it to be gained only so long as the gaining represents benefit to the community. This, I know, implies a policy of a far more active governmental interference with social and economic conditions in this country than we have yet had, but I think we have got to face the fact that such an increase in governmental control is now necessary.

No man should receive a dollar unless that dollar has been fairly earned. Every dollar received should represent a dollar's worth of service rendered—not gambling in stocks, but service rendered. The really big fortune, the swollen fortune, by the mere fact of its size acquires qualities which differentiate it in kind as well as in degree from what is possessed by men of relatively small means. Therefore, I believe in a graduated income tax on big fortunes, and in another tax which is far more easily collected and far more effective—a graduated inheritance tax on big fortunes, properly safeguarded against evasion and increasing rapidly in amount with the size of the estate.

The people of the United States suffer from periodical financial panics to a degree substantially unknown among the other nations which approach us in financial strength. There is no reason why we should suffer what they escape. It is of profound importance that our financial system should be promptly investigated, and so thoroughly and effectively revised as to make it certain that hereafter our currency will no longer fail at critical times to meet our needs.

It is hardly necessary for me to repeat that I believe in an efficient army and a navy large enough to secure for us abroad that respect which is the surest guarantee of peace. A word of special warning to my fellow citizens who are as progressive as I hope I am. I want them to keep up their interest in our internal affairs; and I want them also continually to remember Uncle Sam's interests abroad. Justice and fair dealing among nations rest upon principles identical with those which control justice and fair dealing among the individuals of which nations are composed, with the vital exception that each nation must do its own part in international police work. If you get into trouble here, you can call for the police; but if Uncle Sam gets into trouble, he has got to be his own policeman, and I want to see him strong enough to encourage the peaceful aspirations of other peoples in connection with us. I believe in national friendships and heartiest good will to all nations;

but national friendships, like those between men, must be founded on respect as well as on liking, on forbearance as well as upon trust. I should be heartily ashamed of any American who did not try to make the American government act as justly toward the other nations in international relations as he himself would act toward any individual in private relations. I should be heartily ashamed to see us wrong a weaker power, and I should hang my head forever if we tamely suffered wrong from a stronger power.

Of conservation I shall speak more at length elsewhere. Conservation means development as much as it does protection. I recognize the right and duty of this generation to develop and use the natural resources of our land; but I do not recognize the right to waste them, or to rob, by wasteful use, the generations that come after us. I ask nothing of the nation except that it so behave as each farmer here behaves with reference to his own children. That farmer is a poor creature who skins the land and leaves it worthless to his chilren. The farmer is a good farmer who, having enabled the land to support himself and to provide for the education of his children, leaves it to them a little better than he found it himself. I believe the same thing of a nation.

Moreover, I believe that the natural resources must be used for the benefit of all our people, and not monopolized for the benefit of the few, and here again is another case in which I am accused of taking a revolutionary attitude. People forget now that one hundred years ago there were public men of good character who advocated the nation selling its public lands in great quantities, so that the nation could get the most money out of it, and giving it to the men who could cultivate it for their own uses. We took the proper democratic ground that the land should be granted in small sections to the men who were actually to till it and live on it. Now, with the water power, with the forests, with the mines, we are brought face to face with the fact that there are many people who will go with us in conserving the resources only if they are to be allowed to exploit them for their benefit. That is one of the fundamental reasons why the special interests should be driven out of politics. Of all the questions which can come before this nation, short of the actual preservation of its existence in a great war, there is none which compares in importance with the great central task of leaving this land even a better land for our descendants than it is for us, and training them into a better race to inhabit the land and pass it on. Conservation is a great moral issue, for it involves the patriotic duty of insuring the safety and continuance of the nation. Let me add that the health and vitality of our people are at least as well worth conserving as their forests, waters, lands, and minerals, and in this great work the national government must bear a most important part.

I have spoken elsewhere also of the great task which lies before the farmers of the country to get for themselves and their wives and children not only the benefits of better farming, but also those of better business methods and better conditions of life on the farm. The burden of this great task will fall, as it should, mainly upon the great organizations of the farmers themselves. I am glad it will, for I believe they are all well able to handle it. In particular, there are strong reasons why the Departments of Agriculture of the various states, the United States Department of Agriculture, and the agricultural colleges and experiment stations should extend their work to cover all phases of farm life, instead of limiting themselves, as they have far too often limited themselves in the past, solely to the question of the production of crops. And now a special word to the farmer. I want to see him make the farm as fine a farm as it can be made; and let him remember to see that the improvement goes on indoors as well as out; let him remember that the farmer's wife should have her share of thought and attention just as much as the farmer himself.

Nothing is more true than that excess of every kind is followed by reaction; a fact which should be pondered by reformer and reactionary alike. We are face to face with new conceptions of the relations of property to human welfare, chiefly because certain advocates of the rights of property as against the rights of men have been pushing their claims too far. The man who wrongly holds that every human right is secondary to his profit must now give way to the advocate of human welfare, who rightly maintains that every man holds his property subject to the general right of the community to regulate its use to whatever degree the public welfare may require it.

But I think we may go still further. The right to regulate the use of wealth in the public interest is universally admitted. Let us admit also the right to regulate the terms and conditions of labor, which is the chief element of wealth, directly in the interest of the common good. The fundamental thing to do for every man is to give him a chance to reach a place in which he will make the greatest possible contribution to the public welfare. Understand what I say there. Give him a chance, not push him up if he will not be pushed. Help any man who stumbles; if he lies down, it is a poor job to try to carry him; but if he is a worthy man, try your best to see that he gets a chance to show the worth that is in him. No man can be a good citizen unless he has a wage more than sufficient to cover the bare cost of living, and hours of labor short enough so that after his day's work is done he will have time and energy to bear his share in the management of the community, to help in carrying the general load. We keep countless men from being good citizens by the conditions of life with which we surround them. We need comprehensive workmen's compensation acts, both state and national laws to regulate child labor and work for women, and, especially, we need in our common schools not merely education in book learning, but also practical training for daily life and work. We need to enforce better sanitary conditions for our workers and to extend the use of safety appliances for our workers in industry and commerce, both within and between the states. Also, friends, in the interest of the workingman himself we need to set our faces like flint against mob violence just as against corporate greed; against violence and injustice and lawlessness by wage workers just as much as against lawless cunning and greed and selfish arrogance of employers. If I could ask but one thing of my fellow countrymen, my request would be that, whenever they go in for reform, they remember the two sides, and that they always exact justice from one side as much as from the other. I have small use for the public servant who can always see and denounce the corruption of the capitalist, but who cannot persuade himself, especially before election, to say a word about lawless mob violence. And I have equally small use for the man, be he a judge on the bench, or editor of a great paper, or wealthy and influential private citizen, who can see clearly enough and denounce the lawlessness of mob violence, but whose eyes are closed so that he is blind when the question is one of corruption in business on a gigantic scale.

Also remember what I said about excess in reformer and reactionary alike. If the reactionary man, who thinks of nothing but the rights of property, could have his way, he would bring about a revolution; and one of my chief fears in connection with progress comes because I do not want to see our people, for lack of proper leadership, compelled to follow men whose intentions are excellent, but whose eyes are a little too wild to make it really safe to trust them. Here in Kansas there is one paper which habitually denounces me as a tool of Wall Street, and at the same time frantically repudiates the statement that I am a Socialist on the ground that that is an unwarranted slander of the Socialists.

National efficiency has many factors. It is a necessary result of the principle of conservation widely applied. In the end it will determine our failure or success as a nation. National efficiency has to do, not only with natural resources and with men, but it is equally concerned with institutions. The state must be made efficient for the work which concerns only the people of the state; and the nation for that which concerns all the people. There must remain no neutral ground to serve as a refuge for lawbreakers, and especially for lawbreakers of great wealth, who can hire the vulpine legal cunning which will teach them how to avoid both jurisdictions. It is a misfortune when the national legislature fails to do its duty in providing a national remedy, so that the only national activity is the purely negative activity of the judiciary in forbidding the state to exercise power in the premises.

I do not ask for overcentralization; but I do ask that we work in a spirit of broad and far-reaching nationalism when we work for what concerns our people as a whole. We are all Americans. Our common interests are as broad as the continent. I speak to you here in Kansas exactly as I would speak in New York or Georgia, for the most vital problems are those which affect us all alike. The national government belongs to the whole American people, and where the whole American people are interested, that interest can be guarded effectively only by the national government. The betterment which we seek must be accomplished, I believe, mainly through the national government.

The American people are right in demanding that New Nationalism, without which we cannot hope to deal with new problems. The New Nationalism puts the national need before sectional or personal advantage. It is impatient of the utter confusion that results from local legislatures attempting to treat national issues as local issues. It is still more impatient of the impotence which springs from overdivision of governmental powers, the impotence which makes it possible for local self-ishness or for legal cunning, hired by wealthy special interests, to bring national activities to a deadlock. This New Nationalism regards the executive power as the steward of the public welfare. It demands of the judiciary that it shall be interested primarily in human welfare rather than in property, just as it demands that the representative body shall represent all the people rather than any one class or section of the people.

I believe in shaping the ends of government to protect property as well as human welfare. Normally, and in the long run, the ends are the same; but whenever the alternative must be faced, I am for men and not for property, as you were in the Civil War. I am far from underestimating the importance of dividends; but I rank dividends below human character. Again, I do not have any sympathy with the reformer who says he does not care for dividends. Of course, economic welfare is necessary, for a man must pull his own weight and be able to support his family. I know well that the reformers must not bring upon the people economic ruin, or the reforms themselves will go down in the ruin. But we must be ready to face temporary disaster, whether or not brought on by those who will war against us to the knife. Those who oppose all reform will do well to re-member that ruin in its worst form is inevitable if our national life brings us nothing better than swollen fortunes for the few and the triumph in both politics and business of a sordid and selfish materialism.

If our political institutions were perfect, they would absolutely prevent the political domination of money in any part of our affairs. We need to make our political representatives more quickly and sensitively responsive to the people whose servants they are. More direct action by the people in their own affairs under proper safeguards is vitally necessary. The direct primary is a step in this direction, if it is associated with a corrupt practices act effective to prevent the advantage of the man willing recklessly and unscrupulously to spend money over his more honest competitor. It is particularly important that all moneys received or expended for campaign purposes should be publicly accounted for, not only after election, but before election as well. Political action must be made simpler, easier, and freer from confusion for every citizen. I believe that the prompt removal of unfaithful or incompetent public servants should be made easy and sure in whatever way experience shall show to be most expedient in any given class of cases.

One of the fundamental necessities in a representative government such as ours is to make certain that the men to whom the people delegate their power shall serve the people by whom they are elected, and not the special interests. I believe that every national officer, elected or appointed, should be forbidden to perform any service or receive any compensation, directly or indirectly, from interstate corporations; and a similar provision could not fail to be useful within the states.

The object of government is the welfare of the people. The material progress and prosperity of a nation are desirable chiefly so far as they lead to the moral and material welfare of all good citizens. Just in proportion as the average man and woman are honest, capable of sound judgment and high ideals, active in public affairs,—but, first of all, sound in their home life, and the father and mother of healthy children whom they bring up well,—just so far, and no farther, we may count our civilization a success. We must have—I believe we have already—a genuine and permanent moral awakening, without which no wisdom of legislation or administration really means anything; and, on the other hand, we must try to secure the social and economic legislation without which any improvement due to purely moral agitation is necessarily evanescent. Let me again illustrate by a reference to the Grand Army. You could not have won simply as a disorderly and disorganized mob. You needed generals; you needed careful administration of the most advanced type; and a good commissary—the cracker line. You well remember that success was necessary in many different lines in order to bring about general success. You had to have the administration at Washington good, just as you had to have the administration in the field; and you had to have the work of the generals good. You could not have triumphed without that administration and leadership; but it would all have been worthless if the average soldier had not had the right stuff in him. He had to have the right stuff in him, or you could not get it out of him. In the last analysis, therefore, vitally necessary though it was to have the right kind of organization and the right kind of generalship, it was even more vitally necessary that the average soldier should have the fighting edge, the right character. So it is in our civil life. No matter how honest and decent we are in our private lives, if we do not have the right kind of law and the right kind of administration of the law, we cannot go forward as a nation. That is imperative; but it must be an addition to, and not a substitution for, the qualities that make us good citizens. In the last analysis, the most important elements in any man's career must be the sum of those qualities which, in the aggregate, we speak of as character. If he has not got it, then no law that the wit of man can devise, no administration of the law by the boldest and strongest executive, will avail to help him. We must have the right kind of character—character that makes a man, first of all, a good man in the home, a good father, a good husband—that makes a man a good neighbor. You must have that, and, then, in addition, you must have the kind of law and the kind of administration of the law which will give to those qualities in the private citizen the best possible chance for development. The prime problem of our nation is to get the right type of good citizenship, and, to get it, we must have progress, and our public men must be genuinely progressive.

7

An Affirmation of Faith in Democracy

Woodrow Wilson's "Life Comes From the Soil" and "The Liberation of a People's Vital Energies"

Woodrow Wilson (1856-1924), as with many others of his generation, reflected the evolutionary, progressive temper of the twentieth
century. "We are in the presence of a new organization of society,"
he said on one occasion. "Our life has broken away from the past.
The life of America is not the life that it was twenty years ago; it is
not the life that it was ten years ago. We have changed our economic
conditions, absolutely, from top to bottom; and, with our economic
society, the organization of our life." But obstacles stood in the way
of a realization of America's full potential. The principal enemies of
freedom were monopolists in business and bosses in politics. While
Roosevelt advocated reform to strengthen the nation, Wilson sought
to free men and women from the trammels of modern life that hampered their efforts at individual self-fulfillment. Born and reared in
the South, Wilson made a career for himself in higher education first
as a college professor later as a university president. In 1910 at the
age of 54 he resigned the presidency of Princeton University to enter
politics in New Jersey. In 1912 he became the Democratic Party's
nominee for President of the United States. He published his campaign speeches of 1912 under the title of "The New Freedom," and
this phrase has since been used to characterize the program of his
first administration, 1913-1917. Few men have been able to use words
and phrases as effectively as Woodrow Wilson. He was a master
rhetorician who caught the moods and aspirations of the masses and
fleshed them out in magnificent prose. Arthur S. Link has written a
multivolume biography of Wilson, the best of several. See especially
his *Wilson: The Road to the White House* and his *Wilson: The New
Freedom* (Princeton: Princeton University Press, 1947, 1956). The
same author's °*Woodrow Wilson and the Progressive Era, 1910-1917*
(New York: Harper and Company, 1954) is indispensable to an understanding of the changes that occurred in the New Freedom. A read-

Woodrow Wilson, *The New Freedom, A Call for the Emancipation of the
Generous Energies of a People* (New York: Doubleday, Page and Company,
1913), pp. 79-89; 277-94.

able brief biography is °John M. Blum's *Woodrow Wilson and the Politics of Morality* (Boston: Little, Brown and Company, 1956). In reading these two addresses note (1) the symbolism employed; (2) the measure of faith in the common man; (3) Wilson's sense of the responsibility of power residing in the country; (4) what connection he saw between freedom and progress; (5) how he related sixteenth- and seventeenth-century America to twentieth-century America; (6) what endangered liberty in the modern world; (7) what Wilson understood by liberty; (8) what specifics he proposed to ensure its persistence; (9) the quality of his rhetoric.

Life Comes from the Soil

When i look back on the processes of history, when I survey the genesis of America, I see this written over every page: that the nations are renewed from the bottom, not from the top; that the genius which springs up from the ranks of unknown men is the genius which renews the youth and energy of the people. Everything I know about history, every bit of experience and observation that has contributed to my thought, has confirmed me in the conviction that the real wisdom of human life is compounded out of the experiences of ordinary men. The utility, the vitality, the fruitage of life does not come from the top to the bottom; it comes, like the natural growth of a great tree, from the soil, up through the trunk into the branches to the foliage and the fruit. The great struggling unknown masses of the men who are at the base of everything are the dynamic force that is lifting the levels of society. A nation is as great, and only as great, as her rank and file.

So the first and chief need of this nation of ours to-day is to include in the partnership of government all those great bodies of unnamed men who are going to produce our future leaders and renew the future energies of America. And as I confess that, as I confess my belief in the common man, I know what I am saying. The man who is swimming against the stream knows the strength of it. The man who is in the mêlée knows what blows are being struck and what blood is being drawn. The man who is on the make is the judge of what is happening in

America, not the man who has made good; not the man who has emerged from the flood; not the man who is standing on the bank looking on, but the man who is struggling for his life and for the lives of those who are dearer to him than himself. That is the man whose judgment will tell you what is going on in America; that is the man by whose judgment I, for one, wish to be guided.

We have had the wrong jury; we have had the wrong group —no, I will not say the wrong group, but too small a group— in control of the policies of the United States. The average man has not been consulted, and his heart had begun to sink for fear he never would be consulted again. Therefore, we have got to organize a government whose sympathies will be open to the whole body of the people of the United States, a government which will consult as large a proportion of the people of the United States as possible before it acts. Because the great problem of government is to know what the average man is experiencing and is thinking about. Most of us are average men; very few of us rise, except by fortunate accident, above the general level of the community about us; and therefore the man who thinks common thoughts, the man who has had common experiences, is almost always the man who interprets America aright. Isn't that the reason that we are proud of such stories as the story of Abraham Lincoln—a man who rose out of the ranks and interpreted America better than any man had interpreted it who had risen out of the privileged classes or the educated classes of America?

The hope of the United States in the present and in the future is the same that it has always been: it is the hope and confidence that out of unknown homes will come men who will constitute themselves the masters of industry and of politics. The average hopefulness, the average welfare, the average enterprise, the average initiative, of the United States are the only things that make it rich. We are not rich because a few gentlemen direct our industry; we are rich because of our own intelligence and our own industry. America does not consist of men who get their names into the newspapers; America does not consist politically of the men who set themselves up to be political leaders; she does not consist of the men who do most of her talking— they are important only so far as they speak for that great

voiceless multitude of men who constitute the great body and
the saving force of the nation. Nobody who cannot speak the
common thought, who does not move by the common impulse,
is the man to speak for America, or for any of her future purposes. Only he is fit to speak who knows the thoughts of the
great body of citizens, the men who go about their business
every day, the men who toil from morning till night, the men
who go home tired in the evenings, the men who are carrying
on the things we are so proud of.

You know how it thrills our blood sometimes to think how all
the nations of the earth wait to see what America is going to
do with her power, her physical power, her enormous resources,
her enormous wealth. The nations hold their breath to see what
this young country will do with her young unspoiled strength;
we cannot help but be proud that we are strong. But what has
made us strong? The toil of millions of men, the toil of men
who do not boast, who are inconspicuous, but who live their
lives humbly from day to day; it is the great body of toilers
that constitutes the might of America. It is one of the glories
of our land that nobody is able to predict from what family,
from what region, from what race, even, the leaders of the
country are going to come. The great leaders of this country
have not come very often from the established, "successful"
families.

I remember speaking at a school not long ago where I understood that almost all the young men were the sons of very rich
people, and I told them I looked upon them with a great deal
of pity, because, I said: "Most of you fellows are doomed to
obscurity. You will not do anything. You will never try to do
anything, and with all the great tasks of the country waiting
to be done, probably you are the very men who will decline
to do them. Some man who has been 'up against it,' some man
who has come out of the crowd, somebody who has had the
whip of necessity laid on his back, will emerge out of the crowd,
will show that he understands the crowd, understands the interests of the nation, united and not separated, and will stand up
and lead us."

If I may speak of my own experience, I have found audiences
made up of the "common people" quicker to take a point,

quicker to understand an argument, quicker to discern a tendency and to comprehend a principle, than many a college class that I have lectured to—not because the college class lacked the intelligence, but because college boys are not in contact with the realities of life, while "common" citizens are in contact with the actual life of day by day; you do not have to explain to them what touches them to the quick.

There is one illustration of the value of the constant renewal of society from the bottom that has always interested me profoundly. The only reason why government did not suffer dry rot in the Middle Ages under the aristocratic system which then prevailed was that so many of the men who were efficient instruments of government were drawn from the church—from that great religious body which was then the only church, that body which we now distinguish from other religious bodies as the Roman Catholic Church. The Roman Catholic Church was then, as it is now, a great democracy. There was no peasant so humble that he might not become a priest, and no priest so obscure that he might not become Pope of Christendom; and every chancellery in Europe, every court in Europe, was ruled by these learned, trained and accomplished men—the priesthood of that great and dominant body. What kept government alive in the Middle Ages was this constant rise of the sap from the bottom, from the rank and file of the great body of the people through the open channels of the priesthood. That, it seems to me, is one of the most interesting and convincing illustrations that could possibly be adduced of the thing that I am talking about.

The only way that government is kept pure is by keeping these channels open, so that nobody may deem himself so humble as not to constitute a part of the body politic, so that there will constantly be coming new blood into the veins of the body politic; so that no man is so obscure that he may not break the crust of any class he may belong to, may not spring up to higher levels and be counted among the leaders of the state. Anything that depresses, anything that makes the organization greater than the man, anything that blocks, discourages, dismays the humble man, is against all the principles of progress. When I see alliances formed, as they are now being formed, by successful men

of business with successful organizers of politics, I know that
something has been done that checks the vitality and progress
of society. Such an alliance, made at the top, is an alliance made
to depress the levels, to hold them where they are, if not to sink
them; and, therefore, it is the constant business of good politics
to break up such partnerships, to re-establish and reopen the
connections between the great body of the people and the offices
of government.

To-day, when our government has so far passed into the hands
of special interests; to-day, when the doctrine is implicitly avowed
that only select classes have the equipment necessary for carrying on government; to-day, when so many conscientious citizens,
smitten with the scene of social wrong and suffering, have fallen
victims to the fallacy that benevolent government can be meted
out to the people by kind-hearted trustees of prosperity and
guardians of the welfare of dutiful employees—to-day, supremely,
does it behoove this nation to remember that a people shall be
saved by the power that sleeps in its own deep bosom, or by
none; shall be renewed in hope, in conscience, in strength, by
waters welling up from its own sweet, perennial springs. Not
from above; not by patronage of its aristocrats. The flower does
not bear the root, but the root the flower. Everything that blooms
in beauty in the air of heaven draws its fairness, its vigor, from
its roots. Nothing living can blossom into fruitage unless through
nourishing stalks deep-planted in the common soil. The rose is
merely the evidence of the vitality of the root; and the real
source of its beauty, the very blush that it wears upon its tender
cheek, comes from those silent sources of life that lie hidden in
the chemistry of the soil. Up from that soil, up from the silent
bosom of the earth, rise the currents of life and energy. Up
from the common soil, up from the quiet heart of the people,
rise joyously to-day streams of hope and determination bound to
renew the face of the earth in glory.

I tell you, the so-called radicalism of our times is simply the
effort of nature to release the generous energies of our people.
This great American people is at bottom just, virtuous, and
hopeful; the roots of its being are in the soil of what is lovely,
pure, and of good report, and the need of the hour is just that
radicalism that will clear a way for the realization of the aspirations of a sturdy race.

The Liberation of a People's Vital Energies

No matter how often we think of it, the discovery of America must each time make a fresh appeal to our imaginations. For centuries, indeed from the beginning, the face of Europe had been turned toward the east. All the routes of trade, every impulse and energy, ran from west to east. The Atlantic lay at the world's back-door. Then, suddenly, the conquest of Constantinople by the Turk closed the route to the Orient. Europe had either to face about or lack any outlet for her energies; the unknown sea at the west at last was ventured upon, and the earth learned that it was twice as big as it had thought. Columbus did not find, as he had expected, the civilization of Cathay; he found an empty continent. In that part of the world, upon that new-found half of the globe, mankind, late in its history, was thus afforded an opportunity to set up a new civilization; here it was strangely privileged to make a new human experiment.

Never can that moment of unique opportunity fail to excite the emotion of all who consider its strangeness and richness; a thousand fanciful histories of the earth might be contrived without the imagination daring to conceive such a romance as the hiding away of half the globe until the fulness of time had come for a new start in civilization. A mere sea captain's ambition to trace a new trade route gave way to a moral adventure for humanity. The race was to found a new order here on this delectable land, which no man approached without receiving, as the old voyagers relate, you remember, sweet airs out of woods aflame with flowers and murmurous with the sound of pellucid waters. The hemisphere lay waiting to be touched with life—life from the old centres of living, surely, but cleansed of defilement, and cured of weariness, so as to be fit for the virgin purity of a new bride. The whole thing springs into the imagination like a wonderful vision, an exquisite marvel which once only in all history could be vouchsafed.

One other thing only compares with it; only one other thing touches the springs of emotion as does the picture of the ships of Columbus drawing near the bright shores—and that is the thought of the choke in the throat of the immigrant of to-day as he gazes from the steerage deck at the land where he has been taught to believe he in his turn shall find an earthly paradise, where, a free man, he shall forget the heartaches of the old life, and enter into the fulfilment of the hope of the world. For has not every ship that has pointed her prow westward borne hither the hopes of generation after generation of the oppressed of other lands? How always have men's hearts beat as they saw the coast of America rise to their view! How it has always seemed to them that the dweller there would at last be rid of kings, of privileged classes, and of all those bonds which had kept men depressed and helpless, and would there realize the full fruition of his sense of honest manhood, would there be one of a great body of brothers, not seeking to defraud and deceive one another, but seeking to accomplish the general good!

What was in the writings of the men who founded America—to serve the selfish interests of America? Do you find that in their writings? No; to serve the cause of humanity, to bring liberty to mankind. They set up their standards here in America in the tenet of hope, as a beacon of encouragement to all the nations of the world; and men came thronging to these shores with an expectancy that never existed before, with a confidence they never dared feel before, and found here for generations together a haven of peace, of opportunity, of equality.

God send that in the complicated state of modern affairs we may recover the standards and repeat the achievements of that heroic age!

For life is no longer the comparatively simple thing it was. Our relations one with another have been profoundly modified by the new agencies of rapid communication and transportation, tending swiftly to concentrate life, widen communities, fuse interests, and complicate all the processes of living. The individual is dizzily swept about in a thousand new whirlpools of activities. Tyranny has become more subtle, and has learned to wear the guise of mere industry, and even of benevolence. Freedom has become a somewhat different matter. It cannot—eternal principle that it is—it cannot have altered, yet it shows itself in new aspects. Perhaps it is only revealing its deeper meaning.

What is liberty?

I have long had an image in my mind of what constitutes liberty. Suppose that I were building a great piece of powerful machinery, and suppose that I should so awkwardly and unskilfully assemble the parts of it that every time one part tried to move it would be interfered with by the others, and the whole thing would buckle up and be checked. Liberty for the several parts would consist in the best possible assembling and adjustment of them all, would it not? If you want the great piston of the engine to run with absolute freedom, give it absolutely perfect alignment and adjustment with the other parts of the machine, so that it is free, not because it is let alone or isolated, but because it has been associated most skilfully and carefully with the other parts of the great structure.

What is liberty? You say of the locomotive that it runs free. What do you mean? You mean that its parts are so assembled and adjusted that friction is reduced to a minimum, and that it has perfect adjustment. We say of a boat skimming the water with light foot, "How free she runs," when we mean, how perfectly she is adjusted to the force of the wind, how perfectly she obeys the great breath out of the heavens that fills her sails. Throw her head up into the wind and see how she will halt and stagger, how every sheet will shiver and her whole frame be shaken, how instantly she is "in irons," in the expressive phrase of the sea. She is free only when you have let her fall off again and have recovered once more her nice adjustment to the forces she must obey and cannot defy.

Human freedom consists in perfect adjustments of human interests and human activities and human energies.

Now, the adjustments necessary between individuals, between individuals and the complex institutions amidst which they live, and between those institutions and the government, are infinitely more intricate to-day than ever before. No doubt this is a tiresome and roundabout way of saying the thing, yet perhaps it is worth while to get somewhat clearly in our mind what makes all the trouble to-day. Life has become complex; there are many more elements, more parts, to it than ever before. And, therefore, it is harder to keep everything adjusted—and harder to find out where the trouble lies when the machine gets out of order.

You know that one of the interesting things that Mr. Jefferson said in those early days of simplicity which marked the beginnings of our government was that the best government consisted in as little governing as possible. And there is still a sense in which that is true. It is still intolerable for the government to

interfere with our individual activities except where it is necessary to interfere with them in order to free them. But I feel
confident that if Jefferson were living in our day he would see
what we see: that the individual is caught in a great confused
nexus of all sorts of complicated circumstances, and that to let
him alone is to leave him helpless as against the obstacles with
which he has to contend; and that, therefore, law in our day
must come to the assistance of the individual. It must come to
his assistance to see that he gets fair play; that is all, but that
is much. Without the watchful interference, the resolute interference, of the government, there can be no fair play between
individuals and such powerful institutions as the trusts. Freedom
to-day is something more than being let alone. The program of
a government of freedom must in these days be positive, not
negative merely.

Well, then, in this new sense and meaning of it, are we preserving freedom in this land of ours, the hope of all the earth?

Have we, inheritors of this continent and of the ideals to
which the fathers consecrated it—have we maintained them,
realizing them, as each generation must, anew? Are we, in the
consciousness that the life of man is pledged to higher levels
here than elsewhere, striving still to bear aloft the standards
of liberty and hope, or, disillusioned and defeated, are we feeling the disgrace of having had a free field in which to do new
things and of not having done them?

The answer must be, I am sure, that we have been in a fair
way of failure—tragic failure. And we stand in danger of utter
failure yet except we fulfil speedily the determination we have
reached, to deal with the new and subtle tyrannies according to
their deserts. Don't deceive yourselves for a moment as to the
power of the great interests which now dominate our development. They are so great that it is almost an open question
whether the government of the United States can dominate them
or not. Go one step further, make their organized power permanent, and it may be too late to turn back. The roads diverge
at the point where we stand. They stretch their vistas out to
regions where they are very far separated from one another;
at the end of one is the old tiresome scene of government tied
up with special interests; and at the other shines the liberating
light of individual initiative, of individual liberty, of individual

freedom, the light of untrammeled enterprise. I believe that that light shines out of the heavens itself that God has created. I believe in human liberty as I believe in the wine of life. There is no salvation for men in the pitiful condescensions of industrial masters. Guardians have no place in a land of freemen. Prosperity guaranteed by trustees has no prospect of endurance. Monopoly means the atrophy of enterprise. If monopoly persists, monopoly will always sit at the helm of the government. I do not expect to see monopoly restrain itself. If there are men in this country big enough to own the government of the United States, they are going to own it; what we have to determine now is whether we are big enough, whether we are men enough, whether we are free enough, to take possession again of the government which is our own. We haven't had free access to it, our minds have not touched it by way of guidance, in half a generation, and now we are engaged in nothing less than the recovery of what was made with our own hands, and acts only by our delegated authority.

I tell you, when you discuss the question of the tariffs and of the trusts, you are discussing the very lives of yourselves and your children. I believe that I am preaching the very cause of some of the gentlemen whom I am opposing when I preach the cause of free industry in the United States, for I think they are slowly girding the tree that bears the inestimable fruits of our life, and that if they are permitted to gird it entirely nature will take her revenge and the tree will die.

I do not believe that America is securely great because she has great men in her now. America is great in proportion as she can make sure of having great men in the next generation. She is rich in her unborn children; rich, that is to say, if those unborn children see the sun in a day of opportunity, see the sun when they are free to exercise their energies as they will. If they open their eyes in a land where there is no special privilege, then we shall come into a new era of American greatness and American liberty; but if they open their eyes in a country where they must be employees or nothing, if they open their eyes in a land of merely regulated monopoly, where all the conditions of industry are determined by small groups of men, then they will see an America such as the founders of this Republic would have wept to think of. The only hope is in the

release of the forces which philanthropic trust presidents want
to monopolize. Only the emancipation, the freeing and heartening of the vital energies of all the people will redeem us. In all
that I may have to do in public affairs in the United States I
am going to think of towns such as I have seen in Indiana,
towns of the old American pattern, that own and operate their
own industries, hopefully and happily. My thought is going to
be bent upon the multiplication of towns of that kind and the
prevention of the concentration of industry in this country in
such a fashion and upon such a scale that towns that own themselves will be impossible. You know what the vitality of America
consists of. Its vitality does not lie in New York, nor in Chicago;
it will not be sapped by anything that happens in St. Louis.
The vitality of America lies in the brains, the energies, the
enterprise of the people throughout the land; in the efficiency
of their factories and in the richness of the fields that stretch
beyond the borders of the town; in the wealth which they extract
from nature and originate for themselves through the inventive
genius characteristic of all free American communities.

That is the wealth of America, and if America discourages
the locality, the community, the self-contained town, she will
kill the nation. A nation is as rich as her free communities; she
is not as rich as her capital city or her metropolis. The amount
of money in Wall Street is no indication of the wealth of the
American people. That indication can be found only in the
fertility of the American mind and the productivity of American
industry everywhere throughout the United States. If America
were not rich and fertile, there would be no money in Wall
Street. If Americans were not vital and able to take care of
themselves, the great money exchanges would break down. The
welfare, the very existence of the nation, rests at last upon the
great mass of the people; its prosperity depends at last upon
the spirit in which they go about their work in their several
communities throughout the broad land. In proportion as her
towns and her countrysides are happy and hopeful will America
realize the high ambitions which have marked her in the eyes
of all the world.

The welfare, the happiness, the energy and spirit of the men
and women who do the daily work in our mines and factories,
on our railroads, in our offices and ports of trade, on our farms

and on the sea, is the underlying necessity of all prosperity. There can be nothing wholesome unless their life is wholesome; there can be no contentment unless they are contented. Their physical welfare affects the soundness of the whole nation. How would it suit the prosperity of the United States, how would it suit business, to have a people that went every day sadly or sullenly to their work? How would the future look to you if you felt that the aspiration had gone out of most men, the confidence of success, the hope that they might improve their condition? Do you not see that just so soon as the old self-confidence of America, just as soon as her old boasted advantage of individual liberty and opportunity, is taken away, all the energy of her people begins to subside, to slacken, to grow loose and pulpy, without fibre, and men simply cast about to see that the day does not end disastrously with them?

So we must put heart into the people by taking the heartlessness out of politics, business, and industry. We have got to make politics a thing in which an honest man can take his part with satisfaction because he knows that his opinion will count as much as the next man's, and that the boss and the interests have been dethroned. Business we have got to untrammel, abolishing tariff favors, and railroad discrimination, and credit denials, and all forms of unjust handicaps against the little man. Industry we have got to humanize—not through the trusts—but through the direct action of law guaranteeing protection against dangers and compensation for injuries, guaranteeing sanitary conditions, proper hours, the right to organize, and all the other things which the conscience of the country demands as the workingman's right. We have got to cheer and inspirit our people with the sure prospects of social justice and due reward, with the vision of the open gates of opportunity for all. We have got to set the energy and the initiative of this great people absolutely free, so that the future of America will be greater than the past, so that the pride of America will grow with achievement, so that America will know as she advances from generation to generation that each brood of her sons is greater and more enlightened than that which preceded it, know that she is fulfilling the promise that she has made to mankind.

Such is the vision of some of us who now come to assist in its realization. For we Democrats would not have endured this long burden of exile if we had not seen a vision. We could have traded; we could have got into the game; we could have surrendered and made terms; we could have played the role of patrons to the men who wanted to dominate the interests of the country—and here and there gentlemen who pretended to be of us did make those arrangements. They couldn't stand privation. You never can stand it unless you have within you some imperishable food upon which to sustain life and courage, the food of those visions of the spirit where a table is set before us laden with palatable fruits, the fruits of hope, the fruits of imagination, those invisible things of the spirit which are the only things upon which we can sustain ourselves through this weary world without fainting. We have carried in our minds, after you had thought you had obscured and blurred them, the ideals of those men who first set their foot upon America, those little bands who came to make a foothold in the wilderness, because the great teeming nations that they had left behind them had forgotten what human liberty was, liberty of thought, liberty of religion, liberty of residence, liberty of action.

Since their day the meaning of liberty has deepened. But it has not ceased to be a fundamental demand of the human spirit, a fundamental necessity for the life of the soul. And the day is at hand when it shall be realized on this consecrated soil—a New Freedom—a Liberty widened and deepened to match the broadened life of man in modern America, restoring to him in very truth the control of his government, throwing wide all gates of lawful enterprise, unfettering his energies, and warming the generous impulses of his heart—a process of release, emancipation, and inspiration, full of a breath of life as sweet and wholesome as the airs that filled the sails of the caravels of Columbus and gave the promise and boast of magnificent Opportunity in which America *dare not fail.*

8

Democracy Is a Way of Life
Walter Lippmann's "Drift and Mastery"

Walter Lippmann (1889-   ) has for over a half-century been a steady observer, critic, and commentator; few features of American life in its domestic and foreign manifestations have escaped his attention. A New Yorker with a brilliant Harvard-trained mind, he established for himself early in his career a substantial reputation as a publicist and journalist. Herbert Croly, impressed with Lippmann's youthful enthusiasm and incisive intelligence, invited him to become associated with *The New Republic*, the nation's foremost progressive weekly, founded in 1914. Author of over two dozen books and innumerable articles, editorials, and syndicated columns dealing principally with the theory and practice of politics, Lippmann's influence over the decades has continued to be impressive. He was a true child of his age, and in the volume from which the following selections have been taken, he called upon his readers to recognize that all the fine formulas and rhetoric inherited from the eighteenth and nineteenth centuries had outserved their usefulness. Modern science had produced new tools of thinking as it had fashioned a new urban, industrial world and it was high time to realize that one could not operate a twentieth-century social mechanism with methods and materials appropriate to the eighteenth and nineteenth centuries. America could no longer afford to drift along, depending upon the expansion of the West to save it from the errors that it occasionally committed as it blundered and stumbled from one crisis to the next. The time had come boldly and consciously to master and direct the incomparable forces unleashed by modern science and technology. Marquis Childs and James Reston, editors, have in *Walter Lippmann and His Times* (New York: Harcourt, Brace and Company, 1959) brought together a collection of essays, useful in estimating Lippmann's place in twentieth-century American thought. Charles Forcey's *The Crossroads of Liberalism: Croly, Weyl, Lippmann and the Progressive Era, 1900-1925* (New York: Oxford University Press, 1961) provides an excellent critical

Walter Lippmann, *Drift and Mastery: An Attempt to Diagnose the Current Unrest* (New York: Mitchell Kennerley, 1914), pp. xvi-xxv; 124-48; 154-73; 176-91; 196-97; 206-13; 254-77; 328-34.

study of progressivism and helps locate Lippmann in the movement. Christopher Lasch's *The New Radicalism in America, 1888-1963: The Intellectual As a Social Type* (New York: Alfred A. Knopf, 1965) is an original and very perceptive study of the reformers who came to maturity early in the twentieth century. For comparative purposes one might consult °Herbert Croly's *The Promise of American Life* (New York: The Macmillan Company, 1909) and °Walter Weyl's *The New Democracy: An Essay Concering Certain Political and Economic Conditions in the United States* (New York: The Macmillan Company, 1912). In reading the following selections note (1) what assumptions the author postulates at the outset; (2) evidences of the influence of William James and pragmatism on Lippmann's thought; (3) what he meant by the chapter heading "A Nation of Villagers"; (4) his judgment of the antitrust laws and the bases for his opinions; (5) what he thought of Bryan's and Wilson's programs of action and why; (6) his arguments concerning the inadequacies of current institutions and his prescription for coping with new problems; (7) what he meant by *Drift* and how that situation had come about; (8) what he implied by saying that "All of us are immigrants spiritually"; (9) what he thought was needed in a program of self-government; (10) what he thought should replace tradition in the modern world and why he thought so; (11) what he meant by *Mastery* and what he thought its relation to democracy was; and (12) evidence of his antiformalistic approach to human problems.

Introduction

. . . Without a tyrant to attack an immature democracy is always somewhat bewildered. Yet we have to face the fact in America that what thwarts the growth of our civilization is not the uncanny, malicious contrivance of the plutocracy, but the faltering method, the distracted soul, and the murky vision of what we call grandiloquently the will of the people. If we flounder, it is not because the old order is strong, but because the new one is weak. Democracy is more than the absence of czars, more than freedom, more than equal opportunity. It is a way of life, a use of freedom, an embrace of opportunity. For republics do not come in when kings go out, the defeat of a propertied class is not followed by a cooperative commonwealth, the emancipation of woman is more than a struggle for rights. A servile community will have a master, if not a monarch, then a landlord or a boss, and no legal device will save it. A nation of uncritical drifters can change only the form of tyranny, for like Christian's sword, democracy is a weapon in the hands of those who have the courage and the skill to wield it; in all others it is a rusty piece of junk.

The issues that we face are very different from those of the last century and a half. The difference, I think, might be summed up roughly this way: those who went before inherited a conservatism and overthrew it; we inherit freedom, and have to use it. The sanctity of property, the patriarchal family, hereditary caste, the dogma of sin, obedience to authority—the rock of ages, in brief, has been blasted for us. Those who are young to-day are born into a world in which the foundations of the older order survive only as habits or by default. So Americans can carry through their purposes when they have them. If the standpatter is still powerful amongst us it is because we have not learned to use our power, and direct it to fruitful ends. The American conservative, it seems to me, fills the vacuum where democratic purpose should be.

So far as we are concerned, then, the case is made out against absolutism, commercial oligarchy, and unquestioned creeds. *The rebel program is stated.* Scientific invention and blind social currents have made the old authority impossible in fact, the artillery fire of the iconoclasts has shattered its prestige. We inherit a rebel tradition. The dominant forces in our world are not the sacredness of property, nor the intellectual leadership of the priest; they are not the divinity of the constitution, the glory of industrial push, Victorian sentiment, New England respectability, the Republican Party, or John D. Rockefeller. Our time, of course, believes in change. The adjective "progressive" is what we like, and the word "new," be it the New Nationalism of Roosevelt, the New Freedom of Wilson, or the New Socialism of the syndicalists. The conservatives are more lonely than the pioneers, for almost any prophet to-day can have disciples. The leading thought of our world has ceased to regard commercialism either as permanent or desirable, and the only real question among intelligent people is how business methods are to be altered, not whether they are to be altered. For no one, unafflicted with invincible ignorance, desires to preserve our economic system in its existing form.

The business man has stepped down from his shrine; he is no longer an oracle whose opinion on religion, science, and education is listened to dumbly as the valuable by-product of a paying business. We have scotched the romance of success. In the emerging morality the husband is not regarded as the proprietor of his wife, nor the parents as autocrats over the children. We are met by women who are "emancipated"; for what we hardly know. We are not stifled by a classical tradition in art: in fact artists to-day are somewhat stunned by the rarefied atmosphere of their freedom. There is a wide agreement among thinking people that the body is not a filthy thing, and that to implant in a child the sense of sin is a poor preparation for a temperate life.

The battle for us, in short, does not lie against crusted prejudice, but against the chaos of a new freedom.

This chaos is our real problem. So if the younger critics are to meet the issues of their generation they must give their attention, not so much to the evils of authority, as to the weaknesses of democracy. But how is a man to go about doing such a task? He faces an enormously complicated world, full of stirring and confusion and ferment. He hears of movements and agitations, criticisms and reforms, knows people who are devoted to "causes," feels angry or hopeful at different times, goes to meetings, reads radical books, and accumulates a sense of uneasiness and pending change.

He can't, however, live with any meaning unless he formulates for himself a vision of what is to come out of the unrest. I have tried in this book to sketch such a vision for myself. At first thought it must seem an absurdly presumptuous task. But it is a task that everyone has to attempt if he is to take part in the work of his time. For in so far as we can direct the future at all, we shall do it by laying what we see against what other people see.

This doesn't mean the constructing of utopias. The kind of vision which will be fruitful to democratic life is one that is made out of latent promise in the actual world. There is a future contained in the trust and the union, the new status of women, and the moral texture of democracy. It is a future that can in a measure be foreseen and bent somewhat nearer to our hopes. A knowledge of it gives a sanction to our efforts, a part in a larger career, and an invaluable sense of our direction. We make our vision, and hold it ready for any amendment that experience suggests. It is not a fixed picture, a row of shiny ideals which we can exhibit to mankind, and say: Achieve these or be damned. All we can do is to search the world as we find it, extricate the forces that seem to move it, and surround them with criticism and suggestion. Such a vision will inevitably reveal the bias of its author; that is to say it will be a human hypothesis, not an oracular revelation. But if the hypothesis is honest and alive it should cast a little light upon our chaos. It should help us to cease revolving in the mere routine of the present or floating in a private utopia. For a vision of latent hope would be woven of vigorous strands; it would be concentrated on the crucial points of contemporary life, on that living zone where the present is passing into the future. It is the region where thought and action count. Too far ahead there is nothing but your dream; just behind, there is nothing but your memory. But in the unfolding present, man can be creative if his vision is gathered from the promise of actual things.

The day is past, I believe, when anybody can pretend to have laid down an inclusive or a final analysis of the democratic problem. Everyone is compelled to omit infinitely more than he can deal with; everyone is compelled to meet the fact that a democratic vision must be made by the progressive collaboration of many people. Thus I have touched upon the industrial problem at certain points that seem to me of outstanding importance, but there are vast sections and phases of industrial enterprise that pass unnoticed. The points I have raised are big in the world I happen to live in, but obviously they are not the whole world.

It is necessary, also, to inquire how "practical" you can be in a book of generalizations. That amounts to asking how detailed you can be. Well, it is impossible when you mention a minimum wage law, for example, to append a draft of the bill and a concrete set of rules for its administration. In human problems especially there is a vagueness which no one can escape entirely. Even the most voluminous study in three volumes of some legal question does not meet at every point the actual difficulties of the lawyer in a particular case. Generalization is always rough, and never entirely accurate. But it can be useful if it is made with a sense of responsibility to action. I have tried, therefore, to avoid gratuitously fine sentiments; I have tried to suggest nothing that with the information at my command doesn't seem at least probable.

This book, then, is an attempt to diagnose the current unrest and to arrive at some sense of what democracy implies. It begins with the obvious drift of our time and gropes for the conditions of mastery. I have tried in the essays that follow to enter the American problem at a few significant points in order to trace a little of the immense suggestion that radiates from them. I hope the book will leave the reader, as it does me, with a sense of the varied talents and opportunities, powers and organizations that may contribute to a conscious revolution. I have not been able to convince myself that one policy, one party, one class, or one set of tactics, is as fertile as human need. . . .

"A Nation of Villagers"

. . . If the anti-trust people really grasped the full meaning of what they said, and if they really had the power or the courage to do what they propose, they would be engaged in one of the most destructive agitations that America has known. They would be breaking up the beginning of a collective organization, thwarting the possibility of cooperation, and insisting upon submitting industry to the wasteful, the planless scramble of little profiteers. They would make impossible any deliberate and constructive use of our natural resources, they would thwart any effort to form the great industries into coordinated services, they would preserve commercialism as the undisputed master of our lives, they would lay a premium on the strategy of industrial war—they would, if they could. For these anti-trust people have never seen the possibilities of organized industries. They have seen only the obvious evils, the birth-pains, the undisciplined strut of youth, the bad manners, the greed, and the trickery. The trusts have been ruthless, of course. No one tried to guide them; they have broken the law in a thousand ways, largely because the law was such that they had to.

At any rate, I should not like to answer before a just tribunal for the harm done this country in the last twenty-five years by the stupid hostility of anti-trust laws. How much they have perverted the constructive genius of this country it is impossible to estimate. They have blocked any policy of welcome and use, they have concentrated a nation's thinking on inessentials, they have driven creative business men to underhand methods, and put a high money value on intrigue and legal cunning, demagoguery and waste. The trusts have survived it all, but in mutilated form, the battered make-shifts of a trampled promise. They have learned every art of evasion—the only art reformers allowed them to learn.

It is said that the economy of trusts is unreal. Yet no one has ever tried the economies of the trust in any open, deliberate fashion. The amount of energy that has had to go into repelling stupid attack, the adjustments that had to be made underground —it is a wonder the trusts achieved what they did to bring order out of chaos, and forge an instrument for a nation's business. You have no more right to judge the trusts by what they are than to judge the labor movement by what it is. Both of them are in that preliminary state where they are fighting for existence, and any real outburst of constructive effort has been impossible for them.

But revolutions are not stopped by blind resistance. They are only perverted. And as an exhibition of blind resistance to a great promise, the trust campaign of the American democracy is surely unequalled. Think of contriving correctives for a revolution, such as ordering business men to compete with each other. It is as if we said: "Let not thy right hand know what thy left hand doeth; let thy right hand fight thy left hand, and in the name of God let neither win." Bernard Shaw remarked several years ago that "after all, America is not submitting to the Trusts without a struggle. The first steps have already been taken by the village constable. He is no doubt preparing a new question for immigrants" . . . after asking them whether they are anarchists or polygamists, he is to add " 'Do you approve of Trusts?' but pending this supreme measure of national defense he has declared in several states that trusts will certainly be put in the stocks and whipped."

There has been no American policy on the trust question: there has been merely a widespread resentment. The small local competitors who were wiped out became little centers of bad feeling: these nationally organized industries were looked upon as foreign invaders. They were arrogant, as the English in Ireland or the Germans in Alsace, and much of the feeling for local democracy attached itself to the revolt against these national despotisms. The trusts made enemies right and left: they squeezed the profits of the farmer, they made life difficult for the shopkeeper, they abolished jobbers and travelling salesmen, they closed down factories, they exercised an enormous control over credit through their size and through their eastern connections. Labor was no match for them, state legislatures were impotent before them. They came into the life of the simple American community as a tremendous revolutionary force, upsetting custom, changing men's status, demanding a readjustment for which people were unready. Of course, there was anti-trust feeling; of course, there was a blind desire to smash them. Men had been ruined and they were too angry to think, too hard pressed to care much about the larger life which the trusts suggested.

This feeling came to a head in Bryan's famous "cross of gold" speech in 1896. "When you come before us and tell us that we shall disturb your business interests, we reply that you have disturbed our business interests by your action. . . . The man who is employed for wages is as much a business man as his employers. The attorney in a country town is as much a business man as the corporation counsel in a great metropolis. The merchant at the crossroads store is as much a business man as the merchant of New York. The farmer . . . is as much a business man as the man who goes upon the Board of Trade and bets upon the price of grain. The miners . . . It is for these that we speak . . . we are fighting in the defense of our homes, our families, and posterity." What Bryan was really defending was the old and simple life of America, a life that was doomed by the great organization that had come into the world. He thought he was fighting the plutocracy: as a matter of fact he was fighting something much deeper than that; he was fighting the larger scale of human life. The Eastern money power controlled the new industrial system, and Bryan fought it. But what he and his people hated from the bottom of their souls were the economic conditions which had upset the old life of the prairies, made new demands upon democracy, introduced specialization and science, had destroyed village loyalties, frustrated private ambitions, and created the impersonal relationships of the modern world.

Bryan has never been able to adjust himself to the new world in which he lives. That is why he is so irresistibly funny to sophisticated newspaper men. His virtues, his habits, his ideas, are the simple, direct, shrewd qualities of early America. He is the true Don Quixote of our politics, for he moves in a world that has ceased to exist.

He is a more genuine conservative than some propertied bigot. Bryan stands for the popular tradition of America, whereas most of his enemies stand merely for the power that is destroying that tradition. Bryan is what America was; his critics are generally defenders of what America has become. And neither seems to have any vision of what America is to be.

Yet there has always been great power behind Bryan, the power of those who in one way or another were hurt by the greater organization that America was developing. The Populists were part of that power. La Follette and the insurgent Republicans expressed it. It was easily a political majority of the American people. The Republican Party disintegrated under the pressure of the revolt. The Bull Moose gathered much of its strength from it. The Socialists have got some of it. But in 1912 it swept the Democratic Party, and by a combination of circumstances, carried the country. The plutocracy was beaten in politics, and the power that Bryan spoke for in 1896, the forces that had made muckraking popular, captured the government. They were led by a man who was no part of the power that he represented.

Woodrow Wilson is an outsider capable of skilled interpretation. He is an historian, and that has helped him to know the older tradition of America. He is a student of theory, and like most theorists of his generation he is deeply attached to the doctrines that swayed the world when America was founded.

But Woodrow Wilson at least knows that there is a new world. "There is one great basic fact which underlies all the questions that are discussed on the political platform at the present moment. That singular fact is that nothing is done in this country as it was done twenty years ago. We are in the presence of a new organization of society. . . . We have changed our economic conditions, absolutely, from top to bottom; and, with our economic society, the organization of our life." You could not make a more sweeping statement of the case. The President is perfectly aware of what has happened, and he says at the very outset that "our laws still deal with us on the basis of the old system . . . the old positive formulas do not fit the present problems."

You wait eagerly for some new formula. The new formula is this: "I believe the time has come when the governments of this country, both state and national, have to set the stage, and set it very minutely and carefully, for the doing of justice to men in every relationship of life." Now that is a new formula, because it means a willingness to use the power of government much more extensively.

But for what purpose is this power to be used? There, of course, is the rub. It is to be used to "*restore* our politics to their full spiritual vigor *again,* and our national life, whether in trade, in industry, or in what concerns us only as families and individuals, to its purity, its self-respect, and its *pristine* strength and freedom." The ideal is the old ideal, the ideal of Bryan, the method is the new one of government interference.

That, I believe, is the inner contradiction of Woodrow Wilson. He knows that there is a new world demanding new methods, but he dreams of an older world. He is torn between the two. It is a very deep conflict in him between what he knows and what he feels.

His feeling is, as he says, for "the man on the make." "For my part, I want the pigmy to have a chance to come out" . . . "Just let some of the youngsters I know have a chance and they'll give these gentlemen points. Lend them a little money. They can't get any now. See to it that when they have got a local market they can't be squeezed out of it." Nowhere in his speeches will you find any sense that it may be possible to organize the fundamental industries on some deliberate plan for national service. He is thinking always about somebody's chance to build up a profitable business; he likes the idea that somebody can beat somebody else, and the small business man takes on the virtues of David in a battle with Goliath.

"Have you found trusts that thought as much of their men as they did of their machinery?" he asks, forgetting that few people have ever found competitive textile mills or clothing factories that did. There isn't an evil of commercialism that Wilson isn't ready to lay at the door of the trusts. He becomes quite reckless in his denunciation of the New Devil—Monopoly—and of course, by contrast the competitive business takes on a halo of light. It is amazing how clearly he sees the evils that trusts do, how blind he is to the evils that his supporters do. You would think that the trusts were the first oppressors of labor; you would think they were the first business organization that failed to achieve the highest possible efficiency. The pretty record of competition throughout the Nineteenth Century is forgotten. Suddenly all that is a glorious past which we have lost. You would think that competitive commercialism was really a generous, chivalrous, high-minded stage of human culture.

"We design that the limitations on private enterprise shall be removed, so that the next generation of youngsters, as they come along, will not have to become protégés of benevolent trusts, but will be free to go about making their own lives what they will; so that we shall taste again the full cup, not of charity, but of liberty—the only wine that ever refreshed and renewed the spirit of a people." That cup of liberty—we may well ask him to go back to Manchester, to Paterson to-day, to the garment trades of New York, and taste it for himself.

The New Freedom means the effort of small business men and farmers to use the government against the larger collective organization of industry. Wilson's power comes from them; his feeling is with them; his thinking is for them. Never a word of understanding for the new type of administrator, the specialist, the professionally trained business man; practically no mention of the consumer—even the tariff is for the business man; no understanding of the new demands of labor, its solidarity, its aspiration for some control over the management of business; no hint that it may be necessary to organize the fundamental industries of the country on some definite plan so that our resources may be developed by scientific method instead of by men "on the make"; no friendliness for the larger, collective life upon which the world is entering, only a constant return to the commercial chances of young men trying to set up in business. That is the push and force of this New Freedom, a freedom for the little profiteer, but no freedom for the nation from the narrowness, the poor incentives, the limited vision of small competitors—no freedom from clamorous advertisement, from wasteful selling, from duplication of plants, from unnecessary enterprise, from the chaos, the welter, the strategy of industrial war.

There is no doubt, I think, that President Wilson and his party represent primarily small business in a war against the great interests. Socialists speak of his administration as a revolution within the bounds of capitalism. Wilson doesn't really fight the oppressions of property. He fights the evil done by large property-holders to small ones. The temper of his administration was revealed very clearly when the proposal was made to establish a Federal Trade Commission. It was suggested at once by leading spokesmen of the Democratic Party that corporations with a capital of less than a million dollars should be exempted from supervision. Is that because little corporations exploit labor or the consumer less? Not a bit of it. It is because little corporations are in control of the political situation.

But there are certain obstacles to the working out of the New Freedom. First of all, there was a suspicion in Wilson's mind, even during the campaign, that the tendency to large organization was too powerful to be stopped by legislation. So he left open a way of escape from the literal achievement of what the New Freedom seemed to threaten. *"I am for big business,"* he said, *"and I am against the trusts."* That is a very subtle distinction, so subtle, I suspect, that no human legislation will ever be able to make it. The distinction is this: big business is a business that has survived competition; a trust is an arrangement to do away with competition. But when competition is done away with, who is the Solomon wise enough to know whether the result was accomplished by superior efficiency or by agreement among the competitors or by both?

The big trusts have undoubtedly been built up in part by superior business ability, and by successful competition, but also by ruthless competition, by underground arrangements, by an intricate series of facts which no earthly tribunal will ever be able to disentangle. And why should it try? These great combinations are here. What interests us is not their history but their future. The point is whether you are going to split them up, and if so into how many parts. Once split, are they to be kept from coming together again? Are you determined to prevent men who could cooperate from cooperating? Wilson seems to imply that a big business which has survived competition is to be let alone, and the trusts attacked. But as there is no real way of distinguishing between them, he leaves the question just where he found it: he must choose between the large organization of business and the small.

It's here that his temperament and his prejudices clash with fact and necessity. He really would like to disintegrate large business. "Are you not eager for the time," he asks, "when your sons shall be able to look forward to becoming not employees, but heads of some small, it may be, but hopeful business . . . ?" But to what percentage of the population can he hold out that hope? How many small but hopeful steel mills, coal mines, telegraph systems, oil refineries, copper mines, can this country support? A few hundred at the outside. And for these few hundred sons whose "best energies . . . are inspired by the knowledge that they are their own masters with the paths of the world before them," we are asked to give up the hope of a sane, deliberate organization of national industry brought under democratic control.

I submit that it is an unworthy dream. I submit that the intelligent men of my generation can find a better outlet for their energies than in making themselves masters of little businesses. They have the vast opportunity of introducing order and purpose into the business world, of devising administrative methods by which the great resources of the country can be operated on some thought-out plan. They have the whole new field of industrial statesmanship before them, and those who prefer the egotism of some little business are not the ones whose ambitions we need most to cultivate.

But the distintegration which Wilson promised in the New Freedom is not likely to be carried out. One year of public office has toned down the audacity of the campaign speeches so much that Mr. Dooley says you can play the President's messages on a harp. Instead of a "radical reconstruction" we are engaged in signing a "constitution of peace." These big business men who a few months ago showed not the "least promise of disinterestedness" are to-day inspired by "a spirit of accommodation." The President's own Secretary of Commerce, Mr. Redfield, has said to the National Chamber of Commerce that the number of trusts still operating "is conspicuously small." Was ever wish the father to a pleasanter thought? Was ever greater magic wrought with less effort? Or is it that politicians in office have to pretend that what they can't do has happened anyway?

Wilson is against the trusts for many reasons: the political economy of his generation was based on competition and free trade; the Democratic Party is by tradition opposed to a strong central government, and that opposition applies equally well to strong national business—it is a party attached to local rights, to village patriotism, to humble but ambitious enterprise; its temper has always been hostile to specialization and expert knowledge, because it admires a very primitive man-to-man democracy. Wilson's thought is inspired by that outlook. It has been tempered somewhat by contact with men who have outgrown the village culture, so that Wilson is less hostile to experts, less oblivious to administrative problems than is Bryan. But at the same time his speeches are marked with contempt for the specialist: they play up quite obviously to the old democratic notion that any man can do almost any job. You have always to except the negro, of course, about whom the Democrats have a totally different tradition. But among white men, special training and expert knowledge are somewhat under suspicion in Democratic circles.

Hostility to large organization is a natural quality in village life. Wilson is always repeating that the old personal relationships of employer and employee have disappeared. He deplores the impersonal nature of the modern world. Now that is a fact not to be passed over lightly. It does change the nature of our problems enormously. Indeed, it is just this breakdown of the old relationships which constitutes the modern problem. So the earlier chapters of this book were devoted to showing how in response to new organization the psychology of business men had changed; how the very nature of property had been altered; how the consumer has had to develop new instruments for controlling the market, and how labor is compelled to organize its power in order not to be trodden by gigantic economic forces.

Nobody likes the present situation very much. But where dispute arises is over whether we can by legislation return to a simpler and more direct stage of civilization. Bryan really hopes to do that, Wilson does too, but his mind is too critical not to have some doubts, and that is why he is against trusts but not against big business. But there is a growing body of opinion which says that communication is blotting out village culture, and opening up national and international thought. It says that bad as big business is to-day, it has a wide promise within it, and that the real task of our generation is to realize it. It looks to the infusion of scientific method, the careful application of administrative technique, the organization and education of the consumer for control, the discipline of labor for an increasing share of the management. Those of us who hold such a belief are pushed from behind by what we think is an irresistible economic development, and lured by a future which we think is possible.

We don't imagine that the trusts are going to drift naturally into the service of human life. We think they can be made to serve it if the American people compel them. We think that the American people may be able to do that if they can adjust their thinking to a new world situation, if they apply the scientific spirit to daily life, and if they can learn to cooperate on a large scale. Those, to be sure, are staggering *ifs*. The conditions may never be fulfilled entirely. But in so far as they are not fulfilled we shall drift along at the mercy of economic forces that we are unable to master. Those who cling to the village view of life may deflect the drift, may batter the trusts about a bit, but they will never dominate business, never humanize its machinery, and they will continue to be the playthings of industrial change.

At bottom the issue is between those who are willing to enter upon an effort for which there is no precedent, and those who aren't. In a real sense it is an adventure. We have still to explore the new scale of human life which machinery has thrust upon us. We have still to invent ways of dealing with it. We have still to adapt our abilities to immense tasks. Of course, men shudder and beg to be let off in order to go back to the simpler life for which they were trained. Of course, they hope that competition will automatically produce the social results they desire. Of course, they see all the evils of the trust and none of its promise. They can point to the failure of empires and the success of little cities. They can say that we are obliterating men in the vast organizations we are permitting.

But they are not the only people who realize that man as he is to-day is not big enough to master the modern world. It is this realization which has made men speculate on the development of what they call a "collective mind." They hope that somehow we shall develop an intelligence larger than the individual.

I see no evidence for that. There are no minds but human minds so far as our problems go. It seems to me that this notion of a collective mind over and above men and women is simply a myth created to meet difficulties greater than men and women are as yet capable of handling. It is a *deus ex machina* invented to cover an enormous need—a hope that something outside ourselves will do our work for us. It would be infinitely easier if such a power existed. But I can't see any ground for relying upon it. We shall have, it seems to me, to develop within men and women themselves the power they need. It is an immense ambition, and each man who approaches it must appear presumptuous. But it is the problem of our generation: to analyze the weakness, to attack the obstacles, to search for some of the possibilities, to realize if we can the kind of effort by which we can face the puzzling world in which we live.

A Big World and Little Men

. . . Institutions have developed a thousand inconsistencies. Our schools, churches, courts, governments were not built for the kind of civilization they are expected to serve. In former times you could make some effort to teach people what they needed to know. It was done badly, but at least it could be attempted. Men knew the kind of problems their children would have to face. But to-day education means a radically different thing. We have to prepare children to meet the unexpected, for their problems will not be the same as their fathers'. To prepare them for the unexpected means to train them in method instead of filling them with facts and rules. They will have to find their own facts and make their own rules, and if schools can't give them that power then schools no longer educate for the modern world.

The churches face a dilemma which is a matter of life and death to them. They come down to us with a tradition that the great things are permanent, and they meet a population that needs above all to understand the meaning and the direction of change. No wonder the churces are empty, no wonder their influence has declined, no wonder that men fight against the influence they have. Ministers are as bewildered as the rest of us, perhaps a little more so. For they are expected to stand up every week and interpret human life in a way that will vitalize feeling and conduct. And for this work of interpretation they have the simple rules of a village civilization, the injunctions of a pastoral people. Of course they can't interpret life on Sunday so that the interpretation will mean something on Monday. Even supposing that the average minister understood the scientific spirit, had studied sociology, and knew what are the forces which agitate men, even under those circumstances, interpretation would be an almost impossible task. For the least hampered minds, the most imaginative and experienced men, can only stumble through to partial explanations. To ask the clergy to find adequate meaning in this era is to expect each minister to be an inspired thinker. If the churches really could interpret life they would be unable to make room for the congregations; if men felt that they could draw anything like wisdom from them, they would be besieged by bewildered and inquiring people. Think of the lectures people flock to, the political meetings they throng, the dull books they work their way through. It isn't indifference to the great problems that leaves the churches empty; it is the sheer intellectual failure of the churches to meet a sudden change.

The courts have not been able to adjust themselves either. But while people can ignore the churches, they have to fight the courts. They fight blindly without any clear notion as to what they would like the courts to do. They are irritated and constrained by a legal system that was developed in a different civilization, and they find the courts, as Prof. Roscoe Pound says, "doing nothing and obstructing everything." They find that whenever a legislature makes an effort to fit law to the new facts of life, a court is there to nullify the work. They find the courts masters of our political system, and yet these masters will not really take the initiative. They have enormous power, but they refuse the responsibility that goes with it. The courts are making law all the time, of course. Now if they made law that met the new situations, there would no revolt against the judiciary. The American voters are not doctrinaires. They don't care in any academic way whether Congress, the President, or the courts, frame legislation. They form their opinions almost entirely by the results. If the President can legislate better than Congress, as Roosevelt and Wilson could, the people will support the President no matter how many lawyers shout that the rights of Congress are being usurped. If the courts made law that dealt with modern necessities, the people would, I believe, never question their power. It is the bad sociology of judges and their class prejudices that are destroying the prestige of the bench. That bad sociology and those prejudices are in the main due to the fact that judges have not been trained for the modern world, have never learned how to understand its temper.

And of course, when you come to the political structure of our government you find that it has only the faintest relation to actual conditions. Our political constituencies are to American life what the skeleton of a two-humped camel would be to an elephant. One is not made to fit the other's necessities. Take the City of New York for example. For all practical purposes the metropolitan district extends up into Connecticut and across into New Jersey. By "practical purposes" I mean that as a health problem, a transportation problem, a housing problem, a food problem, a police problem, the city which sprawls across three states ought to be treated as one unit. Or take New England: for any decent solution of its transportation difficulties or for any scientific use of its natural resources its state lines are a nuisance. On the other hand, it mustn't be imagined that the old political units are always too small. Far from it: thus many of the vital functions of New York City are managed by the State legislature. The political system which comes down to us from a totally different civilization is sometimes too large in its unit—sometimes too small, but in a thousand bewildering ways it does not fit. Every statesman is hampered by conflicts of jurisdiction, by divided responsibility, by the fact that when he tries to use the government for some public purpose, the government is a clumsy instrument.

The regulation of the trusts is made immensely difficult by the fact that the states are too small, and the nation is often too large. There are natural sections of the country, like the Pacific Coast, the Ohio, the Mississippi valley, and New England which ought for many purposes to act as a unit. No sane person, I suppose, wishes to centralize at Washington all the power that is needed to control business, and yet everyone knows that if you leave that control to the states, there will be no control.

But the fitting of government to the facts of the modern world is sure to be a very difficult task. In the past governments have been organized as territorial units, but with the development of transportation the importance of geography has declined. Men are bound together to-day by common interests far more than by living in the same place. It is the union, the trade association, the grange, the club and the party that command allegiance rather than the county or the state. To anyone who is not fooled by charters and forms, it is evident that functions of government are being developed in these groups which are not mentioned in theoretical discussions of government. Labor unions legislate, Boards of Trade legislate, cooperative societies are governments in a very real sense. They make rules under which people live, often much more compelling ones than those of some official legislature. Now in the Eighteenth Century there was a strong sentiment against any minor sovereignty within the political state. In France, for example, by a law of 1791 all associations were forbidden. Our common law looked upon them with extreme disfavor, and the Sherman Act is an expression of that same feeling. Theorists like ex-President Eliot in our own day are against unions because they establish little governments within the state. But the facts are against the ideas of the Eighteenth Century. The world is so complex that no official government can be devised to deal with it, and men have had to organize associations of all kinds in order to create some order in the world. They will develop more of them, I believe, for these voluntary groupings based on common interests are the only way yet proposed by which a complicated society can be governed. But of course, unofficial sovereignties within the nation create very perplexing problems. They all tend to be imperious, to reach out and absorb more and more. And the attempt to adjust them to each other is a task for which political science is not prepared.

I have merely touched on some of the difficulties which arise in our domestic affairs because the anatomy of our politics does not correspond to the anatomy of our life. When you come to international affairs confusion is compounded. As I write, we are in the midst of the Mexican problem. No one knows how much authority anyone has in that country. There are all sorts of conflicting interests and all sorts of conflicting governments.

Does the fact that Englishmen invest in Mexico entitle the British Empire to some authority in Mexican affairs? Are we the guardians of Mexico, and if so where does our authority end? The new imperialism is no simple affair: it has innumerable gradations of power. As Prof. Beard says: "This newer imperialism does not rest primarily upon the desire for more territory, but rather upon the necessity for markets in which to sell manufactured goods and for opportunities to invest surplus accumulations of capital. It begins in a search for trade, advances to intervention on behalf of the interests involved, thence to protectorates, and finally to annexation." Diplomacy now talks about "effective occupation," "hinterland," "sphere of influence," and "Sphere of Legitimate Aspiration." *

One of the curious ironies of history is that after many generations of effort to establish popular government in a few countries, the real interests of the world have overflowed frontiers and eluded democracy. We are just about to establish a democratic state, and we find that capitalism has become international. It seems as if we were always a little too late for the facts. We are now engaged in building up for the world a few of the primitive devices of internal affairs. A code of law, a few half-hearted, impotent courts, treaties, and a little international policing. But all these things, many of which express the fondest hopes of sensible men, are very little more than arrangements between antagonistic nations. Anything like a world-wide cooperative democracy is as yet no part of the expectation of any unsentimental person.

Now anyone who has talked as much about the industrial problem as I have in these chapters is, of course, expected to present a "solution." But as a matter of fact there can be no such thing as a "solution" in the sense which most people understand the word. When you solve a puzzle, you're done with it, but the industrial puzzle has no single key. Nor is there such a thing for it as a remedy or a cure. You have in a very literal sense to *educate* the industrial situation, to draw out its promise, discipline and strengthen it.

It means that you have to do a great variety of things to industry, invent new ones to do, and keep on doing them. You have to make a survey of the natural resources of the country. On the basis of that survey you must draw up a national plan for their development. You must eliminate waste in mining, you must conserve the forests so that their fertility is not impaired, so that stream flow is regulated, and the water-power of the country made available. You must bring to the farmer a knowledge of scientific agriculture, help him to organize cooperatively,

---

*See Graham Wallas, *Human Nature in Politics,* p. 161.

use the taxing power to prevent land speculation and force land to the best use, coordinate markets, build up rural credits, and create in the country a life that shall really be interesting.

You have the intricate problem of how to make the railroads serve the national development of our resources. That means the fixing of rates so that railroads become available where they are most needed. Wastes and grafts have to be cut out, and the control of transportation made part of a national economic policy. You have to see to it that technical schools produce men trained for such work; you have to establish institutes of research, that shall stimulate the economic world not only with physical inventions, but with administrative proposals.

You have to go about deliberately to create a large class of professional business men. You have to enlarge the scope and the vision of the efficiency expert so that he can begin to take out of industry the deadening effects of machine production. You have to find vast sums of money for experiment in methods of humanizing labor.

For each industry you must discover the most satisfactory unit, and you must encourage these units to cooperate so that every industry shall be conducted with a minimum of friction. You must devise a banking system so that the nation's capital shall be available, that it shall be there for use at the lowest possible cost.

You have to find ways of making the worker an integral part of his industry. That means allowing him to develop his unions, and supplying the unions with every incentive by which they can increase their responsibility. You have to create an industrial education by which the worker shall be turned, not into an intelligent machine, but into an understanding, directing partner of business. You have to encourage the long process of self-education in democracy through which unions can develop representative government and adequate leadership. You have to support them in their desire to turn themselves from wage-earners into a corporate body that participates in industrial progress.

You have to devise and try out a great variety of consumers' controls. For some industries you may have to use public ownership, for others the cooperative society may be more effective, for others the regulating commission. You will not be able to come out plump for one method as against all the others. It will depend on the nature of the industry which instrument is the most effective. And back of all these methods, there is the need for industrial citizenship, for creating in the consumer a knowledge of what he wants, and of the different ways there are of getting it. Back of that there is the still subtler problem of making the consumer discriminating, of educating his taste and civilizing his desires.

All this is only a little of what has to be done. It has to be done not by some wise and superior being but by the American people themselves. No one man, no one group can possibly do it all. It is an immense collaboration. It will have to be carried out against the active opposition of class interests and sectional prejudices. At every step there will be a clash with old rights and old habits. There will be the cries of the beaten, the protest of the discarded. For men cling passionately to their routines.

But you cannot institute a better industrial order by decree. It is of necessity an educational process, a work of invention, of cooperative training, of battles against vested rights not only in property but in acquired skill as well, a process that is sure to be intricate, and therefore confusing.

But that is the way democracies move: they have in literal truth to lift themselves by their own bootstraps. Those who have some simpler method than the one I have sketched are, it seems to me, either unaware of the nature of the problem, interested only in some one phase of it, or unconsciously impatient with the limitations of democracy. In the next chapter, I shall make an attempt to describe some of the current philosophies which try to shirk the full force of the problem. They are all excuses for trusting to luck, for relying upon something but ourselves. They are all substitutes for the difficulties of self-government, concessions to the drift of our natures.

Here I want only to reach a sense of the complexity of the task, its variety and its challenge. I have skimmed the surface, nothing more. There is no mention of the fearful obstacles of race prejudice in the South, no mention of the threat that recent immigration brings with it, the threat of an alien and defenseless class of servile labor. And there is, of course, always the distracting possibility of a foreign war, of vast responsibilities in the other Americas.

Certainly democracy has a load to carry. It has arisen in the midst of a civilization for which men are utterly unready, a civilization so complex that their minds cannot grasp it, so unexpected that each man is compelled to be something of a prophet. Its future is so uncertain that no one can feel any assurance in the face of it. Precedent has been wrecked because we have to act upon really new facts. Anything like a central authority to guide us has become impossible because no authority is wise enough, because self-government has become a really effective desire. The old shibboleths of conduct are for the most part meaningless: they don't work when they are tried.

Through it all our souls have become disorganized, for they have lost the ties which bound them. In the very period when man most needs a whole-hearted concentration on external affairs, he is disrupted internally by a revolution in the intimacies of his life. He has lost his place in an eternal scheme, he is losing the ancient sanctions of love, and his sexual nature is chaotic through the immense change that has come into the relations of parent and child, husband and wife. Those changes distract him so deeply that the more "advanced" he is, the more he flounders in the bogs of his own soul.

Drift

It seems as if the most obvious way of reacting toward evil were to consider it a lapse from grace. The New Freedom, we are told, is "only the old revived and clothed in the unconquerable strength of modern America." Everywhere you hear it: that the people have been "deprived" of ancient rights, and legislation is framed on the notion that we can recover the alleged democracy of early America.

I once read in a learned magazine an essay on "The Oblivescence of the Disagreeable." As I remember it, the writer was trying to demonstrate what he regarded as a very hopeful truth —that men tend to forget pain more easily than pleasure. That is no doubt a comfortable faculty, but it plays havoc with history. For in regard to those early days of the Republic, most of our notions are marked by a well-nigh total oblivescence of the disagreeable. We find it very difficult to remember that there were sharp class divisions in the young Republic, that suffrage

was severely restricted, that the Fathers were a very conscious
upper class determined to maintain their privileges. Nations
make their histories to fit their illusions. That is why reformers
are so anxious to return to early America. What they know of
it comes to them filtered through the golden lies of school-books
and hallowed by the generous loyalty of their childhood. . . .

He had the American dream, which may be summed up, I
think, in the statement that the undisciplined man is the salt of
the earth. So when the trusts appeared, when the free land was
gone, and America had been congested into a nation, the only
philosophy with any weight of tradition behind it was a belief
in the virtues of the spontaneous, enterprising, untrained and
unsocialized man. Trust promoters cried: Let us alone. The little
business man cried: We're the natural men, so let us alone. And
the public cried: We're the most natural of all, so please do stop
interfering with us. Muck-raking gave an utterance to the small
business men and to the larger public, who dominated reform
politics. What did they do? They tried by all the machinery and
power they could muster to restore a business world in which
each man could again be left to his own will—a world that
needed no cooperative intelligence. In the Sherman Act is sym-
bolized this deliberate attempt to recreate an undeliberate society. No group of people, except the socialists, wished to take
up the enormous task of disciplining business to popular need.
For the real American was dreaming of the Golden Age in which
he could drift with impunity.

But there has arisen in our time a large group of people who
look to the future. They talk a great deal about their ultimate
goal. Many of them do not differ in any essential way from those
who dream of a glorious past. They put Paradise before them
instead of behind them. They are going to be so rich, so great,
and so happy some day, that any concern about to-morrow seems
a bit sordid. They didn't fall from Heaven, as the reactionaries
say, but they are going to Heaven with the radicals. Now this
habit of reposing in the sun of a brilliant future is very ener-
vating. It opens a chasm between fact and fancy, and the whole
fine dream is detached from the living zone of the present. At
the only point where effort and intelligence are needed, that
point where to-day is turning into to-morrow, there these people
are not found. At the point where human direction counts most

they do not direct. So they are like most anarchists, wild in their dreams and unimportant in their deeds. They cultivate a castle in Spain and a flat in Harlem; a princess in the air and a drudge in the kitchen.

Then too there are the darlings of evolution. They are quite certain that evolution, as they put it, is ever onward and upward. For them all things conspire to achieve that well-known, though unmentioned far-off divine event to which the whole creation moves. They seem to imply as Moody suggested:

> I, I, last product of the toiling ages,
>   Goal of heroic feet that never lagged——

though

> A little thing in trousers, slightly jagged.

How the conservative goes to work with the idea of evolution has been ably exposed by William English Walling. First, assume "progress" by calling it inevitable: this obviates the necessity for any practical change just now. Then assert the indubitable fact that real progress is very slow: and infer that wisdom consists in deprecating haste. Now when you have called progress inevitable and imperceptible, you have done about all that philosophy could do to justify impotence.

The radical view of evolution is more optimistic, but not more intelligent. In fact, it is generally all optimism and little else. For though it doesn't quite dare to say that whatever is, is right, it does assume that whatever is going to be, is going to be right. I believe that G. K. Chesterton once called this sort of thing progressivism by the calendar. There is complete confidence that whatever is later in time is better in fact, that the next phase is the desirable one, that all change is "upward," that God and Nature are collaborating in our blithe ascent to the Superman. Such an outlook undermines judgment and initiative, deliberate effort, invention, plan, and sets you adrift on the currents of time, hoping for impossible harbors.

In a constructive social movement the harm done is immeasurable. The most vivid illustration is that of the old-fashioned, fatalistic Marxian socialists. They have an implicit faith that human destiny is merely the unfolding of an original plan, some of the sketches of which are in their possession, thanks to the labors of Karl Marx. Strictly speaking, these men are not revolutionists as they believe themselves to be; they are the interested pedants of destiny. They are God's audience, and they know the plot so well that occasionally they prompt Him. In their system all that education, unions, leadership and thought can do is to push along what by the theory needs no pushing. These social-ists are like the clown Marceline at the Hippodrome, who is always very busy assisting in labor that would be done whether he were there or not. They face the ancient dilemma of fatalism: whatever they do is right, and nothing they do matters. Go to almost any socialist meeting and you'll hear it said that socialism would come if the Socialist Party had never been heard from. Perhaps so. But why organize a Socialist Party?

Of course, socialists don't act upon their theory. They are too deeply impressed with the evil that exists, too eager for the future that they see, to trust entirely in the logic of events. They do try to shape that future. But their old fatalism hampers them enormously the moment any kind of action is proposed. They are out of sympathy with conservative trade unionism, but they are still more hostile to the I. W. W. In politics they despise the reformer, but when they themselves obtain office they do nothing that a hundred "bourgeois" reformers haven't done before them. The Socialist Party in this country has failed to develop a prac-tical program for labor or a practical program for politics. It claims to have a different philosophy from that of trade unionists or reformers, but when you try to judge the difference by its concrete results, it is imperceptible.

The theory and the temper of orthodox socialism are fatalistic, and no fatalist can really give advice. Theory and practice are widely sundered in the American socialist movement. There is a stumbling revolt which lives from hand to mouth, a catch-as-catch-can struggle, and then far removed from it, standing in majesty, a great citadel of dogma almost impervious to new ideas. For in the real world, destiny is one of the aliases of drift.

Closely related in essence, though outwardly quite different, is what might be called the panacea habit of mind. Beginning very often in some penetrating insight or successful analysis, this sort of mind soon becomes incapable of seeing anything beside that portion of reality which sustains the insight and is subject to the analysis. A good idea, in short, becomes a fixed idea. One group of American socialists can see only the advantage of strikes, another of ballots. One reformer sees the advantages of the direct primaries in Wisconsin: they become the universal solvent of political evil. You find engineers who don't see why you can't build society on the analogy of a steam engine; you find lawyers, like Taft, who see in the courts an intimation of heaven; sanitation experts who wish to treat the whole world as one vast sanitarium; lovers who wish to treat it as one vast happy family; education enthusiasts who wish to treat it as one vast nursery. No one who undertook to be the Balzac of reform by writing its Human Comedy could afford to miss the way in which the reformer in each profession tends to make his specialty an analogy for the whole of life. The most amazing of all are people who deal with the currency question. Somehow or other, long meditation seems to produce in them a feeling that they are dealing with the crux of human difficulties.

Then there is the panacea most frequently propounded by voluble millionaires: the high cost of living is the cost of high living, and thrift is the queen of virtues. Sobriety is another virtue, highly commended—in fact there are thousands of people who seriously regard it as the supreme social virtue. To those of us who are sober and still discontented, the effort to found a political party on a colossal Don't is not very inspiring. After thrift and sobriety, there is always efficiency, a word which covers a multitude of confusions. No one in his senses denies the importance of efficient action, just as no one denies thrift and sober living. It is only when these virtues become the prime duty of man that we rejoice in the poet who has the courage to glorify the vagabond, preach a saving indolence, and glorify Dionysus. Be not righteous overmuch is merely a terse way of saying that virtue can defeat its own ends. Certainly, whenever a negative command like sobriety absorbs too much attention, and morality is obstinate and awkward, then living men have become cluttered in what was meant to serve them.

There are thousands to-day who, out of patience with almost everything, believe passionately that some one change will set everything right. In the first rank stand the suffragettes who believe that votes for women will make men chaste. I have just read a book by a college professor which announces that the short ballot will be as deep a revolution as the abolition of slavery. There are innumerable Americans who believe that a democratic constitution would create a democracy. Of course, there are single taxers so single-minded that they believe a happy civilization would result from the socialization of land values. Everything else that seems to be needed would follow spontaneously if only the land monopoly were abolished.

The syndicalists suffer from this habit of mind in an acute form. They refuse to consider any scheme for the reorganization of industry. All that will follow, they say, if only you can produce a General Strike. But obviously you might paralyze society, you might make the proletariat supreme, and still leave the proletariat without the slightest idea of what to do with the power it had won.

What happens is that men gain some insight into society and concentrate their energy upon it. Then when the facts rise up in their relentless complexity, the only way to escape them is to say: Never mind, do what I advocate, and all these other things shall be added unto you.

There is still another way of reacting toward a too complicated world. That way is to see so much good in every reform that you can't make up your mind where to apply your own magnificent talents. The result is that you don't apply your talents at all.

Reform produces its Don Quixotes who never deal with reality; it produces its Brands who are single-minded to the brink of ruin; and it produces its Hamlets and its Rudins who can never make up their minds. What is common to them all is a failure to deal with the real world in the light of its possibilities. To try to follow all the aliases of drift is like attacking the hydra by cutting off its heads. The few examples given here of how men shirk self-government might be extended indefinitely. They are as common to radicals as to conservatives. You can find them flourishing in an orthodox church and among the most rebellious socialists.

Men will do almost anything but govern themselves. They don't want the responsibility. In the main, they are looking for some benevolent guardian, be it a "good man in office" or a perfect constitution, or the evolution of nature. They want to be taken in charge. If they have to think for themselves they turn either to the past or to a distant future: but they manage to escape the real effort of the imagination which is to weave a dream into the turning present. They trust to destiny, a quick one or a slow one, and the whole task of judging events is avoided. They turn to automatic devices: human initiative can be ignored. They forbid evil, and then they feel better. They settle on a particular analogy, or a particular virtue, or a particular policy, and trust to luck that everything else will take care of itself.

But no one of these substitutes for self-government is really satisfactory, and the result is that a state of chronic rebellion appears. That is our present situation. The most hopeful thing about it is that through the confusion we can come to some closer understanding of why the modern man lacks stability, why his soul is scattered. We may, perhaps, be able to see a little better just what self-government implies. . . .

I don't see how this dream [of returning to a past golden age] can succeed. Their solution is built on a wild impossibility, for in order to realize it they will have to abolish machinery and communication, newspapers and popular books. They will have to call upon some fairy to wipe out the memory of the last hundred years, and they will have to find a magician who can conjure up a church and a monarchy that men will obey. They can't do any of these things, though they can bewail the fact and display their grief by unremitting hostility to the modern world.

But though their remedy is, I believe, altogether academic, their diagnosis does locate the spiritual problem. We have lost authority. We are "emancipated" from an ordered world. We drift.

The loss of something outside ourselves which we can obey is a revolutionary break with our habits. Never before have we had to rely so completely upon ourselves. No guardian to think for us, no precedent to follow without question, no lawmaker above, only ordinary men set to deal with heart-breaking perplexity. All weakness comes to the surface. We are homeless in a jungle of machines and untamed powers that haunt and lure the imagination. Of course, our culture is confused, our thinking spasmodic, and our emotion out of kilter. No mariner ever enters upon a more uncharted sea than does the average human being born into the Twentieth Century. Our ancestors thought they knew their way from birth through all eternity: we are puzzled about the day after to-morrow.

What nonsense it is, then, to talk of liberty as if it were a happy-go-lucky breaking of chains. It is with emancipation that real tasks begin, and liberty is a searching challenge, for it takes away the guardianship of the master and the comfort of the priest. The iconoclasts didn't free us. They threw us into the water, and now we have to swim. . . .

The Rock of Ages

. . . A stern commander is just what this age lacks. Liberalism suffuses our lives and the outstanding fact is the decay of authority. But this doesn't mean for one minute that we are able to command ourselves. In fact, if a man dare attempt to sum up the spiritual condition of his time, he might say of ours that it has lost authority and retained the need of it. We are freer than we are strong. We have more responsibility than we have capacity. And if we wish to state what the future sets for us, we might say, I think, that we must find within ourselves the certainty which the external world has lost.

It is not fair to claim that we who attack absolutism are robbing life of its guarantees. It is far truer to say that the enlargement and ferment of the modern world have robbed absolutism of its excuse. To the business man who believes sincerely in the old sanctities of private property, the industrial situation must seem like a mine of explosives. The legalist gasps in panic. And as for these new aspirations of women, this push of the working-class towards an industrial democracy, this faculty of the young for taking an interest in life uncensored, what lamp-post is there that a man can embrace in a giddy and reeling universe? None. It was possible to talk about eternal principles of conduct in an old-world village where the son replaced the father generation after generation, where the only immigrants were babies and the only emigrants the dead. But in the new world, where fifty races meet, and a continent is exploited, ten years is an enormous change, a generation is a revolution.

Life has overflowed the little system of eternity. Thought has become humbler because its task is greater. We can invoke no monumental creeds, because facts smile ironically upon them. And so in a changing world, men have to cast aside the old thick-set forms of their thinking for suppler experimental ones. They think oftener. They think more lavishly, and they don't hang their hope of immortality on the issue of their thoughts. It is not so comfortable. It gives none of that harmony outside which men desire. The challenge is endless, to finer perceptions and sharper insights. Such thinking is more accurate than settled principles can ever be; the restless modern world has made such thinking necessary. But gone are the repose and the sublimity and the shelter of larger creeds. Our thought is homely, of the earth, and not awe-inspiring. No profound homage can go out to ideas that an honest man may have to scrap to-morrow. There is nothing of Gibraltar about to-day's hypothesis.

The most dramatic revelation of this crisis is among the newer immigrants in an American city. They come suddenly from the fixed traditions of peasant life into the distracting variety of a strange civilization. America for them is not only a foreign country where they have to find a living in ways to which they are unaccustomed; America is a place where their creeds do not work, where what at home seemed big and emphatic as the mountains is almost unnoticed. It is a commonplace to say that the tide of emigration has shifted from the Northwest to the Southeast of Europe, and that America to-day is receiving a radically different stock than it did twenty years ago. That is undoubtedly true. But the difference is not only in the immigrants. America itself is different. Those who are coming to-day have to bridge a much greater gap than did those who entered this country when it was a nation of villages.

They come to a country which shatters cynically the whole structure of their emotional life. There is a brave attempt to preserve it in ghettos. But with no great success, and the second generation is drawn unprotected into the new world. Parents and children often hardly understand each others' speech, let alone each others' desires.

In Queenstown harbor I once talked to an Irish boy who was about to embark for America. His home was in the West of Ireland, in a small village where his sister and he helped their father till a meager farm. They had saved enough for a passage to America, and they were abandoning their home. I asked the boy whether he knew anyone in America. He didn't, but his parish priest at home did. He was going to write to Father Riley every week. Would he ever return to Ireland? "Yes," said this boy of eighteen, "I'm going to die in Ireland." Where was he going to in America? To a place called New Haven. He was, in short, going from one epoch into another, and for guidance he had the parish priest at home and perhaps the ward boss in New Haven. His gentleness and trust in the slums of New Haven, assaulted by din and glare, hedged in by ugliness and cynical push—if there is any adventure comparable to his, I have not heard of it. At the very moment when he needed a faith, he was cutting loose from it. If he becomes brutal, greedy, vulgar, will it be so surprising? If he fails to measure up to the requirements of citizenship in a world reconstruction, is there anything strange about it?

Well, he was an immigrant in the literal sense. All of us are immigrants spiritually. We are all of us immigrants in the industrial world, and we have no authority to lean upon. We are an uprooted people, newly arrived, and *nouveau riche*. As a nation we have all the vulgarity that goes with that, all the scattering of soul. The modern man is not yet settled in his world. It is strange to him, terrifying, alluring, and incomprehensibly big. The evidence is everywhere: the amusements of the city; the jokes that pass for jokes; the blare that stands for beauty, the folksongs of Broadway, the feeble and apologetic pulpits, the cruel standards of success, raucous purity. We make love to rag-time and we die to it. We are blown hither and thither like litter before the wind. Our days are lumps of undigested experience. You have only to study what newspapers regard as news to see how we are torn and twisted by the irrelevant: in frenzy about issues that do not concern us, bored with those that do. Is it a wild mistake to say that the absence of central authority has disorganized our souls, that our souls are like Peer Gynt's onion, in that they lack a kernel?

A Note on the Woman's Movement

Liberty may be an uncomfortable blessing unless you know what to do with it. That is why so many freed slaves returned to their masters, why so many emancipated women are only too glad to give up the racket and settle down. For between announcing that you will live your own life, and the living of it lie the real difficulties of any awakening. . . .

Obedience

. . . The first item in the program of self-government is to drag the whole population well above the misery line. To create a minimum standard of life below which no human being can fall is the most elementary duty of the democratic state. For those who go below the line of civilized decency not only suffer wretchedly: they breed the poisons of self-government. They form the famous slum proletariat about whom even the socialists despair. Occasionally some dramatic figure rises out of them, occasionally they mutter and rebel and send the newspapers into a panic. But for the purposes of constructive revolution this submerged mass is of little use, for it is harassed, beaten, helpless. These last will not be first. They may scare the rest of us into a little reform. But out of sheer wretchedness will come little of the material or the power of democracy, for as Walter Weyl has said, "A man or a class, crushed to earth—is crushed to earth."

Unfit for self-government, they are the most easily led, the most easily fooled, and the most easily corrupted. You can't build a modern nation out of Georgia crackers, poverty-stricken negroes, the homeless and helpless of the great cities. They make a governing class essential. They are used by the forces of reaction. Once in a while they are used by revolutionists for agitation, but always they are used. Before you can begin to have democracy you need a country in which everyone has some stake and some taste of its promise.

Now to link chastity with poverty as one of the props of absolutism is to prepare for yourself a peck of trouble. "Do you advocate unchastity?" shrieks the frightened person. As unchastity means to most people promiscuity, I say emphatically, "No, it isn't unchastity that we wish." We don't wish poverty, but that doesn't mean that we are for parvenus and millionaires. And so for sex, we don't seek Don Juans or ascetics, we seek fathers and mothers, and a life that isn't swamped by sex.

Life can be swamped by sex very easily if sex is not normally satisfied. Those who can't have a piece of flesh, said Nietzsche, often grasp at a piece of spirit. I must confess I never saw anything very noble or pure in the dreams of St. Theresa. And as for St. Anthony in the Wilderness—surely that was no solution of the sex problem. But it was a wonderful way of cementing loyalty, to deny men and women a human life, and suggest that they marry the Church. The mediaeval vow of chastity did not mean a sudden disappearance of the sexual life: it meant a concentration of that life upon the spiritual authority.

With poverty and chastity effectively enforced, there would have been very little need to preach obedience. That was necessary only because human nature didn't permit of any thoroughgoing application of the first two vows. Had the Church achieved its full ambition, to be glorious and rich amidst poverty, to offer the only spiritual compensation to thwarted lives, then the Church would have had few disloyal sons. But as it didn't succeed completely, it had to demand the third vow—obedience —as a kind of extra prop if the other two failed.

It is no wonder then, that the upholders of authority recognize in the labor movement and the women's awakening their mortal foes, or that Ibsen in that classic prophecy of his, should have seen in these same movements the two greatest forces for human emancipation. They are the power through which there will be accomplished that transvaluation of values which democracy means. They are pointed toward a frank worldliness, a coöperation among free people, they are pointed away from submissive want, balked impulse, and unquestioned obedience.

We can begin to see, then, a little of what democratic culture implies. There was a time, not so long ago, when scholars, and "cultured people" generally, regarded Ruskin's interest in political economy as the unfortunate perversion of a man who was born to better things. We do no longer regard it as "sordid" to take an interest in economic problems. I have met artists who deplore Mr. George Russell's interest in agricultural cooperation as unworthy of the poet who is known to the world by the mystic letters AE. The interest of the working-class in its bread and butter problem is still occasionally the chance for a scolding about its "materialism." But in the main, modern democrats recognize that the abolition of poverty is the most immediate question before the world to-day, and they have imagination enough to know that the success of the war against poverty will be the conquest of new territory for civilized life.

So too, the day is passing when the child is taught to regard the body as a filthy thing. We train quite frankly for parenthood,

not for the ecstasies of the celibate. Our interest in sex is no
longer to annihilate it, but to educate it, to find civilized opportunities for its expression. We hope to organize industry and
housekeeping so that normal mating shall not be a monstrously
difficult problem. And there is an increasing number of people
who judge sexual conduct by its results in the quality of human
life. They don't think that marriage justifies licentiousness, nor
will they say that every unconventional union is necessarily evil.
They know the tyrannies that indissoluble marriage produces,
and they are beginning to know the equal oppressions of what is
called "Free love." They are becoming concrete and realistic
about sex. They are saying that where love exists with self-
respect and joy, where a fine environment is provided for the
child, where the parents live under conditions that neither
stunt the imagination nor let it run to uncontrolled fantasy, there
you have the family that modern men are seeking to create.
They desire such a family not because they are afraid not to
advocate it, but because they have reason to believe that this is
the most fruitful way of ordering human life.

When we speak of the modern intellect we mean this habit
of judging rules by their results instead of by their sources. The
fact that an idea is old or that it is "advanced," that the Pope
said it or Bernard Shaw, all that is of no decisive importance.
The real question always turns on what an idea is worth in the
satisfaction of human desire.

Objections will arise at once. It will be said that you can't
judge rules of life or beliefs by their results, because many an
idea of the greatest value may at first be very disagreeable. In
other words, it is often necessary to sacrifice immediate advantages to distant results. That is perfectly true, of course, and
the balancing of present wants against the future is really the
central problem of ethics. Will you weigh action by its results on
this particular venture, or on your whole life, or by its results
on your generation, or on the generations to come? There is no
simple answer to those questions. Every human being makes his
own particular compromise. There are few people so concentrated on the immediate that they don't look ahead a little, if
it's only to the extent of taking out a life insurance policy. There
have been a few fanatics who lived so absolutely for the millen-
nium that they made a little hell for their companions. But the

wiser a man is, it seems to me, the more vividly he can see the future as part of the evolving present. He doesn't break the flow of life, he directs it, hastens it, but preserves its continuity. The people who really matter in social affairs are neither those who wish to stop short like a mule, or leap from crag to crag like a mountain goat.

But of course, to act for results instead of in response to authority requires a readiness of thought that no one can achieve at all times. You cannot question everything radically at every moment. You have to do an infinite number of acts without thinking about their results. I have to follow the orders of my physician. We all of us have to follow the lead of specialists.

And so, it is easy to score points against anyone who suggests that modern thought is substituting the pragmatic test by results for the old obedience to authority. It can't do that altogether. We cannot be absolute pragmatists. But we judge by results as much as we can, as much as our human limitations allow. Where we have to accept dogmas without question we do so not because we have any special awe of them, but because we know that we are too ignorant, or too busy, to analyze them through. I know how unphilosophical this will sound to those who worship neatness in thought.

Well, if they can find some surer key to the complexity of life, all power to them. But let them be careful that they are not building a theory which is symmetrical only on the printed page. Nothing is easier than to simplify life and then make a philosophy about it. The trouble is that the resulting philosophy is true only of that simplified life. If somebody can create an absolute system of beliefs and rules of conduct that will guide a business man at eleven o'clock in the morning, a boy trying to select a career, a woman in an unhappy love affair,—well then, surely no pragmatist will object. He insists only that philosophy shall come down to earth and be tried out there.

In some such spirit as I have tried to suggest, the modern world is reversing the old virtues of authority. They aimed deliberately to make men unworldly. They did not aim to found society on a full use of the earth's resources; they did not aim to use the whole nature of man; they did not intend him to think out the full expression of his desires. Democracy is a turning upon those ideals in a pursuit, at first unconsciously, of the richest life that men can devise for themselves.

Mastery

. . . The Dyaks of Borneo, it is said, were not accustomed to chopping down a tree, as white men do, by notching out V-shaped cuts. "Hence," says Mr. Marett in telling the story, "any Dyak caught imitating the European fashion was punished by a fine. And yet so well aware were they that this method was an improvement on their own that, when they could trust each other not to tell, they would surreptitiously use it."

If you went to an elder of the Dyak race and asked him why the newer method was forbidden, he would probably have told you that it was wrong. The answer would not have satisfied you, but the Dyak would have inquired no further. What was wrong was filled with impending calamity. Now, of course, there is no end of conservatism to-day which is just as instinctive, just as fearful of unimagined evil, and just as dumbly irrational as the Dyaks'. I have heard a middle-aged woman say "It isn't done" as if the voice of the universe spoke through her. But there is a rationalized conservatism. If you go to an elder of the Boston race and ask why new projects are so unexceptionally bad, he will tell you that without reverence for tradition life becomes unsettled, and a nation loses itself for lack of cohesion.

These essays are based upon that observation, but added to it is the observation, just as important, that tradition will not work in the complexity of modern life. For if you ask Americans to remain true to the traditions of all their Fathers, there would be a pretty confusion if they followed your advice. There is great confusion, as it is, due in large measure to the persistency which men follow tradition in a world unsuited to it. They modify a bit, however, they apply "the rule of reason" to their old loyalties, and so a little adjustment is possible. But there can be no real cohesion for America in following scrupulously the inherited ideals of our people. Between the Sons of the Revolution, the Ancient Order of Hibernians, the Orangemen, the plantation life of the South, the refugees from Russia, the Balkan Slavs, there is in their traditions a conflict of prejudice and custom that would make all America as clamorous as the Stock Exchange on a busy day. Nor is there going to be lasting inspiration for Bulgarian immigrants in the legend of the Mayflower.

The only possible cohesion now is a loyalty that looks forward. America is preëminently the country where there is practical substance in Nietzsche's advice that we should live not for our fatherland but for our children's land.

To do this men have to substitute purpose for tradition: and that is, I believe, the profoundest change that has ever taken place in human history. We can no longer treat life as something that has trickled down to us. We have to deal with it deliberately, devise its social organization, alter its tools, formulate its method, educate and control it. In endless ways we put intention where custom has reigned. We break up routines, make decisions, choose our ends, select means.

The massive part of man's life has always been, and still is, subconscious. The influence of his intelligence seems insignificant in comparison with attachments and desires, brute forces, and natural catastrophes. Our life is managed from behind the scenes: we are actors in dramas that we cannot interpret. Of almost no decisive event can we say: this was our own choosing. We happen upon careers, necessity pushing, blind inclination pulling. If we stop to think we are amazed that we should be what we are. And so we have come to call mysterious everything that counts, and the more mysterious the better some of us pretend to think it is. We drift into our work, we fall in love, and our lives seem like the intermittent flicker of an obstinate lamp. War panics, and financial panics, revivals, fads sweep us before them. Men go to war not knowing why, hurl themselves at cannon as if they were bags of flour, seek impossible goals, submit to senseless wrongs, for mankind lives to-day only in the intervals of a fitful sleep.

There is indeed a dreaming quality in life: moved as it is from within by unconscious desires and habits, and from without by the brute forces of climate and soil and wind and tide. There are stretches in every day when we have no sense of ourselves at all, and men often wake up with a start: "Have I lived as long as I'm supposed to have lived? . . . Here I am, this kind of person who has passed through these experiences—well, I didn't quite know it."

That, I think, is the beginning of what we call reflection: a desire to realize the drama in which we are acting, to be awake during our own lifetime. When we cultivate reflection by watching ourselves and the world outside, the thing we call science begins. We draw the hidden into the light of consciousness, record it, compare phases of it, note its history, experiment, reflect on error, and we find that our conscious life is no longer a trivial iridescence, but a progressively powerful way of domesticating the brute.

This is what mastery means: the substitution of conscious intention for unconscious striving. Civilization, it seems to me, is just this constant effort to introduce plan where there has been clash, and purpose into the jungles of disordered growth. But to shape the world nearer to the heart's desire requires a knowledge of the heart's desire and of the world. You cannot throw yourself blindly against unknown facts and trust to luck that the result will be satisfactory.

Yet from the way many business men, minor artists, and modern philosophers talk you would think that the best world can be created by the mere conflict of economic egotisms, the mere eruption of fantasy, and the mere surge of blind instinct. There is to-day a widespread attempt to show the futility of ideas. Now in so far as this movement represents a critical insight into the emotional basis of ideas, it is a fundamental contribution to human power. But when it seeks to fall back upon the unconscious, when the return to nature is the ideal of a deliberate vegetable, this movement is like the effort of the animal that tried to eat itself: the tail could be managed and the hind legs, but the head was an insurmountable difficulty. You can have misleading ideas, but you cannot escape ideas. To give up theory, to cease formulating your desire is not to reach back, as some people imagine, to profounder sources of inspiration. It is to put yourself at the mercy of stray ideas, of ancient impositions or trumped-up fads. Accident becomes the master, the accident largely of your own training, and you become the plaything of whatever happens to have accumulated at the bottom of your mind, or to find itself sanctified in the newspaper you read and the suburb that suited your income.

There have been fine things produced in the world without intention. Most of our happiness has come to us, I imagine, by the fortunate meeting of events. But happiness has always been a precarious incident, elusive and shifting in an unaccountable world. In love, especially, men rejoice and suffer through what are to them mysterious ways. Yet when it is suggested that the intelligence must invade our unconscious life, men shrink from it as from dangerous and clumsy meddling. It is dangerous and clumsy now, but it is the path we shall have to follow. We have to penetrate the dreaming brute in ourselves, and make him answerable to our waking life.

It is a long and difficult process, one for which we are just beginning to find a method. But there is no other way that offers any hope. To shove our impulses underground by the taboo is to force them to virulent and uncontrolled expression. To follow impulse wherever it leads means the satisfaction of one impulse at the expense of all the others. The glutton and the rake can satisfy only their gluttonous and rakish impulses, and that isn't enough for happiness. What civilized men aim at is neither whim nor taboo, but a frank recognition of desire, disciplined by a knowledge of what is possible, and ordered by the conscious purpose of their lives.

There is a story that experimental psychology grew from the discovery that two astronomers trying to time the movement of the same heavenly body reached different results. It became necessary then to time the astronomers themselves in order to discount the differences in the speed of their reactions. Now whether the story is literally true or not, it is very significant. For it symbolizes the essential quality of modern science—its growing self-consciousness. There have been scientific discoveries all through the ages. Heron of Alexandria invented a steam-turbine about 200 B.C. They had gunpowder in Ancient China. But these discoveries lay dormant, and they appear to us now as interesting accidents. What we have learned is to organize invention deliberately, to create a record for it and preserve its continuity, to subsidize it, and surround it with criticism. We have not only scientific work, but a philosophy of science, and that philosophy is the source of fruitful scientific work. We have become conscious about scientific method; we have set about studying the minds of scientists. This gives us an infinitely greater control of human invention, for we are learning to control the inventor. We are able already to discount some of the limitations of those engaged in research: we should not, for example, send a man who was color blind to report on the protective coloring of animals; we begin to see how much it matters in many investigations whether the student is an auditory or a visualizing type. Well, psychology opens up greater possibilities than this for the conscious control of scientific progress. It has begun to penetrate emotional prejudice, to show why some men are so deeply attached to authority, why philosophers have such unphilosophical likes and dislikes. We ask now of an economist, who his friends are, what his ambitions, his class bias. When one thinker exalts absolute freedom, another violent repression, we have ceased to take such ideas at their face value, and modern psychology, especially the school of Freud, has begun to work out a technique for cutting under the surface of our thoughts.

The power of criticizing the scientific mind is, I believe, our best guarantee for the progress of scientific discovery. This is the inner sanctuary of civilized power. For when science becomes its own critic it assures its own future. It is able, then, to attack the source of error itself; to forestall its own timidities, and control its own bias.

If the scientific temper were as much a part of us as the faltering ethics we now absorb in our childhood, then we might hope to face our problems with something like assurance. A mere emotion of futurity, that sense of "vital urge" which is so common to-day, will fritter itself away unless it comes under the scientific discipline, where men use language accurately, know fact from fancy, search out their own prejudice, are willing to learn from failures, and do not shrink from the long process of close observation. Then only shall we have a substitute for authority. Rightly understood science is the culture under which people can live forward in the midst of complexity, and treat life not as something given but as something to be shaped. Custom and authority will work in a simple and unchanging civilization, but in our world only those will conquer who can understand.

There is nothing accidental then in the fact that democracy in politics is the twin-brother of scientific thinking. They had to come together. As absolutism falls, science arises. It *is* self-government. For when the impulse which overthrows kings and priests and unquestioned creeds becomes self-conscious we call it science.

Inventions and laboratories, Greek words, mathematical formulae, fat books, are only the outward sign of an attitude toward life, an attitude which is self-governing, and most adequately named humanistic. Science is the irreconcilable foe of bogeys, and therefore, a method of laying the conflicts of the soul. It is the unfrightened, masterful and humble approach to reality—the needs of our natures and the possibilities of the world. The scientific spirit is the discipline of democracy, the escape from drift, the outlook of a free man. Its direction is to distinguish fact from fancy; its "enthusiasm is for the possible", its promise is the shaping of fact to a chastened and honest dream.

Fact and Fancy

. . . The method of a self-governing people is to meet every issue with an affirmative proposal which draws its strength from some latent promise. Thus the real remedy for violence in industrial disputes is to give labor power that brings responsibility. The remedy for commercialism is collective organization in which the profiteer has given way to the industrial statesman. The incentive to efficiency is not alone love of competent work but a desire to get greater social values out of human life. The way out of corrupt and inept politics is to use the political state for interesting and important purposes. The unrest of women cannot be met by a few negative freedoms: only the finding of careers and the creation of positive functions can make liberty valuable. In the drift of our emotional life, the genuine hope is to substitute for terror and weakness, a frank and open worldliness, a love of mortal things in the discipline of science.

These are not idle dreams: they are, it seems to me, concrete possibilities of the actual world in which we live. I have tried in this book to suggest a few of them, to make clearer to myself by illustrations, the attitude of mind with which we can begin to approach our strangely complex world. It lacks precision, it lacks the definiteness of a panacea, and all of us rebel against that. But mastery in our world cannot mean any single, neat and absolute line of procedure. There is something multitudinous about the very notion of democracy, something that offends our inherited intellectual prejudices. This book would have a more dramatic climax if I could say that mastery consisted in some one thing: say in a big union of the working class, or the nationalization of all business. But it isn't possible to say that because there are too many factors which compete for a place, too many forces that disturb a simple formula. Mastery, whether we like it or not, is an immense collaboration, in which all the promises of to-day will have their vote.

Our business as critics is to make those promises evident, to give to the men who embody them a consciousness of them, to show how they clash with facts, to bathe them in suggestion. In that atmosphere we can go about organizing the new structure of society, building up producers' and consumers' controls, laying down plans for wise uses of our natural resources, working wherever we happen to be, or wherever our abilities call us, on the substitution of design for accident, human purposes for brute destiny. It is not easy, nor as yet a normal attitude toward life. The sustained effort it requires is so great that few can maintain it for any length of time. Anyone who has tried will report that no intellectual discipline is comparable in the severity of its demands: from the weariness it engenders men fall either into sheer speculation or mechanical repetition. How often does a book begin truly, and turn off exhausted into a conventional ending. You can almost see the point where the author gave up his struggle, and called in the claptrap of a happy accident. How often does a reformer begin with penetration, entangle himself in officialdom, and end in excuses for uninspired deeds. Who has not wept over the critical paper which started off so bravely, handling each event with freshness and skill, only to become cluttered in its own successes and redundant with stale virtues. Everyone has met the man who approached life eagerly and tapered off to a middle age where the effort is over, his opinions formed, his habits immutable, with nothing to do but live in the house he has built, and sip what he has brewed.

Effort wells up, beats bravely against reality, and in weariness simmers down into routine or fantasy. No doubt much of this is due to physiological causes, some of which lie beyond our present control. And yet in large measure the explanation lies elsewhere. There are fine maturities to give our pessimism the lie. This abandonment of effort is due, I imagine, to the fact that the conscious mastery of experience is, comparatively speaking, a new turn in human culture. The old absolutisms of caste and church and state made more modest demands than democracy does: life was settled and fantasy was organized into ritual and riveted by authority. But the modern world swings wide and loose, it has thrown men upon their own responsibility. And for that gigantic task they lack experience, they are fettered and bound and finally broken by ancient terrors that huddle about them. Think of the enormous effort that goes into mere rebellion, think of the struggle that young men and women go through in what they call a fight for independence, independence which is nothing but an opportunity to begin. They have to break with habits rooted in the animal loyalties of their childhood, and the rupture has consequences greater than most people realize. The scars are very deep, even the most successful rebel is somewhat crippled. No wonder then that those who win freedom are often unable to use it; no wonder that liberty brings its despair.

There are people who think that rebellion is an inevitable accompaniment of progress. I don't see why it should be. If it is possible to destroy, as I think we are doing, the very basis of authority, then change becomes a matter of invention and deliberate experiment. No doubt there is a long road to travel before we atttain such a civilization. But it seems to me that we have every right to look forward to it—to a time when childhood will cease to be assaulted by bogeys, when eagerness for life will cease to be a sin. There is no more reason why everyone should go through the rebellions of our time than that everyone should have to start a suffrage movement to secure his vote.

To idealize rebellion is simply to make a virtue out of necessity. It shows more clearly than anything else that the sheer struggle for freedom is an exhausting thing, so exhausting that the people who lead it are often unable to appreciate its uses. But just as the men who founded democracy were more concerned with the evils of the kingly system than they were with the possibilities of self-government, so it is with working men and women, and with all those who are in revolt against the subtle tyrannies of the school and the home and the creed. Only with difficulty does the affirmative vision emerge.

Each of us contributes to it what he can in the intervals of his battle with surviving absolutisms. The vision is clearer to-day than it was to the rebels of the Nineteenth Century. We are more used to freedom than they were. But in comparison with what we need our vision is murky, fragmentary, and distorted. We have dared to look upon life naturally, we have exorcised many bogeys and laid many superstitions, we have felt reality bend to our purposes. We gather assurance from these hints.

9

Wilson Pleads for a Peace Without Victory

Woodrow Wilson's Address to the Senate, January 22, 1917

The European war that broke out in the late summer of 1914 caught most Americans by surprise. Before going to Washington President Wilson had remarked that "it would be the irony of fate if my administration had to deal chiefly with foreign affairs." His administration was scarcely eighteen months old when World War I exploded and dumped a host of problems on the President's desk. "The United States," the President said as the fighting in Western Europe began, "must be neutral in fact as well as in name. . . ." This proved no easy undertaking; even the President himself was unequal to the task, for eventually he became convinced that right was on the side of England and France. Meanwhile, however, he maintained an official policy of neutrality while increasing the effort to end the war before the United States should be drawn into it. Wilson assiduously sought to bring the warring parties to the conference table. Time and again he offered the good offices of the nation to the belligerents; time and again they rebuffed his advances. The address reprinted here was his last major appeal to end the war before the United States accepted "the gauge of battle." The literature relating to the causes of the war and to the causes of American entry into the conflict is voluminous. Charles Seymour's *American Neutrality, 1914-1917; Essays on the Causes of American Intervention in the World War* (New Haven: Yale University Press, 1935) treats American efforts to avoid involvement in the war. Arthus S. Link's *Wilson: The Struggle for Neutrality 1914-1915* (Princeton: Princeton University Press, 1960) and *Wilson: Confusions and Crises, 1915-1916* (Priceton: Princeton University Press, 1964) provide the best account of Wilson during the years 1914-1916. A study of larger scope is R. E. Osgood's *Ideals and Self-Interest in America's Foreign Relations: The Great Transformation of the Twentieth Century* (Chicago: The University of Chicago Press, 1953). In reading this address note (1) what efforts Wilson had made to promote peace talks and with what results; (2) what

Woodrow Wilson, Address, January 22, 1917, Senate Document, 685, U.S. 64 Cong., 2 sess., pp. 3-8.

he thought was America's duty in the situation and why; (3) what role he envisioned for new-world nations in keeping the peace; (4) what he hoped to substitute for the balance of power; (5) what unique American principle Wilson advocated as a basis for peace; (6) other aims he advanced as conditions of American participation in peace making; and (7) elements of idealism in his address.

GENTLEMEN OF THE SENATE: ON THE EIGHTEENTH of December last [1916] I addressed an identic note to the governments of the nations now at war requesting them to state, more definitely than they had yet been stated by either group of belligerents, the terms upon which they would deem it possible to make peace. I spoke on behalf of humanity and of the rights of all neutral nations like our own, many of whose most vital interests the war puts in constant jeopardy. The Central Powers united in a reply which stated merely that they were ready to meet their antagonists in conference to discuss terms of peace. The Entente Powers have replied much more definitely and have stated, in general terms, indeed, but with sufficient definiteness to imply details, the arrangements, guarantees, and acts of reparation which they deem to be the indispensable conditions of a satisfactory settlement. We are that much nearer a definite discussion of the peace which shall end the present war. We are that much nearer the discussion of the international concert which must thereafter hold the world at peace. In every discussion of the peace that must end this war it is taken for granted that that peace must be followed by some definite concert of power which will make it virtually impossible that any such catastrophe should ever overwhelm us again. Every lover of mankind, every sane and thoughtful man must take that for granted.

I have sought this opportunity to address you because I thought that I owed it to you, as the council associated with me in the final determination of our international obligations, to disclose to you without reserve the thought and purpose that have been taking form in my mind in regard to the duty of our Government in the days to come when it will be necessary to lay afresh and upon a new plan the foundations of peace among the nations.

It is inconceivable that the people of the United States should play no part in that great enterprise. To take part in such a service will be the opportunity for which they have sought to prepare themselves by the very principles and purposes of their polity and the approved practices of their Government ever since the days when they set up a new nation in the high and honourable hope that it might in all that it was and did show mankind the way to liberty. They cannot in honour withhold the service to which they are now about to be challenged. They do not wish to withhold it. But they owe it to themselves and to the other nations of the world to state the conditions under which they will feel free to render it.

That service is nothing less than this, to add their authority and their power to the authority and force of other nations to guarantee peace and justice throughout the world. Such a settlement cannot now be long postponed. It is right that before it comes this Government should frankly formulate the conditions upon which it would feel justified in asking our people to approve its formal and solemn adherence to a League for Peace. I am here to attempt to state those conditions.

The present war must first be ended; but we owe it to candour and to a just regard for the opinion of mankind to say that, so far as our participation in guarantees of future peace is concerned, it makes a great deal of difference in what way and upon what terms it is ended. The treaties and agreements which bring it to an end must embody terms which will create a peace that is worth guaranteeing and preserving, a peace that will win the approval of mankind, not merely a peace that will serve the several interests and immediate aims of the nations engaged. We shall have no voice in determining what those terms shall be, but we shall, I feel sure, have a voice in determining whether they shall be made lasting or not by the guarantees of a universal covenant; and our judgment upon what is fundamental and essential as a condition precedent to permanency should be spoken now, not afterwards when it may be too late.

No covenant of cooperative peace that does not include the peoples of the New World can suffice to keep the future safe against war; and yet there is only one sort of peace that the peoples of America could join in guaranteeing. The elements of that peace must be elements that engage the confidence and satisfy the principles of the American governments, elements consistent with their political faith and with the practical convictions which the peoples of America have once for all embraced and undertaken to defend.

I do not mean to say that any American government would throw any obstacle in the way of any terms of peace the governments now at war might agree upon, or seek to upset them when made, whatever they might be. I only take it for granted that mere terms of peace between the belligerents will not satisfy even the belligerents themselves. Mere agreements may not make peace secure. It will be absolutely necessary that a force be created as a guarantor of the permanency of the settlement so much greater than the force of any nation now engaged or any alliance hitherto formed or projected that no nation, no probable combination of nations could face or withstand it. If the peace presently to be made is to endure, it must be a peace made secure by the organized major force of mankind.

The terms of the immediate peace agreed upon will determine whether it is a peace for which such a guarantee can be secured. The question upon which the whole future peace and policy of the world depends is this: Is the present war a struggle for a just and secure peace, or only for a new balance of power? If it be only a struggle for a new balance of power, who will guarantee, who can guarantee, the stable equilibrium of the new arrangement? Only a tranquil Europe can be a stable Europe. There must be, not a balance of power, but a community of power; not organized rivalries, but an organized common peace.

Fortunately we have received very explicit assurances on this point. The statesmen of both of the groups of nations now arrayed against one another have said, in terms that could not be misinterpreted, that it was no part of the purpose they had in mind to crush their antagonists. But the implications of these assurances may not be equally clear to all—may not be the same on both sides of the water. I think it will be serviceable if I attempt to set forth what we understand them to be.

They imply, first of all, that it must be a peace without victory. It is not pleasant to say this. I beg that I may be permitted to put my own interpretation upon it and that it may be understood that no other interpretation was in my thought. I am seeking only to face realities and to face them without soft concealments. Victory would mean peace forced upon the loser, a victor's terms imposed upon the vanquished. It would be accepted in humiliation, under duress, at intolerable sacrifice, and would leave a sting, a resentment, a bitter memory upon which terms of peace would rest, not permanently, but only as upon quicksand. Only a peace between equals can last. Only a peace the very principle of which is equality and a common participation in a common benefit. The right state of mind, the right feeling between nations, is as necessary for a lasting peace as is the just settlement of vexed questions of territory or of racial and national allegiance.

The equality of nations upon which peace must be founded if it is to last must be an equality of rights; the guarantees exchanged must neither recognize nor imply a difference between big nations and small, between those that are powerful and those that are weak. Right must be based upon the common strength, not upon the individual strength, of the nations upon whose concert peace will depend. Equality of territory or of resources there of course cannot be; nor any other sort of equality not gained in the ordinary peaceful and legitimate development of the peoples themselves. But no one asks or expects anything more than an equality of rights. Mankind is looking now for freedom of life, not for equipoises of power.

And there is a deeper thing involved than even equality of right among organized nations. No peace can last, or ought to last, which does not recognize and accept the principle that governments derive all their just powers from the consent of the governed, and that no right anywhere exists to hand peoples about from sovereignty to sovereignty as if they were property. I take it for granted, for instance, if I may venture upon a single example, that statesmen everywhere are agreed that there should be a united, independent, and autonomous Poland, and that henceforth inviolable security of life, of worship, and of industrial and social development should be guaranteed to all peoples who have lived hitherto under the power of governments devoted to a faith and purpose hostile to their own.

I speak of this, not because of any desire to exalt an abstract political principle which has always been held very dear by those who have sought to build up liberty in America, but for the same reason that I have spoken of the other conditions of peace which seem to me clearly indispensable—because I wish frankly to uncover realities. Any peace which does not recognize and accept this principle will inevitably be upset. It will not rest upon the affections or the convictions of mankind. The ferment of spirit of whole populations will fight subtly and constantly against it, and all the world will sympathize. The world can be at peace only if its life is stable, and there can be no stability where the will is in rebellion, where there is not tranquility of spirit and a sense of justice, of freedom, and of right.

So far as practicable, moreover, every great people now struggling towards a full development of its resources and of its powers should be assured a direct outlet to the great highways of the sea. Where this cannot be done by the cession of territory, it can no doubt be done by the neutralization of direct rights of way under the general guarantee which will assure the peace itself. With a right comity of arrangement no nation need be shut away from free access to the open paths of the world's commerce.

And the paths of the sea must alike in law and in fact be free. The freedom of the seas is the *sine qua non* of peace, equality, and cooperation. No doubt a somewhat radical reconsideration of many of the rules of international practice hitherto thought to be established may be necessary in order to make the seas indeed free and common in practically all circumstances for the use of mankind, but the motive for such changes is convincing and compelling. There can be no trust or intimacy between the peoples of the world without them. The free, constant, unthreatened intercourse of nations is an essential part of the process of peace and of development. It need not be difficult either to define or to secure the freedom of the seas if the governments of the world sincerely desire to come to an agreement concerning it.

It is a problem closely connected with the limitation of naval armaments and the cooperation of the navies of the world in keeping the seas at once free and safe. And the question of limiting naval armaments opens the wider and perhaps more difficult question of the limitation of armies and of all programmes of military preparation. Difficult and delicate as these questions are, they must be faced with the utmost candour and decided in a spirit of real accommodation if peace is to come with healing in its wings, and come to stay. Peace cannot be had without concession and sacrifice. There can be no sense of safety and equality among the nations if great preponderating armaments are henceforth to continue here and there to be built up and maintained. The statesmen of the world must plan for peace and nations must adjust and accommodate their policy to it as they have planned for war and made ready for pitiless contest and rivalry. The question of armaments, whether on land or sea, is the most immediately and intensely practical question connected with the future fortunes of nations and of mankind.

I have spoken upon these great matters without reserve and with the utmost explicitness because it has seemed to me to be necessary if the world's yearning desire for peace was anywhere to find free voice and utterance. Perhaps I am the only person in high authority amongst all the peoples of the world who is at liberty to speak and hold nothing back. I am speaking as an individual, and yet I am speaking also, of course as the responsible head of a great government, and I feel confident that I have said what the people of the United States would wish me to say. May I not add that I hope and believe that I am in effect speaking for liberals and friends of humanity in every nation and of every programme of liberty? I would fain believe that I am speaking for the silent mass of mankind everywhere who have as yet had no place or opportunity to speak their real hearts out concerning the death and ruin they see to have come already upon the persons and the homes they hold most dear.

And in holding out the expectation that the people and Government of the United States will join the other civilized nations of the world in guaranteeing the permanence of peace upon such terms as I have named I speak with the greater boldness and confidence because it is clear to every man who can think that there is in this promise no breach in either our traditions or our policy as a nation, but a fulfilment, rather, of all that we have professed or striven for.

I am proposing, as it were, that the nations should with one accord adopt the doctrine of President Monroe as the doctrine of the world: that no nation should seek to extend its polity over any other nation or people, but that every people should be left free to determine its own polity, its own way of development, unhindered, unthreatened, unafraid, the little along with the great and powerful.

I am proposing that all nations henceforth avoid entangling alliances which would draw them into competitions of power, catch them in a net of intrigue and selfish rivalry, and disturb their own affairs with influences intruded from without. There is no entangling alliance in a concert of power. When all unite to act in the same sense and with the same purpose all act in the common interest and are free to live their own lives under a common protection.

I am proposing government by the consent of the governed; that freedom of the seas which in international conference after conference representatives of the United States have urged with the eloquence of those who are the convinced disciples of liberty; and that moderation of armaments which makes of armies and navies a power for order merely, not an instrument af aggression or of selfish violence.

These are American principles, American policies. We could stand for no others. And they are also the principles and policies of forward looking men and women everywhere, of every modern nation, of every enlightened community. They are the principles of mankind and must prevail.

10

Wilson Asks for a Declaration of a State of War

Woodrow Wilson's Address to Congress, April 2, 1917

President Wilson was the critical figure in America's decision to enter the war against Germany. Wilson had won the presidential race in 1916 partly on the slogan "He kept us out of war." The phrase, however, in no way tied his hands as to the future. The President continued his peace offensive following his second inauguration in March, 1917. Moreover, he continued to press the preparedness program initiated early in 1916. A number of factors operated to move the country toward war. Perhaps the most significant was the President's conviction that only if the United States helped negotiate the peace after the defeat of Germany would there be a chance of a just and durable settlement. Only belligerents put their feet under the peace table at the end of a war; if the United States and Wilson were to direct the treaty settlement the nation must enter the war. Germany provided the occasion for the decision to fight by resuming early in 1917 unrestricted submarine warfare against all shipping, belligerent and neutral, trading with her enemies. The President appeared before a joint session of Congress on April 2, 1917, to deliver the address reprinted below. Walter Millis in his best-selling *The Road to War* (Boston and New York: Houghton Mifflin Company, 1935), written in the full bloom of the isolationist mood of the 1930's, describes the diplomatic prelude to war. Mark Sullivan's *Our Times* (New York: Charles Scribner's Sons, 1935), Vol. V, gives a colorful account of the United States at war. See also Ernest R. May, *The World War and American Isolation* (Cambridge: Harvard University Press, 1959). In reading this selection note (1) the President's report concerning the renewal of submarine warfare; (2) his characterization of that kind of war; (3) the mood he hoped to engender in his listeners; (4) upon whom he thought the burden of first waging war rested; (5) what some of the implications were of accepting a belligerent status; (6) his statement of American motives and objectives; (7) what disclosures he made of recent machinations of the German government;

Congressional Record, Vol. 55, Part 1, April 2, 1917, pp. 102-04.

(8) ways in which he placed the war in a universal setting; (9) his attitude toward the German people; and (10) the quality of Wilson's rhetoric in this address.

GENTLEMEN OF THE CONGRESS: I HAVE CALLED THE Congress into extraordinary session because there are serious, very serious, choices of policy to be made, and made immediately, which it was neither right nor constitutionally permissible that I should assume the responsibility of making.

On the third of February last I officially laid before you the extraordinary announcement of the Imperial German Government that on and after the first day of February it was its purpose to put aside all restraints of law or of humanity and use its submarines to sink every vessel that sought to approach either the ports of Great Britain and Ireland or the western coasts of Europe or any of the ports controlled by the enemies of Germany within the Mediterranean. That had seemed to be the object of the German submarine warfare earlier in the war, but since April of last year the Imperial Government had somewhat restrained the commanders of its undersea craft in conformity with its promise then given to us that passenger boats should not be sunk and that due warning would be given to all other vessels which its submarines might seek to destroy, when no resistance was offered or escape attempted, and care taken that their crews were given at least a fair chance to save their lives in their open boats. The precautions taken were meagre and haphazard enough, as was proved in distressing instance after instance in the progress of the cruel and unmanly business, but a certain degree of restraint was observed. The new policy has swept every restriction aside. Vessels of every kind, whatever their flag, their character, their cargo, their destination, their errand, have been ruthlessly sent to the bottom without warning and without thought of help or mercy for those on board, the vessels of friendly neutrals along with those of belligerents. Even hospital ships and ships carrying relief to the sorely bereaved and stricken people of Belgium, though the latter were provided with safe conduct through the proscribed areas by the German Government itself and were distinguished by unmistakable marks of identity, have been sunk with the same reckless lack of compassion or of principle.

I was for a little while unable to believe that such things would in fact be done by any government that had hitherto subscribed to the humane practices of civilized nations. International law had its origin in the attempt to set up some law which would be respected and observed upon the seas, where no nation had right of dominion and where lay the free highways of the world. By painful stage after stage has that law been built up, with meagre enough results, indeed, after all was accomplished that could be accomplished, but always with a clear view, at least, of what the heart and conscience of mankind demanded. This minimum of right the German Government has swept aside under the plea of retaliation and necessity and because it had no weapons which it could use at sea except these which it is impossible to employ as it is employing them without throwing to the winds all scruples of humanity or of respect for the understandings that were supposed to underlie the intercourse of the world. I am not now thinking of the loss of property involved, immense and serious as that is, but only of the wanton and wholesale destruction of the lives of non-combatants, men, women, and children, engaged in pursuits which have always, even in the darkest periods of modern history, been deemed innocent and legitimate. Property can be paid for; the lives of peaceful and innocent people cannot be. The present German submarine warfare against commerce is a warfare against mankind.

It is a war against all nations. American ships have been sunk, American lives taken, in ways which it has stirred us very deeply to learn of, but the ships and people of other neutral and friendly nations have been sunk and overwhelmed in the waters in the same way. There has been no discrimination. The challenge is to all mankind. Each nation must decide for itself how it will meet it. The choice we make for ourselves must be made with a moderation of counsel and a temperateness of judgment befitting our character and our motives as a nation. We must put excited feeling away. Our motive will not be revenge or the victorious assertion of the physical might of the nation, but only the vindication of right, of human right, of which we are only a single champion.

When I addressed the Congress on the twenty-sixth of February last I thought that it would suffice to assert our neutral rights with arms, our right to use the seas against unlawful interference, our right to keep our people safe against unlawful violence. But armed neutrality, it now appears, is impracticable. Because submarines are in effect outlaws when used as the German submarines have been used against merchant shipping, it is impossible to defend ships against their attacks as the law of nations has assumed that merchantmen would defend themselves against privateers or cruisers, visible craft giving chase upon the open sea. It is common prudence in such circumstances, grim necessity indeed, to endeavor to destroy them before they have shown their own intention. They must be dealt with upon sight if dealt with at all. The German Government denies the right of neutrals to use arms at all within the areas of the sea which it has proscribed, even in the defense of rights which no modern publicist has ever before questioned their right to defend. The intimation is conveyed that the armed guards which we have placed on our merchant ships will be treated as beyond the pale of law and subject to be dealt with as pirates would be. Armed neutrality is ineffectual enough at best; in such circumstances and in the face of such pretensions it is worse than ineffectual: it is likely only to produce what it was meant to prevent; it is practically certain to draw us into the war without either the rights or the effectiveness of belligerents. There is one choice we cannot make, we are incapable of making: we will not choose the path of submission and suffer the most sacred rights of our nation and our people to be ignored or violated. The wrongs against which we now array ourselves are no common wrongs; they cut to the very roots of human life.

With a profound sense of the solemn and even tragical character of the step I am taking and of the grave responsibilities which it involves, but in unhesitating obedience to what I deem my constitutional duty, I advise that the Congress declare the recent course of the Imperial German Government to be in fact nothing less than war against the government and people of the United States; that it formally accept the status of belligerent which has thus been thrust upon it; and that it take immediate steps not only to put the country in a more thorough state of

defense but also to exert all its power and employ all its resources to bring the Government of the German Empire to terms
and end the war.

What this will involve is clear. It will involve the utmost practicable cooperation in counsel and action with the governments
now at war with Germany, and, as incident to that, the extension to those governments of the most liberal financial credits, in
order that our resources may so far as possible be added to
theirs. It will involve the organization and mobilization of all
the material resources of the country to supply the materials of
war and serve the incidental needs of the nation in the most
abundant and yet the most economical and efficient way possible.
It will involve the immediate full equipment of the navy in all
respects but particularly in supplying it with the best means of
dealing with the enemy's submarines. It will involve the immediate addition to the armed forces of the United States already
provided for by law in case of war at least five hundred thousand men, who should, in my opinion, be chosen upon the principle of universal liability to service, and also the authorization
of subsequent additional increments of equal force so soon as
they may be needed and can be handled in training. It will involve also, of course, the granting of adequate credits to the
Government, sustained, I hope, so far as they can equitably be
sustained by the present generation, by well-conceived taxation.

I say sustained so far as may be equitable by taxation because
it seems to me that it would be most unwise to base the credits
which will now be necessary entirely on money borrowed. It is
our duty, I most respectfully urge, to protect our people so far
as we may against the very serious hardships and evils which
would be likely to arise out of the inflation which would be
produced by vast loans.

In carrying out the measures by which these things are to be
accomplished we should keep constantly in mind the wisdom
of interfering as little as possible in our own preparation and in
the equipment of our own military forces with the duty—for it
will be a very practical duty—of supplying the nations already
at war with Germany with the materials which they can obtain
only from us or by our assistance. They are in the field and we
should help them in every way to be effective there.

I shall take the liberty of suggesting, through the several

executive departments of the Government, for the consideration of your committees, measures for the accomplishment of the several objects I have mentioned. I hope that it will be your pleasure to deal with them as having been framed after very careful thought by the branch of the Government upon which the responsibility of conducting the war and safeguarding the nation will most directly fall.

While we do these things, these deeply momentous things, let us be very clear, and make very clear to all the world what our motives and our objects are. My own thought has not been driven from its habitual and normal course by the unhappy events of the last two months, and I do not believe that the thought of the nation has been altered or clouded by them. I have exactly the same things in mind now that I had in mind when I addressed the Senate on the twenty-second of January last; the same that I had in mind when I addressed the Congress on the third of February and on the twenty-sixth of February. Our object now, as then, is to vindicate the principles of peace and justice in the life of the world as against selfish and autocratic power and to set up amongst the really free and self-governed peoples of the world such a concert of purpose and of action as will henceforth ensure the observance of those principles. Neutrality is no longer feasible or desirable where the peace of the world is involved and the freedom of its peoples, and the menace to that peace and freedom lies in the existence of autocratic governments backed by organized force which is controlled wholly by their will, not by the will of their people. We have seen the last of neutrality in such circumstances. We are at the beginning of an age in which it will be insisted that the same standards of conduct and of responsibility for wrong done shall be observed among nations and their governments that are observed among the individual citizens of civilized states.

We have no quarrel with the German people. We have no feeling towards them but one of sympathy and friendship. It was not upon their impulse that their government acted in entering this war. It was not with their previous knowledge or approval. It was a war determined upon as wars used to be determined upon in the old, unhappy days when peoples were nowhere consulted by their rulers and wars were provoked and waged in the interest of dynasties or of little groups of ambitious men who were accustomed to use their fellow men as pawns and tools. Self-governed nations do not fill their neighbour states with spies or set the course of intrigue to bring about some critical posture of affairs which will give them an opportunity to strike and make conquest. Such designs can be successfully worked out only under cover and where no one has the right to ask questions. Cunningly contrived plans of deception or aggression, carried, it may be, from generation to generation, can be worked out and kept from the light only within the privacy of courts or behind the carefully guarded confidences of a narrow and privileged class. They are happily impossible where public opinion commands and insists upon full information concerning all the nation's affairs.

A steadfast concert for peace can never be maintained except by a partnership of democratic nations. No autocratic government could be trusted to keep faith within it or observe its covenants. It must be a league of honour, a partnership of opinion. Intrigue would eat its vitals away; the plottings of inner circles who could plan what they would and render account to no one would be a corruption seated at its very heart. Only free peoples can hold their purpose and their honour steady to a common end and prefer the interests of mankind to any narrow interest of their own.

Does not every American feel that assurance has been added to our hope for the future peace of the world by the wonderful and heartening things that have been happening within the last few weeks in Russia?* Russia was known by those who knew it best to have been always in fact democratic at heart, in all the vital habits of her thought, in all the intimate relationships of her people that spoke their natural instinct, their habitual attitude towards life. The autocracy that crowned the summit of her political structure, long as it had stood and terrible as was the reality of its power, was not in fact Russian in origin, character, or purpose; and now it has been shaken off and the great, generous Russian people have been added in all their naive

---

*Editor's note: The overthrow of the Czarist government and the establishment of a provisional government under the liberal leadership of Alexander Kerensky occurred in March 1917. Kerensky's government in turn fell during the October-November 1917 Bolshevik revolution. The present Soviet regime in Russia arose out of this second revolution.

majesty and might to the forces that are fighting for freedom in the world, for justice, and for peace. Here is a fit partner for a League of Honour.

One of the things that has served to convince us that the Prussian autocracy was not and could never be our friend is that from the very outset of the present war it has filled our unsuspecting communities and even our offices of government with spies and set criminal intrigues everywhere afoot against our national unity of counsel, our peace within and without, our industries and our commerce. Indeed it is now evident that its spies were here even before the war began; and it is unhappily not a matter of conjecture but a fact proved in our courts of justice that the intrigues which have more than once come perilously near to disturbing the peace and dislocating the industries of the country have been carried on at the instigation, with the support, and even under the personal direction of official agents of the Imperial Government accredited to the Government of the United States. Even in checking these things and trying to extirpate them we have sought to put the most generous interpretation possible upon them because we knew that their source lay, not in any hostile feeling or purpose of the German people towards us (who were, no doubt as ignorant of them as we ourselves were), but only in the selfish designs of a Government that did what it pleased and told its people nothing. But they have played their part in serving to convince us at last that that Government entertains no real friendship for us and means to act against our peace and security at its convenience. That it means to stir up enemies against us at our very doors the intercepted note to the German Minister at Mexico City is eloquent evidence.

We are accepting this challenge of hostile purpose because we know that in such a government, following such methods, we can never have a friend; and that in the presence of its organized power, always lying in wait to accomplish we know not what purpose, there can be no assured security for the democratic governments of the world. We are now about to accept the gauge of battle with this natural foe to liberty and shall, if necessary, spend the whole force of the nation to check and nullify its pretensions and its power. We are glad, now that we see the facts with no veil of false pretence about them, to fight thus for the ultimate peace of the world and for the liberation of its peoples, the German peoples included: for the rights of nations great and small and the privilege of men everywhere to choose their way of life and of obedience. The world must be made safe for democracy. Its peace must be planted upon the tested foundations of political liberty. We have no selfish ends to serve. We desire no conquest, no dominion. We seek no indemnities for ourselves, no material compensation for the sacrifices we shall freely make. We are but one of the champions of the rights of mankind. We shall be satisfied when those rights have been made as secure as the faith and the freedom of nations can make them.

Just because we fight without rancour and without selfish object, seeking nothing for ourselves but what we shall wish to share with all free peoples, we shall, I feel confident, conduct our operations as belligerents without passion and ourselves observe with proud punctilio the principles of right and of fair play we profess to be fighting for.

I have said nothing of the governments allied with the Imperial Government of Germany because they have not made war upon us or challenged us to defend our right and our honour. The Austro-Hungarian Government has, indeed, avowed its unqualified endorsement and acceptance of the reckless and lawless submarine warfare adopted now without disguise by the Imperial German Government, and it has therefore not been possible for this Government to receive Count Tarnowski, the Ambassador recently accredited to this Government by the Imperial and Royal Government of Austria-Hungary; but that Government has not actually engaged in warfare against citizens of the United States on the seas, and I take the liberty, for the present at least, of postponing a discussion of our relations with the authorities at Vienna. We enter this war only where we are clearly forced into it because there are no other means of defending our rights.

It will be all the easier for us to conduct ourselves as belligerents in a high spirit of right and fairness because we act without animus, not in enmity towards a people or with the desire to bring any injury or disadvantage upon them, but only in armed opposition to an irresponsible government which has thrown aside all considerations of humanity and of right and is running amuck. We are, let me say again, the sincere friends of the German people, and shall desire nothing so much as the early re-establishment of intimate relations of mutual advantage between us—however hard it may be for them, for the time being, to believe that this is spoken from our hearts. We have borne with their present government through all these bitter months because of that friendship—exercising a patience and forbearance which would otherwise have been impossible. We shall, happily, still have an opportunity to prove that friendship in our daily attitude and actions towards the millions of men and women of German birth and native sympathy who live amongst us and share our life, and we shall be proud to prove it towards all who are in fact loyal to their neighbours and to the Government in the hour of test. They are, most of them, as true and loyal Americans as if they had never known any other fealty or allegiance. They will be prompt to stand with us in rebuking and restraining the few who may be of a different mind and purpose. If there should be disloyalty, it will be dealt with with a firm hand of stern repression; but, if it lifts its head at all, it will lift it only here and there and without countenance except from a lawless and malignant few.

It is a distressing and oppressive duty, Gentlemen of the Congress, which I have performed in thus addressing you. There are, it may be, many months of fiery trial and sacrifice ahead of us. It is a fearful thing to lead this great peaceful people into war, into the most terrible and disastrous of all wars, civilization itself seeming to be in the balance. But the right is more precious than peace, and we shall fight for the things which we have always carried nearest our hearts—for democracy, for the right of those who submit to authority to have a voice in their own governments, for the rights and liberties of small nations, for a universal dominion of right by such a concert of free peoples as shall bring peace and safety to all nations and make the world itself at last free. To such a task we can dedicate our lives and our fortunes, everything that we are and everything that we have, with the pride of those who know that the day has come when America is privileged to spend her blood and her might for the principles that gave her birth and happiness and the peace which she has treasured. God helping her, she can do no other.

11

A Progressive Opposes the War
Randolph S. Bourne's "The War and the Intellectuals"

President Wilson phrased the war aims of the United States in masterful phrases that stirred his fellow citizens to strong emotional support for the crusade to save the world for democracy. Opposition to America's entry into the war, however, persisted despite the President's efforts. Among the opposition were those having strong and sincere pacifist convictions. Others rejected the President's theory of the war and argued that England, France, and Russia were equally guilty with Germany and her allies and that the United States should refuse to become embroiled in the family quarrels of Europe. Randolph S. Bourne (1886-1918), a liberal intellectual, contributor to magazines and journals of opinion, represented the views of those Progressives who doubted the possibility of building a new society through the instrumentality of war. He, and they, recalled William James's influential essay "The Moral Equivalent of War." They recognized the principle that ends are means and that when ends and means diverge sharply in any program the chances of success are seriously compromised. Louis Filler's *Randolph Bourne* (Washington: American Council on Public Affairs, 1943) is our only full-length biography of Bourne. The student will find a collection of Bourne's essays in °Carl Resek, ed., *War and the Intellectuals: Essays by Randolph S. Bourne, 1915-1919* (New York: Harper and Row, 1964). A more extensive collection will be found in °Lillian Schlissel, ed., *The World of Randolph Bourne: An Anthology* (New York: E. P. Dutton and Co., 1965). °Jane Addams's *Peace and Bread in Time of War* (Boston: G. K. Hall and Co., 1960) can also be read with profit. A general account of opposition to the war is Gilbert C. Fite's and H. C. Peterson's *Opponents of War, 1917-18* (Madison: University of Wisconsin Press, 1957). In reading this selection note (1) the tone with which Bourne observed the intellectuals' confessed role in bringing on the war; (2) what clarification he asked for; (3) what irony he saw in the role of leadership of the intellectuals; (4) what he regarded as the real task of the intellectuals in the crisis; (5) what he meant by

Randolph Bourne, "The War and the Intellectuals," *The Seven Arts*, II (June 1917), pp. 133-46.

saying that the American intellectuals acted like colonials; (6) what he thought of the League idea; (7) his analysis of the intellectuals' thought processes in time of crises; and (8) what tasks he saw for the intellectuals who refused to support the war.

To those of us who still retain an irreconcil-able animus against war, it has been a bitter experience to see the unanimity with which the American intellectuals have thrown their support to the use of war-technique in the crisis in which America found herself. Socialists, college professors, publicists, new-republicans, practitioners of literature, have vied with each other in confirming with their intellectual faith the collapse of neutrality and the riveting of the war-mind on a hundred million more of the world's people. And the intellectuals are not content with confirming our belligerent gesture. They are now complacently asserting that it was they who effectively willed it, against the hesitation and dim perceptions of the American democratic masses. A war made deliberately by the intellectuals! A calm moral verdict, arrived at after a penetrating study of inexorable facts! Sluggish masses, too remote from the world-conflict to be stirred, too lacking in intellect to perceive their danger! An alert intellectual class, saving the people in spite of themselves, biding their time with Fabian strategy until the nation could be moved into war without serious resistance! An intellectual class, gently guiding a nation through sheer force of ideas into what the other nations entered only through predatory craft or popular hysteria or militarist madness! A war free from any taint of self-seeking, a war that will secure the triumph of democracy and internationalize the world! This is the picture which the more self-conscious intellectuals have formed of themselves, and which they are slowly impressing upon a population which is being led no man knows whither by an indubitably intellectualized President. And they are right, in that the war certainly did not spring from either the ideals or the prejudices, from the national ambitions or hysterias, of the American people, however acquiescent the masses prove to be, and however clearly the intellectuals prove their putative intuition.

Those intellectuals who have felt themselves totally out of

sympathy with this drag toward war will seek some explanation for this joyful leadership. They will want to understand this willingness of the American intellect to open the sluices and flood us with the sewage of the war spirit. We cannot forget the virtuous horror and stupefaction which filled our college professors when they read the famous manifesto of their ninety-three German colleagues in defense of their war. To the American academic mind of 1914 defense of war was inconceivable. From Bernhardi it recoiled as from a blasphemy, little dreaming that two years later would find it creating its own cleanly reasons for imposing military service on the country and for talking of the rough rude currents of health and regeneration that war would send through the American body politic. They would have thought any one mad who talked of shipping American men by the hundreds of thousands—conscripts—to die on the fields of France. Such a spiritual change seems catastrophic when we shoot our minds back to those days when neutrality was a proud thing. But the intellectual progress has been so gradual that the country retains little sense of the irony. The war sentiment, begun so gradually but so perseveringly by the preparedness advocates who came from the ranks of big business, caught hold of one after another of the intellectual groups. With the aid of Roosevelt, the murmurs became a monotonous chant, and finally a chorus so mighty that to be out of it was at first to be disreputable and finally almost obscene. And slowly a strident rant was worked up against Germany which compared very creditably with the German fulminations against the greedy power of England. The nerve of the war-feeling centered, of course, in the richer and older classes of the Atlantic seaboard, and was keenest where there were French or English business and particularly social connections. The sentiment then spread over the country as a class-phenomenon, touching everywhere those upper-class elements in each section who identified themselves with this Eastern ruling group. It must never be forgotten that in every community it was the least liberal and least democratic elements among whom the preparedness and later the war sentiment was found. The farmers were apathetic, the small business men and workingmen are still apathetic towards the war. The election was a vote of confidence of these latter classes in a President who would keep the faith of neutrality. The intellectuals, in other words, have identified themselves with the least democratic forces in American life. They have assumed the leadership for war of those very classes whom the American democracy has been immemorially fighting. Only in a world where irony was dead could an intellectual class enter war at the head of such illiberal cohorts in the avowed cause of world-liberalism and world-democracy. No one is left to point out the undemocratic nature of this war-liberalism. In a time of faith, skepticism is the most intolerable of all insults.

Our intellectual class might have been occupied, during the last two years of war, in studying and clarifying the ideals and aspirations of the American democracy, in discovering a true Americanism which would not have been merely nebulous but might have federated the different ethnic groups and traditions. They might have spent the time in endeavoring to clear the public mind of the cant of war, to get rid of old mystical notions that clog our thinking. We might have used the time for a great wave of education, for setting our house in spiritual order. We could at least have set the problem before ourselves. If our intellectuals were going to lead the administration, they might conceivably have tried to find some way of securing peace by making neutrality effective. They might have turned their intellectual energy not to the problem of jockeying the nation into war, but to the problem of using our vast neutral power to attain democratic ends for the rest of the world and ourselves without the use of the malevolent technique of war. They might have failed. The point is that they scarcely tried. The time was spent not in clarification and education, but in a mulling over of nebulous ideals of democracy and liberalism and civilization which had never meant anything fruitful to those ruling classes who now so glibly used them, and in giving free rein to the elementary instinct of self-defense. The whole era has been spiritually wasted. The outstanding feature has been not its Americanism but its intense colonialism. The offense of our intellectuals was not so much that they were colonial—for what could we expect of a nation composed of so many national elements?—but that it was so one-sidedly and partisanly colonial. The official, reputable expression of the intellectual class has been that of the English colonial. Certain portions of it have been even more loyalist than the King, more British even than Australia. Other colonial attitudes have been vulgar. The colonialism of the other American stocks was denied a hearing from the start. America might have been made a meeting-ground for the different national attitudes. An intellectual class, cultural colonists of the different European nations, might have threshed out the issues here as they could not be threshed out in Europe. Instead of this, the English colonials in university and press took command at the start, and we became an intellectual Hungary where thought was subject to an effective process of Magyarization. The reputable opinion of the American intellectuals became more and more either what could be read pleasantly in London, or what was written in an earnest effort to put Englishmen straight on their war-aims and war-technique. This Magyarization of thought produced as a counter-reaction a peculiarly offensive and inept German apologetic, and the two partisans divided the field between them. The great masses, the other ethnic groups, were inarticulate. American public opinion was almost as little prepared for war in 1917 as it was in 1914.

The sterile results of such an intellectual policy are inevitable. During the war the American intellectual class has produced almost nothing in the way of original and illuminating interpretation. Veblen's "Imperial Germany," Patten's "Culture and War," and addresses, Dewey's "German Philosophy and Politics," a chapter or two in Weyl's "American Foreign Policies"—is there much else of creative value in the intellectual repercussion of the war? It is true that the shock of war put the American intellectual to an unusual strain. He had to sit idle and think as spectator not as actor. There was no government to which he could docilely and loyally tender his mind as did the Oxford professors to justify England in her own eyes. The American's training was such as to make the fact of war almost incredible. Both in his reading of history and in his lack of economic perspective he was badly prepared for it. He had to explain to himself something which was too colossal for the modern mind, which outran any language or terms which we had to interpret it in. He had to expand his sympathies to the breaking-point, while pulling the past and present into some sort of interpretative order. The intellectuals in the fighting countries had only to rationalize and justify what their country was already doing. Their task was easy. A neutral, however, had really to search out the truth.

Perhaps perspective was too much to ask of any mind. Certainly the older colonials among our college professors let their prejudices at once dictate their thought. They have been comfortable ever since. The war has taught them nothing and will teach them nothing. And they have had the satisfaction, under the rigor of events, of seeing prejudice submerge the intellects of their younger colleagues. And they have lived to see almost their entire class, pacifists and democrats too, join them as apologists for the "gigantic irrelevance" of war.

We have had to watch, therefore, in this country the same process which so shocked us abroad,—the coalescence of the intellectual classes in support of the military programme. In this country, indeed, the socialist intellectuals did not even have the grace of their German brothers and wait for the declaration of war before they broke for cover. And when they declared for war they showed how thin was the intellectual veneer of their socialism. For they called us in terms that might have emanated from any bourgeois journal to defend democracy and civilization, just as if it was not exactly against those very bourgeois democracies and capitalist civilizations that socialists had been fighting for decades. But so subtle is the spiritual chemistry of the "inside" that all this intellectual cohesion—herd-instinct become herd-intellect—which seemed abroad so hysterical and so servile, comes to us here in highly rational terms. We go to war to save the world from subjugation! But the German intellectuals went to war to save their culture from barbarization! And the French went to war to save their beautiful France! And the English to save international honor! And Russia, most altruistic and self-sacrificing of all, to save a small State from destruction! Whence is our miraculous intuition of our moral spotlesssness? Whence our confidence that history will not unravel huge economic and imperialist forces upon which our rationalizations float like bubbles? The Jew often marvels that his race alone should have been chosen as the true people of the cosmic God. Are not our intellectuals equally fatuous when they tell us that our war of all wars is stainless and thrillingly achieving for good?

An intellectual class that was wholly rational would have called insistently for peace and not for war. For months the crying need has been for a negotiated peace, in order to avoid the ruin of a deadlock. Would not the same amount of resolute statesmanship thrown into intervention have secured a peace that would have been a subjugation for neither side? Was the terrific bargaining power of a great neutral ever really used? Our war followed, as all wars follow, a monstrous failure of diplomacy. Shamefacedness should now be our intellectuals' attitude, because the American play for peace was made so little more than a polite play. The intellectuals have still to explain why, willing as they now are to use force to continue the war to absolute exhaustion, they were not willing to use force to coerce the world to a speedy peace.

Their forward vision is no more convincing than their past rationality. We go to war now to internationalize the world! But surely their League to Enforce Peace is only a palpable apocalyptic myth, like the syndicalists' myth of the "general strike." It is not a rational programme so much as a glowing symbol for the purpose of focusing belief, of setting enthusiasm on fire for international order. As far as it does this it has pragmatic value, but as far as it provides a certain radiant mirage of idealism for this war and for a world-order founded on mutual fear, it is dangerous and obnoxious. Idealism should be kept for what is ideal. It is depressing to think that the prospect of a world so strong that none dare challenge it should be the immediate ideal of the American intellectual. If the League is only a makeshift, a coalition into which we enter to restore order, then it is only a description of existing fact, and the idea should be treated as such. But if it is an actually prospective outcome of the settlement, the keystone of American policy, it is neither realizable nor desirable. For the programme of such a League contains no provision for dynamic national growth or for international economic justice. In a world which requires recognition of economic internationalism far more than of political internationalism, an idea is reactionary which proposes to petrify and federate the nations as political and economic units. Such a scheme for international order is a dubious justification for American policy. And if American policy had been sincere in its belief that our participation would achieve international beatitude, would we not have made our entrance into the war conditional upon a solemn general agreement to respect in the final settlement these principles of international order? Could we have afforded, if our war was to end war by the establishment of a league of honor, to risk the defeat of our vision and our betrayal in the settlement? Yet we are in the war, and no such solemn agreement was made, nor has it even been suggested.

The case of the intellectuals seems, therefore, only very speciously rational. They could have used their energy to force a just peace or at least to devise other means than war for carrying through American policy. They could have used their intellectual energy to ensure that our participation in the war meant the international order which they wish. Intellect was not so used. It was used to lead an apathetic nation into an irresponsible war, without guarantees from those belligerents whose cause we were saving. The American intellectual, therefore, has been rational neither in his hindsight nor his foresight. To explain him we must look beneath the intellectual reasons to the emotional disposition. It is not so much what they thought as how they felt that explains our intellectual class. Allowing for colonial sympathy, there was still the personal shock in a world-war which outraged all our preconceived notions of the way the world was tending. It reduced to rubbish most of the humanitarian internationalism and democratic nationalism which had been the emotional thread of our intellectuals' life. We had suddenly to make a new orientation. There were mental conflicts. Our latent colonialism strove with our longing for American unity. Our desire for peace strove with our desire for national responsibility in the world. That first lofty and remote and not altogether unsound feeling of our spiritual isolation from the conflict could not last. There was the itch to be in the great experience which the rest of the world was having. Numbers of intelligent people who had never been stirred by the horrors of capitalistic peace at home were shaken out of their slumber by the horrors of war in Belgium. Never having felt responsibility for labor wars and oppressed masses and excluded races at home, they had a large fund of idle emotional capital to invest in the oppressed nationalities and ravaged villages of Europe. Hearts that had felt only ugly contempt for democratic strivings at home beat in tune with the struggle for freedom abroad. All this was natural, but it tended to over-emphasize our responsibility. And it threw our thinking out of gear. The task of making our own country detailedly fit for peace was abandoned in favor of a feverish concern for the management of the war, advice to the fighting governments on all matters, military, social and political, and a gradual working up of the conviction that we were ordained as a nation to lead all erring brothers towards the light of liberty and democracy. The failure of the American intellectual class to erect a creative attitude toward the war can be explained by these sterile mental conflicts which the shock to our ideals sent raging through us.

Mental conflicts end either in a new and higher synthesis or adjustment, or else in a reversion to more primitive ideas which have been outgrown but to which we drop when jolted out of our attained position. The war caused in America a recrudescence of nebulous ideals which a younger generation was fast outgrowing because it had passed the wistful stage and was discovering concrete ways of getting them incarnated in actual institutions. The shock of the war threw us back from this pragmatic work into an emotional bath of these old ideals. There was even a somewhat rarefied revival of our primitive Yankee boastfulness, the reversion of senility to that republican childhood when we expected the whole world to copy our republican institutions. We amusingly ignored the fact that it was just that Imperial German régime, to whom we are to teach the art of self-government, which our own Federal structure, with its executive irresponsible in foreign policy and with its absence of parliamentary control, most resembles. And we are missing the exquisite irony of the unaffected homage paid by the American democratic intellectuals to the last and most detested of Britain's tory premiers as the representative of a "liberal" ally, as well as the irony of the selection of the best hated of America's bourbon "old guard" as the missionary of American democracy to Russia.

The intellectual state that could produce such things is one where reversion has taken place to more primitive ways of thinking. Simple syllogisms are substituted for analysis, things are known by their labels, our heart's desire dictates what we shall see. The American intellectual class, having failed to make the higher syntheses, regresses to ideas that can issue in quick, simplified action. Thought becomes any easy rationalization of what is actually going on or what is to happen inevitably tomorrow. It is true that certain groups did rationalize their colonialism and attach the doctrine of the inviolability of British sea-power to the doctrine of a League of Peace. But this agile resolution of the mental conflict did not become a higher synthesis, to be creatively developed. It gradually merged into a justification for our going to war. It petrified into a dogma to be propagated. Criticism flagged and emotional propaganda began. Most of the socialists, the college professors and the practitioners of literature, however, have not even reached this high-water mark of synthesis. Their mental conflicts have been resolved much more simply. War in the interests of democracy! This was almost the sum of their philosophy. The primitive idea to which they regerssed became almost insensibly translated into a craving for action. War was seen as the crowning relief of their indecision. At last action, irresponsibility, the end of anxious and torturing attempts to reconcile peace-ideals with the drag of the world towards Hell. An end to the pain of trying to adjust the facts to what they ought to be! Let us consecrate the facts as ideal! Let us join the greased slide towards war! The momentum increased. Hesitations, ironies, consciences, considerations—all were drowned in the elemental blare of doing something aggressive, colossal. The new-found Sabbath "peacefulness of being at war"! The thankfulness with which so many intellectuals lay down and floated with the current betrays the hesitation and suspense through which they had been. The American university is a brisk and happy place these days. Simple, unquestioning action has superseded the knots of thought. The thinker dances with reality.

With how many of the acceptors of war has it been mostly a dread of intellectual suspense? It is a mistake to suppose that intellectuality necessarily makes for suspended judgments. The intellect craves certitude. It takes effort to keep it supple and pliable. In a time of danger and disaster we jump desperately for some dogma to cling to. The time comes, if we try to hold out, when our nerves are sick with fatigue, and we seize in a great healing wave of release some doctrine that can be immediately translated into action. Neutrality meant suspense, and so it became the object of loathing to frayed nerves. The vital myth of the League of Peace provides a dogma to jump to. With war the world becomes motor again and speculation is brushed aside like cobwebs. The blessed emotion of self-defense intervenes too, which focused millions in Europe. A few keep up a critical pose after war is begun, but since they usually advise action which is in one-to-one correspondence with what the mass is already doing, their criticism is little more than a rationalization of the common emotional drive.

The results of war on the intellectual class are already apparent. Their thought becomes little more than a description and justification of what is going on. They turn upon any rash one who continues idly to speculate. Once the war is on, the conviction spreads that individual thought is helpless, that the only way one can count is as a cog in the great wheel. There is no good holding back. We are told to dry our unnoticed and ineffective tears and plunge into the great work. Not only is every one forced into line, but the new certitude becomes idealized. It is a noble realism which opposes itself to futile obstruction and the cowardly refusal to face facts. This realistic boast is so loud and sonorous that one wonders whether realism is always a stern and intelligent grappling with realities. May it not be sometimes a mere surrender to the actual, an abdication of the ideal through a sheer fatigue from intellectual suspense? The pacifist is roundly scolded for refusing to face the facts, and for retiring into his own world of sentimental desire. But is the realist, who refuses to challenge or criticize facts, entitled to any more credit than that which comes from following the line of least resistance? The realist thinks he at least can control events by linking himself to the forces that are moving. Perhaps he can. But if it is a question of controlling war, it is difficult to see how the child on the back of a mad elephant is to be any more effective in stopping the beast than is the child who tries to stop him from the ground. The ex-humanitarian, turned realist, sneers at the snobbish neutrality, colossal conceit, crooked thinking, dazed sensibilities, of those who are still unable to find any balm of consolation for this war. We manufacture consolations here in America while there are probably not a dozen men fighting in Europe who did not long ago give up every reason for their being there except that nobody knew how to get them away.

But the intellectuals whom the crisis has crystallized into an acceptance of war have put themselves into a terrifyingly strategic position. It is only on the craft, in the stream, they say, that one has any chance of controlling the current forces for liberal purposes. If we obstruct, we surrender all power for influence. If we responsibly approve, we then retain our power for guiding.

We will be listened to as responsible thinkers, while those who obstructed the coming of war have committed intellectual suicide and shall be cast into outer darkness. Criticism by the ruling powers will only be accepted from those intellectuals who are in sympathy with the general tendency of the war. Well, it is true that they may guide, but if their stream leads to disaster and the frustration of national life, is their guiding any more than a preference whether they shall go over the right-hand or the left-hand side of the precipice? Meanwhile, however, there is comfort on board. Be with us, they call, or be negligible, irrelevant. Dissenters are already excommunicated. Irreconcilable radicals, wringing their hands among the débris, become the most despicable and impotent of men. There seems no choice for the intellectual but to join the mass of acceptance. But again the terrible dilemma arises—either support what is going on, in which case you count for nothing because you are swallowed in the mass and great incalculable forces bear you on; or remain aloof, passively resistant, in which case you count for nothing because you are outside the machinery of reality.

Is there no place left, then, for the intellectual who cannot yet crystallize, who does not dread suspense, and is not yet drugged with fatigue? The American intellectuals, in their preoccupation with reality, seem to have forgotten that the real enemy is War rather than imperial Germany. There is work to be done to prevent this war of ours from passing into popular mythology as a holy crusade. What shall we do with leaders who tell us that we go to war in moral spotlessness, or who make "democracy" synonymous with a republican form of government? There is work to be done in still shouting that all the revolutionary by-products will not justify the war, or make war anything else than the most noxious complex of all the evils that afflict men. There must be some to find no consolation whatever, and some to sneer at those who buy the cheap emotion of sacrifice. There must be some irreconcilables left who will not even accept the war with walrus tears. There must be some to call unceasingly for peace, and some to insist that the terms of settlement shall be not only liberal but democratic. There must be some intellectuals who are not willing to use the old discredited counters again and to support a peace which would leave all the old inflammable materials of armament lying about the world. There must still be opposition to any contemplated "liberal" world-order founded on military coalitions. The "irreconcilable" need not be disloyal. He need not even be "impossibilist." His apathy towards war should take the form of a heightened energy and enthusiasm for the education, the art, the interpretation that make for life in the midst of the world of death. The intellectual who retains his animus against war will push out more boldly than ever to make his case solid aginst it. The old ideals crumble; new ideals must be forged. His mind will continue to roam widely and ceaselessly. The thing he will fear most is premature crystallization. If the American intellectual class rivets itself to a "liberal" philosophy that perpetuates the old errors, there will then be need for "democrats" whose task will be to divide, confuse, disturb, keep the intellectual waters constantly in motion to prevent any such ice from ever forming.

12

Freedom of Speech in Time of War
Justice Oliver Wendell Holmes's Opinions in
Schenck v. United States and Abrams v. United States

Oliver Wendell Holmes (1841-1935) enjoyed a long and varied life. He fought in the American Civil War, practiced law, taught at Harvard, and capped his legal career by serving for 30 years (1902-1932) as an Associate Justice of the United States Supreme Court. As a friend of Charles Peirce and William James he early became acquainted with the new philosophy of pragmatism, to which he seemed to have a natural affinity. Espousing the cause of legal realism, Holmes argued that the law was made for man and not man for the law. Law and legal institutions were made by men for men; they were products of society and must shift to suit changing social objectives. Experience was the best teacher. During World War I the Wilson administration in its zeal regimented the American people to an unprecedented degree. In the process, civil liberties became an early casualty of the crusade to save the world for democracy. Among the cases in which the defendants claimed the protection of the First Amendment these two have justly become famous. Holmes wrote the opinion for the court in the first, and prepared a dissent from the majority in the second. In his opinions Holmes advanced a new principle which in general subsequent courts have followed. Mark De Wolfe Howe's *Justice Oliver Wendell Holmes* (Cambridge: Harvard University Press, 1957) is one of many biographies of the colorful Justice. Harry N. Scheiber in *The Wilson Administration and Civil Liberties: 1917-1921* (Ithaca: Cornell University Press, 1957) gives a thorough treatment of this complex subject. Zechariah Chaffee's *Free Speech in the United States* (Cambridge: Harvard University Press, 1941) is an older study which sets the problem in a larger framework than Scheiber's book. In reading Holmes's opinions note (1) whether or not he thought the evidence sufficient to connect the defendants with the mailing of circulars aimed at obstructing the draft; (2) under what circumstances Holmes thought restricting the freedom of speech was justified; (3) in

Schenck *v.* United States, 249 U.S., 47, 1919, October term 1918.
Abrams *v.* United States. 250 U.S. 616, 1919, October, term, 1919.

the Abrams opinion upon what grounds the indictment was found; (4) why he thought the leaflets innocuous; (5) what observations he made concerning the principle of free speech; (6) what he thought of the contents of the leaflets and their authors; and (7) his philosophical justification of his belief in freedom of speech.

Schenck v. United States.
Baer v. United States.

ERROR TO THE DISTRICT COURT OF THE UNITED STATES FOR
THE EASTERN DISTRICT OF PENNSYLVANIA.

Nos. 437, 438. Argued January 9, 10, 1919.—Decided March 3, 1919.

THE case is stated in the opinion. . . .

MR. JUSTICE HOLMES delivered the opinion of the court.

This is an indictment in three counts. The first charges a conspiracy to violate the Espionage Act of June 15, 1917, c. 30, § 3, 40 Stat. 217, 219, by causing and attempting to cause insubordination, &c., in the military and naval forces of the United States, and to obstruct the recruiting and enlistment service of the United States, when the United States was at war with the German Empire, to-wit, that the defendants wilfully conspired to have printed and circulated to men who had been called and accepted for military service under the Act of May 18, 1917, a document set forth and alleged to be calculated to cause such insubordination and obstruction. The count alleges overt acts in pursuance of the conspiracy, ending in the distribution of the document set forth. The second count alleges a conspiracy to commit an offence against the United States, to-wit, to use the mails for the transmission of matter declared to be non-mailable by Title XII, § 2 of the Act of June 15, 1917, to-wit, the above mentioned document, with an averment of the same overt acts. The third count charges an unlawful use of the mails for the transmission of the same matter and otherwise as above. The defendants were found guilty on all the counts. They set up the First Amendment to the Constitution forbidding Congress to make any law abridging the freedom of speech, or of the press, and bringing the case here on that ground have argued some other points also of which we must dispose.

It is argued that the evidence, if admissible, was not sufficient to prove that the defendant Schenck was concerned in sending the documents. According to the testimony Schenck said he was general secretary of the Socialist party and had charge of the Socialist headquarters from which the documents were sent. He identified a book found there as the minutes of the Executive Committee of the party. The book showed a resolution of August 13, 1917, that 15,000 leaflets should be printed on the other side of one of them in use, to be mailed to men who had passed exemption boards, and for distribution. Schenck personally attended to the printing. On August 20 the general secretary's report said "Obtained new leaflets from printer and started work addressing envelopes" &c.; and there was a resolve that Comrade Schenck be allowed $125 for sending leaflets through the mail. He said that he had about fifteen or sixteen thousand printed. There were files of the circular in question in the inner office which he said were printed on the other side of the one sided circular and were there for distribution. Other copies were proved to have been sent through the mails to drafted men. Without going into confirmatory details that were proved, no reasonable man could doubt that the defendant Schenck was largely instrumental in sending the circulars about. As to the defendant Baer there was evidence that she was a member of the Executive Board and that the minutes of its transactions were hers. The argument as to the sufficiency of the evidence that the defendants conspired to send the documents only impairs the seriousness of the real defence.

It is objected that the documentary evidence was not admissible because obtained upon a search warrant, valid so far as appears. The contrary is established. *Adams* v. *New York,* 192 U. S. 585; *Weeks* v. *United States,* 232 U. S. 383, 395, 396. The search warrant did not issue against the defendant but against the Socialist headquarters at 1326 Arch Street and it would seem that the documents technically were not even in the defendants' possession. See *Johnson* v. *United States,* 228 U. S. 457. Notwithstanding some protest in argument the notion that evidence even directly proceeding from the defendant in a criminal proceeding is excluded in all cases by the Fifth Amendment is plainly unsound. *Holt* v. *United States,* 218 U. S. 245, 252, 253.

The document in question upon its first printed side recited the first section of the Thirteenth Amendment, said that the idea embodied in it was violated by the Conscription Act and that a conscript is little better than a convict. In impassioned language it intimated that conscription was despotism in its worst form and a monstrous wrong against humanity in the interest of Wall Street's chosen few. It said "Do not submit to intimidation," but in form at least confined itself to peaceful measures such as a petition for the repeal of the act. The other and later printed side of the sheet was headed "Assert Your Rights." It stated reasons for alleging that any one violated the Constitution when he refused to recognize "your right to assert your opposition to the draft," and went on "If you do not assert and support your rights, you are helping to deny or disparage rights which it is the solemn duty of all citizens and residents of the United States to retain." It described the arguments on the other side as coming from cunning politicians and a mercenary capitalist press, and even silent consent to the conscription law as helping to support an infamous conspiracy. It denied the power to send our citizens away to foreign shores to shoot up the people of other lands, and added that words could not express the condemnation such cold-blooded ruthlessness deserves, &c., &c., winding up "You must do your share to maintain, support and uphold the rights of the people of this country." Of course the document would not have been sent unless it had been intended to have some effect, and we do not see what effect it could be expected to have upon persons subject to the draft except to influence them to obstruct the carrying of it out. The defendants do not deny that the jury might find against them on this point.

But it is said, suppose that that was the tendency of this circular, it is protected by the First Amendment to the Constitution. Two of the strongest expressions are said to be quoted respectively from well-known public men. It well may be that the prohibition of laws abridging the freedom of speech is not confined to previous restraints, although to prevent them may have been the main purpose, as intimated in *Patterson* v. *Colorado,* 205 U. S. 454, 462. We admit that in many places and in ordinary times the defendants in saying all that was said in the circular would have been within their constiutional rights. But the character of every act depends upon the circumstances in which it is done. *Aikens* v. *Wisconsin,* 195 U. S. 194, 205, 206. The most stringent protection of free speech would not protect a man in falsely shouting fire in a theatre and causing a panic. It does not even protect a man from an injunction against uttering words that may have all the effect of force. *Gompers* v. *Bucks Stove & Range Co.,* 221 U. S. 418, 439. The question in every case is whether the words used are used in such circumstances and are of such a nature as to create a clear and present danger that they will bring about the substantive evils that Congress has a right to prevent. It is a question of proximity and degree. When a nation is at war many things that might be said in time of peace are such a hindrance to its effort that their utterance will not be endured so long as men fight and that no Court could regard them as protected by any constitutional right. It seems to be admitted that if an actual obstruction of the recruiting service were proved, liability for words that produced that effect might be enforced. The statute of 1917 in § 4 punishes conspiracies to obstruct as well as actual obstruction. If the act (speaking, or circulating a paper) its tendency and the intent with which it is done are the same, we perceive no ground for saying that success alone warrants making the act a crime. *Goldman* v. *United States,* 245 U. S. 474, 477. Indeed that case might be said to dispose of the preesnt contention if the precedent covers all *media concludendi.* But as the right to free speech was not referred to specially, we have thought fit to add a few words.

It was not argued that a conspiracy to obstruct the draft was not within the words of the Act of 1917. The words are "obstruct the recruiting or enlistment service," and it might be suggested that they refer only to making it hard to get volunteers. Recruiting heretofore usually having been accomplished by getting volunteers the word is apt to call up that method only in our minds. But recruiting is gaining fresh supplies for the forces, as well by draft as otherwise. It is put as an alternative to enlistment or voluntary enrollment in this act. The fact that the Act of 1917 was enlarged by the amending Act of May 16, 1918, c. 75, 40 Stat. 553, of course, does not affect the present indictment and would not, even if the former act had been repealed. Rev. Stats., § 13.

Judgments affirmed.

Abrams v. United States*

MR. JUSTICE HOLMES dissenting.

This indictment is founded wholly upon the publication of two leaflets which I shall describe in a moment. The first count charges a conspiracy pending the war with Germany to publish abusive language about the form of government of the United States, laying the preparation and publishing of the first leaflet as overt acts. The second count charges a conspiracy pending the war to publish language intended to bring the form of government into contempt, laying the preparation and publishing of the two leaflets as overt acts. The third count alleges a conspiracy to encourage resistance to the United States in the same war and to attempt to effectuate the purpose by publishing the same leaflets. The fourth count lays a conspiracy to incite curtailment of production of things necessary to the prosecution of the war and to attempt to accomplish it by publishing the second leaflet to which I have referred.

The first of these leaflets says that the President's cowardly silence about the intervention in Russia reveals the hypocrisy of the plutocratic gang in Washington. It intimates that "German militarism combined with allied capitalism to crush the Russian revolution"—goes on that the tyrants of the world fight each other until they see a common enemy—working class enlightenment, when they combine to crush it; and that now militarism and capitalism combined, though not openly, to crush the Russian revolution. It says that there is only one enemy of the workers of the world and that is capitalism; that it is a crime for workers of America, &c., to fight the workers' republic of Russia, and ends "Awake! Awake, you Workers of the World! Revolutionists." A note adds "It is absurd to call us pro-German. We hate and despise German militarism more than do you hypocritical tyrants. We have more reasons for denouncing German militarism than has the coward of the White House."

The other leaflet, headed "Workers—Wake Up," with abusive language says that America together with the Allies will march

---

*Editor's Note: The Supreme Court sustained the District Court's verdict holding the defendants guilty of violating statutes making it an offense to interfere with the war effort.

for Russia to help the Czecko-Slovaks in their struggle against the Bolsheviki, and that this time the hypocrites shall not fool the Russian emigrants and friends of Russia in America. It tells the Russian emigrants that they now must spit in the face of the false military propaganda by which their sympathy and help to the prosecution of the war have been called forth and says that with the money they have lent or are going to lend "they will make bullets not only for the Germans but also for the Workers Soviets of Russia," and further, "Workers in the ammunition factories, you are producing bullets, bayonets, cannon, to murder not only the Germans, but also your dearest, best, who are in Russia and are fighting for freedom." It then appeals to the same Russian emigrants at some length not to consent to the "inquisitionary expedition to Russia," and says that the destruction of the Russian revolution is "the politics of the march to Russia." The leaflet winds up by saying "Workers, our reply to this barbaric intervention has to be a general strike!" and after a few words on the spirit of revolution, exhortations not to be afraid, and some usual tall talk ends "Woe unto those who will be in the way of progress. Let solidarity live! The Rebels."

No argument seems to me necessary to show that these pronunciamentos in no way attack the form of government of the United States, or that they do not support either of the first two counts. What little I have to say about the third count may be postponed until I have considered the fourth. With regard to that it seems too plain to be denied that the suggestion to workers in the ammunition factories that they are producing bullets to murder their dearest, and the further advocacy of a general strike, both in the second leaflet, do urge curtailment of production of things necessary to the prosecution of the war within the meaning of the Act of May 16, 1918, c. 75, 40 Stat. 553, amending § 3 of the earlier Act of 1917. But to make the conduct criminal that statute requires that it should be "with intent by such curtailment to cripple or hinder the United States in the prosecution of the war." It seems to me that no such intent is proved.

I am aware of course that the word intent as vaguely used in ordinary legal discussion means no more than knowledge at the time of the act that the consequences said to be intended will ensue. Even less than that will satisfy the general principle of civil and criminal liability. A man may have to pay damages, may be sent to prison, at common law might be hanged, if at the time of his act he knew facts from which common experience showed that the consequences would follow, whether he individually could foresee them or not. But, when words are used exactly, a deed is not done with intent to produce a consequence unless that consequence is the aim of the deed. It may be obvious, and obvious to the actor, that the consequence will follow, and he may be liable for it even if he regrets it, but he does not do the act with intent to produce it unless the aim to produce it is the proximate motive of the specific act, although there may be some deeper motive behind.

It seems to me that this statute must be taken to use its words in a strict and accurate sense. They would be absurd in any other. A patriot might think that we were wasting money on aeroplanes, or making more cannon of a certain kind than we needed, and might advocate curtailment with success, yet even if it turned out that the curtailment hindered and was thought by other minds to have been obviously likely to hinder the United States in the prosecution of the war, no one would hold such conduct a crime. I admit that my illustration does not answer all that might be said but it is enough to show what I think and to let me pass to a more important aspect of the case. I refer to the First Amendment to the Constitution that Congress shall make no law abridging the freedom of speech.

I never have seen any reason to doubt that the questions of law that alone were before this Court in the cases of *Schenck*, *Frohwerk* and *Debs*, 249 U. S. 47, 204, 211, were rightly decided. I do not doubt for a moment that by the same reasoning that would justify punishing persuasion to murder, the United States constitutionally may punish speech that produces or is intended to produce a clear and imminent danger that it will bring about forthwith certain substantive evils that the United States constitutionally may seek to prevent. The power undoubtedly is greater in time of war than in time of peace because war opens dangers that do not exist at other times.

But as against dangers peculiar to war, as against others, the principle of the right to free speech is always the same. It is only the present danger of immediate evil or an intent to bring it about that warrants Congress in setting a limit to the expression of opinion where private rights are not concerned. Congress certainly cannot forbid all effort to change the mind of the country. Now nobody can suppose that the surreptitious publishing of a silly leaflet by an unknown man, without more, would present any immediate danger that its opinions would hinder the success of the government arms or have any appreciable tendency to do so. Publishing those opinions for the very purpose of obstructing however, might indicate a greater danger and at any rate would have the quality of an attempt. So I assume that the second leaflet if published for the purposes alleged in the fourth count might be punishable. But it seems pretty clear to me that nothing less than that would bring these papers within the scope of this law. An actual intent in the sense that I have explained is necessary to constitute an attempt, where a further act of the same individual is required to complete the substantive crime, for reasons given in *Swift & Co.* v. *United States,* 196 U. S. 375, 396. It is necessary where the success of the attempt depends upon others because if that intent is not present the actor's aim may be accomplished without bringing about the evils sought to be checked. An intent to prevent interference with the revolution in Russia might have been satisfied without any hindrance to carrying on the war in which we were engaged.

I do not see how anyone can find the intent required by the statute in any of the defendants' words. The second leaflet is the only one that affords even a foundation for the charge, and there, without invoking the hatred of German militarism expressed in the former one, it is evident from the beginning to the end that the only object of the paper is to help Russia and stop American intervention there against the popular government—not to impede the United States in the war that it was carrying on. To say that two phrases taken literally might import a suggestion of conduct that would have interference with the war as an indirect and probably undesired effect seems to me by no means enough to show an attempt to produce that effect.

I return for a moment to the third count. That charges an intent to provoke resistance to the United States in its war with Germany. Taking the clause in the statute that deals with that in connection with the other elaborate provisions of the act, I think that resistance to the United States means some forcible act of opposition to some proceeding of the United States in pursuance of the war. I think the intent must be the specific intent that I have described and for the reasons that I have given I think that no such intent was proved or existed in fact. I also think that there is no hint at resistance to the United States as I construe the phrase.

In this case sentences of twenty years imprisonment have been imposed for the publishing of two leaflets that I believe the defendants had as much right to publish as the Government has to publish the Constitution of the United States now vainly invoked by them. Even if I am technically wrong and enough can be squeezed from these poor and puny anonymities to turn the color of legal litmus paper; I will add, even if what I think the necessary intent were shown; the most nominal punishment seems to me all that possibly could be inflicted, unless the defendants are to be made to suffer not for what the indictment alleges but for the creed that they avow—a creed that I believe to be the creed of ignorance and immaturity when honestly held, as I see no reason to doubt that it was held here, but which, although made the subject of examination at the trial, no one has a right even to consider in dealing with the charges before the Court.

Persecution for the expression of opinions seems to me perfectly logical. If you have no doubt of your premises or your power and want a certain result with all your heart you naturally express your wishes in law and sweep away all opposition. To allow opposition by speech seems to indicate that you think the speech impotent, as when a man says that he has squared the circle, or that you do not care whole-heartedly for the result, or that you doubt either your power or your premises. But when men have realized that time has upset many fighting faiths, they may come to believe even more than they believe the very foundations of their own conduct that the ultimate good desired is better reached by free trade in ideas—that the best test of truth is the power of the thought to get itself accepted in the competition of the market, and that truth is the only ground upon which their wishes safely can be carried out. That at any rate is the theory of our Constitution. It is an experiment, as all life is an experiment. Every year if not every day we have to wager our salvation upon some prophecy based upon imperfect knowledge. While that experiment is part of our system I think that we should be eternally vigilant against attempts to check the expression of opinions that we loathe and believe to be fraught with death, unless they so imminently threaten immediate interference with the lawful and pressing purposes of the law that an immediate check is required to save the country. I wholly disagree with the argument of the Government that the First Amendment left the common law as to seditious libel in force. History seems to me against the notion. I had conceived that the United States through many years had shown its repentance for the Sedition Act of 1798, by repaying fines that it imposed. Only the emergency that makes it immediately dangerous to leave the correction of evil counsels to time warrants making any exception to the sweeping command, "Congress shall make no law . . . abridging the freedom of speech." Of course I am speaking only of expressions of opinion and exhortations, which were all that were uttered here, but I regret that I cannot put into more impressive words my belief that in their conviction upon this indictment the defendants were deprived of their rights under the Constitution of the United States.

MR. JUSTICE BRANDEIS concurs with the foregoing opinion.

13

An Irreconcilable Opposes the League of Nations
Senator William E. Borah's Address to the Senate, February 21, 1919

William E. Borah (1865-1940), a Progressive Republican Senator from Idaho (1903-1940), was one of those in the forefront of the campaign to prevent the United States from joining the League of Nations. Less than one month after the Paris Peace Conference voted to make the Covenant of the League of Nations an integral part of the treaty settlement and five months before the covenant was sent to the United States Senate for action, Borah made his first major speech against the League. Borah, as one of the leading isolationists, brought his unusual oratorical talents into the fight against President Wilson, who led the forces favoring America's adherence to the League. The Senator from Idaho was partly motivated by politics in opposing the President, but he was also a sincere and devoted nationalist. The standard biography of him is Claudius O. Johnson, *Borah of Idaho* (New York: Longman's Green and Company, 1936). Marian Cecilia McKenna's *Borah* (Ann Arbor: University of Michigan Press, 1961) is the most recent study of him. Alexander De Conde has edited a survey of isolationism entitled *Isolation and Security; Ideas and Interests in 20th Century American Foreign Policy* (Durham: Duke University Press, 1957) that may be considered with profit. Thomas A. Bailey's *Wilson and the Peacemakers* . . . (New York: The Macmillan Company, 1947) tells the story of the President's vain crusade for the treaty and the League. In reading this selection note (1) whom Borah wanted to pass judgment on the League; (2) on what argument he based this proposal; (3) what historical events and traditions he used to support his position; (4) his interpretation of the Monroe Doctrine; (5) the implications for America that Borah drew from the League Covenant; (6) what in particular he disliked about Article X of the Covenant; (7) what Borah objected to in the voting provisions of the League; (8) what implications for nationalism he saw in the League; and (9) the quality and content of his peroration.

Senator William E. Borah, Address, February 21, 1919, *Congressional Record*, 65 Cong., 3 sess., vol. 57, pt. 5, pp. 3910-15.

Mr. borah. mr. president, the people of the
United States have the undoubted right to change
their form of government and to renounce established customs or
long-standing policies whenever in their wisdom they see fit to
do so. As a believer in democratic government, I readily acknowledge the right of the people to make in an orderly fashion
such changes as may be approved by their judgment at any time.
I contend, moreover, that when radical and important departures
from established national policies are proposed, the people ought
to be consulted.

We are now proposing what to my mind is the most radical
departure from our policies hitherto obtaining that has ever
been proposed at any time since our Government was established. I think the advocates of the league will agree with me
that it is a pronounced departure from all the policies which we
have heretofore obtained.

It may be wise, as they contend; nevertheless, it involves a
different course of conduct upon the part of the Government and
of our people for the future, and the people are entitled to pass
judgment upon the advisability of such a course.

It seems clear, also, that this proposed program, if it is to be
made effective and operative under the proposed constitution
of the league, involves a change in our Constitution. Certainly,
questions of that kind ought to be submitted to a plebiscite or to
a vote of the people, and the Constitution amended in the manner provided for amending that instrument. We are merely
agents of the people; and it will not be contended that we have
received any authority from the principal, the people, to proceed
along this line. It is a greater responsibility than an agent ought
to assume without express authority or approval from his principal to say nothing of the want of authority. Preliminary to a
discussion of this question, therefore, I want to declare my belief
that we should arrange the machinery for taking a vote of the
people of the United States upon this stupendous program. I am
aware that the processes by which that may be accomplished
involve some difficulties; but they are not insurmountable, and
they are by no means to be compared in their difficulty with the
importance of being right and in harmony with the judgment of
the people before we proceed to a final approval. We should

have the specific indorsement of those whose agents we are, and we should have the changes in our Constitution that we may have sanction under the Constitution for the fearful responsibility we propose to assume. If we can effectuate this change now proposed without direct authority from the people I can not think of a question of sufficient moment to call for their indorsement.

It must be conceded that this program can never be a success unless there is behind it the intelligent and sustained public opinion of the United States. If the voters do not have their voice before the program is initiated, they will certainly have an opportunity to give expression to their views in the future. They are still the source of power, and through their votes they effectuate the policies under which we must live. From the standpoint, therefore, of expediency and from the standpoint of fairness to those who are most concerned, to wit, the people, those who must carry the burdens, if there be burdens, and suffer the consequences, if there should be ill consequences to suffer, as well as from the standpoint of insuring success, if possible, the mass of the people ought to be consulted and their approval had before we proceed. I, therefore, in the very beginning of this procedure, declare in favor of that program.

Mr. President, I think I should have deferred any remarks I had to make upon this subject until a later day had it not been for an interview which was put out by Mr. [William Howard] Taft some two or three days ago upon this question. I felt, in view of that statement, that those who were opposed to the program were justified in proceeding at once to the debate, because it is a statement which in my judgment is not founded upon fact. In saying that I do not charge a conscious purpose upon the part of Mr. Taft to mislead, but I am sure it can not be sustained by the historic facts at the command of anyone who desires to examine the subject; and as it can not be sustained, it is to the utmost degree misleading.

Mr. Taft informs the American people, from the pedestal of an ex-President, that this program does not destroy the policy announced by Washington in his Farewell Address and does not renounce the doctrine known as the Monroe doctrine—two fundamental principles underlying our foreign policy for more than 100 years in one instance and nearly 100 years in the other; two policies to which the American people have long been committed, and which, in my judgment, they still believe to be indispensable to their happiness and future tranquillity. If, indeed, this program does dispose of these policies, it presents an entirely different question to the American people than if the reverse were true. This is one of the first things to be settled in this controversy. It meets us at the very threshold of all discussion and all consideration. It is of such moment as to call for clear statement and candid presentation. What is the effect of this proposed program upon these ancient and most vital policies?

Mr. Taft says:

Article 10 covers the Monroe doctrine and extends it to the world. . . . The league is to be regarded as in conflict with the advice of Washington only with a narrow and reactionary viewpoint.

"Reactionary" is not a familiar term in the ex-President's vocabulary. I think he has unintentionally misused it.

Mr. President, prior to the administration of Washington, America had been involved in every European war since colonization began. When a difficulty arose in Europe, whatever might be the subject of the difficulty, whether dynastic quarrels or territorial aggrandizement, it spread at once to the American Continent. Although we might be wholly unconcerned in the controversy upon its merits, nevertheless the evil effects of the conflict in Europe enveloped the people of this country in its consequences. As you recall, Macaulay, in his graphic way in the essay upon Frederick the Great, said:

In order that he might rob a neighbor whom he had promised to defend, black men fought on the coast of Coromandel and red men scalped each other by the Great Lakes of North America.

When Washington assumed the responsibilties as administrator of this Government, he immediately set about to change that condition of affairs; to wit, to separate the European system from the American system, to withdraw our people from her broils, to individualize the American Nation, and to divorce us from the quarrels and turmoils of European life. This was peculiarly and distinctly a policy originating with the Father of our Country. If there is any one thing in his entire career, marvelous as it was, which can be said to be distinctly his, it is the foreign policy which characterized his administration. His idea almost alone in the first instance was that we never could become a nation with a national mind, a national purpose, and national ideals until we divorce ourselves from the European system. He entertained this view before he became President. I venture to recall to your minds a letter which he wrote, prior to the Presidency, to Sir Edward Newenham, in which he says:

I hope the United States of America will be able to keep disengaged from the labyrinth of European politics and wars. . . . It should be the policy of the United States to administer to their wants without being engaged in their quarrels.

In 1791 he addressed a letter to Mr. Morris, in which he said:

I trust we shall never so far lose sight of our own interest and happiness as to become unnecessarily a party to these political disputes. Our local situation enables us to maintain that state with respect to them which otherwise could not, perhaps, be preserved by human wisdom.

The author from whom I quote, Senator [Henry Cabot] LODGE, commenting upon this, says:

The world was told that a new power had come into being, which meant to hold aloof from Europe, and which took no interest in the balance of power or the fate of dynasties, but looked only to the welfare of its own people and to the conquest and mastery of a continent as its allotted tasks. The policy declared by the proclamation was purely American in its conception, and severed the colonial tradition at a stroke.

I digress to say I wish every boy and girl over the age of 15 years could be induced to read the brilliant story of Washington as it is found in those two volumes. If they were not better Americans, with higher ideals, after they had read it, nothing could make them so.

Again, Mr. President, in a letter to Patrick Henry, dated later, he says:

I can most religiously aver that I have no wish that is incompatible with the dignity, happiness, and true interest of the people of this country. My ardent desire is, and my aim has been, so far as dependent on the executive department, to comply strictly with all our engagements, foreign and domestic, but to keep the United States free from any political connections with every other country, to see it independent of all, and under the influence of none. In a word, I want an American character, that the powers of Europe may be convinced that we act for ourselves.

Pursuing this thought and this great principle throughout his administration until he had fairly established it as a part of our foreign policy—the initiatory step of the same—he referred particularly to it in his Farewell Address. I shall detain the Senate by reading a single paragraph only. This was the conclusion of Washington after years of observation, after the most pointed experience, after eight years of administration of public affairs, and with as wide a vision and with as far-seeing a vision as ever accompanied a human mind upon this mundane sphere:

Why quit our own to stand upon foreign ground? Why, by interweaving our destiny with that of any part of Europe, entangle our peace and prosperity in the toils of European ambition, rivalship, interest, humor, or caprice?

Are there people in this day who believe that Europe now and in the future shall be free of selfishness, of rivalship, of humor, of ambition, of caprice? If not, are we not undertaking the task against which the Father of our Country warned when he bade farewell to public service? "Why quit our own to stand upon foreign ground?" And yet in this proposed league of nations, in the very beginning, we are advised of an executive council which shall dominate and control its action, three members of which are Europeans, one member Asiatic, and one American.

If a controversy ever arises in which there is a conflict between the European system and the American system, or if a conflict ever arises in which their interests, their humor, their caprice, and their selfishness shall attempt to dominate the situation, shall we not have indeed quit our own to stand upon foreign ground?

Why should we interweave our destiny with the European destiny? Are we not interweaving our future and our destiny with European powers when we join a league of nations the constitution of which gives a majority vote in every single instance in which the league can ever be called into action to European powers?

Does the ex-President mean to say to an intelligent and thinking people that this league which thus grants this power to European governments is not interweaving our destiny with European destiny? Does he assume to say that that is not a departure from the plain terms of Washington's Farewell Address?

I repeat what I said upon the floor of the Senate a few weeks ago. It may be that the people of America want to do this; it may be that they think their future happiness and tranquillity necessitate their doing it, but I inveigh against the misleading statement that we do not propose to do it by this league of nations. Let us be candid with those upon whom must rest the future burdens and obligations and not undertake to advise them that that is not going to happen which must necessarily and inevitably happen.

Mr. President, Washington succeeded in establishing the policy that we should not interfere in European affairs. It would have served no good purpose and would not have been beneficial to the American people in the least had we simply remained aloof from European affairs but had permitted Europe to transfer her system to the American Continent. Therefore, the Monroe doctrine. It was designed to support the policy of Washington. He had warned against the danger of entering Europe—the Monroe doctrine declared that Europe should not enter America. Permit me to say that one of these can not stand, in my judgment, without the support of the other. It is an inevitable result of Washington's teaching that the Monroe doctrine should exist. Indeed, such men as Mr. Coudert, the great lawyer, say that Washington's policy incorporated and included the Monroe doctrine; that Monroe's statement was simply an exemplification and application of the principle.

So, sir, in order that we might become a nation free from European broils and cease forever to have to do with European affairs, the Washington policy and the Monroe doctrine were announced and have ever since been maintained. The great question now is, Are they policies which we should still maintain; are they in all essential particulars still indispensable to our well-being as a people and to our strength and permanency as a nation? The present war has drawn us to Europe, but only temporarily. The question is, Shall we enter European affairs permanently, and shall we invite Europe, with her systems of government, some more pernicious than in the days of Washington, to America? We had a temporary alliance with France when Washington became President, but he fought against the making of these alliances permanent. That is the question here.

What is the Monroe doctrine? I apologize to the Senate for going into that question. I do so more for others than my colleagues, but I will be brief. Before the exigencies arising out of the conditions connected with a defense of this league it would not have been necessary to discuss it. All understood it alike. The Monroe doctrine is simply the principle of self-defense applied to a people, and the principle of self-defense can not be the subject of arbitration or of enforcement by any one other than that one who is to claim and enforce the principle of self-defense.

The ex-President said the Monroe doctrine is covered and extended to the world. That was the condition before Monroe announced it. The world was one. Monroe determined to separate it and divide it, and that was the very object of it. It was a distinct announcement that the European system could not be transferred to America. The rest was simply detail. It was the division of two systems; it was the political partition of two continents. Monroe or Jefferson never would have contemplated for a moment sharing the enforcement of the Monroe doctrine with any nation of Europe. We would not even join with England in announcing it.

May I read here in connection with my remarks a statement by ex-Senator [Elihu] Root upon this particular feature? Before I do that, however, I desire to call attention to the language of Thomas Jefferson. It precedes the remark which I was about to make. This letter of Jefferson states as clearly as can be stated the prime object of the announcement of this doctrine:

The question presented by the letters you have sent me is the most momentous which has ever been offered to my contemplation since that of independence.

Why does the Sage of Monticello rank the Monroe doctrine next to the Declaration of Independence? Because he believed as that genius of constructive government, Hamilton, believed, and Washington believed, that we could not maintain our independence without the Monroe doctrine. He believed that it was an indispensable pillar to our national independence, and second only to it in the catalogue of responsibilities and duties and obligations which rested upon us:

That made us a nation.

This sets our compass and points the course which we are to steer through the ocean of time opening on us. And never could we embark upon it under circumstances more auspicious. Our first and fundamental maxim should be never to entangle ourselves in the broils of Europe;

The Washington policy—

our second, never to suffer Europe to intermeddle with cis-Atlantic affairs.

Yet the ex-President says notwithstanding this we carry out this discrimination and distinction between European affairs and American affairs when we permit the two systems to be united, to be organized and administered by a common authority. He declares that although we do entangle ourselves in the broils of Europe, although we do suffer Europe to intermeddle with cis-Atlantic affairs, it is not in conflict with the Monroe doctrine.

I now call your attention to the statement of Senator Root upon the proposition advanced by the ex-President—of sharing with other nations responsibility in enforcing this doctrine. Mr. Root says:

Since the Monroe doctrine is a declaration based upon this Nation's right of self-protection, it can not be transmuted into a joint or common declaration by American States or any number of them.

We could not even share the responsibility and the execution of the Monroe doctrine with our Commonwealths here upon the Western Continent. It is personal; it is individual; it is the law of self-defense. It belongs to us, and we alone must determine when it shall be enforced or when it shall not apply. It is the same rule and principle which Australia invokes, and correctly invokes, with reference to the German islands near Australia. It is the same principle which Japan sought to have established in the Orient. It is the principle of self-defense and not of common defense, or defense by common authority invoked and sustained by the joint act of many nations.

Yet we are solemnly advised that although we should share it with all the Governments of Europe and Asia and all the tribes of the different races which may in the future be organized into some form of government, it is still the doctrine of self-defense which Jefferson and Monroe announced and which Mr. Root so clearly explained.

I read another paragraph from Mr. Root's speech, which leaves nothing further to be said both as to the meaning and the worth of this policy:

The familiar paragraphs of Washington's Farewell Address upon this subject were not rhetoric. They were intensely practical rules of conduct for the future guidance of the country:

"Europe has a set of primary interests which to us have none, or a very remote, relation. Hence, she must be engaged in frequent controversies, the causes of which are essentially foreign to our concerns. Hence, therefore, it must be unwise in us to implicate ourselves, by artificial ties, in the ordinary vicissitudes of her politics, or the ordinary combinations and collisions of her friendships or enmities. Our detached and distant situation invites and enables us to pursue a different course."

It was the same instinct which led Jefferson, in the letter to Monroe already quoted, to say:

"Our first and fundamental maxim should be, never to entangle ourselves in the broils of Europe; our second, never to suffer Europe to intermeddle with cis-Atlantic affairs."

The concurrence of Washington and Hamilton and Jefferson in the declaration of this principle of action entitles it to great respect. . . . Separation of influences as absolute and complete as possible was the remedy which the wisest of Americans agreed upon. It was one of the primary purposes of Monroe's declaration to insist upon this separation, and to accomplish it he drew the line at the water's edge. The problem of national protection in the distant future is one not to be solved by the first impressions of the casual observer, but only by profound study of the forces which, in the long life of nations, work out results. In this case the results of such a study by the best men of the formative period of the United States are supported by the instincts of the American democracy holding steadily in one direction for almost a century. The problem has not changed essentially. If the declaration of Monroe was right when the message was sent, it is right now.

We come now to the constitution of the proposed league of nations, which has been submitted to us. I shall not undertake to go into details; indeed, time would not permit to take up the many different phases which this constitution presents for consideration. I want only to call attention to some features of it bearing upon this particular subject matter—that is, the effect it has upon these two great policies.

The mere reading of the constitution of the league will convince any reasonable mind, any unprejudiced mind, that if put into effect the policy of Washington and the policy of Monroe must depart. The propositions are irreconcilable and can not exist together. In the first place, the league provides for an organization composed principally of five great nations, three of them European, one Asiatic, and one American. Every policy determined upon by the league and every movement made by it could be, and might be, controlled solely by European powers, whether the matter dealt with had reference to America or Europe. The league nowhere distinguishes or discriminates between European and American affairs. It functions in one continent the same as another. It compounds all three continents into a single unit, so far as the operations of the league are concerned. The league interferes in European affairs and in American affairs upon the same grounds and for the same reasons. If the territorial integrity of any member of the league is threatened or involved, whether that territory be in America or Europe, the league deals with the subject. If it becomes necessary for the league to act through economic pressure, or finally through military power, although the procedure may be voted by European powers alone, it may exert that pressure in America the same as in Europe. The very object and purpose of the league is to eliminate all differences between Europe and America and place all in a common liability to be governed and controlled by a common authority. If the United States, for instance, should disregard its covenants, as provided in the league, it would be deemed to have committed an act of war against all other members of the league; and under our solemn obligation and agreement we would have authorized the European powers to wage war against us and upon the American Continent. And yet men deliberately and blandly state to the American people that this league constitution preserves the Monroe doctrine and the doctrine given us by Washington.

I read from article 10 as an illustration:

> The high contracting parties shall undertake to respect and preserve as against external aggression the territorial existence and existing political independence of all States members of the league.

Take for illustration one of our own associates and allies. England has possessions in three continents. As has been said, the sun never sets upon her possessions. They dot every sea and are found in every land. She to-day holds possession of one-fifth of the habitable globe, and we in article 10 guarantee the integrity of her possessions in the three continents of the earth.

Mr. [Gilbert M.] HITCHCOCK. Will the Senator state what he is reading from?

MR. BORAH. I am reading from article 10 of the constitution of the league.

Mr. HITCHCOCK. That is not the language of article 10 as printed in the Senate document at the request of the Senator from Massachusetts (Mr. LODGE). There is nothing said about possessions there at all.

Mr. BORAH. Did I read possessions?

Mr. HITCHCOCK. I understood the Senator to say possessions.

Mr. BORAH. No; I think the Senator is mistaken. I will read it again.

The high contracting parties shall undertake to respect and preserve as against external aggression the territorial integrity and existing political independence of all States members of the league.

Mr. HITCHCOCK. That is correct.

Mr. BORAH. I presume that her territorial integrity necessarily involves her territorial possessions.

So, Mr. President, the first obligation which we assume is to to protect the territorial integrity of the British Empire. That takes us into every part of the civilized world. That is the most radical departure from the Washington policy. I will come to the Monroe policy in a minute. Now, how are we to determine that?

In case of any such aggression or in case of any threat or danger of such aggression the executive council shall advise upon the means by which the obligation shall be fulfilled.

Does that mean what it says, and is it to be executed in accordance with its plain terms? If the territorial integrity of any part of the British Empire shall be threatened, not the Congress of the United States, not the people of the United States, not the Government of the United States determines what shall be done, but the executive council, of which the American people have one member. We, if we mean what we say in this constitution, are pledging ourselves, our honor, our sacred lives, to the preservation of the territorial possessions the world over and not leaving it to the judgment and sense of the American people but to the diplomats of Europe.

Mr. HITCHCOCK. The Senator again uses the words "territorial possessions." That is what I am objecting to.

Mr. BORAH. Mr. President, I will leave it to an intelligent

audience to determine whether or not "territorial integrity" does not include "territorial possessions."

Mr. HITCHCOCK. If the Senator will refer to article 7, the indications are there that the dominions of the British Empire are to be regarded as separate and independent self-governing countries.

Mr. BORAH. Mr. President, I am coming to that in a few moments. I admire the careful use of language by the Senator from Nebraska when he says there are "indications." This constitution is prolific indeed of "indications."

That is the duty devolving upon us by virtue of the league, to enter European affairs. What would be the duty and the obligation of England, of France, of Italy, and of Japan to the other member should a disturbance arise upon the Western Continent? Suppose some threat of danger to the Republic should come from Mexico or from Mexico and its allies. We are not even consulted as to whether we shall call in help, but the duty devolves upon the council, in its initiative capacity, to at once assume jurisdiction of it and to proceed to the American Continent to determine what its duties shall be with reference to American affairs. This league operates upon the Western Continent with the same jurisdiction and power and the same utter disregard of which continent it is upon as it does in the European Continent. Does anybody deny that proposition?

Let us take a homely illustration; perhaps it may better illustrate the argument. A great many years ago a man by the name of Europe opened a farm. He begins the tillage of his great farm, but turmoil, strife, and dissension arise among his tenants. Finally a dissatisfied European by the name of, we will call him, America, determines to leave these turmoils on the European farm to go into the forest, open a clearing, and establish a new farm. He says, "I shall go where I can worship God according to the dictates of my own conscience. I shall go where I can set up a new system of farming." He goes into the wilderness and sacrifices and finally establishes a farm of his own. After he has established it he declares, after reflection, "I am afraid those Europeans will come here and cause me the same disturbance and trouble and establish the same kind of a system which we had in Europe; so I will establish a partition fence." He does establish a partition fence. When he has finished the fence he says, "I will neither go to your farm nor shall you come to mine; I have had some experience with you, and I do not want to try it again." So he builds an insurmountable wall or fence between his neighbor Europe and himself. It stands for a hundred years. People sit about and discuss it, and pass many eulogies, declaring over and over again that it was one of the wisest things that a farmer ever did. But suddenly a new inspiration dawns, and it is thought that it would be a good idea to tear down the wall or fence and to commingle and intermingle the systems; to join one farm to another and have one superintendent. It is said to the farmer America, "Let us tear down this fence." He replies in surprise and consternation, "I built it for a purpose." "Well," it is contended by the idealist, "we think it is better to tear it down." At this time there rises up a man by the name of William Howard. He says to farmer America, "Let us tear down that wall fence of yours. It must be done right away. Anyone who opposes can not be trusted overnight." The farmer says, "I do not think it would be well." "But," William Howard replies, "it is just the same after it is torn down as it is when it is standing up. We are going to put a fence around both farms, and that will be the same as a fence between the farms." William Howard further says, "Let us go into partnership with your neighbor Europe." America says, "I do not want any partnership. I came here to get away from that very thing." William Howard urges, with a spirit of unselfishness and good-naturedly, "It is just the same without a partnership as it is with it. Let us transmute or combine these two systems and make them one." "But," farmer America says, "I came to this country to get away from that system. I do not want one system; I want two systems. I do not like their system of farming." William Howard replies, "One system is just the same as two systems." He declares, furthermore, "I know something about this; I ran this farm for four years myself [laughter]; I know how to run it; and I declare to you that the best thing for you to do is to tear down your wall fence, to unite your two systems, and make one farm out of it and one common overseer." He further, by way of a profound argument, casually remarks, "I had such remarkable success while I was running this farm and received such universal commendation upon my work after it was over, having received the approval of 2 tenants out of 48, that I am sure that I can run both farms; at least, I am anxious to try." [Laughter.]

The VICE-PRESIDENT. The galleries must preserve order.

Mr. BORAH. Mr. President, some of us declare that this proposition tears down the farmer's fence. We say furthermore that we do not want two farms made into one. If you want to do so, all right, go ahead; but let us make no mistake about what we are doing. Let us not try to fool ourselves or anyone else.

What do other countries think about it, Mr. President? I should like to call in outside witnesses, notwithstanding the very profound respect that I have for the ex-President. The English press, we are informed, in so far as it has commented upon this subject at all, has regarded it as an abrogation of the Monroe doctrine. Mr. Lloyd George [British Prime Minister, December 1916-January 1919] said in the very beginning of these conferences that Great Britain could concede much to the United States if, as the result, they were to draw the United States out of her isolation and away from her traditional foreign policies. Japan has practically announced semiofficially that it is the abolishment of the Monroe doctrine. The Brazilian Minister at The Hague has announced that it is the end of the Monroe doctrine. Why leave it in doubt? Do you, Senators, or those who are in favor of the league of nations, want to destroy the Monroe doctrine? If you do not, why leave it in doubt? Why leave it to the construction of European diplomats sitting behind closed doors? By the insertion of three lines in this constitution you can place it beyond peradventure, beyond contention or cavil. The question which I submit now is, if you are unwilling to do this, is it not proof conclusive that you intend to destroy the policy and wipe out this long-standing doctrine?

Let us go to another feature of this league. I am not here to-day to criticize in any way, either directly or by inference, the great English nation or the great English people. They are among, not excepting our own, the most powerful and admirable people upon the globe. Every man must pay his profound respect to their genius and to their capacity for Government and for mastery of great problems. But when we come to deal with England, we must deal with her intelligently and with a due regard for our own interests and our own rights, for one of the distinguishing characteristics of that proud nation is that England always looks after England's interests. I admire her for doing so.

Her national spirit never fails her. The talents and genius of her statesmen never betray her. She has signed many treaties which have been worthless in the hour of peril. She has entered into many leagues and combinations which have dissolved, but her proud national spirit never forsakes her. Ultimately she relies upon this instead of treaties and leagues. She has passed through many a crisis, she has seen dark hours; but in every crisis, however severe, and in the darkest hour every Englishman is expected to do his duty and does it. I admire her for her national spirit, for her vigilance in guarding the interests of the Empire.

Mr. President, this constitution of the league of nations is the greatest triumph for English diplomacy in three centuries of English diplomatic life. This constitution, in the first place, is lifted almost bodily, as you will see if you will compare the two, from the constitution proposed in January by Gen. [Jan Christiaan] Smuts.* There is not an organic, a vital principle incorporated in this constitution that is not found in Gen. Smuts' constitution. As is known to all, Gen. Smuts, a South African, is one of the most remarkable men under the English rule to-day. That you may not think I am stating it strongly, let me read a word from the London *Times* on the second day after this constitution was adopted:

The project, if not the same as that outlined by Gen. Smuts, is like it as its brother. . . . It is a cause for legitimate pride to recognize in the covenant so much of the work of Englishmen. . . . It is again a source of legitimate pride to Englishmen that article 19 in the covenant might almost be taken as an exposition of the principles animating the relations of Great Britain with India and the dominions.

Listen to this language—

That the dominions are in this document recognized as nations before the world is also a fact of profound significance in the history of these relations.

The gentleman who wrote that editorial had not acquired the capacity of using language to conceal his thoughts; he labored

---

*EDITOR'S NOTE: Smuts represented South Africa in the Imperial War Cabinet 1917-1918 and at the Paris Peace Conference.

under the disadvantage of having to use language to convey his thoughts. The fact that the dominions of Great Britain and her colonies are recognized as nations is a matter of "profound significance." Yes; when they finally settle down to business England will have one vote, Canada one vote, New Zealand one vote, Australia one vote, and South Africa one vote, whilst the American Nation, brought into being by our fathers at so much cost of blood and treasure and preserved through the century by the vigilance and sacrifice of our forbears, this Nation with all her wealth and resources will have one vote. In both the executive council and the delegate body the same proportion obtains, and those two bodies direct, dominate, and mark out the policy of this entire program, whatever it is to be, under the league. A matter of "profound significance!"

I ask you who are in favor of this league, Are you willing to give to any nation five votes against our one? Do you presume that the questions of interest, of ambition, of selfishness, of caprice, of humor will not arise in the future? Have they not already, in a proper way, but none the less in an unmistakable way, made their appearance since the armistice was signed? Are we not already advised that we must use the same intelligence, the same foresight, the same prevision, and the same patriotism that our fathers used against the inherent, the inevitable selfishness of all nations? Yet we are seriously proposing that we shall join a league whose constitutional powers shall determine—what? Shall determine policies, politic and economic, upon the two continents and shall give to our greatest commercial rival five votes to our one.

Mr. President, I have called attention to some of the obligations which we assume. Let me repeat a single statement. You have now observed the number of votes in the executive council, but that is not all. There are Italy and Japan associated with England, and more nearly like her in their systems and in their policies than they are like the United States. There are already treaties between those nations and England, which Mr. Balfour frankly says are not to be abrogated; in other words, we are in the very beginning put up not only against this extraordinary vote by one nation but we have the disadvantage of contending against a system, which system covers other nations as well as that of Great Britain.

We all want the friendship and the respect of and future amicable relations between Great Britain and this country. That also was Washington's wish; that was Jefferson's wish; that was also Lincoln's wish; but never for a moment did they surrender any power or any authority or compromise their capacity in any way to take care of the situation in case there should not be an agreement between the two powers.

What has England given up in this league of nations? What has she surrendered? Will some one advise me? Did she surrender the freedom of the seas? That was pushed aside at the first meetings of the conference as not subject to its jurisdiction. Has she surrendered her claim for the largest navy? What has she surrendered?

On the other hand, we have surrendered the traditional foreign policy of this country, which has been established for 100 years; and we have gone behind these powers and placed at their disposal our finances, our man power, and our full capacity to guarantee the integrity of their possessions all over the globe. Is it an even balance? Is it an equitable, is it an honest, arrangement between these great powers and the United States?

I come now to another feature, which to me is even more interesting, more menacing, than those over which we have passed. Conceal it as you may, disguise it as some will attempt to do, this is the first step in internationalism and the first distinct effort to sterilize nationalism. This is a recognized fact, tacitly admitted by all who support it and expressly admitted by many, that the national state has broken down and that we must now depend upon the international state and international power in order to preserve our interests and our civilization. The national state can no longer serve the cause of civilization, and therefore we must resort to the international state. That is disclosed in every line and paragraph of this instrument. It begins with the preamble and ends with the last article—a recognition that internationalism must take the place of nationalism.

May I call attention to a statement from perhaps the most famous international now living? I read from a book entitled "The Bolsheviki and World Peace," by Trotzky.* He says:

*EDITOR'S NOTE: Leon Trotsky (1877-1940), Russian communist leader, associated with Lenin in effecting the October-November 1917 Bolshevik revolution.

The present war is at bottom a revolt of the forces of production against the political form of nation and State. It means the collapse of the national state as an independent economic unit.

In another paragraph:

The war proclaims the downfall of the national state. . . . We Russian Socialists stand firmly on the ground of internationalism. . . . The German social democracy was to us not only *a* party of the international—it was *the* party par excellence.

Again, he declares:

The present war signalizes the collapse of the national states.

He proceeds to argue that the only thing which can take the place of the national state is internationalism, to internationalize our governments, internationalize our power, internationalize production, internationalize our economic capacity, and become an international state the world over. That is at the bottom of this entire procedure, whether consciously or unconsciously, upon the part of those who are advocating it. It will be the fruit of this effort if it succeeds—the dead-sea fruit for the common people everywhere. It is a distinct announcement that the intense nationalism of Washington, the intense nationalism of Lincoln, can no longer serve the cause of the American people, and that we must internationalize and place the sovereign powers of this Government to make war and control our economic forces in an international tribunal.

A few days ago one of the boldest and most brilliant internationalists of this country—a man, no doubt, who believes in it as firmly as I believe in nationalism—wrote this paragraph:

The death of Col. [Theodore] Roosevelt was a shock, I think, to everybody who loves life. No man ever lived who had more fun in 61 years; and yet his death, with that last frantic reiteration of Americanism and nothing but Americanism, fresh from his pen, was like a symbol of the progress of life. The boyish magnetism is all gone out of those words. They die in the dawn of revolutionary internationalism.

I sometimes wonder, Can it be true? Are we, indeed, yielding our Americanism before the onrushing tide of revolutionary internationalism? Did the death of this undaunted advocate of American nationalism mark an epoch in the fearful, damnable, downward trend?

Yes, Mr. President, this many-sided man touched life at every point, and sometimes seemed inconsistent; but there was one supreme passion which gave simplicity and singleness of purpose to all he said or did—his abounding Americanism. In this era of national infidelity let us be deeply grateful for this. Though he had erred a thousand times, and grievously erred, we would still pay sincere tribute to his memory for holding aloft at all times, and especially in the world's greatest turmoil, the banner of the true faith. Huntsman, plainsman, author, political leader, governor, Vice-President, President, and ex-President, this was always the directing and dominating theme. Even in his full, rich life, replete with noble deeds and brilliant achievements, it runs like a golden thread through all of the bewildering activities of his wide-ranging genius. It gave consistency to every change of view and justified what sometimes seemed his merciless intolerance. When the final estimate is placed upon his career, and all his services to his fellows are weighed and judged, his embodiment of the national spirit, his vigilant defense of our national integrity, his exemplification of our national ideals will distinguish him, as says in effect this internationalist, from all the men of his day and generation.

Mr. President, I am not a pessimist. I find neither solace nor guidance in the doleful doctrine. But who will gainsay that we have reached a supreme hour in the history of the Republic he loved? There is not a Government in existence to-day but feels the strain of those inscrutable forces which are working their willful way through all the established institutions of men. Church and creed, ancient governments and new, despotic and liberal, order and law, at this time stand under challenge. Hunger and disease, business anxiety, and industrial unrest threaten to demobilize the moral forces of organized society. In all of this turmoil and strife, in all this chaos of despair and hope, there is much that is good if it can be brought under direction and subordinated to the sway of reason. At the bottom of it all there is the infinite longing of oppressed humanity seeking in madness to be rid of oppression and to escape from these centuries of injustice. How shall we help to bring order out of chaos? Shall we do so by becoming less or more American? Shall we entangle and embarrass the efforts of a powerful and independent people, or shall we leave them in every emergency and in every crisis to do in that particular hour and in that supreme moment what the conscience and wisdom of an untrammeled and liberty-loving people shall decide is wise and just? Or shall we yoke our deliberations to forces we can not control and leave our people to the mercy of powers which may be wholly at variance with our conception of duty? I may be willing to help my neighbor, though he be improvident or unfortunate, but I do not necessarily want him for a business partner. I may be willing to give liberally of my means, of my council and advice, even of my strength or blood, to protect his family from attack or injustice, but I do not want him placed in a position where he may decide for me when and how I shall act or to what extent I shall make sacrifice. I do not want this Republic, its intelligence and its patriotism, its free people and its institutions, to go into partnership with and to give control of the partnership to those many of whom have no conception of our civilization and no true insight into our destiny. What we want is what Roosevelt taught and urged—a free, untrammeled Nation, imbued anew and inspired again with the national spirit; not isolation but freedom to do as our own people think wise and just; not isolation but simply the unembarrassed and un-entangled freedom of a great Nation to determine for itself and in its own way where duty lies and where wisdom calls. There is not a supreme council possible of creation or conceivable equal in wisdom, in conscience, and humanitarianism to the wisdom and conscience and humanitarianism of the hundred million free and independent liberty-loving souls to whom the living God has intrusted the keeping of this Nation. The moment this Republic comes to any other conclusion it has forfeited its right to live as an independent and self-respecting Republic.

It was not, one likes to believe, a mere incident, but a significant though strangely arranged fact that the last message to the American people from the illustrious dead who, the internationalists tell us, was the last of the great Americans should have been upon this particular subject. I believe it was the night of his death that this message which I shall now read to you was read at a public meeting to which he had been invited but was unable to attend:

Any man who says he is an American but something else also isn't an American at all. We have room for but one flag, the American flag. . . . We have room for but one language, and that is the English language; for we intend to see that the crucible turns our people out as Americans, of American nationality, and not as dwellers in a polyglot boarding house; and we have room for but one soul loyalty to the American people.

Let us inscribe this upon our banner and hang it upon the outer wall. In all the vicissitudes of our national life, in all the duties which may come to us as a people, in all the future, filled, as it will be, with profound and perplexing problems, let us cling uncompromisingly to this holy creed. In these times, when ancient faiths are disappearing and governments are crumbling, when institutions are yielding to the tread of the mad hosts of disorder, let us take our stand on the side of orderly liberty, on the side of constitutional government. Let us range ourselves along with Washington and Jefferson and Jackson and Lincoln and Roosevelt. Let us be true to ourselves; and, whatever the obligations of the future, we can not then be false to others.

14

An Economic Revolution in America
Wesley C. Mitchell's "Review" of Recent Economic Changes

The Conference on Unemployment, called in 1921 by President Warren G. Harding, established three surveys to enlarge the general understanding of the American economy. The first investigated Business Cycles and Unemployment, the second studied Seasonal Operations in the Construction Industry, and the third surveyed Recent Economic Changes. The third comittee, for a time chaired by Herbert Hoover (1874-1964), began its work in January, 1928, and completed its report a year later. Charged with making "a critical appraisal of the factors of stability and instability," it was "to observe and to describe the American economy as a whole, suggesting rather than developing recommendations." The National Bureau of Economic Research sponsored the basic investigations; a dozen social scientists prepared special studies on specific problems or aspects of the economy. Wesley C. Mitchell (1874-1948), for many years Professor of Sociology at New York University and Director of Research for the National Bureau of Economic Research, summarized the work of the others and prepared a review of the report, most of which is reprinted here. The nation's leaders took a lively interest in the American economy during the 1920's. The United States had emerged from the war relatively unscathed and, despite a primary postwar depression of sharp intensity, the country quickly recovered and went on to chalk up new records of production and consumption. The unparalleled prosperity seemed the more remarkable in view of continued economic sluggishness abroad. How could this situation be explained, and what was more important, how could this situation be maintained were questions asked by many thoughtful Americans. *Recent Economic Changes in the United States* provided some answers. One might also consult George Soule's *Prosperity Decade, From War to Depression, 1917-1929* (New York: Rinehart and Com-

Wesley C. Mitchell, "Review," in the President's Conference on Unemployment, *Recent Economic Changes in the United States* (New York: McGraw-Hill Book Company, 1929), II, 841-54, 856-57, 859-68, 873-90, 909-10.

pany, 1947.) Arthur Schlesinger, Jr., in *The Crisis of the Old Order
1919-1933*, Vol. I of his *The Age of Roosevelt* (Boston: Houghton
Mifflin Company, 1957) has written a brilliant though not unprejudiced account of the 1920's. For changes in agriculture one should
see the U.S. Department of Agriculture's *The Yearbook of Agriculture,
1940, Farmers in a Changing World* (Washington: Government Printing Office, 1940). Theodore Saloutos and John Hicks wrote a penetrating study of *Agricultural Discontent in the Middle West,
1900-1939* (Madison: University of Wisconsin Press, 1951). In reading this selection note (1) what the author thought was the principal
factor in producing major economic changes; (2) what effects World
War I had upon the economies of Europe and the United States;
(3) what happened when peace broke out in 1919; (4) what, in the
author's judgment, prevented the crisis from degenerating into a
panic; (5) what unfavorable and what favorable conditions affected
the American economy after the depression of 1921; (6) what the
author regarded as the prime factor responsible for American prosperity; (7) what novel developments he observed in the realm of
economic policy; (8) what hardships were produced by increasing
efficiency; (9) what was the influence of new products and new
tastes; (10) what were the effects of population changes on the
economy; (11) what prospects he saw for the future; and (12) the
general tone and spirit of the "Review."

I. The Maze of Economic Changes and a Clue

THE PRECEDING CHAPTERS FORM A MOVING PICTURE
of the economic changes now going on in the
United States. They show scenes from real life registered from
various angles by a group of skilled observers. Starting with a
survey of the kinds and quantities of goods American families
are consuming, the scene shifts to the work people are doing in
factories and mines, on construction jobs, railways, ships and
farms. Another shift focuses attention upon the activities of
labor organizations and of management. Then come the impersonal records of price fluctuations, capital accumulations,
banking and international dealings. The close links into the
beginning—it shows the inflow of incomes which enable American families to sustain their varied consumption.

This record presents striking contrasts. Consumption as a
whole has increased, but the consumption of certain great
staples has shrunk. While trade at large has flourished, certain

branches have languished—notably ship building, the railway equipment industry, and agriculture; in less measure the textile, coal and shoe trades. Pay-roll disbursements of factories have expanded, but manufacturing employment has diminished. Business profits have been large, but so also have been the number of bankruptcies. Great quantities of gold have flowed into the country, but wholesale prices have sagged much of the time. Income as a whole has grown larger, but important sections of the country have made little gain, and important occupations have suffered loss.

Impressionistic writers often disregard such diversities of fortune. One can paint a glowing picture of American prosperity which emphasizes the triumphs of mass production in automatic factories, the success of large-scale farming with power machinery, the rapid spread of chain stores, the co-operation of labor unions in enlarging output, the economy of high wages, our new position in international finance. Or one can paint a picture of average and subaverage performance by ordinary men struggling with difficult circumstances and ending in discouragement or failure. Both pictures may be true to life, so far as they go. Both are easy to make—one has only to select from the abundant materials those which harmonize with the chosen theme. Both are easy to understand because they show no incompatible elements. But neither picture satisfies an observer who uses his eyes.

A just picture is neither easy to make nor easy to understand after it has been made. Trustworthy general impressions must be based upon study of what is happening in different geographical sections, in different industries, business enterprises, labor organizations, markets, professional societies, trade associations, and Government bureaus. No individual is equipped to gather and to analyze all of the evidence which should be canvassed. For that there is needed the critical skill of engineers, business executives, public officials, bankers, economists, statisticians, labor specialists and agricultural experts. Even in his own department, each of these men finds diverse developments. Often there is a striking contrast between average current performance and exceptional achievements which are important more for what they promise in the future than for what they represent in the present. At times, national totals or averages can be drawn up to summarize the general situation as seen from some angle; but the very estimators who present such figures emphasize the differences hidden in the general results. And when the contributions of numerous specialists have been assembled in one volume, there still remains the task of assimilating all the elements—of understanding the picture as a whole.*

The best clue to the maze of recent economic changes is supplied by economic history. What has been happening in the United States is the latest phase of cumulative processes which have dominated western life since the Industrial Revolution got under way. Powerful as these processes are, they were appreciably influenced by the sudden outbreak of the war and by the sudden return of peace. By changing the conditions amidst which the old influences worked, these world shocks contributed to strange results.

II. The Continuing Forces—Science and Economic Change

The nineteenth century brought an unprecedented increase in the number of Europeans, an unprecedented spread of Europeans over the earth, and marked changes in their relation to other peoples. These multiplying numbers, moreover, gradually attained a higher level of material comfort than the mass of their progenitors had ever enjoyed.

These great changes in the fortunes of mankind were made possible by the application of science to the work of producing, transporting, manufacturing, and distributing goods. Increasingly wide and exact knowledge of natural processes underlay the

---

*Not that all factors which have affected the economic fortunes of the United States in recent years are adequately presented in the survey. We have had to shape our inquiries according to our means. Little is said about the enormous advantages which this country, in sharp contrast to Europe, enjoys from the absence of internal tariff barriers, or about the mixed effects of the tariff upon imports. The influence of Federal, state and local taxation is mentioned here and there; but it is not systematically discussed. Previous inquiries had shown how difficult it would be to get conclusive data concerning the economic reactions of the Eighteenth Amendment; with the limited time and money at our disposal it seemed futile to scratch the skin of that controverted issue. Immigration restriction is dealt with incidentally; it merits far closer analysis than we have been able to provide. But even with these omissions and others of less moment, we have a rather bewildering array of factors to set in order.

invention of the steam engine, the locomotive, the steamship; the smelting of iron with coal; the improvements in mining and metallurgy; the development of the telegraph, ocean cable, telephone, dynamo, transmission line, radio; the industrial applications of chemistry and biology, the increasing precision of work, the system of interchangeable parts, the progress toward automatic mechanisms, the linking of machines into continuous processes for mass production; the rise of the oil and rubber industries; the perfecting of the internal combustion engine, the automobile and the airplane.

In the course of the century, a technique of material progress was developed. Science spread from its ancient stronghold of mathematics into a systematic study of the most varied phenomena, including the phenomena of living processes and consciousness. The industrial application of scientific discoveries was secured by the rise and differentiation of the engineering professions. From the parent stock of military engineers there developed in turn civil engineers, mechanical, mining, marine, sanitary, gas, chemical, electrical, efficiency and production engineers—each group trained in the fundamental sciences and experienced in industrial practice. Business men were prompt to see the profit which could be drawn from the use of the new methods. Indeed, the Industrial Revolution had been preceded by a Commercial Revolution. Encouraged by the gradual expansion of demand, business leaders had been reorganizing methods of producing, transporting and distributing goods to secure greater efficiency. But this quiet process was enormously stimulated by the "great inventions" and the numberless inventions which followed. For these technical improvements not only increased efficiency more than mere reorganization of old processes could do; they also widened the markets at surprising speed and thus created ever larger opportunities for the business organizer to seize.

Not only did the new technique enable men to produce more from their known resources, it also brought distant resources within reach and discovered new treasures which were turned to human use. Vast new granaries were developed in the Mississippi Valley, Argentina and Canada; vast new ranges for cattle and sheep stretched from Texas to Montana and over much of Argentina and Australia. The textile mills of England were fed cotton from the South Atlantic and Gulf states, Egypt and India; silk from China and Japan; wool from Argentina and Australia; coarser fibers from Mexico and the Philippines. European soils were replenished from Chilean nitrates. Iron ranges of great extent were found in North America; copper came from Michigan, Montana, Arizona, Utah, Chile and Peru; gold flowed from Brazil, California, Australia, Alaska and South Africa; petroleum pools were found dotted over the globe. Most important of all for the new technique, coal deposits, surpassing those of England in extent, were developed in Europe and America. Science enabled the generations which applied it to tap energy from the sun, accumulated through millions of years. As research, engineering and business enterprise were developed, so also was prospecting. The world was combed over as never before by men with piercing eyes and long plans.

By no means all the increase in efficiency took the form of a net gain in current livelihood. To use the technique founded on science, men had to build machines, factories, railways, roads, warehouses and sewers. In developing new resources, they had to dig mines; to break the prairies and fence in farms; to make homes in strange habitats. And this work of re-equipping themselves for making consumers' goods was never done. Every discovery put to use on a commercial scale meant a new equipment job, often of great extent. But after all this work on the means of production was done, there remained an ever larger flow of the things men eat and wear, house and amuse themselves with.

The net gain in ability to provide for their desires brought men the possibility of raising their standard of consumption, of reducing their hours of work, of giving their children more education, of increasing their numbers. They took a slice of each of these goods, rather than all of one. They worked somewhat less hard as the decades went by; they raised their standards of consumption appreciably; they established compulsory education and reduced illiteracy; they added to the population. Any one of these changes might have been made on a larger scale had not men taken their gains in various forms.

The pace at which the sciences grow, and the pace at which their discoveries are applied to the work of the world, keep changing. In any given field of scientific discovery or commercial application, a period of revolutionary changes is followed by rapid expansion as the new discovery is fitted into the existing body of knowledge or the existing structure of industry; then expansion tends to slow down. One after another, many of our leading industries have gone through this cycle of changes since 1800. In any given decade in any given country, some parts of its economic mechanism were being made over, some parts were growing steadily, some parts were changing little. Hence the growth of industry as a whole has been less unsteady than the growth of its component parts. The pace has not been uniform, however; even from the national viewpoint there have been periods of more rapid and less rapid advance.

Population growth also has its changes of pace. The nations which lead in science and industry have been increasing their numbers more slowly of late than in the earlier part of the nineteenth century. This change is explained by experts as so many modern changes are explained—it is attributed in large part to the practical application of scientific knowledge. From a critical study of European evidence, Sir William Beveridge concludes: "The practice of birth control, that is to say, the deliberate prevention of fertilization, suddenly increased about 1880, not because there was then any change of economic conditions making restriction of families suddenly more desirable than before, but because the means of birth control were perfected and the knowledge of them was spread, both by those interested in their sale and by disinterested propagandists."* That may not be all of the story, but, whatever its causes, the reduction of the birth rate meant that as men acquired more knowledge they absorbed a smaller share of the gains from applied science in propagating their kind, and thereby increased the possibility of shortening hours and of raising the standard of living.

The whole process of gaining new knowledge and putting it to use has had to make headway against other human interests—particularly man's interest in getting the better of his fellowmen. Business friction, class struggles, and national wars check science and the peaceful arts; they impoverish the participants and usually injure the bystanders as well.

---

*"The Fall of Fertility among European Races," *Economica*, March, 1925, No. 13, p. 20.

III. The War and Economic Changes

Of the checks which economic progress has suffered since the Industrial Revolution began, the gravest was inflicted by the war of 1914-1918. For all the great nations which lead in science and industry were directly involved in this desperate struggle, and all the lesser nations on the same cultural plane were either belligerents or harassed neighbors of the belligerents. Never had warring powers mobilized their brains and brawn, their industrial equipment, and their financial resources so skillfully to harm the persons and property of their enemies. Of the damages inflicted and suffered, we need here note only such items as help to account for the postwar changes in American conditions and practices.

The elaborate equipment for attack and defense demanded by up-to-date standards of military efficiency meant that every soldier at the front had to be served by several workers behind the lines. In desperate haste, each belligerent organized its industry and trade to produce a maximum output of military supplies and the indispensable minimum of goods for civilians. A large part of the most efficient workers had to be withdrawn from production and others hurriedly trained to take their places. Old factories had to be remodeled for war uses and new plants built that would serve no peace-time purpose. Governments had to intervene on a grand scale in operations where private initiative had been deemed more effective. Long-run advantages and deliberate planning had to be sacrificed to immediate needs. Despite prodigies of energy on the part of many leaders and devotion on the part of the masses, the industrial changes of the war were attended by enormous wastes, in addition to the wastes which the reorganization was intended to effect.

In finance the war brought even wilder confusion than in industry. Monetary and banking policies were dictated, not by the economic interests of peoples, but by the pressure of circumstances. Specie payments were suspended in several countries almost immediately. Wholesale prices, wages, and costs of living, in terms of the irredeemable paper currencies, underwent fantastic fluctuations, and made necessary awkward schemes of government control. Millions of people had much of their property quietly confiscated through no fault of their own, and thousands grew suddenly rich not by virtue of service. Taxes mounted to heights which seemed unbearable, but public debts swelled faster still. No rule of rational finance could be followed when it ran counter to the plea of necessity.

The latest estimates indicate that "the war carried off in round numbers thirteen million mobilized men." The war is charged further with a large share of responsibility for the ten million deaths during the influenza epidemic of 1918, and the scarcely less destructive epidemics which followed in Eastern Europe. Census figures show that the total population of Europe declined more than ten millions between 1910 and 1920. The loss from 1917 to 1920 must have been considerably greater.

Thus the war left Europe with fewer people; these people were less well-nourished, less able-bodied, less self-reliant; their industrial equipment was in poor physical condition and in good part useless for peace-time production; their soils were depleted from the lack of fertilizers; they had sacrificed a large part of their farm animals; they had laid waste considerable stretches of land and ruined many towns. When peace returned, they faced the task of demobilizing their soldiers and war workers, releasing their government controls, reorganizing their industrial forces, and restoring their capital equipment while prices were still fluctuating violently, and while political prospects, domestic and international, were most uncertain. Economic welfare in Europe had received a setback indeed.

The economic position of the United States improved greatly in comparison with Europe's during the war. But that was more because European losses were staggering than because American gains were spectacular.

Business in this country recovered from depression in the second half of 1915 with remarkable rapidity, thanks largely to war orders. Then we had a year of intense business prosperity in 1916, followed in 1917-18 by the hectic economic activity which prevailed among all the belligerents. If taxes were heavy, current profits were very large. Nor were the gains confined to the profit-making classes. Wage rates may not have kept even pace with the cost of living, but employment was full and there was a widespread reduction in standard working time between 1914 and 1920, which Dr. Leo Wolman estimates at five hours a week.

Listing the deductions is a more complicated matter. There was an uncommonly large share of haste and waste, as well as of profits, in war-contract work during 1915 and 1916. Though we were not forced to suspend specie payments, our whole system of prices suffered convulsions almost matching those of the Civil War. In 1917 we sought to mobilize all our economic resources in a hurry for military ends, and had to demobilize the war workers, as well as the army, in 1919. Our railways declined in efficiency. We poured millions into war plants and ships that had to be scrapped after the armistice. We took about 5,000,000 of our best producers out of civilian life. We lost 116,000 soldiers and sailors, and shared in the influenza epidemic of 1918. These costs were real, and must be considered in any accounting of the economic effects of the war just as much as the profits which the war brought to American business enterprises.

Even if items which cannot be expressed adequately in dollars were set aside, it would be exceedingly difficult to strike a balance between the war gains and the war losses. That task is not attempted here. But it is proper to note the fluctuations in the country's "real" income during the war, that is, income in dollars of constant purchasing power. . . . In the last full year before the war, a year which began with brisk trade but ended in dullness, the per capita income of Americans, taken at the retail prices of 1925, was $621. Starting with this figure as 100, per capita income shrank to 97 in 1914, rose to 99 in 1915, to 106 in 1916, remained constant at that level in 1917, and then declined to 105 in 1918. On this showing, we were far from impoverished during the war; but our economic progress was not remarkably rapid.

Nor can we close the reckoning of the war's influence upon real income with 1918, either in the United States or in other countries. The readjustment of economic activities to peace is one of the costs of war. And that readjustment is more than a matter of beating swords into ploughshares. In proportion as the belligerent nations had succeeded in mobilizing all their economic resources for war, not only their governments, but also their business enterprises and individual citizens had to reorganize their plans after the armistice. The business mistakes made during this period of confusion are largely chargeable to the confusion itself. Other countries found the process of re-adjusting even more difficult than did the United States. All our allies made matters worse, as did we, by committing economic blunders in 1919 for which they paid in 1921. What happened is sketched briefly in the next section. But here we should note that income in the United States sank in the early years of peace. Indeed, average real income per capita in the United States during the eight years of war and postwar readjustments, 1914 to 1921, was less than the per capita income of 1913. That is not a record of prosperity.

IV. Peace and the Economic Convulsions of 1919-1921

Readily as they had accepted the economic regulations and restrictions imposed during the war, the American people threw off the yoke eagerly after the armistice. The "dollar-a-year" men returned to their offices; the munitions plants closed and their workers dispersed; the soldiers in training camps and in France were sent back to their homes as rapidly as might be. Government price-fixing ended, and everyone was at liberty to charge what he could get for his goods. The rationing of raw materials, the granting of transportation "priorities," the conservation program, the Federal regulation of imports and exports, and the Government control over shipping stopped at various dates. When the Transportation Act of February, 1920, provided for returning the railroads to private control, practically nothing was left of the war-time mobilization.

It was not "business as usual," however, to which Americans returned in 1919, but business as dominated by postwar conditions. Early in the year there was grave uncertainty regarding the trend of affairs. Wholesale prices declined from December to February or March; there was much loose talk about the necessity of "liquidating labor;" the prevailing business attitude was one of "watchful waiting." But, early in the spring, signs of eager demand for consumers' goods began to appear. In April, Federal Reserve agents reported that "the business community has given up the thought that it may profitably await a further considerable reduction in prices . . ."* In July, the Bureau of

---
*Federal Reserve Bulletin, May, 1919.

Labor Statistics wholesale price index (as then constituted) jumped from 207 to 219, and business boomed.

The extraordinary demand for goods, which produced this sudden transition from hesitation to feverish activity, came partly from foreign countries. The underfed European populations bid eagerly for our foodstuffs; also they were short of raw materials for their mills. Aided by American credits, governmental and private, they could pay for what they needed. So the physical volume of exports and their prices rose together. The value of shipments to Europe reached nearly $5,200,000,000 in 1919, 25 per cent higher than the preceding record, and double the money value in any year since then. The removal of restrictions upon foreign trade enabled our other customers also to buy in proportion to their respective needs. The increase in the value of total exports over 1918 reached $1,771,000,000.

Domestic demands were scarcely less keen. Economies in consumption, partly voluntary and partly forced, had been practiced widely in 1917-18. Hence there was need for buying more than the customary quantities of clothing, household furnishings and other semidurable comforts. Ordinary building had been discouraged during the war as a nonessential industry, and there was pressing call for more houses. Crops in 1918 had been but moderately good; stocks had been kept low; numerous branches of civilian production had been purposely restricted. High prices were asked, for the current supply of finished commodities soon proved inadequate. But for a time customers were willing to pay almost any price for prompt deliveries. Employment had been full for three years, soldiers commonly had substantial sums due them when mustered out, new jobs were readily had at high money wages, everyone seemed tired of economizing.

Under these circumstances, 1919 developed into a great trading year. Interest rates remained fairly low until late autumn; the Treasury was floating its great Victory loans that summer and wanted easy money to facilitate subscriptions. Orders for goods from merchants, contractors and manufacturers promised a continuation of good times. A run-away market developed on the New York Stock Exchange for industrials. Paper profits, present and prospective, seemed very high.

But 1919 was a poor year from the point of view of production. The harvests, indeed, turned out well; there was a large yield of wheat and there were fair crops of corn and cotton. It was in mining and industry that the record was bad. . . . By strenuous effort we had kept production at a high level in 1917 and 1918, despite the withdrawal of more than a million men from our mines and factories. In the first year of peace, when many of these men got back to work, efficiency declined. These indexes of physical production confirm and are confirmed by the estimates of per capita income in dollars of constant purchasing power. The figure for 1918 had been $651. For 1919 it was $611.

More insight into the nature of the industrial inefficiency of 1919 is provided by the indexes from the censuses of manufactures. . . . The most significant figures for the present purpose relate to productivity per wage earner. Of course one expects average productivity per worker to rise gradually in a country which keeps abreast of technical progress. Such an advance we find from 1899 to 1909—the index of productivity per worker in this period runs 100 in 1899, 104 in 1904, and 110 in 1909. We may explain the relapse to 108 in 1914 by the business depression of that year. But the further decline to 104 in the boom year 1919 must mean that both management and labor were deplorably lax. Probably it means also that, during the war, we had neglected our industrial equipment for civilian production and made but few improvements in method.

The business boom of 1919 developed with extraordinary quickness, and in rather extreme form, the internal stresses characteristic of such episodes. A rapid expansion of commercial loans reduced the reserve ratios of the Federal Reserve banks below 50 per cent in October. On November 3, the New York bank raised its rediscount rate. Stock prices tumbled promptly. But as usually happens in booms, commercial activity continued to expand for some months after the stock-market collapse. The further expansion of commitments added to the accumulating tension. Though the other Reserve banks followed the example of New York in raising their rediscount rates, the Reserve ratio continued to sag. By February, 1920, the figure was below 43 per cent, and there it remained for several months of growing uneasiness. Meanwhile, prices at wholesale climbed unsteadily to 247 in May—an advance of 54 points on the prewar base since the dizzy rise had started in March of the preceding year. Then came the turn. Slowly at first, soon rapidly, prices gave way. In half the time it had taken prices to rise 54 points, they dropped 68 points.

At the close of the Civil War, wholesale prices had fallen from 216 in January, 1865, to 158 in July—a drop of over 25 per cent in six months. That fall produced no grave crisis. The business community had expected the greenback dollar to appreciate in gold when the Confederacy collapsed. Grant's successes against Lee and Sherman's march to the sea gave timely warning of what was coming, both at the front and behind the lines. Because business men prepared for the worst, keeping commitments and inventories at a minimum, the country passed through this sudden fall of prices with extraordinary success.

The corresponding drop of prices in 1920-21 caught the business community in a different frame of mind and in a different technical position. Perhaps if the fall had come soon after the armistice, when many expected it and almost everyone was cautious, it would have passed off much as in 1865. But prices had risen in 1919, the volume of trade had expanded, profits had been high, the preliminary warnings of the Federal Reserve banks had been ineffectual, and, when the turn came, many business enterprises were caught with heavy inventories and heavy future commitments. So the fall of prices, which started gently enough, was accentuated by the efforts of embarrassed houses to turn commodities into cash. Every price decline made the financial position of overexpanded enterprises worse, reinforced the fears of insolvency and the pressure for liquidating indebtedness, thus increased the pressure to realize upon stocks of goods, and so forced prices lower still.

Three favorable factors prevented this crisis from degenerating into a panic. Though European demand for our goods declined somewhat from the high level of 1919, the demand from other countries scored a more than compensating increase. The total value of our exports exceeded $8,228,000,000 in 1920—which still stands as the record figure. Second, retail demand from domestic consumers remained active to the end of the year. The Federal Trade Commission estimates total retail sales as nearly 35 billion dollars in 1919 and over 38 billions in 1920. Third, and probably most important, the Federal Reserve System, with its organization of banking reserves, enabled our banks to meet the emergency needs of business far more effectively than in previous crises. There was no such suspension of payments by banks, no such refusal of credit to solvent enterprises, as in 1893 and 1907.

The net resultant of the complex of forces was a drastic financial liquidation, which presently produced, and was then aggravated by, a severe industrial depression. Business enterprises, fearing for their solvency, canceled orders freely; enterprises in a less precarious condition bought hand-to-mouth on the falling markets; concerns which had been making up stocks of raw materials reduced their working forces instead of buying new stocks. Discharges mounted month by month, until the number of unemployed in 1921 alarmed the nation.* In consequence, retail buying fell off—by 7.6 billion dollars, according to the Federal Trade Commission. Thus one of the timbers which had shored up business in 1920 gave way under the prolongation of the strain. A second support failed; other countries were suffering misfortunes like our own, so that our exports dropped 3.7 billion dollars, 45 per cent, below the preceding year.

Amidst these unfavorable circumstances, business losses swelled to prodigious figures. The rise of prices from the middle of 1915 to May, 1920, had rendered money-making overeasy. Speculation in commodities had been encouraged; the penalties

---

*President Harding called a Conference on Unemployment, of which Mr. Hoover was chairman. For a committee of the conference, the National Bureau of Economic Research made a fact-finding study, published in 1923 under the title *Business Cycles and Unemployment*. In this report, the best estimates we could make of the extent of unemployment in 1921 were summarized thus:

"There seems good ground for believing that, in actual diminution of employment, the depression of 1921 was almost twice as acute as that of 1908 and at least twice as acute as that of 1914-15." William A. Berridge (p. 59).

"The figures show that the depression brought about a reduction in the number employed in every industry except the hand trades, and the trivial increase in that one field is scarcely sufficient to keep pace with the growth of population. The reduction in all industries amounted to about 4,000,000 workers, or nearly one-seventh of all persons employed at the crest of the 1920 boom." Willford I. King (p. 86).

The new estimate, given in the chapter on labor in the present report, states the "average minimum volume of unemployment" at 4,225,000 in 1921 as compared with 1,305,000 in 1920. These figures are not inconsistent with the earlier ones; for they give averages for years on a minimum basis, whereas King used quarterly data and attempted to reach a maximum figure.

for inefficient operation and risky financing had been relaxed. The numbers and the liabilities of bankruptcies had declined to half their prewar levels. Thus, when prices began their precipitous fall, the American business community contained a dangerously large proportion of weak enterprises. Despite the extraordinary efforts of bankers, supported by the Federal Reserve System, to prevent avoidable failures, business mortalities trebled between 1919 and 1921. Liabilities increased more than fivefold. What happened to the bulk of enterprises is perhaps best indicated by the reports of corporations to the Internal Revenue Office, though even these official returns must be accepted with reservations. . . . more than half of the corporations reported that they lost money in 1921. If we subtract the deficits of the losers from the net incomes of the concerns which admitted making money, we find that the balance of profits falls from eight billions of dollars in 1919 to less than half a billion in 1921. Probably that statement exaggerates the drop in net corporate income. But it is safe to say that, in the course of the drastic readjustment, a considerable fraction of the accumulated war-time profits was swallowed up.

Though the boom of 1919, the crisis of 1920, and the depression of 1921 followed the pattern of earlier cycles, we have seen how much this cycle was influenced by economic conditions resulting from the war and its sudden ending. These influences were world-wide. If American business men were betrayed by postwar demands into unwise courses, so were business men in all countries similarly situated. . . . The course of business affairs in the United States from 1919 to 1921 was almost exactly paralleled by the course of affairs in the leading European allies, in four great British dependencies on four continents, in the two European neutrals studied, in two South American nations, in Japan and in China. Each of these thirteen countries had its ordinary supplies for civilian uses gravely restricted during the war; to each peace brought a hectic season of activity (mildest in Italy); each suffered a recession in 1920 and a depression in 1921. In only three countries does the record differ widely from that of the United States, and these are countries where the fortunes of war and peace had an opposite cast. Russia's internal troubles kept her economic life in disorder. Germany and Austria suffered depression in 1919-1920 while their victorious opponents enjoyed prosperity, and emerged into revivals in 1920-1921 while their opponents were liquidating postwar booms. Not until this liquidation was finished did economic life resume its independent way. Even then, factors arising from the war continued to exercise an important influence.

V. Factors Affecting American Fortunes in 1922-1927

Among the factors which have shaped economic developments in the United States since the first postwar cycle ended its wild career, we may note first certain unfavorable conditions which business has had to surmount.

Conditions in Other Countries. Prosperity in other countries to which it sells its products tends to beget prosperity in the producing nation. Similarly, depression in foreign markets reacts unfavorably upon domestic business. These international influences gain in scope and energy as nations are drawn closer together by improvements in transportation and communications. Hence the business annals of the nineteenth century show a secular trend toward increasing similarity of economic fortunes among trading nations. Though capable of meeting most of its own needs and separated from the other leaders in commerce by broad oceans, the United States feels the reflex influence of business conditions in every country with which it deals on an appreciable scale. Prosperity here is heightened by active foreign demand for our products, and depression abroad is an unfavorable factor in our home affairs.

Such prosperity as the United States has enjoyed since 1922 owes less than usual to foreign stimulation and support. . . . Few countries have fared so well as we in the last six years. Compared with most of the nations represented, if not judged by the standard we like to set for American prosperity, the United States has been well off.

Department of Commerce figures support this inference from business annals. After an extraordinary fall from 1920 to 1921 or 1922, the value of American exports and imports began to increase again. But imports increased at the more rapid rate. In 1919-1921, the value of our imports made only 56 per cent of the value of our exports. In 1922-1927, this percentage rose to 86. That figure is decidedly higher than the prewar average of 78 per cent in 1910-1914. When 1913 records are taken as 100, the averages for 1922-1927 show the following changes:

The physical volume of imports has increased 66 per cent.
The physical volume of exports has increased 33 per cent.

The prices of imports have increased 31 per cent.
The prices of exports have increased 38 per cent.

The dollar values of imports have increased 117 per cent.
The dollar values of exports have increased 81 per cent.

If we grant that the real goal of economic effort is to secure goods for meeting human wants, it follows that a country's gains from international trade consist of its imports. Exports represent costs—prices paid for the goods desired. In this sense, the fact that our imports have grown faster than our exports means that the outside world had increased its contribution to our economic welfare more rapidly than we have increased our contribution to the economic welfare of other countries. But from the business point of view, the preceding figures mean that by enlarging our purchases more than our sales we have stimulated trade in other countries more than other countries have stimulated trade here.

Further, unless the most inclusive of statistical indexes are grievously in error, our domestic business as a whole has grown faster than our foreign business. Comparisons like those just given, which credit exports with an 81 percent increase, show that on the basis of 1913 records as 100:

The dollar volume of the average national income per year in 1922-1926 increased 121 per cent.

The dollar volume of average yearly bank clearings outside of New York in 1922-1927 increased 175 per cent.

So, too, the Department of Commerce finds that the value of manufactured goods produced in the United States has grown much faster since 1919 than the value of manufactured exports. Indeed, the fraction of these products exported in 1925 was smaller than the prewar average.

In particular, American prosperity has been marred by agricultural depression, and agricultural depression has been due in part to foreign conditions.

The war brought an increased export demand for American breadstuffs and meat. When the United States entered the struggle, and millions of tons of shipping were required for transporting our army to France, there was further reason for avoiding the long hauls of food from Argentina, Australia and India. There was danger also that enlistments would reduce our harvests. One of the first war measures of the Government was the creation of a Food Administration. In other industries, price-fixing meant setting of maximum prices; Congress itself set a minimum price of $2 a bushel on wheat, and authorized the President to raise the minimum higher if need be.

Farmers responded to these war demands as fully as they could. According to the census returns, they had increased the area harvested by 28 million acres between 1899 and 1909; between 1909 and 1919 they added 37 million acres. Yields are always at the mercy of the weather; but the Harvard index of physical production in agriculture shows an acceleration in the rate of growth when averages are taken for several years. This index rose 5 points on the 1899 basis between 1904-1908 and 1909-1913, 12 points between 1909-1913 and 1914-1918, and 2 points more between the war period and 1919-1921—though the last year was one of poor crops.

Thus the war left American agriculture with expanded facilities for production. And the good times had lasted long enough to let even this occupation, which must wait upon nature, base its finances on the unstable prospect of continued high prices and high profits. In the corn belt, the regions where wheat growing was expanding, and in certain tobacco-planting sections, farm lands had risen to prices unheard of before, and thousands of enterprising men had bought all the land they could acquire by stretching their credit to the utmost.

The imperious needs of underfed Europeans had swelled our agricultural exports in 1919 to more than 4 billion dollars—much more than the war-year figures. Even in 1920, agricultural exports were valued at nearly 3.5 billions. But then came a sudden fall in the foreign demand. The total value of agricultural exports shrank in 1921 by 1.3 billion dollars, and in 1922-1927 it fluctuated about an average lower than that of 1921—1.9 billions as compared with 2.1.

For this shrinkage in exports it is easy to account. Price reductions are a large part, but not all, of the story. After demobilization, European farmers could get all the labor they required;

gradually they restored their depleted stocks of farm animals and their accustomed use of fertilizers. Also there were fewer European mouths to feed in 1920 than there had been in 1917, or even in 1910. Thus Europe became less dependent on foreign countries for food than it had been during the war. Second, shipping became superabundant, freights fell to very low levels, and the world's commerce slipped back toward its old channels. The United States lost most of its war-time advantage from a short haul. Third, our competitors in food production—especially Argentina, Canada and Australia—were expanding their output of meat and cereals vigorously. With cheaper lands, they could make things most uncomfortable in world markets for farmers in the United States. Finally, cotton crops were small in these years, manly because of the boll weevil, and the high level of prices made it difficult for the impoverished countries of Europe to buy the quantity needed to furnish employment in their factories and cotton fabrics to their people.

Reckoned in physical units, our agricultural exports remained above the prewar levels in 1922-1927. But they fell below the levels to which American farmers had adjusted their output in 1917-1920. To sell even these reduced quantities, they have had to accept prices which in most cases were low in comparison with the prices of other commodities. . . .

More than in average prewar years, American farmers, with their increased output, had to depend on the domestic markets. They fared ill, and their hard times created more difficulties for other American industries than the prevalence of depression in foreign countries.

The Prime Factor Making for Prosperity. Past experience has taught us that a period of depression will presently be followed by a business revival. But when this revival will come, and whether it will develop into full-blown prosperity, are matters which the past does not tell. Each cycle has its own special features which require special explanations. How the United States managed to attain a higher per capita income in 1922-1927 than ever before, though conditions in most other countries were not favorable, and though its basic industry, agriculture, was depressed, is the outstanding problem of the cycles of 1921-1924, 1924-1927 and 1927 to date [1929].

The preceding chapters give many partial answers to this

question. All these answers may be condensed into one: Since 1921, Americans have applied intelligence to the day's work more effectively than ever before. Thus the prime factor in producing the extraordinary changes in the economic fortunes of the European peoples during the nineteenth century is the prime factor in producing the prosperity of the United States in recent years. The old process of putting science into industry has been followed more intensively than before; it has been supplemented by tentative efforts to put science into business management, trade-union policy, and Government administration.

Concrete instances of technical improvements in many mining, metallurgical, and fabricating processes are given in the chapters on industry. The remarkable results achieved are demonstrated statistically from census data showing output per worker. Similar, though less striking, instances appear in the chapter on construction. Without help from any extraordinary invention, the railroads also have attained a higher level of operating efficiency. In farming there is an intriguing report of new machines and new methods coming into use. Here too, the record of average output per worker shows considerable gains.

All this means that since 1921 Americans have found ways of producing more physical goods per hour of labor than before. They have received larger average incomes because they have produced more commodities and services. That is true in the aggregate, although not all who have contributed to the increase in physical production have shared in the increase of real income. The important exceptions to the general rule will be discussed presently.

The reality of the gains made by improving the technique of farming, railroading, manufacturing, and building seems to be established beyond question. There is room for doubt only concerning the pace of recent progress in comparison with earlier spurts of technical improvement. Comparisons between output per worker in later years and in 1919 often show sensational gains. But that is largely because 1919 made a wretched record of physical inefficiency. . . . The census of manufactures places this year below 1914, and still further below 1909, in output per worker. The above-cited estimates of national income per capita in dollars of constant purchasing power confirm this showing. . . . Nor does 1921, a year of severe depression, afford a satisfactory basis of comparison. Thus it is difficult to measure the technical progress of 1922-1927, with the data now available. It is still more difficult to make reliable measurements for earlier years, when censuses were taken at longer intervals and fewer supplementary figures were published. But doubts whether the rate of improvement in the past six years is unprecedented are not of great moment. It remains clear that the Industrial Revolution is not a closed episode; we are living in the midst of it, and the economic problems of to-day are largely problems of its making.

While the details of the latest technical advances always possess thrilling interest, perhaps there is more of promise for the future in the chapters on recent changes in economic policy. The efforts to apply scientific methods to such matters are in an early stage of development. The sciences which underlie these efforts—psychology, sociology, economics—are far less advanced than physics and chemistry. The experts who are making the applications—personnel managers, advertising specialists, sales directors, business economists and statisticians—are less rigorously trained than engineers. It is even harder to measure the results they achieve than to determine what difference a new machine makes in unit costs. Nor are business executives so generally convinced of the practical value of the rather intangible services which the new professions can render as they are of the indispensability of engineering advice. Yet it is conceivable that applications of the social sciences, now in their tentative stage, will grow into contributions of great moment to economic welfare. Certainly the chapters in this report on marketing, management and labor show that many enterprising business concerns and some enterprising trade unions are trying new policies, and often getting results which they deem good.

Perhaps none of the changes reported here will prove more important in the long run than the change in the economic theories on which the American Federation of Labor and certain outside unions are acting. That organizations of wage earners should grasp the relations between productivity and wages, and that they should take the initiative in pressing constructive plans for increasing efficiency upon employers, is not wholly without precedent; but the spread of such ideas and the vigor with which they are acted on by large organizations must startle those who have believed that trade unions are brakes upon economic progress.

Scarcely less significant is the report from the employing side. Our investigators believe that the art of business management turned a corner in 1921, cultivating since then more skillful understanding of the whole situation and nicer adjustment of means to the immediate environment. Numerous corporations and some trade associations are maintaining research bureaus of their own. Among the managerial devices experimented with, are coordinated staffs in place of one "big boss," bonus payments to executives and "incentive wages" for the rank and file, operating budgets, forecasts of business conditions, close inventory control, personnel management and employee representation. Most of these devices are attempts to understand and to utilize the psychological forces which control human behavior, or the economic forces which control business activity. "There is today not only more production per man, more wages per man and more horse power per man; there is also more management per man."*
Marketing—traditionally the part of business in which native shrewdness, experience and "personal magnetism" have been held all-important—even marketing is being permeated by ap-

---

*On this passage Colonel M. C. Rorty comments as follows:

One of the most significant results arising from improvements in the science of management has been an increasing ability to secure from large units or "chains" the type of individual efficiency that a few years ago could be secured only in the small organization working under the direct supervision of a competent employer-owner. Under the older type of organization there was a gain in efficiency with size, up to the point where the reductions in costs, through ability to specialize and functionalize the work of a larger group of workers and the increases in process, purchasing and selling efficiency under larger scale operation, began to be more than offset by a reduced general efficiency due to the inability of the employer-owner to maintain close contacts with the members of the enlarged organization. Recent developments in management methods, and in accounting and statistical control, have apparently broken down these former economic limitations on the size of the individual organization or "chain," with the result that practically all types of business and industry are now open to efficient large-scale corporate control. If this tendency persists, it may represent a fundamental economic change having very far-reaching consequences. The field of operations for the independent owner-manager will be steadily restricted, and the young man of capacity and intelligence will have to look forward more than ever before to a career in which, except by some rare combination of good fortune and adaptability to circumstances, he will continue throughout to be a subordinate worker in a large corporation organization.

plied psychology. Costly investigations of "consumer appeal," of advertising "pull," of "sales resistance"—the very terms would have been unintelligible to our fathers—show that sales managers are trying to base their planning upon factual studies of human behavior. And the rapid spread of chain stores and of installment selling show that marketing methods are no more standing still than is industrial technique.

By the side of these rather definite changes in trade-union and in business policy, we may set the influence of certain general ideas which have gained wide currency in the last few years.

First, there is the spirit of caution, manifested in minimizing future commitments, in hand-to-mouth buying by merchants, in efforts to keep down inventories or to pass the need for keeping large stocks on to the concern from which one buys. This lesson is taught afresh by every great crisis. The staggering financial losses of 1920-21 enforced the old moral emphatically; the sagging course of commodity prices has kept it in mind, and the increased operating efficiency of producers and railroads has made possible close scheduling of merchandise transactions. The Florida land boom and the stock-market adventure of 1928 indicate the course American business might have taken in the absence of all restraint.

Associated with the prudence which has tempered enterprise is a more systematic effort to learn from experience. Here there seems to be a new emphasis, if not a new practice. Most can be learned from experience when it is exactly known, and seen in relation to its environment. The most exact records of economic experience are statistical in form. Since the war, an increasing number of officials, publicists and business men have fostered the keeping of better statistical records, and have analyzed past experience as a guide to future planning. Every reader must realize that, without the aid of the new statistics which this widespread effort has provided, the present survey of recent economic changes would be more imperfect than it is. What is of use in providing a factual basis for determining economic trends at large is not less useful in determining the factors which affect the success of private enterprises.

More publicity concerning business operations and closer co-operation among business enterprises should also be noted as characteristic of the day. These are features of American practice

which impress all our foreign visitors; the older rules of
secretiveness and rivalry seem to have maintained themselves
more rigidly in other countries. Perhaps the growth of trade
associations and the expansion of their programs is the clearest
evidence of the new attitude. No doubt every industry has its
recalcitrants who, for one reason or another, refuse to play
on the team; but certainly there is a marked increase of
readiness to join co-operative programs of research and publicity, to interchange trade information, to standaradize products
where standardization is good business, to consult about methods
and practices—in short, to treat the industry for many purposes
as a unit in whose prosperity all members have a common interest, and to inspire good will in the public by open dealings.

Fourth, belief in the economy of high wages has become
prevalent among the abler business executives, much as belief
in increasing productivity has become prevalent among the abler
trade-union leaders. To find a market for the wares turned out
by mass production and urged on consumers by national advertising, it is patently necessary to have corresponding purchasing
power in the hands of consumers. Since studies of the national
income have demonstrated that wages constitute by far the
largest stream of personal income, it follows that wages per man
—or rather, wages per family—must be increased as production is
expanded. Perhaps most people would have accepted this argument in the abstract at any time in the last hundred years. But
many employers in the past would have retorted with the assertion that high wages undermine the moral stamina of the
masses. To-day such talk is far less common in the United States.
Not only do many business executives admit the general principle that paying high wages is good policy; they are ready to
assume what they consider their share of the responsibility for
putting the principle into practice.

The share of Government in recent economic changes has not
been made the subject of a separate chapter. . . . If the prime
factor making for prosperity has been the application of intelligence to the day's work, then Government agencies must be
credited with an indispensable, though indirect, part in what has
been accomplished.

Further, our Federal Government has of late years manifested
a more intelligent attitude toward problems of economic organi-

zation than it has manifested in the past. To treat business enterprises as agencies for performing social services, to facilitate their operations, and to hold them to this conception of their function, is a policy exceedingly difficult to carry out. It requires a delicate combination of constructive intervention at some points and of clearing away obstacles at other points. No one can say that this policy has become characteristic of Government in all of its dealings with business, any more than one can say that the doctrine of high wages is accepted by all employers, or the theory that increased productivity benefits labor is accepted by all trade-unionists. Yet no one who has watched Federal policy, as practiced by the numerous agencies which have to deal with economic issues, will question that a change has occurred. Efforts to check extortion have not ceased; but more regularly than in the past they are accompanied by active efforts to heighten the efficiency of what are judged to be legitimate enterprises. Farmers and exporters are not the only beneficiaries.

To repeat: all of the changes making for prosperity which have been recalled in this section, together with many others noted in preceding chapters, can be summed up under a single head—applying fresh intelligence to the day's work. From the use of abstruse researches in pure science to the use of broad economic conceptions and the use of common sense, the method of American progress in 1922-1928 has been the old method of taking thought. Peace let us turn our thoughts to common matters, the hard times of 1921 spurred our efforts, and the complicated consequences our efforts produced have kept us thinking.

VI. Hardships Caused by Increasing Efficiency

Among the consequences which improvements in industrial technique or in business methods produce in an individualistic state, are hardships of various kinds. The victims are partly business competitors who are a bit slow in adopting new methods; partly industries or geographic regions affected indirectly; partly individuals who find their services no longer needed. To follow all the complicated difficulties produced by recent economic advances in the United States is out of the question; but a few chains of cause and effect may be traced link by link. For the queer mixture of prosperity and depression noted at the outset of this chapter is due largely to the pressure which some group's growing efficiency puts upon other groups.

Reductions in Unit-costs, Prices and Profits. The technical advances of recent years in the United States have been largely advances in the direction of more economical production. A greater volume of goods has been turned out at lower costs per unit. Now larger supplies sent to market tend to depress prices.

In most periods of prosperity this tendency has been more than offset by an increase in demand. The cases have been few indeed when the index numbers of wholesale prices have failed to rise in the prosperous phase of a cycle. And there are clear marks of the standard reaction in our period. The Bureau of Labor Statistics index number advanced from 91.4 in January, 1922, to 104.5 in March, 1923. On the mild recession of that year it reversed its course and declined to 94.9 in June, 1924. When business picked up again, the index began to climb once more, reaching 104.8 in March, 1925. From that point it receded unsteadily to 93.7 in April and May, 1927. Judged by prewar standards, these fluctuations have about the average amplitude. The remarkable fact is that prices sagged through the prosperous year 1926. Taking the whole period from 1922 to 1927, the trend has been a gently declining one. Prices at wholesale have fallen at the rate of 0.1 per cent per annum.

Monetary factors, which are often held responsible for changes in wholesale price levels, can scarcely be held repsonsible in this case. In 1922-1927 international gold movements added $760,000,000 net to our stock, and "earmarking" operations took less than $200,000,000 of this sum out of monetary use. The banks suffered no stringency; indeed they increased their other investments, because commercial borrowers asked less credit than the banks would have been glad to lend. So far as domestic conditions are concerned, business activity and the easy money market might have combined to produce a vigorous advance of prices.

But, though the fact is commonly overlooked, the course of prices cannot be explained in any commercial nation of these days by domestic conditions alone. Commodities subject to international trade on a considerable scale cannot long maintain prices higher in one country than in another by margins which exceed costs of carriage and handling, plus import duties. Price fluctuations in different countries are tied even closer to each other, as a rule, than actual prices; for though import duties may establish a considerable spread between market prices in two countries, these duties are not subject to very frequent change. Shipping charges have been particularly low in the period under review, so that this factor has interfered less than usual with market uniformity. Even countries with inconvertible currencies are bound to the world system of prices, and to its fluctuations, through the rate of exchange.

It is true that a large proportion of the articles dealt in on wholesale markets, in such a country as the United States, are not exported or imported on an appreciable scale. But economists have long since shown that the prices of different goods prevailing in any country at any time are closely related to each other through the channels of supply and demand. Domestic prices thus constitute a system, in the sense that a change in the price of any commodity affects, and is in turn affected by, changes in the prices of a host of other goods. The statistical aspect of these interrelations is briefly developed in the preceding chapter on price movements. Since all domestic prices are thus related to each other, and since a considerable fraction of these prices are related to foreign prices, changes in the general level of wholesale prices in any one country must be related to the changes taking place in the wholesale price levels of other countries. . . .

Thus the reduction in unit costs, and the increase in the supply of wares turned out by improved methods, combined with international forces to keep the American price level from rising buoyantly in the active years of our period, as it has done in most periods of prosperity. Presumably, the international factors have been more potent than the domestic factors in producing the results. Yet we may count the reductions in cost by industrial leaders and the increases in output among the manifestations of efficiency which have contributed to the difficulties of making money in this period.

Sagging prices make it harder to conduct business with profit because many of the expenses of an enterprise are fixed by long contracts or by understandings hard to alter, and cannot be cut to offset a reduction in selling rates. Above, we noticed how the rapidly rising prices of the war and of 1919 swelled paper profits and reduced bankruptcies. Also we noted how the sudden fall of prices in 1920-21 turned profits into losses and swelled bankruptcies. In 1922-1927, we find an intermediate result. Concerns in the van of technical progress have done handsomely. But the prices at which they could market their large outputs with profit to themselves have meant loss and even failure to less aggressive rivals. . . . The average number of failures in 1922-1927 has actually exceeded the number in 1921, but the total and the average liabilities have grown smaller.

"Profitless prosperity," like so many popular paradoxes, combines an element of truth with an element of falsehood. One expects a period of unusually rapid increase in efficiency to be a period of more than usual inequality of profits. This expectation has been borne out by the experience of 1922-1927. As a whole, corporate incomes reported to the Internal Revenue Bureau . . . have been large in the latest years for which we have data; but they have not equaled the records of 1916-1919.

Whether the enterprises which have lagged behind in cost reductions and in earnings are mainly smaller enterprises, as has been contended, is less sure. Of course this contention tends to become true with the lapse of time, for the simple reason that the exceptionally profitable enterprises grow exceptionally fast. The profitable enterprises of to-day tend to become the large enterprises of tomorrow. . . .

The Competition of New Products and New Tastes. Scarcely less characteristic of our period than unit-cost reductions is the rapid expansion in the production and sale of products little used or wholly unknown a generation or even a decade ago. Among consumers' goods, the conspicuous instances are automobiles, radios and rayon. But the list includes also oil-burning furnaces, gas stoves, household electrical appliances in great variety, automobile accessories, antifreezing mixtures, cigarette lighters, propeller pencils, wrist watches, airplanes, and what not. Among producers' goods we have the truck and the tractor competing with the horse and the mule, reinforced concrete competing with brick and lumber, the high-tension line competing with the steam engine, fuel oil competing with coal, not to mention excavating machines, belt conveyors, paint sprayers, and "automatics" of many sorts competing with manual labor.

Changes in taste are in large part merely the consumers' response to the solicitation of novel products, effectively presented by advertising. But that is not all of the story; the consumer is free to choose what he likes among the vociferous offerings, and sometimes reveals traces of initiative. In what other terms can one explain the changes in diet . . . ? Americans are consuming fewer calories per capita; they are eating less wheat and corn but more dairy products, vegetable oils, sugar, fresh vegetables and fruit. More families than ever before are sending their sons and daughters to college—surely that is not a triumph of "high-powered" salesmanship. Young children, girls and women, are wearing lighter and fewer clothes. The short skirt, the low shoe, the silk or rayon stocking, "athletic" underwear, the soft collar, sporting suits and sporting goods, have an appeal which makers of rival articles have not been able to overcome. And, in a sense, every consumers' good, from college to candy, is a rival of every other consumers' good, besides being a rival of the savings bank.

"When the makers of one product get a larger slice of the consumer's dollar, the slices left for the makers of other products get smaller." This way of accounting for the hardships met by certain long-established industries in 1922-1927, such, for example, as the leather and woolen trades, is popular and sound, so far as it goes. But it does not take account of the fact that desire for new goods, or the pressure of installment purchases once made, may lead people to work harder or more steadily, and so get more dollars to spend. Presumably the enticements of automobiles and radios, of wrist watches and electric refrigerators, of correspondence courses and college, have steadied many youths, set many girls hunting for jobs and kept many fathers of families to the mark. Also a considerable part of the country's former bill for intoxicants has been available to spend in other ways. How much allowance we should make for these factors nobody knows. All one can say with assurance is that consumption per capita has increased in volume to match the increased per capita output of consumers' goods taken altogether. Yet the increase in consumption has not been rapid enough to prevent shifts in the kind of goods bought from pressing hard upon the makers of articles waning in popular favor.

So too in the realm of producers' goods. Despite the active building campaign, the lumber industry has had hard sledding.

Coal mining has not prospered, and can attribute part of its difficulties to other fuels, water power, and more economical ways of burning coal itself. Breeders of draft animals have found their markets cut into by motor vehicles. Railways have lost traffic to trucks and omnibusses—though the loss in freight tonnage is held by Professor Cunningham to be less than the public supposes. Steam-engine builders have had to change their products or reduce their output. It is not necessary to multiply examples; most technical improvements reduce the demand for some other good, and so create difficulties for those who supply the latter.

Geographical Shifts in Industry and Trade. Just as definite a gain may be made in productivity by shifting factories to better locations, or by reorganizing channels of supply, as by installing automatic machines. Besides the drift of cotton manufacturing to the South, of which everyone thinks, and the more recent drift of shoe manufacturing to the West, the chapter on industry shows a prevailing tendency toward geographical decentralizing of production. The proportion of the output of many goods coming from the old headquarters is on the decline. The chapter on agriculture indicates a parallel development in farming. The cotton belt is stretching west, the wheat belt west and northwest; the dairying and the market-garden areas are moving in various directions. Finally, the chapter on marketing shows a concentration of trade in cities and towns at the expense of villages.

Doubtless these changes are to the advantage of those who make them. If they proved unprofitable, they would be abandoned. But it is equally clear that we have here another feature of increasing efficiency which brings losses as well as gains. New England may not lose as much as North Carolina and St. Louis gain from the shifts in the cotton and shoe trades—that is a question of the totals. And New England may devise new ways of using its labor, its capital, its manufacturing sites, and its ingenuity, more profitable than the old—necessity is often the mother of invention. If these efforts succeed, they may create fresh difficulties felt elsewhere. Similar truisms might be recited concerning the other cases in point. But whatever happens in the future, we must not let the dazzle of the high lights blind us to the sectional shadows.

"Technological Unemployment." Among all the hardships im-

posed by increasing efficiency, most publicity has been given to the decline in the number of wage earners employed by factories. That is a matter of the gravest concern in view of the millions of families affected or threatened by the change, and in view of their slender resources. To it special attention has been paid in this investigation.

The new phrase coined to describe what is happening, "technological unemployment," designates nothing new in the facts, though the numbers affected may be large beyond precedent. Ever since Ricardo shocked his rigid disciples by admitting that the introduction of "labor-saving" machinery may cause a temporary diminution of employment, economists have discussed this problem. Granting Ricardo's admission, they have nevertheless held that, in the long run, changes in method which heighten efficiency tend to benefit wage earners. English experience since Ricardo's day seems to bear out this contention. The power looms, which put an end to hand-loom weaving after tragic struggles, have not reduced the number of British workers employed in weaving, or cut their average earnings. The railways, which displaced the old mail coaches and carters, have not reduced the number of transport workers or made them poorer. And the new trades of building and caring for the elaborate modern equipment must not be forgotten. There doubtless are cases in which improvements in methods have caused what promises to be a permanent reduction in the number of persons employed in an industry. By defining industry narrowly, these cases can be made numerous. But the broad result plainly has been that the industrial triumphs of the nineteenth century increased the demand for labor and increased its rewards. "Labor-saving" machinery has turned out to be job-making machinery.

To recall these familiar facts should not diminish by one jot our rating of the hardships suffered by men who are thrown out of jobs. They and their families often undergo severe privation before new employment can be found; the new jobs may pay less than the old or be less suitable; too often the displaced man never finds a new opening. Technical progress is continually made at cost to individuals who have committed no fault and committed no avoidable error of judgment. No organized plan has been evolved for preventing such hardships, aside from the schemes devised by some trade unions for tiding their members over mechanical revolutions in their crafts. The nations have left the remedy to "natural forces;" they have trusted that the expansion of production, which improvements bring about, will presently open new places for the displaced workers.

The problem of what happened in the short period 1922-1927, then, is to find how many wage earners were displaced in that time, how many of the displaced found new jobs promptly, and what these new jobs were. To answer these questions accurately would require far better data than are to be had. There are few branches of statistics in which the United States lags further behind the leaders than in statistics of employment. What we have been able to learn comes to this:

Starting with the 1920 census of occupations and reckoning forward, it is estimated that by 1927 there had been an increase of about 5,100,000 employees 16 years of age and over, who looked to nonagricultural occupations for a living. The figure allows for the fact that some 860,000 persons had left the farms to seek livelihoods elsewhere, and the more than offsetting fact that the number of pupils over 15, enrolled in schools and colleges, had risen by 1,430,000 between 1920 and 1927.

Of the 5,100,000 net additions to nonagricultural job seekers, a few turned to mining and allied occupations; 100,000 entered public services, over 600,000 engaged in construction work of some sort, nearly a million attached themselves to "transportation and communications," 1,400,000 became mercantile employees, and more than two and a half millions took to miscellaneous occupations in hotels, restaurants, garages, repair shops, moving-picture places, barber shops, hospitals, insurance work, professional offices, and the like. Manufacturing is the only large occupational group, aside from farming, to show a decline. There the number of employees fell from about 11,200,000 in 1920 to about 10,600,000 in 1927—a drop of 600,000.

All these data are estimates of the net changes in numbers of persons "attached to" the occupations in question. They show that American wage earners met "technological unemployment" in manufacturing mainly by turning to other ways of making a living. The decline from 1920 to 1927 in the number of persons actually at work in manufacturing enterprises is put at 825,000, but the number of *unemployed* among the people who depended on factory work for a living increased only 240,000 between

1920 and 1927, according to the best figures available. If these estimates are approximately correct, then some 585,000 of the workers laid off by factories had taken up other occupations. That is, 71 per cent of the workers displaced had attached themselves to new trades by 1927.

Adopting a new occupation, however, does not guarantee getting a new job. The surplus workers from our farms and factories who hunted for fresh openings increased unemployment in other fields. The expansion of business, particularly the expansion of miscellaneous and mercantile occupations, made places for perhaps four and a half million new wage earners. But the supply of new jobs has not been equal to the number of new workers plus the old workers displaced. Hence there has been a net increase of unemployment, between 1920 and 1927, which exceeds 650,000 people.

The number of the unemployed has varied from year to year with cyclical changes in business activity. It surpassed all previous records in the depression of 1921 [ca. 15.3%]; it declined rather slowly in the revival of 1922; even in the busy year 1923 it remained higher than in 1920; it rose in the mild recession of 1924, declined on the return of activity in 1925-26, and then mounted again in 1927 [ca. 6.3%]. . . .

One may wonder at the versatility, initiative and mobility of Americans, as evidenced afresh by their prompt shifting of occupations on so great a scale in recent years. One may wonder also at the rapid expansion of the trades which have absorbed some five million employees in seven years without reducing wage rates. But one must not forget that these shiftings have been compulsory in large measure; men have been forced out of farming and forced out of factories as well as pulled into automobile services, shops and restaurants. And the employment balance is on the unfavorable side. While our economic progress has meant larger per capita earnings for all workers taken together, it has imposed severe suffering upon hundreds of thousands of individuals.

The Domestic Difficulties of Agriculture. It was noted above that American farming owes part of its difficulties in 1922-1927 to reductions in foreign demand and increases in foreign supply. It must now be added that fresh difficulties have been created for farmers by changes in domestic demand, and by the successful

efforts of farmers to increase their own efficiency as producers.
. . . All in all, the standard of living has been rising in the
United States of late. But Americans have been eating less food
per capita than once they did. The greater diversification of diet
has been advantageous to dairymen, market gardeners and fruit
growers; but the bulk of farmers have lost more than they have
gained from the changes. Americans have also been wearing less
clothing than formerly, and that hurts the market for cotton
planters and wool growers. Moreover, there has been a shift from
cotton and woolen fabrics toward silk and rayon. Finally, the
goods on which American families have spent freely—automobiles and their accessories, gasoline, household furnishings
and equipment, radios, travel, amusements and sports—are goods
in which little agricultural produce is used.

To make matters harder, the firmness of wage rates in the
flourishing industries has forced farmers to pay relatively high
wages for such hired labor as they have needed. Taxes on farm
property have risen in every year covered by the record. While
the prices farmers had to pay for operating supplies and equipment, as well as for consumers' goods, dropped sharply in 1921,
they did not drop nearly so much as the prices which farmers
received for their products. . . .

It is a grave error to think of American farmers as the passive
but complaining victims of calamity. . . . they have exhibited as
vigorous a capacity for self-help as any other large section of the
community. The qualities which enabled their forerunners to
subdue the wilderness reappear in the efforts of the present
generation to work a way out of the postwar tangle.

But agriculture is a business of very slow turnover. Agriculture
is also an extrahazardous business, which depends for results on
averages over a series of harvests. The dislocations it faces at
present are partly the result of continuing secular trends, rather
than cyclical fluctuations which reverse themselves every few
years. And agriculture is a business in which millions of producers are working each on his own account. A concerted policy
is exceedingly difficult to organize. What one farmer does to help
himself often makes matters harder for other farmers. That is the
aspect of the farm problem which requires attention here.

The individual farmer, hard pressed by low prices and high
fixed costs, has tried several ways to better his fortunes. One way

alleviates the lot of other farmers, whether it turns out well for himself or not. It is to give up farming. Dr. C. J. Galpin estimates that there was a net decrease of farm population amounting to 460,000 persons in 1922, perhaps a larger number in 1923, 182,000 in 1924 when city jobs were harder to get, and 479,000 in 1926. We have already noticed Dr. M. B. Givens' estimate that in 1920-27 upwards of a million migrants from the farm sought other occupations. So far as reduction in number of workers goes, there is a close parallel between the record of farming and of manufacturing.

This considerable shift in population has been accompanied by a much slighter decline in the area of land cultivated. The abandonment of poor farms has unquestionably been accelerated by hard times, though we lack comprehensive data to show on what scale. On the other hand, wide tracts of former waste lands have been reclaimed and wider tracts of former cattle ranges have been brought under the plow. . . .

But the smaller numbers of workers left on farms, cultivating slightly less land, have increased their output—again paralleling developments in manufacturing. The Department of Agriculture's index showing "mass of crop production" mounted from 100 in 1919—a year of fair harvests—to 102 in 1922, 104 in 1925, and 106 in 1927. If these figures were reduced to a per capita basis, the rate of increase would be decidedly greater. Of course, every farmer who has enlarged his output has contributed his mite toward keeping down prices. Agricultural depression had forced the individual farmer to meet his narrow margins above cost by raising more units to sell, and selling more units has tended to make these margins narrower still.

Increased productivity per worker in agriculture has been achieved in the same way as increased productivity per worker in manufacturing—by putting more intelligence into the work. For decades, agricultural experiment stations, colleges, state bureaus, farm papers, and the Department of Agriculture in Washington have been actively seeking to learn and to teach better methods of farming. From drainage to the choice of crops, the breeding of stock and the building of fireplaces, scarcely any feature of farming as a technical process, as a business enterprise, or as a way of making a home but has been studied intensively and written up extensively. Slowly the lessons have been learned by an increasing number of farmers and farmers' wives. The pressure of hard times speeded up the application of knowledge to practice, despite the fact that hard times cut down the farmers' ability to accumulate the capital which many of the changes require.

One of the conspicuous changes in methods of farming has reacted most unfavorably upon the demand for farm products. The number of tractors in use on farms is estimated to have increased from 80,000 in January, 1918, to 380,000 in 1922, and 770,000 in January, 1928. This change has been accompanied by a decrease in the number of horses and mules on farms from about 26,400,000 in 1918 and 1919 to 20,100,000 in 1928. An even greater decline was occurring at the same time in the number of horses and mules in cities. A not inconsiderable branch of animal husbandry thus lost much of its market. What was worse, at least 15 to 18 million acres of hay and grain land lost its market also. . . . .

That with all their courage and ability they [farmers] have not yet succeeded in regaining their former measure of prosperity, must be ascribed partly to the slowness of agricultural processes themselves, partly to the halting recuperation of Europe and its reactions on other countries, and partly to the fact that increasing efficiency has added to the supply of farm products or cut down the demand.

Agricultural depression has not been confined to the United States. In many other countries, the tillers of the soil have been engaged in a similar struggle with unfavorable conditions of supply and demand. Their efforts to make up for the relatively low prices received for their products by marketing larger quantities, and their compulsory retrenchments of expenditure, have reacted unfavorably upon the fortunes of American farmers, just as the similar actions of American farmers have made conditions harder for them. Round a good part of the globe, the productivity of agriculture has been rising, while in most of the leading industrial nations other branches of production have grown slowly if at all. The effect upon prices in the great world markets has been striking. The demand for agricultural products as a whole is inelastic compared with the demand for many industrial products. That is, a relatively small increase in the current supply of foodstuffs, the great agricultural staple, brings a relatively large decline in market prices. Hence the change in the international balance of agricultural and nonagricultural output has created a difficult situation for farmers, even in the few countries, like the United States, where production in other lines has increased rapidly.

What has been the net effect of all the factors, domestic and foreign, influencing the economic fortunes of American farmers, is hard to ascertain.

. . . American farmers gained greatly in relative economic status between the beginning and the end of the war, though, even at their peak, agricultural incomes per capita remained far below the national average. The catastrophic drop from 1919 to 1921 wiped out all of this gain and considerably more. If our estimates are reliable, by 1925 farmers had won back to their prewar position in comparison with average per capita incomes in other occupations, but they were by no means so well off as in 1919-20. . . .

Even if these results be accepted as probably more reliable than general impressions, they do not represent adequately the farmer's relative position in the national economy. In particular, they show nothing of the financial entanglements into which many of the most enterprising American farmers were drawn in the flush years. A man may make as good a current income now as before the war and still be far worse off, if he is carrying a greatly increased load of debts. And quite apart from that, the not unfavorable income comparison which 1925 makes with prewar years is due to the use of shrinking per capita figures for farmers and swelling per capita figures for the total population. An industry which keeps up its per capita quota of the national income because thousands of workers withdraw from it cannot be regarded as flourishing.

VII. The Interrelations Among Economic Changes

The Factors Already Discussed. So far, the contrasts noted at the outset of this chapter between the economic fortunes of different income groups, different industries, and different sections of the United States in 1922-1927, have been traced to three factors—or rather to three great complexes of factors. (1) Foreign conditions on the whole have been none too favorable to American business, and they have been eminently unfavorable to American agriculture. Important branches of industry have enjoyed a large increase in foreign sales; but had Europe been prosperous, American prosperity would have been less "spotty" and more intense. (2) Such prosperity as we have enjoyed has been earned by many-sided and strenuous efforts, in which millions of people have shared, to improve our technical methods, our business management, our trade-union policy, and our Government administration. (3) While increasing efficiency has added to real income, it has put pressure, often rising to severe hardship, upon competitors, direct and indirect. The factory hand competing with the "automatic" machine, the horse farmer competing with the tractor farmer, the lumber industry competing with the cement industry, the New England cotton mill competing with the North Carolina cotton mill, the independent retailer competing with the chain store, the clothing trade competing with the makers of automobiles and radios for slices of the consumers' dollars, have had a hard time.

This analysis is not simple, but it is still too schematic. There is no hope of learning and telling the whole story in realistic detail. Yet one further factor of great moment and two sets of "economic reactions" must be introduced before a summing up is attempted.

Retardation in the Growth of Population and Its Effects. The additional factor to be taken into account concerns population growth. In sketching the main lines of nineteenth century experience, it was noted that the fruits of the tree of applied knowledge can be consumed in several ways. One way is to increase population as fast as the tree increases its yield. If that course is pushed to the limit, there can be no reduction of working hours and no advance in the standard of living. The latter gains are contingent upon keeping the growth of population slower than the gain in productive efficiency. And before the close of the century the European stock had sensibly reduced its birth rate.

This reduction of birth rates has been going on during our period in most of the states of the Union. The decline seems to be more rapid than the decline in death rates. Moreover, first the war and then legislation restricted immigration. . . . Combined, the birth-rate and death-rate changes and the changes in migration reduced the average annual increase of population from 1,800,000 in 1920-1925 to 1,545,000 in 1925-1928.

The retardation in population growth has affected the whole social situation profoundly in ways which concern the student of sociology and politics quite as deeply as they concern the economist. It will be long before the full effects upon national life become clear. But certain prompt economic consequences must be noted.

At the close of the war, when a fall in the price level like that of 1865 was expected by many, business executives frequently said that the first task of reorganization was to "liquidate labor." The great buying campaign of 1919 and the accompanying up-rush of prices caused a postponement of this program. For a time it was hard to get men enough, even at rising rates. When prices fell precipitously in 1920-21 and unemployment was rife, the moment to insist on wage reductions seemed to have come. But the trade unions offered strenuous resistance, despite the number of the temporarily idle. Their resistance was more effective than it could have been had not the growth of population been retarded for some years. The prices of labor were cut, to be sure, but not cut as much as the prices of consumers' goods. Hence, when employment became tolerably full again toward the close of 1922, wage earners found themselves in possession of relatively large purchasing power. Then the economic advantages of a broad consumers' market began to appear. Employers discovered that their inability to "liquidate labor" had been fortunate for themselves, as well as for their employees. The doctrine of high wages found conspicuous champions among the business leaders, and their formulations favored its spread. Discoveries in science, as well as in practical life, have often been made thus by observing the consequences of a thwarted effort.

In most periods of prosperity, wage rates lag somewhat behind living costs on the rise. The indications are that these paradoxical "prosperity losses" to wage earners have not cut much figure during 1922-1927. Wholesale prices have sagged slightly, and living costs have advanced but little. Though the percentage of unemployment has risen since 1923, wage rates have been firmly maintained on the whole, if not increased somewhat.

This result also must be ascribed in part to the relatively slow increase in the number of job hunters. Had there been no legal check on immigration in 1922-1927, unemployment would have attained large proportions, and the difficulty of maintaining wage rates would have been greater.

Moreover, it seems sound to ascribe a part of the gains in technical efficiency, which have been so characteristic of recent years, to the high price of labor. An employee to whom one pays high wages may represent low labor cost. But if he is to be so efficient as to be cheap, he must be provided with good equipment and aided by good management. More horse power per man and better management per man, to twist Mr. Dennison's flexible phrase, are needed to secure more production per man; and more production must be had per man when more wages are paid per man.

All this discussion on a per capita basis is proper; to make clear how proper, consider the effect of retardation in population growth upon aggregate production and wealth. Had there been no reduction in birth rates and no restriction of immigration, the United States would contain several millions more people than it does. As large or a larger fraction of the greater population would be "engaged in gainful occupations," and, despite more unemployment and a less advanced stage of industrial technique, the workers would probably be producing a greater volume of goods. Thus, the national income would be rising faster than it is; but per capita income would be growing slower than it is. Since birth-rate restriction seems to be voluntary, and since immigration restriction certainly is, we must conclude that Americans are preferring to raise the economic level of average life rather than to maximize national wealth.

Mutually Moderating and Mutually Intensifying Reactions. The two sets of economic reactions still to be noted may be thought of as the mutually moderating effects of factors opposing each other, and as the mutually intensifying effects of factors working in the same direction.

Like the set of economic reactions already discussed—the pressure exerted on competitors by those who increase their own efficiency—these moderating and intensifying effects arise from the basic feature of economic organization. Though modern society accepts the principle of individual responsibility, each individual gets his money income wholly by serving others, and gets his real income mainly by consuming goods other people have made. Thus everyone depends both on the buying power of other consumers and on the efficiency of other producers. And what is true of every individual is true, *mutatis mutandis,* of every business enterprise. These intricate relations of interdependence tangle the skein of economic causes and effects beyond the present power of man to unravel. Every development is the net resultant of numerous causes and also the cause of numerous effects. But though we can not disentangle all the crisscrossing influences of the factors which have shaped American fortunes in 1922-1927, we can follow certain of their salient reactions upon each other.

To take first the moderating effects of opposing factors: American prosperity in 1922-1927, in nonagricultural lines, would have been decidedly greater had the six million American farmers been flourishing. Every man thrown out of work has subtracted an iota from the national dividend and an iota from the demand for goods. Every business that has failed has made a tiny difference in our ability to provide for our wants and to market our products. The United States as a whole would have been better off if all foreign countries had enjoyed fortunes equal to its own.

On the other hand, the farmers would have been in far worse plight if the majority of Americans had not been receiving relatively large incomes, and if American factories and railways had not been highly efficient as servants of agriculture. So too, the unemployed would have been more numerous, and their difficulties in getting new jobs greater, had the country suffered from industrial depression. Finally, other countries would have been worse off, had we not been in position to import freely, and to make large loans.

There can be no doubt about the reality or the importance of these reactions of hardship in diminishing prosperity, and of prosperity in diminishing hardship. But there seems to be no way of measuring such complicated influences with the data available.

Clearer still are the effects of one favorable development in reinforcing other favorable developments, and the corresponding intensification of misfortune by misfortune. In this period and in our country, the former set of cumulations has been more in evidence than the latter. And it is necessary to bring these reactions of favorable developments upon each other into the foreground of our final picture. For we cannot understand any single factor in the situation, such as increasing technological efficiency, the rising standard of living, the relatively stable price level, the large volume of construction, the abundance of capital and credit, or large income disbursements, without noting how other factors favored its development.

Take, for example, keener intelligence applied to the day's work, which increased the physical output of goods. That has meant the possibility of larger average real incomes per capita. To distribute these goods, market experts cultivated the desires of the people for a freer and more varied consumption; they developed plans by which the eager could satisfy wants before they could pay. A sound monetary and banking system provided the requisite currency and credit to run this whole process of producing and distributing a swelling river of goods. Price fluctuations were held within narrow limits by a combination of prudence among business men, unit-cost reductions by technical experts, skill on the part of bankers, and the course of foreign markets. This relative stability of prices reinforced the pressure upon all parties to exercise caution, calculate closely, and watch costs; it also helped to keep world prices relatively stable. Since prices were not buoyant, business enterprises had to maintain a high level of efficiency in order to make profits, and that fact intensified the application of intelligence with which this paragraph started. By the aid of the reinforced efficiency, it has been possible to pay high wages and salaries, meet interest and rental charges, distribute liberal dividends, and still retain large surpluses for protecting or expanding business ventures. The large income disbursements provided the purchasing power to which the market experts appealed for the purchase of the increased physical output of goods. Meanwhile, the considerable profits reaped by the large number of efficient enterprises made them eager to grow. At the same time, prosperous families wanted better housing; prosperous communities wanted larger schools; prosperous states wanted hard-surfaced roads. So the routine business of providing current income was supplemented by an exceptional volume of new construction to provide industrial equipment of all kinds, office buildings, single dwellings, apartments, hotels, theaters, schools and highways. That required capital running into billions of dollars. The demand was met without strain from the surpluses of business enterprises and the savings of individuals whose higher standards of living had not absorbed all of their money incomes. And of course the construction work, as it proceeded, enlarged the market for a vast variety of goods, and enlarged the disbursements of income.

So one might go on indefiintely, tracing the fashion in which each of the prosperity-producing factors in the situation has increased the activity out of which it grew, and thus promoted conditions which heightened its own efficiency. The broad facts, however, are patent. And no elaboration would lead to a convincing evaluation of what credit belongs to any single factor taken by itself. Drop out any of the developments recalled in the preceding paragraph, and the process as a whole would be altered. It is just as impossible to say what high wages, large construction, skillful marketing, railroad efficiency, or abundant credit contributed to prosperity, as it is to say how much agricultural depression, technological unemployment, or the lingering troubles of Europe have diminished the prosperity which might have been attained but for these drawbacks.

Net Effects upon Average Per Capita Income. Reasons were given above for accepting the estimate of per capita income, expressed in dollars of constant purchasing power, as the most inclusive, and probably the most reliable, summary of the net results flowing from all the myriad changes which affect the economic welfare of the country's people. Accordingly, we return to these figures as the best general conclusion of the whole investigation. Two series of figures are given. The first shows income received in money; the second "disbursed income"—that is, money receipts plus the value of income yielded by homes occupied by their owners and by household goods, the value of farm produce consumed by the producers and minor items of similar nature. The first series corresponds closely to the common conception of income, but the other is a better index of economic welfare. The following comments refer to the second series.

Per Capita Income in the United States Expressed in 1925 Dollars

	Income received in money ($)	Disbursed income ($)
1913	554	621
1917	579	656
1919	510	611
1920	520	600
1921	500	576
1922	557	625
1923	616	679
1924	628	697
1925	647	714
1926	659*	733*

* Preliminary.

From the trough in which the war and the war-dominated cycle of 1919-1921 left the country, Americans raised their average fortunes to the prewar level in a single year of reviving activity. A second year of great gains left the old records far behind. Since 1923, progress has been steady, but less rapid.

Unless these figures are very far in error, not only absolutely but also relatively, the final verdict upon the years 1922-1926, and presumably upon 1927 and 1928, for which the income record is yet incomplete, must be that they brought good times to the majority of our people—though by no means to all. . . .

VIII. How Matters Stand in the Spring of 1929

Forecasting the future is no part of the present task. But we should not close the record without noting that recent developments may appear less satisfactory in retrospect than they appear at present.

Even on the face of affairs, all is not well. Americans have seen more uniformly fortunate times: for example, in 1906, when the Secretary of the Treasury was praying that the country might be delivered from more prosperity. The condition of agriculture, the volume of unemployment, the textile trades, coal mining, the leather industries, present grave problems not only to the people immediately concerned, but also to their fellow citizens. How rapidly these conditions will mend, we do not know. Some may grow worse.

Nor can we be sure that the industries now prosperous will prolong indefinitely their recent record of stability. That we have not had a serious crisis since 1920 or a severe depression since 1921 is no guarantee that we shall be equally prudent, skillful and fortunate in the years to come. If we are to maintain business prosperity, we must continue to earn it month after month and year after year by intelligent effort. The incomes disbursed to consumers, and to wage earners in particular, must be increased on a scale sufficient to pay for the swelling volume of consumers' goods sent to market. The credit structure must be kept in due adjustment to the earnings of business enterprises. Security prices must not outrun prospective profits capitalized at the going rate of interest. Commodity stocks must be held in line with current sales. Overcommitments of all sorts must be avoided. The building of new industrial equipment must not be overrapid. These and the similar matters which might be mentioned present delicate problems of management which will find their practical solutions in the daily decisions of business executives. Perhaps errors are being kept within the limits of tolerance. Perhaps no serious setback will occur for years to come. But we are leaving 1921 well behind us, and there are signs that the caution inspired by that disastrous year is wearing thin.

Whether the recent rate of progress in the arts of industry and business can be maintained is another uncertainty. Past experience, as summed up in the introductory chapter, suggests that the pace will slacken presently, and that years may pass before we see such another well-maintained advance. But that is a matter in which experience is not a trustworthy guide. Scientific research, industrial invention and business pioneering all lead into the unknown. They are fascinating ventures which energetic minds will ever be trying, whether the tangible rewards prove great or small. All that is certain is that whatever progress in efficiency we continue to make must be won by the same type of bold and intelligent work that has earned our recent successes.

15

The Sanctity of Freedom of Contract Upheld
Adkins v. Children's Hospital

Protection of workers against the more rapacious of the new business entrepreneurs was one of the objectives of the early twentieth-century social reformers. The campaign for women's rights was related to the efforts to upgrade the conditions and rewards for labor. Inherited traditions of freedom proved a major stumbling block hampering the reformers in their efforts to aid the working man and working woman. Some accomplishments had been made on the state level before 1920, and in response to pressure exerted by women's rights associations, Congress in 1918, as the legislature for the District of Columbia, sought to provide a minimum wage law for women and minors working in the District. The constitutionality of the act was denied in 1921, and in due time the matter came before the United States Supreme Court. Despite the cogency of the arguments presented, the Court by a vote of 5 to 3 concluded that the act was indeed unconstitutional. The case became the classic statement of judicial support of *laissez-faire* principles. For a useful introduction to pre-New Deal reform see Clarke A. Chambers' excellent study, *Seedtime of Reform: American Social Service and Social Action, 1918-1933* (Minneapolis: University of Minnesota Press, 1963). °Robert Green McCloskey in *American Conservatism in the Age of Enterprise: A Study of William Graham Sumner, Stephen J. Field and Andrew Carnegie* (Cambridge: Harvard University Press, 1951) provides a convenient summary of late nineteenth-century conservative thought. The same author's °*The American Supreme Court* (Chicago: University of Chicago Press, 1960) is a readable survey of the court with an emphasis on the recent past. For a critical exposition of business ideals during the twenties see James W. Prothro's *The Dollar Decade: Business Ideas in the 1920's* (Baton Rouge: Louisiana State University Press, 1954). In reading this selection note (1) what arguments counsel for the appellants presented to the court; (2) the extent to which precedent was cited by counsel; (3) what arguments counsel for the appellees presented; (4) how Justice Sutherland interpreted the doctrine of freedom of contract; (5) what he thought were

Adkins *v.* Children's Hospital, 261 U.S. 525, 1923 (October term, 1922).

permissible restraints on free contract; (6) why he thought the minimum wage law unconstitutional; (7) what bearing on the case he saw in the XIXth Amendment to the Constitution; (8) what he thought of all minimum wage legislation; (9) what prompted chief Justice William Howard Taft (1857-1930) to dissent; and (10) what arguments Justice Holmes used in his dissent.

APPEALS FROM DECREES OF THE COURT OF APPEALS of the District of Columbia, affirming two decrees, entered, on mandate from that court, by the Supreme Court of the District, permanently enjoining the appellants from enforcing orders fixing minimum wages under the District of Columbia Minimum Wage Act.

Mr. Felix Frankfurter, with whom *Mr. Francis H. Stephens* was on the brief, for appellants.

The presumption to be accorded an act of Congress—that it be respected unless transgression of the Constitution is shown "beyond a rational doubt"—amply sustains the District of Columbia Minimum Wage Law, particularly in view of the circumstances of its enactment. Congress, under Art. I, § 8, cl. 17, is possessed of the same power and charged with the same duty of legislating within the District as belongs to the States within their respective boundaries. Congress, in dealing with a practical problem, followed the example of many States in passing the act in question. Such legislation has uniformly been sustained by the courts. *State* v. *Crow,* 130 Ark. 272; *Holcombe* v. *Creamer,* 231 Mass. 99; *Williams* v. *Evans,* 139 Minn. 32; *Miller Telephone Co.* v. *Minimum Wage Commission,* 145 Minn. 262; *Stettler* v. *O'Hara,* 69 Ore. 519; and *Simpson* v. *O'Hara,* 70 Ore. 261, affirmed by divided court in 243 U. S. 629; *Larson* v. *Rice,* 100 Wash. 642; *Spokane Hotel Co.* v. *Younger,* 113 Wash. 359; *Poye* v. *State,* 89 Tex. Crim. Rep. 182. Congress did not, however, rely upon a body of state laws sustained by the courts and vindicated by experience. Senate and House Committees held hearings on the needs of this legislation, in view of the conditions prevailing in the District. No one appeared to oppose the bill. An organized body of employers endorsed the bill and urged its passage. The Committees unanimously recommended the legislation. H. Rep. No. 571, 65th Cong., 2d sess.; S. Rep. No. 562, 65th Cong., 2d sess. And the bill was passed without opposition in the House, and only twelve "nays" in the Senate. Moreover, the judgment of Congress has now been vindicated by the results of over four years in the actual operation of the law, and ten years of extensive experience with such legislation in California, Massachusetts, Minnesota, Oregon, Washington and Wisconsin. Unfair depression in the wages of many women workers has been significantly reduced, without adversely affecting industry or diminishing appreciably employment for employables. The legislation has also successfully weathered the severest strains of "hard times." It is urged with confidence that no such body of laws "attesting a widespread belief in the necessities of such legislation," *Prudential Insurance Co.* v. *Cheek,* 259 U.S. 530, supported by uniform judicial approval, subjected to so long, extensive, fair and favorable a test of actual experience, has ever been before this Court, to vindicate the reasonableness of the legislative intervention and to negative the claim that Congress was guilty of "a purely arbitrary or capricious exercise of that [legislative] power." *Truax* v. *Corrigan,* 257 U.S. 312, 329.

Congress aimed at "ends" that are "legitimate and within the scope of the Constitution." *McCulloch* v. *Maryland,* 4 Wheat. 316, 421. Charged with the responsibility of safeguarding the welfare of the women and children of the District of Columbia, it found that alarming public evils had resulted, and threatened in increasing measure, from the widespread existence of a deficit between the essential needs for decent life and the actual earnings of large numbers of women workers of the District. In the judgment of Congress, based upon unchallenged facts, these conditions impaired the health of this generation of women and thereby threatened the coming generation through undernourishment, demoralizing shelter and insufficient medical care. In its immediate effects, also, financial burdens were imposed upon the District, involving excessive and unproductive taxation, for the support of charitable institutions engaged in impotent amelioration rather than prevention. Here, if ever, was presented a community problem of a most compelling kind, calling for legislation "greatly and immediately necessary to the public welfare." *Noble State Bank* v. *Haskell,* 219 U.S. 104, 111. The purpose of the act was to provide for the deficit between the cost of women's labor, i. e., the means necessary to keep labor going—and any rate of women's pay below the minimum level for living, and thereby to eliminate all the evils attendant upon such deficit upon a large scale. There is no dispute that Congress was acting in good faith, after mature deliberation, in avowing the purposes which it did in the enactment of this law, to wit: "To protect the women and minors of the District from conditions detrimental to their health and morals, resulting from wages which are inadequate to maintain decent standards of life." Having regard to the concrete situation, the judgment of Congress that such legislation was necessary cannot in reason be stigmatized as unreasonable.

The means selected by Congress "are appropriate" and "plainly adapted" (*McCulloch* v. *Maryland, supra*) to accomplish the legitimate ends. The possible alternatives open to Congress in this situation were: (1) to submit to the evils as inevitable human misfortunes, subject only to alleviation through public and private charity; (2) provide a direct subsidy out of the public treasury to pay a wage equal to the necessary cost of living; (3) adopt the Massachusetts method, which seeks to compel for women workers a minimum wage through the pressure of public exposure of offending employers; or, (4) take the method it did take, which involved a prohibition of the use of women's labor for less than its cost except by special license from the Board.

There was cumulative testimony, both in the belief of those entitled to express an opinion and in the actual record of experience, that these evils are not inevitable human misfortune. Congress was entitled to disprove that lazy gospel of fatalism as other English-speaking countries equally jealous of safeguarding liberty and property, and many American States, had disproved it. From the point of view of effectiveness in accomplishing its purposes, the choice of Congress, among the three remedial methods, surely was not "arbitrary" or "unreasonable." It had the support of a great body of public opinion, (see *Jacobson* v. *Massachusetts,* 197 U.S. 11, 31, 34-35; *Muller* v. *Oregon,* 208 U.S. 412, 420; *McLean* v. *Arkansas,* 211 U.S. 539, 548-9; *Tanner* v. *Little,* 240 U.S. 369, 385-6), crystallized in the extensive and successful experience of English countries with such legislation, in the fact of such legislation in other States, in the successful working of such legislation. In other words, Congress rested upon the appeal "from judgment by speculation to judgment by experience." *Tanner* v. *Little,* 240 U.S. 369, 386.

Where a law has been long on the statute books, speculative claims of injustice must yield to the results of actual experience. Cf. *National Union Fire Ins. Co.* v. *Wanberg,* 260 U.S. 71.

No rights of plaintiffs secured under the Constitution prohibit the use of the means adopted by Congress in the Minimum Wage Law to accomplish legitimate public ends. It is for the plaintiff to show some explicit withdrawal of the legislative power as exercised in this case. The only alleged obstruction is the "due process" clause. And the only point for consideration is whether the deprivation of "liberty" or "property" which is involved is "without due process of law."

This Court has consistently recognized the futility of defining "due process." The "due process" clauses embody a standard of fair dealing to be applied to the myriad variety of facts that are involved in modern legislation. That is why this Court has refused to draw lines in advance. The impact of facts must establish the line in each case. The application of "due process" clauses is, in the last analysis, a process of judgment by this Court. In the application of the varying facts to the test of fair dealing the ultimate question in this Court is, does legislation, or its actual operation, "shock the sense of fairness the Fourteenth Amendment was intended to satisfy in respect to state legislation"? *Chicago & N. W. Ry. Co.* v. *Nye Schneider Fowler Co.,* 260 U.S. 35. During the fifty years of extensive judicial unfolding, the central ideas that inhere in this constitutional safeguard have become manifest. A careful study of the long line of cases especially dealing with the "due process" clause, beginning with the *Slaughter-House Cases,* 16 Wall. 36, shows two dominant ideas conceived to be fundamental principles: (1) Freedom from arbitrary or wanton interference, and (2) protection against spoliation of property. "Arbitrary," "wanton" and "spoliation" are the words which are the motif of the decisions under the "due process" clauses. That is as close as we can get to it; it is close enough when dealing with the great questions of government. What it means is that the Fourteenth Amendment intended to leave the States the free play necessary for effective dealing with the constant shift of governmental problems, and not to hamper the States except where it would be obvious to disinterested men that the action was arbitrary and wanton, and therefore spoliative and unjustified. Of course exactly the same freedom of action, the same scope for legislation, belongs to Congress when dealing with the District.

It is not arbitrary, wanton or spoliative for Congress to require the consent of the Board before allowing a wage contract affecting women at below cost, but a valid exercise of the "police power," because of the actual handicaps of women in industry. This was one of the principal grounds of the state courts in sustaining this legislation. This is legislation of the same nature as that revealed by a long line of cases upholding limitations placed upon freedom of contract with women in various ways. They rest upon a realization of the fact that the mass of women workers cannot secure terms of employment needful from the point of view of public welfare without the weight of legislation being thrown into the scales. *Muller* v. *Oregon*, 208 U.S. 412; *Riley* v. *Massachusetts*, 232 U.S. 671; *Hawley* v. *Walker*, 232 U.S. 718; *Miller* v. *Wilson*, 236 U.S. 373; *Bosley* v. *McLaughlin*, 236 U.S. 385.

It is not arbitrary, wanton or spoliative for Congress to require employers to pay the cost of women's labor. The employer, and the employer alone, receives the benefit of the woman's working energy, which cannot be produced or maintained by less than the reasonably ascertained minimum cost of her labor. Since he has her product he ought to pay for its cost, unless and until the employer, by special license, is given the right to use labor at less than its usual cost.

The action of Congress is not arbitrary, wanton, or spoliative; because the direct interest of the District in these particular wage contracts affecting women gave it a special justification for controlling them. A contract for labor below its cost must inevitably rely upon a subsidy from outside or result in human deterioration. To the extent of the subsidy or the deterioration the public is necessarily concerned. The employer has no constitutional right to such an indirect subsidy or to cause such deterioration. Nor has a woman any absolute "right" to give her energies to the employer if she cannot keep her side of the bargain without indirect subsidy or without incurring physical or moral impairment.

It is not arbitrary, wanton or spoliative to require the employer to obtain a license from the Board before he can buy a woman's labor at less than cost; because that is a reasonable means of preventing cut-throat and unfair competition between manufacturers. Congress legislated in the light of actual industrial conditions which denied the abstract equality of bargaining power among women. Congress found that women, in substantial numbers, were under a handicap because they were women. Therefore by legislation it sought to fill the gaps caused by the ignorance or helplessness of women workers, and the ignorance or avarice of some employers. In this it merely followed a long line of legislation which has restricted the field of unregulated competition by prohibitions enforced through a great variety of remedies. The Constitution does not require that right standards should prevail solely through their inherent reasonableness or through enlightened self-interest.

It is not arbitrary, wanton or spoliative for Congress to require the consent of the Board before allowing a woman employee to sell labor below cost; because that is a reasonable means for preventing unfair competition between women employees. The underlying principle is the same as that which eliminates prison labor from competition against free labor. The essential purpose is to compel employers to pay the living cost to all their women employees whose product is worth it, and thereby correspondingly protect the efficient against ruinous competition.

It is not arbitrary, wanton or spoliative for Congress to require the consent of the Board before allowing wage contracts to women workers at below cost; because that is a reasonable exercise of power to foster the productivity of industry. This is a measure of conservation and preservation of the human resources of the State, which is of even more primary importance than the conservation of natural resources. And so its constitutionality follows *a fortiori* from the line of cases which support statutes passed for the preservation and effective utilization of natural resources. *Hudson Water Co.* v. *McCarter,* 209 U.S. 349; *Mt. Vernon Co.* v. *Alabama Power Co.,* 240 U.S. 30; *Pacific Live Stock Co.* v. *Oregon Water Board,* 241 U.S. 440; *Walls* v. *Midland Carbon Co.,* 254 U.S. 300.

The majority opinion of the District Court of Appeals erects its own notions of policy into constitutional prohibitions. It assumes a specific constitutional prohibition against interference with the wage contracts. But there is no specific prohibition against dealing with a wage contract, as such. There is only the general guarantee of fair dealing,—the satisfaction of a "sense of fairness" of the "due process" clauses; and so we find that the wage contract has been interfered with frequently by legislation with the sanction of this Court—legislation which directly affected the money value of the wage contracts, which operated to the financial advantage of one side and was of alleged cost to the other. Payment in cash as against store orders, *Knoxville Iron Co.* v. *Harbison,* 183 U.S. 13; *Dayton Coal Co.* v. *Barton,* 183 U.S. 24; *Keokee Co.* v. *Taylor,* 234 U.S. 227; payment on basis of coal mined before being screened, *McLean* v. *Arkansas,* 211 U.S. 539; *Rail and River Co.* v. *Yaple,* 236 U.S. 338; semi-monthly cash payments, *Erie R. R. Co.* v. *Williams,* 233 U.S. 685—all these requirements affected money terms, cash value, dollars and cents; all involved legislative interferences with wage contracts; all were sustained because each was found a not unreasonable means to safeguard a public interest. Each case was dealt with, not on any absolutist assumption of immunity of wage contracts from legislative interference, but quite the opposite; the concrete circumstances of each case were found to negative arbitrary restraint.

The great fact that this legislation applies solely to women has no relevance for the Court of Appeals. "If it [Congress] may regulate wages for women, it may by the exercise of the same power establish the wages to be paid men." This argument is founded upon the Nineteenth Amendment. But the political equality of woman is an irrelevant factor. The argument was long ago anticipated and answered, in classic language, by this Court. Men and women remain men and women forever. *Muller* v. *Oregon,* 208 U.S. 412, 422-23.

Adair v. *United States,* 208 U.S. 161, and *Coppage* v. *Kansas,* 236 U.S. 1, are wholly inapplicable. The considerations of public health, morals and the general welfare which are the basis and immediate aims of the Minimum Wage Law for women are not presented by the statutes involved in the earlier cases. The restricted scope of these cases, dealing with a purpose "to favor the employee at the expense of the employer and to build up the labor organizations" was carefully pointed out in a recent decision by the Justice who wrote for the court in the *Coppage Case. Prudential Insurance Co.* v. *Cheek,* 259 U.S. 530.

Neither in reason nor in experience does the Minimum Wage Law for women imply, as the court below indicated, power "to fix the prices of all commodities entering into the determination of an equitable wage." Nor is there any basis for the claim that "experience has demonstrated that a fixed minimum wage means in the last analysis a fixed wage."

On all these questions we appeal from "judgment by speculation" to "judgment by experience." *Tanner* v. *Little,* 240 U.S. 369, 386.

Mr. Wade H. Ellis and *Mr. Challen B. Ellis,* with whom *Mr. Joseph W. Folk* was on the brief, for appellees.

The Minimum Wage Law of the District of Columbia is unconstitutional because it is a price-fixing law, directly interfering with freedom of contract, which is a part of the liberty of the citizen guaranteed in the Fifth Amendment, and no exercise of the police power justifies the fixing of prices either of property or of services in a private business, not affected with a public interest, and as a permanent measure.

The protection of liberty and property guaranteed in the Fifth and Fourteenth Amendments includes freedom of contract, embracing contract for personal services. *Coppage* v. *Kansas,* 236 U.S. 1, 14; *Truax* v. *Raich,* 239 U.S. 33; *Prudential Insurance Co.* v. *Cheek,* 259 U.S. 530. These principles apply to legislation by Congress for the District of Columbia. *Callan* v. *Wilson,* 127 U.S. 540, 550; *Wight* v. *Davidson,* 181 U.S. 371.

That a law fixing wages generally in private employment would be beyond legislative power is uniformly assumed or indicated in the decisions of this Court. Cooley, Const. Lim., 7th ed., p. 870; Labatt, Master and Servant, 2nd ed., § 846; *Frisbie* v. *United States,* 157 U.S. 160, 166; *Coppage* v. *Kansas,* 236 U.S. 1; *Bunting* v. *Oregon,* 243 U.S. 426. In decisions of this Court where wage laws or price-fixing laws have been sustained, such laws were sustained solely on the ground that they were to tide over a temporary emergency and in business affected with a public interest. *Wilson* v. *New,* 243 U.S. 332; *Ft. Smith & Western R. R.*

Co. v. *Mills*, 253 U.S. 206; *Block* v. *Hirsh*, 256 U.S. 135; *Pennsylvania Coal Co.* v. *Mahon*, 260 U.S. 393.

There is a clear distinction between "hours-of-service," and similar laws directly promoting health or safety or preventing fraud and only indirectly affecting the cost of labor, on the one hand, and on the other hand "wage laws," directly fixing the price in the bargain between employer and employee, and only indirectly or remotely effecting some other purpose. The distinction is pointed out in *Coppage* v. *Kansas*, 236 U.S. 1; *Frisbie* v. *United States*, 157 U.S. 160, 166. The mere freedom to contract secured in the constitutional guaranty cannot itself be said to be inimical to the public welfare and restricted under the guise of an exercise of the police power, for the police power cannot be used to amend the Constitution. *Pennsylvania Coal Co.* v. *Mahon*, 260 U.S. 393; *Truax* v. *Corrigan*, 257 U.S. 312.

If a law fixing prices or wages is not a health law, because the mere freedom to determine the amount that should be charged in the exchange of property or services for money cannot itself be dangerous to health, morals or safety, then manifestly it is not a health law for women any more than it would be for men, and it does not become valid by having it apply to women only. "Hours-of-service" laws are distinguishable in this respect. "Hours-of-service" laws, being clearly health laws within the police power, permit the exercise of legislative discretion to determine the extent to which they shall go and to take into account the differences in physical nature of the persons to whom they shall apply. They may be in a particular instance justified as to women, where they might not be as to men. *Muller* v. *Oregon*, 208 U.S. 412. But, being proper exercises of the police power, as health laws, they would also be valid when appropriately applied to men. *Bunting* v. *Oregon*, 243 U.S. 426. But the general rule that a person has the right to sell his labor upon such terms as he deems proper, is a fundamental rule applying to men and women alike. *Adair* v. *United States*, 208 U.S. 161, 174.

The contention that this Court must consider only the reasonableness of the law, so as to determine whether it is arbitrary, wanton or spoliative, and cannot consider the power of Congress to deal at all with the subject, is answered in the decisions.

Holden v. *Hardy,* 169 U.S. 366; *Pollock* v. *Farmers' Loan & Trust Co.,* 157 U.S. 429; *Coppage* v. *Kansas,* 236 U.S. 1; *Truax* v. *Raich,* 239 U.S. 33; *Mugler* v. *Kansas,* 123 U.S. 623; *Child Labor Tax Case,* 259 U.S. 20. If every law which expedience may suggest may be called a health law, or a public welfare law, and thus become an exercise of the police power, the constitutional limitations break down, and no action of the legislative body is in any way restricted by the positive guaranties of the fundamental law. *Truax* v. *Corrigan,* 257 U.S. 312; *Pennsylvania Coal Co.* v. *Mahon,* 260 U.S. 393; *Child Labor Tax Case, supra.*

The contention that the consequences of sustaining the power of the legislative body to fix wages for women cannot be considered, is wholly at variance with the decisions of this Court in numerous cases. In testing the constitutionality of any leigslative act, we have the right to inquire, as this Court did, in *Adair* v. *United States,* 208 U.S. 161; *Coppage* v. *Kansas,* 236 U.S. 1; *Truax* v. *Raich,* 239 U.S. 33; *Truax* v. *Corrigan,* 257 U.S. 312; *Child Labor Tax Case,* 259 U.S. 20, to what distance and in what direction the departure from familiar standards may lead us, and what precedents may be established by sustaining the power claimed, which may be cited hereafter as authority for further legislation of wider scope or more extended character.

Requirement of a minimum wage, without corresponding requirement of amount or efficiency of service in return, is the taking of property without just compensation, and not even for a public purpose, but for private purpose, contrary to the Fifth Amendment and the Ninth Amendment.

The requirement that wages shall be fixed at a sum to maintain health and protect morals, provides a vague and uncertain standard incapable of application and renders the act void for this reason alone. 40 Stat. 960, §§ 9, 11.

The contention that employer or employee are not deprived of property rights because special licenses for defectives are provided for in the act, is unsound, because special licenses can not be obtained by the employer, nor by the employee as such, and, in any event, the wage is still fixed by the Board. 40 Stat. 960, 963, § 13.

The assignment of error in the action of the Court of Appeals in granting a rehearing on the first appeal from the Supreme Court of the District is without merit, because the present review is from the second appeal in the lower court, and not from the first appeal, and no question can be raised as to the authority of the court below to hear and determine the second appeal. *Rooker* v. *Fidelity Trust Co.*, 261 U.S. 114. Further it is elementary that the granting or refusing of a rehearing in an equity suit is not the subject of review. *Steines* v. *Franklin County*, 14 Wall. 15; *Roemer* v. *Neumann*, 132 U.S. 103.

Mr. William L. Brewster, by leave of court, on behalf of the States of Oregon, New York, California, Kansas, Wisconsin and Washington, as *amicus curiae*.

By leave of court, briefs were filed by counsel, appearing as *amici curiae*, as follows: *Mr. Isaac H. Van Winkle*, Attorney General of the State of Oregon, *Mr. Joseph N. Teal* and *Mr. William L. Brewster*, on behalf of the Industrial Welfare Commission of Oregon. *Mr. Carl Sherman*, Attorney General of the State of New York, and *Mr. Edward G. Griffin*, Deputy Attorney General, on behalf of that State. *Mr. Hiram Johnson* and *Mr. Jesse Steinhart*, on behalf of the Industrial Welfare Commission of California. *Mr. John G. Egan*, Assistant Attorney General of the State of Kansas, on behalf of that State. *Mr. Herman L. Ekern*, Attorney General of the State of Wisconsin, *Mr. J. E. Messerschmidt*, Assistant Attorney General, and *Mr. Fred M. Wilcox*, on behalf of that State. *Mr. Edward Clifford* and *Mr. Kenneth Durham* on behalf of the Minimum Wage Committee of the State of Washington.

MR. JUSTICE SUTHERLAND delivered the opinion of the Court.*

The question presented for determination by these appeals is the constitutionality of the Act of September 19, 1918, providing for the fixing of minimum wages for women and children in the District of Columbia. 40 Stat. 960, c. 174.

The act provides for a board of three members, to be constituted, as far as practicable, so as to be equally representative of employers, employees and the public. The board is authorized

---

*Editor's Note: George Sutherland (1862-1942), a conservative railroad lawyer and United States Senator from Utah, was appointed by President Harding to the court in 1922.

to have public hearings, at which persons interested in the matter being investigated may appear and testify, to administer oaths, issue subpoenas requiring the attendance of witnesses and production of books, etc., and to make rules and regulations for carrying the act into effect.

By § 8 the board is authorized—

"(1) To investigate and ascertain the wages of women and minors in the different occupations in which they are employed in the District of Columbia; (2) to examine, through any member or authorized representative, any book, pay roll or other record of any employer of women or minors that in any way appertains to or has a bearing upon the question of wages of any such women or minors; and (3) to require from such employer full and true statements of the wages paid to all women and minors in his employment."

And by § 9, "to ascertain and declare, in the manner hereinafter provided, the following things: (a) Standards of minimum wages for women in any occupation within the District of Columbia, and what wages are inadequate to supply the necessary cost of living to any such women workers to maintain them in good health and to protect their morals; and (b) standards of minimum wages for minors in any occupation within the District of Columbia, and what wages are unreasonably low for any such minor workers."

The act then provides (§ 10) that if the board, after investigation, is of opinion that any substantial number of women workers in any occupation are receiving wages inadequate to supply them with the necessary cost of living, maintain them in health and protect their morals, a conference may be called to consider and inquire into and report on the subject investigated, the conference to be equally representative of employers and employees in such occupation and of the public, and to include one or more members of the board.

The conference is required to make and transmit to the board a report including, among other things, "recommendations as to standards of minimum wages for women workers in the occupation under inquiry and as to what wages are inadequate to supply the necessary cost of living to women workers in such occupation and to maintain them in health and to protect their morals." § 11.

The board is authorized (§ 12) to consider and review these

recommendations and to approve or disapprove any or all of them. If it approve any recommendations it must give public notice of its intention and hold a public hearing at which the persons interested will be heard. After such hearing, the board is authorized to make such order as to it may appear necessary to carry into effect the recommendations, and to require all employers in the occupation affected to comply therewith. It is made unlawful for any such employer to violate in this regard any provision of the order or to employ any woman worker at lower wages than are thereby permitted.

There is a provision (§ 13) under which the board may issue a special license to a woman whose earning capacity "has been impaired by age or otherwise," authorizing her employment at less than the minimum wages fixed under the act.

All questions of fact (§ 17) are to be determined by the board, from whose decision there is no appeal; but an appeal is allowed on questions of law.

Any violation of the act (§ 18) by an employer or his agent or by corporate agents is declared to be a misdemeanor, punishable by fine and imprisonment.

Finally, after some further provisions not necessary to be stated, it is declared (§ 23) that the purposes of the act are "to protect the women and minors of the District from conditions detrimental to their health and morals, resulting from wages which are inadequate to maintain decent standards of living; and the Act in each of its provisions and in its entirety shall be interpreted to effectuate these purposes."

The appellee in the first case is a corporation maintaining a hospital for children in the District. It employs a large number of women in various capacities, with whom it had agreed upon rates of wages and compensation satisfactory to such employees, but which in some instances were less than the minimum wage fixed by an order of the board made in pursuance of the act. The women with whom appellee had so contracted were all of full age and under no legal disability. The instant suit was brought by the appellee in the Supreme Court of the District to restrain the board from enforcing or attempting to enforce its order on the ground that the same was in contravention of the Constitution, and particularly the due process clause of the Fifth Amendment.

In the second case the appellee, a woman twenty-one years of age, was employed by the Congress Hall Hotel Company as an elevator operator, at a salary of $35 per month and two meals a day. She alleges that the work was light and healthful, the hours short, with surroundings clean and moral, and that she was anxious to continue it for the compensation she was receiving and that she did not earn more. Her services were satisfactory to the Hotel Company and it would have been glad to retain her but was obliged to dispense with her services by reason of the order of the board and on account of the penalties prescribed by the act. The wages received by this appellee were the best she was able to obtain for any work she was capable of performing and the enforcement of the order, she alleges, deprived her of such employment and wages. She further averred that she could not secure any other position at which she could make a living, with as good physical and moral surroundings, and earn as good wages, and that she was desirous of continuing and would continue the employment but for the order of the board. An injunction was prayed as in the other case.

The Supreme Court of the District denied the injunction and dismissed the bill in each case. Upon appeal the Court of Appeals by a majority first affirmed and subsequently, on a rehearing, reversed the trial court. Upon the first argument a justice of the District Supreme Court was called in to take the place of one of the Appellate Court justices, who was ill. Application for rehearing was made and, by the court as thus constituted, was denied. Subsequently, and during the term, a rehearing was granted by an order concurred in by two of the Appellate Court justices, one being the justice whose place on the prior occasion had been filled by the Supreme Court member. Upon the rehearing thus granted, the Court of Appeals, rejecting the first opinion, held the act in question to be unconstitutional and reversed the decrees of the trial court. Thereupon the cases were remanded, and the trial court entered decrees in pursuance of the mandate, declaring the act in question to be unconstitutional and granting permanent injunctions. Appeals to the Court of Appeals followed and the decrees of the trial court were affirmed. It is from these final decrees that the cases come here.

Upon this state of facts the jurisdiction of the lower court to grant a rehearing, after first denying it, is challenged. We do not deem it necessary to consider the matter farther than to say that we are here dealing with the second appeals, while the proceedings complained of occurred upon the first appeals. That the lower court could properly entertain the second appeals and decide the cases does not admit of doubt; and this the appellants virtually conceded by having themselves invoked the jurisdiction. See *Rooker v. Fidelity Trust Co., ante,* 114.

We come then, at once, to the substantive question involved.

The judicial duty of passing upon the constitutionality of an act of Congress is one of great gravity and delicacy. The statute here in question has successfully borne the scrutiny of the legislative branch of the government, which, by enacting it, has affirmed its validity; and that determination must be given great weight. This Court, by an unbroken line of decisions from Chief Justice Marshall to the present day, has steadily adhered to the rule that every possible presumption is in favor of the validity of an act of Congress until overcome beyond rational doubt. But if by clear and indubitable demonstration a statute be opposed to the Constitution we have no choice but to say so. The Constitution, by its own terms, is the supreme law of the land, emanating from the people, the repository of ultimate sovereignty under our form of government. A congressional statute, on the other hand, is the act of an agency of this sovereign authority and if it conflict with the Constitution must fall; for that which is not supreme must yield to that which is. To hold it invalid (if it be invalid) is a plain exercise of the judicial power—that power vested in courts to enable them to administer justice according to law. From the authority to ascertain and determine the law in a given case, there necessarily results, in case of conflict, the duty to declare and enforce the rule of the supreme law and reject that of an inferior act of legislation which, transcending the Constitution, is of no effect and binding on no one. This is not the exercise of a substantive power to review and nullify acts of Congress, for no such substantive power exists. It is simply a necessary concomitant of the power to hear and dispose of a case or controversy properly before the court, to the determination of which must be brought the test and measure of the law.

The statute now under consideration is attacked upon the ground that it authorizes an unconstitutional interference with the freedom of contract included within the guaranties of the due process clause of the Fifth Amendment. That the right to contract about one's affairs is a part of the liberty of the individual protected by this clause, is settled by the decisions of this Court and is no longer open to question. *Allgeyer* v. *Louisiana,* 165 U.S. 578, 591; *New York Life Insurance Co.* v. *Dodge,* 246 U.S. 357, 373-374; *Coppage* v. *Kansas,* 236 U.S. 1, 10, 14; *Adair* v. *United States,* 208 U.S. 161; *Lochner* v. *New York,* 198 U.S. 45; *Butchers' Union Co.* v. *Crescent City Co.,* 111 U.S. 746; *Muller* v. *Oregon,* 208 U.S. 412, 421. Within this liberty are contracts of employment of labor. In making such contracts, generally speaking, the parties have an equal right to obtain from each other the best terms they can as the result of private bargaining.

In *Adair* v. *United States, supra,* Mr. Justice Harlan (pp. 174, 175), speaking for the Court, said:

"The right of a person to sell his labor upon such terms as he deems proper is, in its essence, the same as the right of the purchaser of labor to prescribe the conditions upon which he will accept such labor from the person offering to sell. . . . In all such particulars the employer and employé have equality of right, and any legislation that disturbs that equality is an arbitrary interference with the liberty of contract which no government can legally justify in a free land."

In *Coppage* v. *Kansas, supra* (p. 14), this Court, speaking through Mr. Justice Pitney, said:

"Included in the right of personal liberty and the right of private property—partaking of the nature of each—is the right to make contracts for the acquisition of property. Chief among such contracts is that of personal employment, by which labor and other services are exchanged for money or other forms of property. If this right be struck down or arbitrarily interfered with, there is a substantial impairment of liberty in the long-established constitutional sense. The right is as essential to the laborer as to the capitalist, to the poor as to the rich; for the vast majority of persons have no other honest way to begin to acquire property, save by working for money.

"An interference with this liberty so serious as that now under consideration, and so disturbing of equality of right, must be deemed to be arbitrary, unless it be supportable as a reasonable exercise of the police power of the State."

There is, of course, no such thing as absolute freedom of contract. It is subject to a great variety of restraints. But freedom of contract is, nevertheless, the general rule and restraint the exception; and the exercise of legislative authority to abridge it can be justified only by the existence of exceptional circumstances. Whether these circumstances exist in the present case constitutes the question to be answered. It will be helpful to this end to review some of the decisions where the interference has been upheld and consider the grounds upon which they rest.

(1) *Those dealing with statutes fixing rates and charges to be exacted by businesses impressed with a public interest.* There are many cases, but it is sufficient to cite *Munn* v. *Illinois,* 94 U.S. 113. The power here rests upon the ground that where property is devoted to a public use the owner thereby, in effect, grants to the public an interest in the use which may be controlled by the public for the common good to the extent of the interest thus created. It is upon this theory that these statutes have been upheld and, it may be noted in passing, so upheld even in respect of their incidental and injurious or destructive effect upon preëxisting contracts. See *Louisville & Nashville R. R. Co.* v. *Mottley,* 219 U.S. 467. In the case at bar the statute does not depend upon the existence of a public interest in any business to be affected, and this class of cases may be laid aside as inapplicable.

(2) *Statutes relating to contracts for the performance of public work. Atkin* v. *Kansas,* 191 U.S. 207; *Heim* v. *McCall,* 239 U.S. 175; *Ellis* v. *United States,* 206 U.S. 246. These cases sustain such statutes as depending, not upon the right to condition private contracts, but upon the right of the government to prescribe the conditions upon which it will permit work of a public character to be done for it, or, in the case of a State, for its municipalities. We may, therefore, in like manner, dismiss these decisions from consideration as inapplicable.

(3) *Statutes prescribing the character, methods and time for payment of wages.* Under this head may be included *McLean* v. *Arkansas,* 211 U.S. 539, sustaining a state statute requiring coal to be measured for payment of miners' wages before screening; *Knoxville Iron Co.* v. *Harbison,* 183 U.S. 13, sustaining a Tennessee statute requiring the redemption in cash of store orders issued in payment of wages; *Erie R. R. Co.* v. *Williams,* 233 U.S. 685, upholding a statute regulating the time within which wages

shall be paid to employees in certain specified industries; and other cases sustaining statutes of like import and effect. In none of the statutes thus sustained, was the liberty of employer or employee to fix the amount of wages the one was willing to pay and the other willing to receive interfered with. Their tendency and purpose was to prevent unfair and perhaps fraudulent methods in the payment of wages and in no sense can they be said to be, or to furnish a precedent for, wage-fixing statutes.

(4) *Statutes fixing hours of labor.* It is upon this class that the greatest emphasis is laid in argument and therefore, and because such cases approach most nearly the line of principle applicable to the statute here involved, we shall consider them more at length. In some instances the statute limited the hours of labor for men in certain occupations and in others it was confined in its application to women. No statute has thus far been brought to the attention of this Court which by its terms, applied to all occupations. In *Holden* v. *Hardy,* 169 U.S. 366, the Court considered an act of the Utah legislature, restricting the hours of labor in mines and smelters. This statute was sustained as a legitimate exercise of the police power, on the ground that the legislature had determined that these particular employments, when too long pursued, were injurious to the health of the employees, and that, as there were reasonable grounds for supporting this determination on the part of the legislature, its decision in that respect was beyond the reviewing power of the federal courts.

That this constituted the basis of the decision is emphasized by the subsequent decision in *Lochner* v. *New York,* 198 U.S. 45, reviewing a state statute which restricted the employment of all persons in bakeries to ten hours in any one day. The Court referred to *Holden* v. *Hardy, supra,* and, declaring it to be inapplicable, held the statute unconstitutional as an unreasonable, unnecessary and arbitrary interference with the liberty of contract and therefore void under the Constitution.

Mr. Justice Peckham, speaking for the Court (p. 56), said:

"It must, of course, be conceded that there is a limit to the valid exercise of the police power by the State. There is no dispute concerning this general proposition. Otherwise the Fourteenth Amendment would have no efficacy and the legislatures of the States would have unbounded power, and it would be enough to say that any piece of legislation was enacted to conserve the morals, the health or the safety of the people; such legislation would be valid, no matter how absolutely without foundation the claim might be. The claim of the police power would be a mere pretext—become another and delusive name for the supreme sovereignty of the State to be exercised free from constitutional restraint."

And again (pp. 57-58):

"It is a question of which of two powers or rights shall prevail—the power of the State to legislate or the right of the individual to liberty of person and freedom of contract. The mere assertion that the subject relates though but in a remote degree to the public health does not necessarily render the enactment valid. The act must have a more direct relation, as a means to an end, and the end itself must be appropriate and legitimate, before an act can be held to be vaild which interferes with the general right of an individual to be free in his person and in his power to contract in relation to his own labor."

Coming then directly to the statute (p. 58), the Court said:

"We think the limit of the police power has been reached and passed in this case. There is, in our judgment, no reasonable foundation for holding this to be necessary or appropriate as a health law to safeguard the public health or the health of the individuals who are following the trade of a baker. If this statute be valid, and if, therefore, a proper case is made out in which to deny the right of an individual, *sui juris,* as employer or employé, to make contracts for the labor of the latter under the protection of the provisions of the Federal Constitution, there would seem to be no length to which legislation of this nature might not go."

And, after pointing out the unreasonable range to which the principle of the statute might be extended, the Court said (p. 60):

"It is also urged, pursuing the same line of argument, that it is to the interest of the State that its population should be strong and robust, and therefore any legislation which may be said to tend to make people healthy must be valid as health laws, enacted under the police power. If this be a valid argument and a justification for this kind of legislation, it follows that the protection of the Federal Constitution from undue interference with liberty of person and freedom of contract is visionary, wherever the law is sought to be justified as a valid exercise of the police power. Scarcely any law but might find shelter under such assumptions, and conduct, properly so called, as well as contract, would come under the restrictive sway of the legislature."

And further (p. 61):

"Statutes of the nature of that under review, limiting the hours in which grown and intelligent men may labor to earn their living, are mere meddlesome interferences with the rights of the individual, and they are not saved from condemnation by the claim that they are passed in the exercise of the police power and upon the subject of the health of the individual whose rights are interfered with, unless there be some fair ground, reasonable in and of itself, to say that there is material danger to the public health or to the health of the employés, if the hours of labor are not curtailed."

Subsequent cases in this Court have been distinguished from that decision, but the principles therein stated have never been disapproved.

In *Bunting* v. *Oregon*, 243 U.S. 426, a state statute forbidding the employment of any person in any mill, factory or manufacturing establishment more than ten hours in any one day, and providing payment for overtime not exceeding three hours in any one day at the rate of time and a half of the regular wage, was sustained on the ground that, since the state legislature and State Supreme Court had found such a law necessary for the preservation of the health of employees in these industries, this Court would accept their judgment, in the absence of facts to support the contrary conclusion. The law was attacked on the ground that it constituted an attempt to fix wages, but that contention was rejected and the law sustained as a reasonable regulation of hours of service.

Wilson v. *New*, 243 U.S. 332, involved the validity of the so-called Adamson Law, which established an eight-hour day for employees of interstate carriers for which it fixed a scale of minimum wages with proportionate increases for overtime, to be enforced, however, only for a limited period. The act was sustained primarily upon the ground that it was a regulation of a business charged with a public interest. The Court, speaking through the Chief Justice, pointed out that regarding "the private right and private interest as contradistinguished from the public interest the power exists between the parties, the employers and employees, to agree as to a standard of wages free from legislative interference" but that this did not affect the power to deal with the matter with a view to protect the public right, and then said (p. 353):

"And this emphasizes that there is no question here of purely private right since the law is concerned only with those who are engaged in a business charged with a public interest where the subject dealt with as to all the parties is one involved in that business and which we have seen comes under the control of the right to regulate to the extent that the power to do so is appropriate or relevant to the business regulated."

Moreover, in sustaining the wage feature of the law, emphasis was put upon the fact (p. 345) that it was in this respect temporary "leaving the employers and employees free as to the subject of wages to govern their relations by their own agreements after the specified time." The act was not only temporary in this respect, but it was passed to meet a sudden and great emergency. This feature of the law was sustained principally because the parties, for the time being, could not or would not agree. Here they are forbidden to agree.

The same principle was applied in the *Rent Cases* (*Block* v. *Hirsh*, 256 U.S. 135, and *Marcus Brown Holding Co.* v. *Feldman,* 256 U.S. 170), where this Court sustained the legislative power to fix rents as between landlord and tenant upon the ground that the operation of the statutes was temporary to tide over an emergency and that the circumstances were such as to clothe "the letting of buildings . . . with a public inteerst so great as to justify regulation by law." The Court said (p. 157):

"The regulation is put and justified only as a temporary measure [citing *Wilson* v. *New, supra*]. A limit in time, to tide over a passing trouble, well may justify a law that could not be upheld as a permanent change."

In a subsequent case, *Pennsylvania Coal Co.* v. *Mahon,* 260 U.S. 393, 416, this Court, after saying "We are in danger of forgetting that a strong public desire to improve the public condition is not enough to warrant achieving the desire by a shorter cut than the constitutional way of paying for the change," pointed out that the *Rent Cases* dealt with laws intended to meet a temporary emergency and "went to the verge of the law."

In addition to the cases cited above, there are the decisions of this Court dealing with laws especially relating to hours of labor for women: *Muller* v. *Oregon,* 208 U.S. 412; *Riley* v. *Massachusetts,* 232 U.S. 671; *Miller* v. *Wilson,* 236 U.S. 373; *Bosley* v. *McLaughlin,* 236 U.S. 385.

In the *Muller Case* the validity of an Oregon statute, forbidding the employment of any female in certain industries more than ten hours during any one day was upheld. The decision proceeded upon the theory that the difference between the sexes may justify a different rule respecting hours of labor in the case of women than in the case of men. It is pointed out that these consist in differences of physical structure, especially in respect of the maternal functions, and also in the fact that historically woman has always been dependent upon man, who has established his control by superior physical strength. The cases of *Riley, Miller* and *Bosley* follow in this respect the *Muller Case.* But the ancient inequality of the sexes, otherwise than physical, as suggested in the *Muller Case* (p. 421) has continued "with diminishing intensity." In view of the great—not to say revolutionary—changes which have taken place since that utterance, in the contractual, political and civil status of women, culminating in the Nineteenth Amendment, it is not unreasonable to say that these differences have now come almost, if not quite, to the vanishing point. In this aspect of the matter, while the physical differences must be recognized in appropriate cases, and legislation fixing hours or conditions of work may properly take them into account, we cannot accept the doctrine that women of mature age, *sui juris,* require or may be subjected to restrictions upon their liberty of contract which could not lawfully be imposed in the case of men under similar circumstances. To do so would be to ignore all the implications to be drawn from the present day trend of legislation, as well as that of common thought and usage, by which woman is accorded emancipation from the old doctrine that she must be given special protection or be subjected to special restraint in her contractual and civil relationships. In passing, it may be noted that the instant statute applies in the case of a woman employer contracting with a woman employee as it does when the former is a man.

The essential characteristics of the statute now under consideration, which differentiate it from the laws fixing hours of labor, will be made to appear as we proceed. It is sufficient now to point out that the latter as well as the statutes mentioned under paragraph (3) deal with incidents of the employment having no necessary effect upon the heart of the contract, that is, the amount of wages to be paid and received. A law forbidding work to continue beyond a given number of hours leaves the parties free to contract about wages and thereby equalize whatever additional burdens may be imposed upon the employer as a result of the restrictions as to hours, by an adjustment in respect of the amount of wages. Enough has been said to show that the authority to fix hours of labor cannot be exercised except in respect of those occupations where work of long continued duration is detrimental to health. This Court has been careful in every case where the question has been raised, to place its decision upon this limited authority of the legislature to regulate hours of labor and to disclaim any purpose to uphold the legislation as fixing wages, thus recognizing an essential difference between the two. It seems plain that these decisions afford no real support for any form of law establishing minimum wages.

If now, in the light furnished by the foregoing exceptions to the general rule forbidding legislative interference with freedom of contract, we examine and analyze the statute in question, we shall see that it differs from them in every material respect. It is not a law dealing with any business charged with a public interest or with public work, or to meet and tide over a temporary emergency. It has nothing to do with the character, methods or periods of wage payments. It does not prescribe hours of labor or conditions under which labor is to be done. It is not for the protection of persons under legal disability or for the prevention of fraud. It is simply and exclusively a price-fixing law, confined to adult women (for we are not now considering the provisions relating to minors), who are legally as capable of contracting for themselves as men. It forbids two parties having lawful capacity —under penalties as to the employer—to freely contract with one another in respect of the price for which one shall render service to the other in a purely private employment where both are willing, perhaps anxious, to agree, even though the consequence may be to oblige one to surrender a desirable engagement and the other to dispense with the services of a desirable employee.* The price fixed by the board need have no relation to the capacity or earning power of the employee, the number of hours which may happen to constitute the day's work, the character of the place where the work is to be done, or the circumstances or surroundings of the employment; and, while it has no other basis to support its validity than the assumed necessities of the employee, it takes no account of any independent resources she may have. It is based wholly on the opinions of the members of the board and their advisers—perhaps an average of their opinions, if they do not precisely agree—as to what will be necessary to provide a living for a woman, keep her in health and preserve her morals. It applies to any and every occupation in the District, without regard to its nature or the character of the work.

The standard furnished by the statute for the guidance of the board is so vague as to be impossible of practical application with any reasonable degree of accuracy. What is sufficient to supply the necessary cost of living for a woman worker and maintain her in good health and protect her morals is obviously not a precise or unvarying sum—not even approximately so. The amount will depend upon a variety of circumstances: the individual temperament, habits of thrift, care, ability to buy necessaries intelligently, and whether the woman live alone or with her family. To those who practice economy, a given sum will afford comfort, while to those of contrary habit the same sum will be wholly inadequate. The cooperative economies of the family group are not taken into account though they constitute an important consideration in estimating the cost of living, for it is obvious that the individual expense will be less in the case of a member of a family than in the case of one living alone. The relation between earnings and morals is not capable of standardization. It cannot be shown that well paid women safeguard their morals more carefully than those who are poorly paid. Morality rests upon other considerations than wages; and there is, certainly, no such prevalent connection between the two as to justify a broad attempt to adjust the latter

---

*This is the exact situation in the Lyons case, as is shown by the statement in the first part of this opinion.

with reference to the former. As a means of safeguarding morals the attempted classification, in our opinion, is without reasonable basis. No distinction can be made between women who work for others and those who do not; nor is there ground for distinction between women and men, for, certainly, if women require a minimum wage to preserve their morals men require it to preserve their honesty. For these reasons, and others which might be stated, the inquiry in respect of the necessary cost of living and of the income necessary to preserve health and morals, presents an individual and not a composite question, and must be answered for each individual considered by herself and not by a general formula prescribed by a statutory bureau.

This uncertainty of the statutory standard is demonstrated by a consideration of certain orders of the board already made. These orders fix the sum to be paid to a woman employed in a place where food is served or in a mercantile establishment, at $16.50 per week; in a printing establishment, at $15.50 per week; and in a laundry, at $15 per week, with a provision reducing this to $9 in the case of a beginner. If a woman employed to serve food requires a minimum of $16.50 per week, it is hard to understand how the same woman working in a printing establishment or in a laundry is to get on with an income lessened by from $1 to $7.50 per week. The board probably found it impossible to follow the indefinite standard of the statute, and brought other and different factors into the problem; and this goes far in the direction of demonstrating the fatal uncertainty of the act, an infirmity which, in our opinion, plainly exists.

The law takes account of the necessities of only one party to the contract. It ignores the necessities of the employer by compelling him to pay not less than a certain sum, not only whether the employee is capable of earning it, but irrespective of the ability of his business to sustain the burden, generously leaving him, of course, the privilege of abandoning his business as an alternative for going on at a loss. Within the limits of the minimum sum, he is precluded, under penalty of fine and imprisonment, from adjusting compensation to the differing merits of his employees. It compels him to pay at least the sum fixed in any event, because the employee needs it, but requires no service of equivalent value from the employee. It therefore undertakes to solve but one-half of the problem. The other half is the establishment of a corresponding standard of efficiency, and this forms no part of the policy of the legislation, although in practice the former half without the latter must lead to ultimate failure, in accordance with the inexorable law that no one can continue indefinitely to take out more than he puts in without ultimately exhausting the supply. The law is not confined to the great and powerful employers but embraces those whose bargaining power may be as weak as that of the employee. It takes no account of periods of stress and business depression, of crippling losses, which may leave the employer himself without adequate means of livelihood. To the extent that the sum fixed exceeds the fair value of the services rendered, it amounts to a compulsory exaction from the employer for the support of a partially indigent person, for whose condition there rests upon him no peculiar responsibility, and therefore, in effect, arbitrarily shifts to his shoulders a burden which, if it belongs to anybody, belongs to society as a whole.

The feature of this statute which, perhaps more than any other, puts upon it the stamp of invalidity is that it exacts from the employer an arbitrary payment for a purpose and upon a basis having no causal connection with his business, or the contract or the work the employee engages to do. The declared basis, as already pointed out, is not the value of the service rendered, but the extraneous circumstance that the employee needs to get a prescribed sum of money to insure her subsistence, health and morals. The ethical right of every worker, man or woman, to a living wage may be conceded. One of the declared and important purposes of trade organizations is to secure it. And with that principle and with every legitimate effort to realize it in fact, no one can quarrel; but the fallacy of the proposed method of attaining it is that it assumes that every employer is bound at all events to furnish it. The moral requirement implicit in every contract of employment, viz, that the amount to be paid and the service to be rendered shall bear to each other some relation of just equivalence, is completely ignored. The necessities of the employee are alone considered and these arise outside of the employment, are the same when there is no employment, and as great in one occupation as in another. Certainly the employer by paying a fair equivalent for the service rendered, though not sufficient to support the employee, has neither caused nor contributed to her poverty. On the contrary, to the extent of what he pays he has relieved it. In principle, there can be no difference between the case of selling labor and the case of selling goods. If one goes to the butcher, the baker or grocer to buy food, he is morally entitled to obtain the worth of his money but he is not entitled to more. If what he gets is worth what he pays he is not justified in demanding more simply because he needs more; and the shopkeeper, having dealt fairly and honestly in that transaction, is not concerned in any peculiar sense with the question of his customer's necessities. Should a statute undertake to vest in a commission power to determine the quantity of food necessary for individual support and require the shopkeeper, if he sell to the individual at all, to furnish that quantity at not more than a fixed maximum, it would undoubtedly fall before the constitutional test. The fallacy of any argument in support of the validity of such a statute would be quickly exposed. The argument in support of that now being considered is equally fallacious, though the weakness of it may not be so plain. A statute requiring an employer to pay in money, to pay at prescribed and regular intervals, to pay the value of the services rendered, even to pay with fair relation to the extent of the benefit obtained from the service, would be understandable. But a statute which prescribes payment without regard to any of these things and solely with relation to circumstances apart from the contract of employment, the business affected by it and the work done under it, is so clearly the product of a naked, arbitrary exercise of power that it cannot be allowed to stand under the Constitution of the United States.

We are asked, upon the one hand, to consider the fact that several States have adopted similar statutes, and we are invited, upon the other hand, to give weight to the fact that three times as many States, presumably as well informed and as anxious to promote the health and morals of their people, have refrained from enacting such legislation. We have also been furnished with a large number of printed opinions approving the policy of the minimum wage, and our own reading has disclosed a large number to the contrary. These are all proper enough for the consideration of the lawmaking bodies, since their tendency is to establish the desirability or undesirability of the legislation; but they reflect no legitimate light upon the question of its validity, and that is what we are called upon to decide. The elucidation of that question cannot be aided by counting heads.

It is said that great benefits have resulted from the operation of such statutes, not alone in the District of Columbia but in the several States, where they have been in force. A mass of reports, opinions of special observers and students of the subject, and the like, has been brought before us in support of this statement, all of which we have found interesting but only mildly persuasive. That the earnings of women now are greater than they were formerly and that conditions affecting women have become better in other respects may be conceded, but convincing indications of the logical relation of these desirable changes to the law in question are significantly lacking. They may be, and quite probably are, due to other causes. We cannot close our eyes to the notorious fact that earnings everywhere in all occupations have greatly increased—not alone in States where the minimum wage law obtains but in the country generally—quite as much or more among men as among women and in occupations outside the reach of the law as in those governed by it. No real test of the economic value of the law can be had during periods of maximum employment, when general causes keep wages up to or above the minimum; that will come in periods of depression and struggle for employment when the efficient will be employed at the minimum rate while the less capable may not be employed at all.

Finally, it may be said that if, in the interest of the public welfare, the police power may be invoked to justify the fixing of a minimum wage, it may, when the public welfare is thought to require it, be invoked to justify a maximum wage. The power to fix high wages connotes, by like course of reasoning, the power to fix low wages. If, in the face of the guaranties of the Fifth Amendment, this form of legislation shall be legally justified, the field for the operation of the police power will have been widened to a great and dangerous degree. If, for example, in the opinion of future lawmakers, wages in the building trades shall become so high as to preclude people of ordinary means from building and owning homes, an authority which sustains the minimum wage will be invoked to support a maximum wage for building laborers and artisans, and the same argument which has been here urged to strip the employer of his constitutional liberty of contract in one direction will be utilized to strip the employee of his constitutional liberty of contract in the opposite direction. A wrong decision does not end with itself: it is a precedent, and, with the swing of sentiment, its bad influence may run from one extremity of the arc to the other.

It has been said that legislation of the kind now under review is required in the interest of social justice, for whose ends freedom of contract may lawfully be subjected to restraint. The liberty of the individual to do as he pleases, even in innocent matters, is not absolute. It must frequently yield to the common good, and the line beyond which the power of interference may not be pressed is neither definite nor unalterable but may be made to move, within limits not well defined, with changing need and circumstance. Any attempt to fix a rigid boundary would be unwise as well as futile. But, nevertheless, there are limits to the power, and when these have been passed, it becomes the plain duty of the courts in the proper exercise of their authority to so declare. To sustain the individual freedom of action contemplated by the Constitution, is not to strike down the common good but to exalt it; for surely the good of society as a whole cannot be better served than by the preservation against arbitrary restraint of the liberties of its constituent members.

It follows from what has been said that the act in question passes the limit prescribed by the Constitution, and, accordingly, the decrees of the court below are

Affirmed.

Mr. Justice Brandeis took no part in the consideration or decision of these cases.

Mr. Chief Justice Taft, dissenting.

I regret much to differ from the Court in these cases.

The boundary of the police power beyond which its exercise becomes an invasion of the guaranty of liberty under the Fifth and Fourteenth Amendments to the Constitution is not easy to mark. Our Court has been laboriously engaged in pricking out a line in successive cases. We must be careful, it seems to me, to follow that line as well as we can and not to depart from it by suggesting a distinction that is formal rather than real.

Legislatures in limiting freedom of contract between employee and employer by a minimum wage proceed on the assumption that employees, in the class receiving least pay, are not upon a full level of equality of choice with their employer and in their necessitous circumstances are prone to accept pretty much anything that is offered. They are peculiarly subject to the overreaching of the harsh and greedy employer. The evils of the sweating system and of the long hours and low wages which are characteristic of it are well known. Now, I agree that it is a disputable question in the field of political economy how far a statutory requirement of maximum hours or minimum wages may be a useful remedy for these evils, and whether it may not make the case of the oppressed employee worse than it was before. But it is not the function of this Court to hold congressional acts invalid simply because they are passed to carry out economic views which the Court believes to be unwise or unsound.

Legislatures which adopt a requirement of maximum hours or minimum wages may be presumed to believe that when sweating employers are prevented from paying unduly low wages by positive law they will continue their business, abating that part of their profits, which were wrung from the necessities of their employees, and will concede the better terms required by the law; and that while in individual cases hardship may result, the restriction will enure to the benefit of the general class of employees in whose interest the law is passed and so to that of the community at large.

The right of the legislature under the Fifth and Fourteenth Amendments to limit the hours of employment on the score of the health of the employee, it seems to me, has been firmly established. As to that, one would think, the line had been pricked out so that it has become a well formulated rule. In *Holden* v. *Hardy*, 169 U.S. 366, it was applied to miners and rested on the unfavorable environment of employment in mining and smelting. In *Lochner* v. *New York*, 198 U.S. 45, it was held that restricting those employed in bakeries to ten hours a day was an arbitrary and invalid interference with the liberty of contract secured by the Fourteenth Amendment. Then followed a number of cases beginning with *Muller* v. *Oregon,* 208 U.S. 412, sustaining the validity of a limit on maximum hours of labor for women to which I shall hereafter allude, and following these cases came *Bunting* v. *Oregon,* 243 U.S. 426. In that case, this Court sustained a law limiting the hours of labor of any person, whether man or woman, working in any mill, factory or manufacturing establishment to ten hours a day with a proviso as to further hours to which I shall hereafter advert. The law covered the whole field of industrial employment and certainly covered the case of persons employed in bakeries. Yet the opinion in the *Bunting Case* does not mention the *Lochner Case.* No one can suggest any constitutional distinction between employment in a bakery and one in any other kind of a manufacturing establishment which should make a limit of hours in the one invalid, and the same limit in the other permissible. It is impossible for me to reconcile the *Bunting Case* and the *Lochner Case* and I have always supposed that the *Lochner Case* was thus overruled *sub silentio.* Yet the opinion of the Court herein in support of its conclusion quotes from the opinion in the *Lochner Case* as one which has been sometimes distinguished but never overruled. Certainly there was no attempt to distinguish it in the *Bunting Case.*

However, the opinion herein does not overrule the *Bunting Case* in express terms, and therefore I assume that the conclusion in this case rests on the distinction between a minimum of wages and a maximum of hours in the limiting of liberty to contract. I regret to be at variance with the Court as to the substance of this distinction. In absolute freedom of contract the one term is as important as the other, for both enter equally into the consideration given and received, a restriction as to one is not any greater in essence than the other, and is of the same kind. One is the multiplier and the other the multiplicand.

If it be said that long hours of labor have a more direct effect upon the health of the employee than the low wage, there is very respectable authority from close observers, disclosed in the record and in the literature on the subject quoted at length in the briefs, that they are equally harmful in this regard. Congress took this view and we can not say it was not warranted in so doing.

With deference to the very able opinion of the Court and my brethren who concur in it, it appears to me to exaggerate the importance of the wage term of the contract of employment as more inviolate than its other terms. Its conclusion seems influenced by the fear that the concession of the power to impose a minimum wage must carry with it a concession of the power to fix a maximum wage. This, I submit, is a *non sequitur*. A line of distinction like the one under discussion in this case is, as the opinion elsewhere admits, a matter of degree and practical experience and not of pure logic. Certainly the wide difference between prescribing a minimum wage and a maximum wage could as a matter of degree and experience be easily affirmed.

Moreover, there are decisions by this Court which have sustained legislative limitations in respect to the wage term in contracts of employment. In *McLean* v. *Arkansas,* 211 U.S. 539, it was held within legislative power to make it unlawful to estimate the graduated pay of miners by weight after screening the coal. In *Knoxville Iron Co.* v. *Harbison,* 183 U.S. 13, it was held that store orders issued for wages must be redeemable in cash. In *Patterson* v. *Bark Eudora,* 190 U.S. 169, a law forbidding the payment of wages in advance was held valid. A like case is *Strathearn S. S. Co.* v. *Dillon,* 252 U.S. 348. While these did not impose a minimum on wages, they did take away from the employee the freedom to agree as to how they should be fixed, in what medium they should be paid, and when they should be paid, all features that might affect the amount or the mode of enjoyment of them. The first two really rested on the advantage the employer had in dealing with the employee. The third was deemed a proper curtailment of a sailor's right of contract in his own interest because of his proneness to squander his wages in port before sailing. In *Bunting* v. *Oregon, supra,* employees in a mill, factory or manufacturing establishment were required if they worked over ten hours a day to accept for the three additional hours permitted not less than fifty per cent. more than their usual wage. This was sustained as a mild penalty imposed on the employer to enforce the limitation as to hours; but it necessarily curtailed the employee's freedom to contract to work for the wages he saw fit to accept during those three hours. I do not feel, therefore, that either on the basis of reason, experience or authority, the boundary of the police power should be drawn to include maximum hours and exclude a minimum wage.

Without, however, expressing an opinion that a minimum wage limitation can be enacted for adult men, it is enough to say that the case before us involves only the application of the minimum wage to women. If I am right in thinking that the legislature can find as much support in experience for the view that a sweating wage has as great and as direct a tendency to bring about an injury to the health and morals of workers, as for the view that long hours injure their health, then I respectfully submit that *Muller* v. *Oregon,* 208 U.S. 412, controls this case. The law which was there sustained forbade the employment of any female in any mechanical establishment or factory or laundry for more than ten hours. This covered a pretty wide field in women's work and it would not seem that any sound distinction between that case and this can be built up on the fact that the law before us applies to all occupations of women with power in the board to make certain exceptions. Mr. Justice Brewer, who spoke for the Court in *Muller* v. *Oregon,* based its conclusion on the natural limit to women's physical strength and the likelihood that long hours would therefore injure her health, and we have had since a series of cases which may be said to have established a rule of decision. *Riley* v. *Massachusetts,* 232 U.S. 671; *Miller* v. *Wilson,* 236 U.S. 373; *Bosley* v. *McLaughlin,* 236 U.S. 385. The cases covered restrictions in wide and varying fields of employment and in the later cases it will be found that the objection to the particular law was based not on the ground that it had general application but because it left out some employments.

I am not sure from a reading of the opinion whether the Court thinks the authority of *Muller* v. *Oregon* is shaken by the adoption of the Nineteenth Amendment. The Nineteenth Amendment did not change the physical strength or limitations of women upon which the decision in *Muller* v. *Oregon* rests. The Amendment did give women political power and makes more certain that legislative provisions for their protection will be in accord with their interests as they see them. But I don't think we are warranted in varying constitutional construction based on physical differences between men and women, because of the Amendment.

But for my inability to agree with some general observations in the forcible opinion of Mr. Justice Holmes who follows me, I should be silent and merely record my concurrence in what he says. It is perhaps wiser for me, however, in a case of this importance, separately to give my reasons for dissenting.

I am authorized to say that Mr. Justice Sanford concurs in this opinion.

Mr. Justice Holmes, dissenting.

The question in this case is the broad one, Whether Congress can establish minimum rates of wages for women in the District of Columbia with due provision for special circumstances, or whether we must say that Congress has no power to meddle with the matter at all. To me, notwithstanding the deference due to the prevailing judgment of the Court, the power of Congress seems absolutely free from doubt. The end, to remove conditions leading to ill health, immorality and the deterioration of the race, no one would deny to be within the scope of constitutional legislation. The means are means that have the approval of Congress, of many States, and of those governments from which we have learned our greatest lessons. When so many intelligent persons, who have studied the matter more than any of us can, have thought that the means are effective and are worth the price, it seems to me impossible to deny that the belief reasonably may be held by reasonable men. If the law encountered no other objection than that the means bore no relation to the end or that they cost too much I do not suppose that anyone would venture to say that it was bad. I agree, of course, that a law answering the foregoing requirements might be invalidated by specific provisions of the Constitution. For instance it might take private property without just compensation. But in the present instance the only objection that can be urged is found within the vague contours of the Fifth Amendment, prohibiting the depriving any person of liberty or property without due process of law. To that I turn.

The earlier decisions upon the same words in the Fourteenth Amendment began within our memory and went no farther than an unpretentious assertion of the liberty to follow the ordinary callings. Later that innocuous generality was expanded into the dogma, Liberty of Contract. Contract is not specially mentioned in the text that we have to construe. It is merely an example of doing what you want to do, embodied in the word liberty. But pretty much all law consists in forbidding men to do some things that they want to do, and contract is no more exempt from law than other acts. Without enumerating all the restrictive laws that have been upheld I will mention a few that seem to me to have interfered with liberty of contract quite as seriously and directly as the one before us. Usury laws prohibit contracts by which a man receives more than so much interest for the money that he lends. Statutes of frauds restrict many contracts to certain forms. Some Sunday laws prohibit practically all contracts during one-seventh of our whole life. Insurance rates may be regulated. *German Alliance Insurance Co.* v. *Lewis,* 233 U.S. 389. (I concurred in that decision without regard to the public interest with which insurance was said to be clothed. It seemed to me that the principle was general.) Contracts may be forced upon the companies. *National Union Fire Insurance Co.* v. *Wanberg,* 260 U.S. 71. Employers of miners may be required to pay for coal by weight before screening. *McLean* v. *Arkansas,* 211 U.S. 539. Employers generally may be required to redeem in cash store orders accepted by their employees in payment. *Knoxville Iron Co.* v. *Harbison,* 183 U.S. 13. Payment of sailors in advance may be forbidden. *Patterson* v. *Bark Eudora,* 190 U.S. 169. The size of a loaf of bread may be established. *Schmidinger* v. *Chicago,* 226 U.S. 578. The responsibility of employers to their employees may be profoundly modified. *New York Central R. R. Co.* v. *White,* 243 U.S. 188. *Arizona Employers' Liability Cases,* 250 U.S. 400. Finally women's hours of labor may be fixed; *Muller* v. *Oregon,* 208 U.S. 412; *Riley* v. *Massachusetts,* 232 U.S. 671, 679; *Hawley* v. *Walker,* 232 U.S. 718; *Miller* v. *Wilson,* 236 U.S. 373; *Bosley* v. *McLaughlin,* 236 U.S. 385; and the principle was extended to men with the allowance of a limited overtime to be paid for "at the rate of time and one-half of the regular wage," in *Bunting* v. *Oregon,* 243 U.S. 426.

I confess that I do not understand the principle on which the power to fix a minimum for the wages of women can be denied by those who admit the power to fix a maximum for their hours of work. I fully assent to the proposition that here as elsewhere the distinctions of the law are distinctions of degree, but I perceive no difference in the kind or degree of interference with liberty, the only matter with which we have any concern, between the one case and the other. The bargain is equally affected whichever half you regulate. *Muller* v. *Oregon,* I take it, is as good law today as it was in 1908. It will need more than the Nineteenth Amendment to convince me that there are no differences between men and women, or that legislation cannot take those differences into account. I should not hesitate to take them into account if I thought it necessary to sustain this act. *Quong Wing* v. *Kirkendall,* 223 U.S. 59, 63. But after *Bunting* v. *Oregon,* 243 U.S. 426, I had supposed that it was not necessary, and that *Lochner* v. *New York,* 198 U.S. 45, would be allowed a deserved repose.

This statute does not compel anybody to pay anything. It simply forbids employment at rates below those fixed as the minimum requirement of health and right living. It is safe to assume that women will not be employed at even the lowest wages allowed unless they earn them, or unless the employer's business can sustain the burden. In short the law in its character and operation is like hundreds of so-called police laws that have been upheld. I see no greater objection to using a Board to apply the standard fixed by the act than there is to the other commissions with which we have become familiar, or than there is to the requirement of a license in other cases. The fact that the statute warrants classification, which like all classifications may bear hard upon some individuals, or in exceptional cases, notwithstanding the power given to the Board to issue a special license, is no greater infirmity than is incident to all law. But the ground on which the law is held to fail is fundamental and therefore it is unnecessary to consider matters of detail.

The criterion of constitutionality is not whether we believe the law to be for the public good. We certainly cannot be prepared to deny that a reasonable man reasonably might have that belief in view of the legislation of Great Britain, Victoria and a number of the States of this Union. The belief is fortified by a very remarkable collection of documents submitted on behalf of the appellants, material here, I conceive, only as showing that the belief reasonably may be held. In Australia the power to fix a minimum for wages in the case of industrial disputes extending beyond the limits of any one State was given to a Court, and its President wrote a most interesting account of its operation. 29 Harv. Law Rev. 13. If a legislature should adopt what he thinks the doctrine of modern economists of all schools, that "freedom of contract is a misnomer as applied to a contract between an employer and an ordinary individual employee," *ibid.* 25, I could not pronounce an opinion with which I agree impossible to be entertained by reasonable men. If the same legislature should accept his further opinion that industrial peace was best attained by the device of a Court having the above powers, I should not feel myself able to contradict it, or to deny that the end justified restrictive legislation quite as adequately as beliefs concerning Sunday or exploded theories about usury. I should have my doubts, as I have them about this statute—but they would be whether the bill that has to be paid for every gain, although hidden as interstitial detriments, was not greater than the gain was worth: a matter that it is not for me to decide.

I am of opinion that the statute is valid and that the decree should be reversed.

16

A Study of Social Objectives
Robert S. and Helen M. Lynd's "Why Do They Work So Hard?"

Robert S. (1892-   ) and Helen Merrell (1897-   ) Lynd are American sociologists trained to the discipline after it shifted its emphasis from a quest for general laws of social development to the less glamorous search for sociological data and techniques of scientific analysis of the information collected. American society had undergone great changes as industrialism and urbanism exerted powerful influences upon the agrarian-commercial culture inherited from the eighteenth and nineteenth centuries. As an author reported in *Recent Social Trends in the United States* (1933), "Modern life is everywhere complicated, but especially so in the United States, where immigration . . . rapid mobility . . . the lack of established classes or castes to act as a brake on social changes, the tendency to seize upon new types of machines, rich natural resources and vast driving power, have hurried us dizzily away from the days of the frontier into a whirl of modernisms which almost passes belief." The Lynds made a sociological study of Muncie, Indiana of unusual value to the historian. Their investigations in depth of this community provide the student of social change with a wealth of information concerning the influence of industrialism upon American life. The student might also consult the President's Research Committee on Social Trends, *Recent Social Trends in the United States* 2 vols. (New York: McGraw Hill Book Company, 1933), an indispensable summary of information collected by the committee. Two useful surveys providing a background for the selection printed below are °Henry Pelling's *American Labor* (Chicago: University of Chicago Press, 1960) and Philip Taft's *Organized Labor in American History* (New York: Harper and Row, 1964). Irving Bernstein's *The Lean Years: A History of the American Worker, 1920-1933* (Boston: Houghton Mifflin Company, 1960) deals more particularly with the 1920's. In reading the Lynds' chapter note (1) what answer the authors found to their question; (2) what contrast they saw in the status of workers in the 1890's and in the 1920's

Robert S. and Helen Merrell Lynd, *Middletown: A Study in Contemporary American Culture* (New York: Harcourt, Brace and Company, 1929), pp. 73-89.

and to what factors they attributed the cause of the shift; (3) what had happened to the trade unions since the 1890's and why; (4) what they saw occurring to the standards of living and what pressures for change they observed; (5) what effects they saw on the role of money as an object of work; (6) what they learned about income, its distribution, and its buying power; (7) how the pursuit of money affected the quality of living; and (8) what they observed concerning the extent to which industry had come to dominate Middletown's life.

ONE EMERGES FROM THE OFFICES, STORES, AND factories of Middletown asking in some bewilderment why all the able-bodied men and many of the women devote their best energies for long hours day after day to this driving activity seemingly so foreign to many of the most powerful impulses of human beings. Is all this expenditure of energy necessary to secure food, clothing, shelter, and other things essential to existence? If not, precisely what over and beyond these subsistence necessaries is Middletown getting out of its work?

For very many of those who get the living for Middletown the amount of robust satisfaction they derive from the actual performance of their specific jobs seems, at best, to be slight. Among the business men the kudos accruing to the eminent in getting a living and to some of their minor associates yields a kind of incidental satisfaction; the successful manufacturer even tends today to supplant in local prestige and authority the judge, preacher, and "professor" of thirty-five to forty years ago. But for the working class both any satisfactions inherent in the actual daily doing of the job and the prestige and kudos of the able worker among his associates would appear to be declining.

The demands of the iron man for swiftness and endurance rather than training and skill have led to the gradual abandonment of the apprentice-master craftsman system; one of the chief characteristics of Middletown life in the nineties, this system is now virtually a thing of the past.[1] The master mechanic was the

---

[1]Less than 1 per cent of those listed by the 1920 Census as engaged in manufacturing and mechanical industries in Middletown were apprentices. Of 429 workers in Middletown wood, glass, and iron and steel industries in 1891, 51 per cent were apprentices or had served apprenticeships. If the

aristocrat among workmen of 1890—"one of the noblest of God's creatures," as one of them put it. But even in the nineties machinery was beginning to undermine the monopolistic status of his skill; he was beginning to feel the ground shifting under his feet. The State Statistician recorded uneasy protests of men from all over the State.[2] Today all that is left of the four-year apprentice system among 9,000 workers in the manufacturing and mechanical industries is three or four score of apprentices scattered through the building and molding trades.[3] "It's 'high speed steel' and specialization and Ford cars that's hit the machinist's union," according to a skilled Middletown worker. "You had to know how to use the old carbon steel to keep it from gettin' hot and spoilin' the edge. But this 'high speed steel' and this new 'stelite' don't absorb the heat and are harder than carbon steel. You can take a boy fresh from the farm and in three days he can manage a machine as well as I can, and I've been at it twenty-seven years."

With the passing of apprenticeship the line between skilled and unskilled worker has become so blurred as to be in some shops almost non-existent. The superintendent of a leading Middletown machine shop says, "Seventy-five per cent of our force of 800 men can be taken from farm or high school and trained in a week's time." In the glass plant . . . 84 per cent of the tool-using personnel, exclusive of foremen, require one month or less of training, another 4 per cent not more than six months, 6 per

---

laborers be excluded from the group, 64 per cent of the remaining 342 either were apprentices or had been apprenticed, and, taking the iron and steel plants and the glass houses separately, this percentage amounts to 79 per cent and 70 per cent respectively. These figures must be used cautiously, since the manner of selecting the sample of 429 workers is not stated. (*Fourth Biennial Report of (the State) Department of Statistics, 1891-2*, pp. 57, 130, 317.)

[2]"It is getting harder to find employment at molding every year." "Machinery and specialty men are used in large establishments altogether. I think in about twenty years a mechanic will be a scarce article in this country." "Men are put in as master mechanics who could not build a wheelbarrow. . . . *Any one can do one thing over and over, so he is just put on a machine at $1.00, or perhaps $1.25, a day.*" (Italics ours.) (*Fourth Biennial Report, 1891-2*, pp. 26-41.)

[3]The Personnel Department of a leading local automobile parts plant listed but four apprentices (all in the tool room) among the more than 2,000 employees on their "normal force." Another plant listed only two apprentices (also in the tool room) in a normal force of 1,000.

cent a year, and the remaining 6 per cent three years.[4] Foundry workers have not lost to the iron man as heavily as machinists, but even here the trend is marked. In Middletown's leading foundry in the early nineties, 47 per cent of the workers (including foremen) had three to six years' training. This trained group today is half as great (24 per cent) and 60 per cent of all the castings produced are made by a group of newcomers who cast with the help of machines and require only a fortnight or so of training.

"Do you think the man who runs a complicated machine takes pride in his work and gets a feeling of proprietorship in his machine?" a responsible executive in charge of personnel in a large machine shop was asked.

"No, I don't," was his ready reply. "There's a man who's ground diameters on gears here for fifteen years and done nothing else. It's a fairly highly skilled job and takes more than six months to learn. But it's so endlessly monotonous! That man is dead, just dead! And there's a lot of others like him, and I don't know what to do for them."

"What," asked the questioner, "do you think most of the men in the plant are working for?—to own a car, or a home, or just to keep their heads above water?"

"They're just working. They don't know what for. They're just in a rut and keep on in it, doing the same monotonous work every day, and wondering when a slump will come and they will be laid off."

"How much of the time are your thoughts on your job?" an alert young Middletown bench molder was asked.

"As long as there happens to be any new problem about the casting I'm making, I'm thinking about it, but as soon as ever I get the hang of the thing there isn't 25 per cent of me paying attention to the job."

The shift from a system in which length of service, craftsmanship, and authority in the shop and social prestige among one's peers tended to go together to one which, in the main, demands little of a worker's personality save rapid, habitual reactions and an ability to submerge himself in the performance of a few routinized easily learned movements seems to have wiped out many of the satisfactions that formerly accompanied the job. Middletown's shops are full of men of whom it may be said that "there isn't 25 per cent of them paying attention to the job."

---

[4]Nearly half the three-year group are carpenters and plumbers, i.e., not primarily factory workers but members of the strongly organized building trades.

And as they leave the shop in the evening, "The work of a modern machine-tender leaves nothing tangible at the end of the day's work to which he can point with pride and say, 'I did that —it is the result of my own skill and my own effort.'"

The intangible income accruing to many of the business group derives in part from such new devices as membership in Rotary and other civic clubs, the Chamber of Commerce, Business and Professional Women's Club, and the various professional clubs.[5] But among the working class not only have no such new groups arisen to reward and bolster their work, but the once powerful trade unions have for the most part either disappeared or persist in attenuated form.

By the early nineties Middletown had become "one of the best organized cities in the United States."[6] By 1897, thirty "locals" totaling 3,766 members were affiliated with the A. F. of L. and the city vied with Detroit and other cities as a labor convention city. In 1899 the first chapter of a national women's organization, the Women's Union Label League, was launched in Middletown. At this time organized labor formed one of the most active coordinating centers in the lives of some thousands of Middletown working class families, touching their getting-a-living, educational, leisure-time, and even in a few cases religious activities. On the getting-a-living sector the unions brought tangible pressure for a weekly pay law, standardized wage scales, factory inspection, safety devices and other things regarded as improvements, and helped in sickness or death, while crowded mass meetings held in the opera house collected large sums for the striking workers in Homestead and elsewhere. A special Workingmen's Library and Reading Room,[7] with a paid librarian and a wide assortment of books, was much frequented. Undoubtedly the religious element in the labor movement of this day was missed by many, but a Middletown old-timer still refers enthusiastically to the Knights of Labor as a "grand organization" with a "fine ritual," and a member of both iron and glass unions

---

[5]For discussion of these groups see [*Middletown,*] Ch. 19.

[6]From a letter from the Secretary of the Glass Bottle Blowers' Association of the U.S. and Canada, Sept. 27, 1924. A member of the executive board of this Association, who came to Middletown in 1893, says the city was "next to Rochester, N.Y., the best organized town in the country."

[7]Cf. [*Middletown,*] Ch. 17.

during the nineties is emphatic regarding the greater importance of the ceremonial aspects of the unions in those days, particularly when new members were received, as compared with the bald meetings of today. As centers of leisure time the unions ranked among the important social factors in the lives of a large number of workers. Such items as these appear in the Middletown press all through the nineties:

A column account of the Ball and Concert given by Midland Lodge No. 20, Amalgamated Association of Iron and Steel Workers in Shirk's Hall, described it as "the largest event of its kind ever given in (Middletown) or the Gas Belt . . . 1,200 to 1,500 present."

An account of the installation of officers and banquet of the Painters' and Decorators' Union records the presence of 200 visitors, including wives and children. A "fine literary program was rendered." The Chief of Police was the guest of honor, and the ex-president and secretary of the Middletown Trades Council spoke. Nearly every member of the police force was present. The hall was decorated with American flags. There was singing, and the new invention, the gramophone, was featured. After the literary program came dancing.

"The Cigar Makers' 'Blue Label' nine played a very hotly contested game with union barbers' nine yesterday (Sunday) P.M."

"Yesterday P.M. (Sunday) the Bakers met at Hummel's Hall on invitation of Aug. Waick, our president, who set up a keg and lunch. We had a meeting, installed officers, then a good time."

Labor Day, a great day in the nineties, is today barely noticed.[8]

From the end of the nineties such laconic reports as "Strike defeated by use of machinery" mark increasingly the failing status of organized labor in Middletown. According to the secretary of one national union, "the organized labor movement in (Middletown) does not compare with that of 1890 as one to one

---

[8]In 1891 the entire city participated in the first Labor Day celebration—commencing at 4 A.M. with an "artillery signal of forty-four rounds" and proceeding throughout a crowded day of bands, parade, greased pole, bicycle races in the street, pie-eating contest, reading of Declaration of Independence, two orations, greased pig, basball, dancing all day, to a grand finale of fireworks at the fair grounds. But today the parade has been abandoned entirely. In 1923 an effort was made to draw a crowd to hear a speaker, free ice cream being used as an inducement, but in 1924 no ceremonies were even attempted.

hundred."[9] The city's civic clubs boast of its being an "open shop town."

The social function of the union has disappeared in this day of movies and automobiles, save for sparsely attended dances at Labor Hall. The strong molders' union, e.g., has to compel attendance at its meetings by making attendance at one or the other of the two monthly meetings compulsory under a penalty of a dollar fine. There is no longer a Workingmen's Library or any other educational activity. Multiple lodge memberships,[10] occasional factory "mutual welfare associations," the diffusion of the habit of carrying life insurance, socialized provision of workmen's compensation, and the beginning of the practice in at least three factories of carrying group life-insurance for all workers, are slowly taking over the insurance function performed by the trade unions. Of the 100 working class families for whom income distribution was secured, only eleven contributed anything to the support of labor unions; amounts contributed ranged from $18.00 to $60.00.

Likewise, public opinion is no longer with organized labor. In the earlier period a prominent Middletown lawyer and the superintendent of schools addressed an open meeting of the Knights of Labor, and the local press commended the "success of the meeting of this flourishing order." When Samuel Gompers came to town in ninety-seven he was dined in the mayor's home

---

[9]From a letter from the Secretary of the Glass Bottle Blowers' Association of the United States and Canada, September 27, 1924.

Numerically at least this is an overstatement, though it may reflect the power of the organized group in the community in the two periods. In 1893 there were 981 union members in Middletown, as against 815 in 1924, when the city was two or three times as large. Some of the present total are aging workers who keep up old union affiliations for the sake of insurance benefits. The building trades, typographical workers, pattern makers, and molders are still well organized, though the first are feeling the competition of non-union workers from outlying small towns who invade the town daily in their Fords, while already, as pointed out above, in a leading foundry 60 per cent of the castings are made by non-union men trained in a fortnight.

[10]Sickness, death, and old-age benefits are with many the sole reason for membership in working class lodges today. Mooseheart and Moosehaven, the two national "homes" for children and the aged maintained by the national order of Moose, are popular in Middletown and offer advantages which only a few of the older and richer unions, inaccessible to the great mass of local workers, can approach.

Cf. discussion of lodges in [*Middletown,*] Ch. 19.

before addressing the great crowd at the opera house. The press carried daily items agitating for stricter local enforcement of the weekly pay law, or urging public support of union solicitations for funds for union purposes, or calling speeches at labor mass-meetings "very able and enjoyable addresses." The proceedings of the Glass Workers' Convention in Baltimore in 1890 were reported in full on the first page. Such a note as this was common: "During the last few months there have been organized in this city several trade organizations and labor unions . . . and much good has resulted therefrom." At a grand Farmers and Knights of Labor picnic in 1890, "a perfect jam, notwithstanding the rain," the speaker "ably denounced trusts, Standard Oil, etc.," according to the leading paper. The largest men's clothing firm presented a union with a silk parade-banner costing nearly $100.[11] Today the Middletown press has little that is good to say of organized labor.[12] The pulpit avoids such subjects, particularly in the churches of the business class, and when it speaks it is apt to do so in guarded, equivocal terms.[13] A prevalent attitude

---

[11]It should not be inferred that the workers had things all their own way. Strikes and lock-outs were frequent, and the boycott was freely and effectively used against local business men who sold non-union goods. The diary of one elderly merchant complains that "a great many were compelled to show a left-handed sneaking approval." But the significant point is that labor was powerful and class-conscious, and the workers apparently gained added stature in many of their vital activities from their membership in this powerful union movement.

[12]One of the two daily papers spoke editorially on one recent occasion of unions as "fine things for those who work with their hands" but went on to decry any activity by the local union "composed of our own 'folks' " in trying "to drag into its own affairs the 'folks' that are international or national and do not know our own local problems."

[13]Cf. the following press report, sent to the paper by the minister himself, which summarizes a sermon in the largest church in Middletown on national "Labor Sunday," 1924: "[The preacher] based his sermon on that portion of the Lord's Prayer which calls upon God 'to give us this day our daily bread.' He pointed out that when this prayer is repeated one does not ask God 'to give me my daily bread' but is broader and takes in all mankind in the words 'us' and 'our.'

"The speaker took up briefly the labor situation in the United States as regards the laborer and the employer, and declared that 'we do not have in [Middletown] the conditions that exist elsewhere,' implying that no serious labor problem is in existence here. Brotherhoods among laboring men have done much good for the laborer and have brought to him certain rights, he said, but in some cases, especially where public welfare is involved, they have gone too far."

among the business class appears in the statement of one of the city's leaders, "Working men don't need unions nowadays. There are no great evils or problems now as there were fifty years ago. We are much more in danger of coddling the working men than abusing them. Working people are just as well off now as they can possibly be except for things which are in the nature of industry and cannot be helped."

This decrease in the psychological satisfactions formerly derived from the sense of craftsmanship and in group solidarity, added to the considerations adduced in the preceding chapters, serves to strengthen the impression gained from talk with families of the working class that, however it may be with their better-educated children, for most of the present generation of workers "there is no break through on their industrial sector." It is important for the consideration of other life-activities to bear in mind this fact, that the heavy majority of the numerically dominant working class group live in a world in which neither present nor future appears to hold as much prospect of dominance on the job or of the breaking through to further expansion of personal powers by the head of the family as among the business group.

Frustrated in this sector of their lives, many workers seek compensations elsewhere. The president of the Middletown Trades Council, an alert and energetic molder of thirty and until now the most active figure in the local labor movement, has left the working class to become one of the minor office-holders in the dominant political machine. Others who do not leave are finding outlets, if no longer in the saloon, in such compensatory devices as hooking up the radio or driving the "old bus." The great pressure toward education on the part of the working class is, of course, another phase of this desire to escape to better things.[14]

For both working and business class no other accompaniment of getting a living approaches in importance the money received for their work. It is more this future, instrumental aspect of work, rather than the intrinsic satisfactions involved, that keeps Middletown working so hard as more and more of the activities of living are coming to be strained through the bars of the dollar

---

[14]Cf. in [*Middletown,*] Ch. 13 the importance to working class parents of education for their children.

sign.[15] Among the business group, such things as one's circle of friends, the kind of car one drives, playing golf, joining Rotary, the church to which one belongs, one's political principles, the social position of one's wife apparently tend to be scrutinized somewhat more than formerly in Middletown for their instrumental bearing upon the main business of getting a living, while, conversely, one's status in these various other activities tends to be much influenced by one's financial position. As vicinage [the neighborhood] has decreased in its influence upon the ordinary social contacts of this group,[16] there appears to be a constantly closer relation between the solitary factor of financial status and one's social status. A leading citizen presented this matter in a nutshell to a member of the research staff in discussing the almost universal local custom of "placing" newcomers in terms of where they live, how they live, the kind of car they drive, and similar externals: "It's perfectly natural. You see, they know money, and they don't know you."

This dominance of the dollar appears in the apparently growing tendency among younger working class men to swap a problematic future for immediate "big money." Foremen complain that Middletown boys entering the shops today are increasingly less interested in being moved from job to job until they have become all-round skilled workers, but want to stay on one machine and run up their production so that they may quickly reach a maximum wage scale.[17]

---

[15]Cf. Maynard Keynes on "the habitual appeal" of our age "to the money motive in nine-tenths of the activities of life . . . the universal striving after individual economic security as the prime object of endeavor . . . the social approbation of money as the measure of constructive success, and . . . the social appeal to the hoarding instinct as the foundation of the necessary provision for the family and for the future." (*New Republic,* Nov. 11, 1925.)

[16]Cf. in [*Middletown,*] Ch. 19 the places where both business and working class men and women see their friends.

[17]According to one veteran foundry foreman: "In the old days of the nineties a boy was shaped and trained by his foreman. When he started his apprenticeship for the molder's trade he was lucky to make $3 or $4 a week. At the end of the first year he was making, maybe, a dollar or $1.25 a day; at the end of the second year perhaps $1.50 or $2.00; the third year, $2.25; and then at the end of the fourth year he received his card and $2.75 a day. Meanwhile his foreman had shifted him about from job to job until, when he became a molder and went on a piece-work basis, he knew his job from every angle and could make big money. But the trouble nowadays is that within a year a machine molder may be making as much

The rise of large-scale advertising, popular magazines, movies, radio, and other channels of increased cultural diffusion from without are rapidly changing habits of thought as to what things are essential to living and multiplying optional occasions for spending money.[18] Installment buying, which turns wishes into horses overnight, and the heavy increase in the number of

---

as a man who has been there fifteen or twenty years. He has his eyes on the money—$40 to $50 a week—and resists the foreman's efforts to put him on bench molding where he would learn the fine points of the molder's trade."

[18]It is perhaps impossible to overestimate the role of motion pictures, advertising, and other forms of publicity in this rise in subjective standards. Week after week at the movies people in all walks of life enter, often with an intensity of emotion that is apparently one of the most potent means of reconditioning habits, into the intimacies of Fifth Avenue drawing rooms and English country houses, watching the habitual activities of a different cultural level. The growth of popular magazines and national advertising involves the utilization through the printed page of the most powerful stimuli to action. In place of the relatively mild, scattered, something-for-nothing, sample-free, I-tell-you-this-is-a-good-article copy seen in Middletown a generation ago, advertising is concentrating increasingly upon a type of copy aiming to make the reader emotionally uneasy, to bludgeon him with the fact that decent people don't live the way *he* does: *decent* people ride on balloon tires, have a second bathroom, and so on. This copy points an accusing finger at the stenographer as she reads her *Motion Picture Magazine* and makes her acutely conscious of her unpolished finger nails, or of the worn place in the living room rug, and sends the housewife peering anxiously into the mirror to see if *her* wrinkles look like those that made Mrs. X—— in the ad "Old at thirty-five" because she did not have a Leisure Hour electric washer.

Whole industries are pooling their strength to ram home a higher standard of living, e.g., the recent nation-wide essay contest among school children on home lighting conducted by all branches of the electrical industry. In addition to the national prizes of a $15,000 house and university scholarships, local prizes ranging all the way from a radio set and dressing table to electric curling irons and basketball season tickets were given to the thirty best Middletown essays. In this campaign 1,500 Middletown children submitted essays on how the lighting of their homes could be improved, and upwards of 1,500 families were made immediately aware of the inadequacies of their homes as regards library table lamps, porch lights, piano lamps, and convenient floor sockets. As one of the winning local essays said: "I and all my family have learned a great deal that we did not know before, and we intend improving the lighting in our own home."

The "style show" is a new and effective form of Middletown advertising that unquestionably influences the local standard of living. On two successive nights at one of these local shows a thousand people—ten-cent store clerks, tired-looking mothers with children, husbands and wives—watched rouged clerks promenade languorously along the tops of the show cases, displaying the latest hats, furs, dresses, shoes, parasols, bags and other accessories, while a jazz orchestra kept everybody "feeling good."

children receiving higher education, with its occasions for breaking with home traditions, are facilitating this rise to new standards of living. In 1890 Middletown appears to have lived on a series of plateaus as regards standard of living; old citizens say there was more contentment with relative arrival; it was a common thing to hear a remark that so and so "is pretty good for people in our circumstances." Today the edges of the plateaus have been shaved off, and every one lives on a slope from any point of which desirable things belonging to people all the way to the top are in view.

This diffusion of new urgent occasions for spending money in every sector of living is exhibited by such new tools and services commonly used in Middletown today, but either unknown or little used in the nineties, as the following:

In the home—furnace, running hot and cold water, modern sanitation, electric appliances ranging from toasters to washing machines, telephone, refrigeration, green vegetables and fresh fruit all the year round, greater variety of clothing, silk hose and underwear, commercial pressing and cleaning of clothes,[19] commercial laundering or use of expensive electrical equipment in the home,[20] cosmetics, manicuring, and commercial hair-dressing.

In spending leisure time—movies (attendance far more frequent than at earlier occasional "shows"), automobile (gas, tires, depreciation, cost of trips), phonograph, radio, more elaborate children's playthings, more club dues for more members of the family, Y.M.C.A. and Y.W.C.A., more formal dances and banquets, including a highly competitive series of "smartly appointed affairs" by high school clubs;[21] cigarette smoking and expensive cigars.

In education—high school and college (involving longer dependence

---

[19]In the Middletown city directory for 1889 there were no dry cleaners and only one dye house. Today a city less than four times the size has twelve dry cleaners and four dye houses. The habit of pressing trousers is said not to have "come in" until about 1895.

[20]The hand-washers of 1890 sold for $7.50 to $10.00, while the modern machines cost $60.00 to $200.00.

[21]A dance no longer costs $0.50, as in the nineties, but the members of clubs are assessed about $4.00 for their Christmas dances today. Music used to be a two- or three-piece affair, but now it is an imported orchestra costing from $150 to $300. A boy has to take a girl in a taxi if he does not have the use of the family car. One does not go home after a dance but spends a dollar or so on "eats" afterwards. Expensive favors are given at annual sorority banquets.

of children), many new incidental costs such as entrance to constant school athletic contests.[22]

In the face of these rapidly multiplying accessories to living, the "social problem" of "the high cost of living" is apparently envisaged by most people in Middletown as soluble if they can only inch themselves up a notch higher in the amount of money received for their work. Under these circumstances, why shouldn't money be important to people in Middletown? "The Bible never spoke a truer word," says the local paper in an editorial headed "Your Bank Account Your Best Friend," "than when it said: 'But money answereth all things.' . . . If it doesn't answer all things, it at least answers more than 50 per cent of them." And again, "Of our happy position in world affairs there need be no . . . further proof than the stability of our money system." One leading Middletown business man summed up this trend toward a monetary approach to the satisfactions of life in addressing a local civic club when he said, "Next to the doctor we think of the banker to help us and to guide us in our wants and worries today."

Money being, then, so crucial, how much money do Middletown people actually receive? The minimum cost of living for a "standard family of five" in Middletown in 1924 was $1,920.87.[23] A complete distribution of the earnings of Middletown is not available. Twelve to 15 per cent of those getting the city's living reported a large enough income for 1923 to make the filing of a Federal income tax return necessary.[24] Of the 16,000-17,000 people gainfully employed in 1923—including, however, somewhere in the neighborhood of a thousand married women, some of whom undoubtedly made joint returns with their husbands— 210 reported net incomes (i.e., minus interest, contributions, etc.) of $5,000 or over, 999 more net incomes less than $5,000 but large enough to be taxable after subtracting allowed exemp-

---

[22]See Table VI [not reproduced here] for distribution of expenditures of 100 working class families.

[23]Based on the budget of the United States Bureau of Labor and computed on the basis of Middletown prices. . . .

[24]These income tax data, fallible as they are, owing to non-reporting and other possible errors, are used here simply as the best rough estimate available. There are at the outside probably not over two- or three-score people in Middletown who made income tax returns who are not actually engaged in getting a living.

tions ($1,000 if single, $2,500 if married, and $400 per dependent), while 1,036 more filed returns but were not taxable after subtracting allowed deductions and exemptions. The other 85-88 per cent of those earning the city's living presumably received either less than $1,000 if single or less than $2,000 if married, or failed to make income tax returns. A cross section of working class earnings is afforded by the following distribution of 100 of the working class families interviewed according to their earnings in the preceding twelve months:[25]

	Distribution of Families by Fathers' Earnings Only	Distribution of Families by Total Family Earnings
Total number of families	100	100
Earning *less* than minimum standard of $1,920.87	— —	— —
Families of 5 members or more	42	39
Families of 4 or 3 members (including families of 2 foremen)	35	35
Earning *more* than minimum standard of $1,920.87		
Families of 5 members or more (including one foreman)	10	13
Families of 4 or 3 members (including 6 foremen)	13	13

The incomes of these 100 families range from $344.50 to $3,460.00, with the median at $1,494.75 and the first and third quartiles respectively at $1,193.63 and $2,006.00.[26]

The relative earning power of males and females in Middle-

---

[25]See Table VI [not reproduced here] for distribution of income of these 100 families by members of family earning and for distribution of certain major items of expenditure throughout the year.

Six of the twelve months (Oct. 1, 1923, to Oct. 1, 1924) covered by these income figures were good times in Middletown and six months were relatively bad times locally, though the latter was not a period of national depression. This would tend to make the 1924 average income less than on a "big year" like 1923—though 50 per cent good and bad times is more representative of the actual chance to get a living in Middletown today than either a completely good or bad year would have been. . . .

The minimum standard for a family of less than five members would be less than $1,920.87, and consequently certain marginal families of three or four grouped above with those earning ·less than the minimum would on a more exact calculation be transferred to the group earning more than the minimum standard.

[26]The incomes of the husbands alone of these 100 families exhibit a spread from $344.50 to $3,200.00, with the median at $1,303.10 and the first and third quartiles at $1,047.50 and $1,856.75 respectively.

town is indicated by the fact that in a characteristic leading Middletown plant during the first six months of 1924 the weighted average hourly wage of all females (excluding office force and forewomen) was $0.31 and of all males (excluding office force and foremen) $0.55. The bulk of this plant is on a ten-hour basis, fifty-five hours per week, making the average annual income for fifty-two weeks, provided work is steady, $886.60 for females and $1,573.00 for males. In three other major plants similar average wages for males were $0.55, $0.54 and $0.59. In general, unskilled female labor gets $0.18 to $0.28 an hour and a few skilled females $0.30 to $0.50.[27] Unskilled males receive $0.35 to $0.40 an hour and skilled males from $0.50 to $1.00 and occasionally slightly more.

As over against these wages of women in industry in Middletown in 1924, ranging from $10.00 to $18.00 a week in the main, the younger clerks in the leading department store received $10.00 a week, and more experienced clerks a flat rate from $8.00 to $17.00 a week plus a bonus, if earned—the whole amounting occasionally "when times are good" for a veteran clerk to $30.00 to $40.00 a week.

A detailed calculation of a cost of living index for Middletown in 1924 on the basis of the cost of living in 1891 reveals an increase of 117 per cent.[28] A comparison of the average yearly earnings of the 100 heads of families in 1924 with available figures for 439 glass, wood, and iron and steel workers in Middletown in 1891 reveals an average of $1,469.61 in the former case and $505.65 in the latter, or an increase of 191 per cent today.[29] Or if we take the earnings of school teachers as an index, probably conservative, of the trend in earnings, as against this rise of 117 per cent in the cost of living, it appears that the minimum

---

[27]Willford I. King says wages of females the country over are "about three-fourths those of males."

[28]See Table VIII [not reproduced here] for the increase by major items and also for the method of computing this index.

[29]The 1891 earnings are taken from the *Fourth Biennial Report* for the state in which Middletown is located, dated 1891-2, pp. 57, 130, and 317. This Report gives the average income of 225 Middletown adult male glass workers as $519.49, of sixty-nine wood workers at $432.32, and of 145 iron and steel workers as $519.06—or an average for the entire 439 of $505.65. Too much weight obviously cannot be put upon these 1891 figures, as nothing is known either as to the method of their collection or as to their accuracy.

salary paid to grade school teachers has risen 143 per cent and
the maximum 159 per cent, and the minimum salary paid to high
school teachers 134 per cent and the maximum 250 per cent.
The median salary for grade school teachers in 1924 was
$1,331.25, with the first and third quartiles at $983.66 and
$1,368.00 respectively. The median salary for high school teach-
ers was $1,575.00, with the first and third quartiles at $1,449.43
and $1,705.50 respectively. Substantial increases in the incomes
of persons in certain other representative occupations are suggested by the fact that the salary of a bank teller has mounted
from $65.00 a month in 1890 to $166.67 a month in 1924, that of
an average male clerk in a leading men's clothing store from
$12.00 a week in 1890 to $35.00 today; a doctor's fee for a normal
delivery with the same amount of accompanying care in both
periods has risen from $10.00 to $35.00, and for a house call from
$1.00 to $3.00.

Thus this crucial activity of spending one's best energies year
in and year out in doing things remote from the immediate concerns of living eventuates apparently in the ability to buy somewhat more than formerly, but both business men and working
men seem to be running for dear life in this business of making
the money they earn keep pace with the even more rapid growth
of their subjective wants. A Rip Van Winkle who fell asleep in
the Middletown of 1885 to awake today would marvel at the
change as did the French economist Say when he revisited England at the close of the Napoleonic Wars; every one seemed to
run intent upon his own business as though fearing to stop lest
those behind trample him down. In the quiet county-seat of the
middle eighties men lived relatively close to the earth and its
products. In less than four decades, business class and working
class, bosses and bossed, have been caught up by Industry, this
new trait in the city's culture that is shaping the pattern of the
whole of living.[30] According to its needs, large numbers of
people anxious to get their living are periodically stopped by the
recurrent phenomenon of "bad times" when the machines stop
running, workers are "laid off" by the hundreds, salesmen sell
less, bankers call in loans, "credit freezes," and many Middle-

---

[30]R. H. Tawney speaks of the rise of industry "to a position of exclusive
prominence among human interests" until the modern world is "like a
hypochrondriac . . . absorbed in the process of his own digestion."

town families may take their children from school, move into
cheaper homes, cut down on food, and do without many of the
countless things they desire.

The working class is mystified by the whole fateful business.
Many of them say, for instance, that they went to the polls and
voted for Coolidge in November, 1924, after being assured daily
by the local papers that "A vote for Coolidge is a vote for prosperity and your job"; puzzled as to why "times" did not improve
after the overwhelming victory of Coolidge, a number of them
asked the interviewers if the latter thought times would be
better "after the first of the year"; the first of the year having
come and gone, their question was changed to "Will business
pick up in the spring?"

The attitude of the business men, as fairly reflected by the
editorial pages of the press which today echo the sentiments
heard at Rotary and the Chamber of Commerce, is more confident but confusing. Within a year the leading paper offered the
following prescriptions for local prosperity: "The first duty of a
citizen is to produce"; and later, "The American citizen's first
importance to his country is no longer that of citizen but that of
consumer. Consumption is a new necessity." "The way to make
business boom is to buy." At the same time the citizen is told to
"consume" he is told, "Better start saving late than never. If you
haven't opened your weekly savings account with some local
bank, trust company, or building and loan, today's the day." Still
within the same year the people of Middletown are told: "The
only true prosperity is that for which can be assigned natural
reasons such as good crops, a demand for building materials . . .
increased need for transportation," and ". . . advancing prices
are due to natural causes which are always responsible for prices.
. . . As all wealth comes from the soil, so does all prosperity,
which is only another way of saying so does all business." But
again, "natural causes" are apparently not the chief essential:
"There can be no greater single contribution to the welfare of
the nation than the spirit of hopefulness. . . ." "[This] will be a
banner year because the people believe it will be, which amounts
to the determination that it shall be. . . ." Still another solution
for securing "good times" appears: "The most prosperous town
is that in which the citizens are bound most closely together. . . .
Loyalty to the home town . . . is intensely practical. . . . The

thing we must get into our heads about this out-of-town buying business is that it hurts the individual who does it and his friends who live here. Spending your money at home in the long run amounts practically to spending it upon yourself, and buying away from home means buying the comforts and luxuries for the other fellow." "A dollar that is spent out of town never returns." One looking on at this procedure may begin to wonder if the business men, too, are not somewhat bewildered.

Although neither business men nor working men like the recurring "hard times," members of both groups urge the maintenance of the present industrial system. The former laud the group leaders who urge "normalcy" and "more business in government and less government in business," while the following sentences from an address by a leading worker, the president of the Trades Council, during the 1924 political campaign, sets forth the same faith in "free competition" on the part of the working class: "The important issue is the economic issue. We can all unite on that. We want a return to active free competition, so that prices will be lower and a man can buy enough for himself and his family with the money he makes." Both groups, as they order a lay-off, cut wages to meet outside competition, or, on the other hand, vote for La Follette in the hope of his being able to "do something to help the working man," appear to be fumbling earnestly to make their appropriate moves in the situation according to the rules of the game as far as they see them; but both appear to be bound on the wheel of this modern game of corner-clipping production. The puzzled observer may wonder how far any of them realizes the relation of his particular move to the whole function of getting a living.[31] He might even be reminded of a picture appearing in a periodical circulated in Middletown during the course of the study: A mother leans over her two absorbed infants playing at cards on the floor and asks, "What are you playing, children?"

"We're playing 'Putcher,' Mamma. Bobby, putcher card down."

In the midst of such a partially understood but earnestly followed scheme of getting a living, the rest of living goes on in Middletown.

---

[31]Cf. Walton Hamilton's *The Case of Bituminous Coal* (The Institute of Economics Series, *Investigations in Industry and Labor*. New York: Macmillan, 1925), pp. 251-2.

17

Defending Immigration Restriction
Henry Pratt Fairchild's "The Melting Pot Mistake"

Henry Pratt Fairchild (1880-1956) was trained as a social scientist and spent the major portion of his career as a professor of sociology at New York University. He was especially interested in population problems and more particularly immigration. American nativism was not new, nor was the idea of immigration restriction novel. For a variety of reasons the two forces coalesced during and after World War I. The "new immigration"—from Eastern and Southeastern Europe dating from the mid-1880's—it seemed to many, was threatening to alter the character of the American nation. The immigration laws of the 1920's sought to limit the flow of immigration and to confine it largely to those peoples who had been prominent in the early settling of North America. Professor Fairchild was one of those who favored the restrictive legislation, bringing to its support some of the conclusions of the science of eugenics. °Maldwyn Allen Jones's *American Immigration* (Chicago: University of Chicago Press, 1960) provides a good survey of the general subject. For the legislation since 1920 see Robert A. Divine, *American Immigration Policy 1924-1952* (New Haven: Yale University Press, 1957). °Oscar Handlin's *The Uprooted* (Boston: Little, Brown and Company, 1951), discusses the problem of immigrant adjustment to new world conditions. The relationship between immigration policy and nativism is fully and ably discussed in °John Higham's *Strangers in the Land: Patterns of American Nativism, 1860-1925* (New Brunswick: Rutgers University Press, 1955). The selection printed below is drawn from portions of the entire book, hence some of the transitions are abrupt; in reading note (1) what Fairchild observed were the uses and abuses of "the melting pot" symbol; (2) what he thought was the role of group unity and what factors engendered and supported that unity; (3) his distinction between race and nationality; and (4) upon what he based his argument that the immigration problem was not a racial problem prior to 1882 and why it was a racial problem after that

Henry Pratt Fairchild, *The Melting Pot Mistake* (Boston: Little, Brown and Company, 1926), pp. 8-15, 20-21, 26-29, 40-47, 105-09, 119-28, 134-35, 247-61.

date; (5) how he used a chemical analogy in his argument; (6) what he thought was the result of indiscriminate mixing of the races; (7) what he predicted would happen should the United States adopt a policy of unlimited immigration; (8) what dire consequences he foresaw based upon his analogies drawn from biology and botany; (9) the distinctions he drew between American and foreign ideas and critics; (10) how he would protect the United States from alien ideas; (11) his summary of those whom he regarded as destructive elements within the nation; and (12) what he thought was the mission of America and what threatened its fulfillment.

DEMOCRATIC PROCESSES, TO BE WHOLLY SAFE AND effective, require that popular decisions should result from the consensus of judgments of the largest possible number and variety of individuals, each forming his conclusions independently on the maximum basis of facts. It is this balancing of individual judgments, rather than any superior mastery of facts, that gives democracy an advantage in stability and soundness over any form of oligarchy. A small, powerful governing clique can very easily acquire a higher average grasp of facts than the common people as a body, but its judgment upon them is bound to be partial. Yet to the extent that any individual in a democratic electorate lacks essential facts his conclusion is quite likely to be erroneous, and the probability of a correct general decision is reduced by just so much.

This brings us back where we started from. We simply can not get all the facts on all the problems. If we are to form independent judgments at all we must of necessity be guided largely by labels and symbols. It is fundamentally important, then, that the interpreters be both honest and acute, and that the symbols be authentic as well as realistic.

These were the facts which gave to Israel Zangwill's little drama, "The Melting-Pot," when it appeared in 1909, a significance quite disproportionate to its literary importance. For one hundred years and more a stream of immigration had been pouring into the United States in constantly increasing volume. At first this movement had attracted little attention, and such feelings as it aroused were mainly those of complacency and satisfaction. As the decades rolled by certain features of the

movement created considerable consternation and a demand
sprang up for some form of governmental relief. In time this
relief was granted, and the popular concern died down. In general, however, during practically the whole of the nineteenth
century the attitude of the American people toward immigration
was one of easy-going, tolerant indifference when it was not actually welcome. But as the century drew to a close evidences of
popular uneasiness and misgiving began to display themselves.
These were due in part to changes in the social and economic
situation in the United States, in part to changes in the personal
and social characteristics of the immigrants, and in part to
repeated warnings issued by those whose professional activities
and opportunities gave them a wider access to the facts of immigration than was possible to the average citizen. In particular
the American people began to ponder about the ultimate effect
upon its own vitality and solidarity of this stupendous injection
of foreign elements. Could we stand it, and if so, how long?
Were not the foundations of our cherished institutions already
partially undermined by all these alien ideas, habits, and customs? What kind of a people were we destined to become physically? Was the American nation itself in danger? Immigration
became a great public problem, calling for judgment.

Then came the symbol, like a portent in the heavens. America
is a Melting-Pot. Into it are being poured representatives of all
the world's peoples. Within its magic confines there is being
formed something that is not only uniform and homogeneous but
also finer than any of the separate ingredients. The nations of
the world are being fused into a new and choicer nation, the
United States.

The figure was a clever one—picturesque, expressive, familiar,
just the sort of thing to catch the popular fancy and lend itself
to a thousand uses. It swept over this country and other countries like wild fire. As always, it was welcomed as a substitute
for both investigation and thought. It calmed the rising wave of
misgiving. Few stopped to ask whether it fitted the phenomena
of assimilation. Few inquired whether Mr. Zangwill's familiarity
with the intricate facts of immigration were such as to justify
him in assuming the heavy responsibility of interpreter. America
was a Melting-Pot, the apparent evidences of national disintegra-
tion were illusions, and that settled it.

It would be hard to estimate the influence of the symbol of the melting pot in staving off the restriction of immigration. It is certain that in the popular mind it offsets volumes of laboriously compiled statistics and carefully reasoned analyses. It is virtually beyond question that restriction would have come in time in any case. How soon it would have come without the Great War must remain a matter of conjecture. Be that as it may, when the concussions of that conflict had begun to die down the melting pot was discovered to be so badly cracked that it is not likely ever to be dragged into service again. Its day was over. But this did not mean that the real facts of immigration had suddenly become public property. Our symbol had been shattered, but we had not yet, as a people, been able to undertake the extensive investigation necessary to reveal the true nature of the case. The history of post-war movements is replete with evidences of the gross misconceptions of the meaning and processes of assimilation which characterized many even of those who devoted themselves directly to the problem. Even to-day, in spite of the fact that there is perhaps no other great public problem on which the American people is so well educated as on immigration, there is yet great need of a clearer understanding of the tremendous task that still confronts us. We know now that the Melting-Pot did not melt, but we are not entirely sure why. We suspect that that particular figure of speech was an anomaly, but we have not yet found a more appropriate one to take its place. We are a little in doubt as to whether so complicated a phenomenon as assimilation can be adequately represented by any symbol at all. Perhaps there is no short cut to a comprehension of this great problem, and he who would form a sound independent judgment must resign himself to the laborious methods of investigation and thought.

There is a general agreement that in connection with its great immigration movement the United States tried to do something and failed. What was this thing that it tried to do? Why did it fail? Is there still a menace in the results of that failure? Was there ever a possibility of success under the old conditions? Is there hope of escaping the consequences of failure under present conditions? If so, by what means may that hope be realized? These are some of the questions intimately bound up with the fallacy of the Melting-Pot.

Race

The central idea of the melting-pot symbol is clearly the idea of unification. That is an idea which needs no logical demonstration to command general acceptance. Every one realizes, almost intuitively, that in any community, particularly a democratic one, unity is one of the essentials of stability, order, and progress. Every American citizen will admit without argument that if immigration threatens the national unity of the United States it is a matter of grave concern. The purpose of the melting-pot figure was to convince the American people that immigration did not threaten its unity, but tended to produce an even finer type of unity. It failed because it did not take account of the true nature of group unity, of the conditions of its preservation, or of the actual consequences of such inroads upon unity as are involved in an immigration movement.

As we survey the world of to-day we are impressed with the fact that group unity is one of the most important factors with which mankind has to reckon. We see the human species divided up into numerous well-defined units, each with certain distinctive characters of its own, each knit together by very powerful ties, each seeking its own interests in preference to, often in opposition to, the interests of others. We call these groups by various names—nations, countries, peoples, races, states, societies. Often one of these names more accurately describes a given group than another. But whatever the name, and whatever the minor distinctions between kinds of groups, the primary fact remains that it is upon the basis of these groups that many vitally important world alignments take place. It is by groups that men trade, develop art and literature, acquire land, seek political aggrandizement, and—most important of all—make war. The world would be an entirely different place to live in if these group demarcations did not exist.

Immigration involves a flow of population between various of these groups. It consequently has an immediate bearing upon group unity, particularly that of the receiving group. In order to understand its significance it is necessary to have in mind the essential facts as to the origin and nature of human groups. As far back as knowledge reaches group organization is found to be characteristic of the human species. In general, as we go back over the course of human evolution we find these groups diminishing in size and eventually in number. The consensus of opinion of scientists is that if we could go back to the very beginning of man's existence we should find a single small group, living probably somewhere on the high central plateau of Asia. Among the members of this group there would be virtually complete unity, with only such minute individual variations as distinguish the members of any restricted species of animals.

It appears, then, that the present varieties of the human family have been developed out of an original uniform type. . . . Differences in environmental features are the cause of changes in the characteristics of species. Variations occur in all directions according to the law of chance, but only those variations are perpetuated which happen to accord with some slightly different environment into which the individual which possesses them may find his way. If for some reason the original environment undergoes a change the same process, of course, takes place. These developments are indescribably slow, but given sufficient time they will eventually produce a distinctly different type. This new type is at first known as a "variety" of the old species. But as the process goes on the changes at last become so marked that the new type can no longer be considered to belong to the old species: a new species has come into being.

It was undoubtedly by such a method as this that mankind first began to separate into distinct types. We know something of the pathways and directions by which the outposts of the species made their way by infinitesimal stages out of the original central Asian habitat into new environments. Certain well-defined channels led northward and northeastward, into the inhospitable plains of Siberia and eventually across the Bering Sea into the northwest corner of the North American continent and thence southward until the whole of the western hemisphere was peopled. Other channels led eastward into the fertile plains of China. Still others took a southwesterly direction and led the primitive pioneers who followed them into Asia Minor, Africa, and thence northward into Europe. In every case the spread of the human species could take place only so fast as the physical variations could be developed necessary for life in each new environment. And in every case it was the contact with a new environment which was responsible for the perpetuation of these variations.

. . . man alone of all the higher species has been able to carry this process of variation to the extremities of the earth without losing his specific unity. Instead of having several more or less closely related species of men, as there are species of wolves, or bears, or sparrows, we have one great inclusive human species divided up into a number of varieties. To these varieties we correctly apply the term "the races of man."

The primary basis of group unity is therefore racial. . . .

Just what the relationship is between the requirements of a given environment and the traits of the race that found its area of characterization there has not yet been fully explained. In a general way it seems clear that the heavily pigmented skin of the Negro is an advantage in the hot, moist climate of the tropics. It is conceivable that the air pockets formed by his kinky hair may also afford protection from the extreme heat of the sun. Conversely the blue eyes and fair skin of the Nordic appear to have some advantage in the less intense, cold light of the north. Yet the Eskimos, in a somewhat similar environment, have dark hair and eyes. There is little doubt that sexual selection also played its part in determining the result. As distinctive traits began to develop in a given group they would naturally come to be thought of as admirable, beautiful, and right. Thus those individuals who possessed them in the most marked degree would be likely to mate earliest and oftenest, and so these traits would tend to be perpetuated and accentuated. If, for example, we can imagine the time when the Nordic race was just beginning to develop, we can easily conceive that men would tend to choose for their mates the lightest-haired members of the opposite sex, and so would the women, in so far as they had anything to say about it. It seems hardly probable, however, that natural selection in its strictest sense and sexual selection, working together, were the sole factors in the development of the characteristic features of the different races. There may have been some inherent predisposition latent in these separate streams of germ plasm, as Bergson has suggested in his stimulating discussion of "Creative Evolution."

Whatever the causes, however, the result is manifest. The racial groups which are characterized by community of physical kinship are also identified by distinct physical features. These are what we ordinarily speak of as "race traits" or "characters," and it is needful to have in mind clearly just what they are and how they operate.

It should be clear by now that all true racial traits are exclusively hereditary. They are carried on from generation to generation by means of "genes" or "determiners" in the germ plasm of each race. Their appearance in the body of any individual is due to the fact that he has the corresponding genes in his germ plasm, and not to any other cause. No racial trait can ever be acquired, nor can it ever be lost by an individual as a result of the experiences of his lifetime. What we are racially, we are from the moment not only of birth, but of conception, and such we remain until we die. It follows that the individual is not in the slightest degree responsible for his racial affiliations or his racial traits. He was not consulted in advance as to what racial traits he would prefer and he has no power to alter or dispose of a single one of them. Moreover, he has no control whatever over the racial traits which he will pass on to his offspring. If any individual is dissatisfied with the racial traits with which he is endowed, his only recourse for himself is artificially to conceal them or inhibit their display in his own person so far as that is possible, and his only hope for his offspring is to mate with a person of a different race, in which case his children get a mixture of racial traits, his own contribution being exactly what it would have been if he had mated with one of his own race. Fortunately, as will appear later, most individuals, at least in an unsophisticated state, are quite content with their racial affiliations and would not change them if they could.

The use of the words "racial traits" and "characters" in the plural suggests the fact that one's racial make-up is a composite of a number of distinct units. This harmonizes with the modern theory of inheritance, which holds that one's entire heredity is composed of separate units—what the biologists call "unit characters"—which are transmitted from generation to generation independently of each other, and never fuse or coalesce, each having its own determiner or gene in the germ plasm. From the point of view of racial interpretation, accordingly, the inherited traits of each individual are composed of two groups. The first group includes all those traits which he as a human being shares with all other human beings, the common features of the species. The second group includes those traits which he shares only with the other members of his racial group, the distinctive features of the race. The narrower the definition of race, obviously, the smaller does this second group become. The first group, however, is vastly larger than the second group even on the most inclusive interpretation of race. Men as a whole are much more alike than they are different. The general structure, all the important organs and members, all the basic life processes are essentially similar if not virtually identical in all the members of all the races.

It is probably much more than a coincidence that most of the important features in which there are characteristic differences between races are associated with the head. It is in the head that the differentiation of the human species from other animal species has been particularly developed, and it is logical that it should be in the head that the specialization of the biological divisions of the human species should be carried to the highest point. The outstanding exception to this rule is found in skin color, which is so very marked as to be adopted as the commonest basis of primary racial classification. . . .

Nationality...

It may be said . . . that *the second great basis of group unity is national.*

As long as human groups remained effectually separated from each other the distinction between race and nationality was of neither academic nor practical importance. The two . . . developed simultaneously and coincidently. Each group which was working out its own peculiar scheme of life was originally a racial group. Consequently a given group was identifiable by either its racial or its national characteristics. The two being practically indistinguishable naturally appeared to be synonymous or identical. Inasmuch as a certain widely penetrating group of roundheaded individuals had the invariable habit of burying their dead in round barrows it was easy to think of the burial customs as being the same sort of a group trait as the head form. Perhaps the most notable—or notorious—instances of this confusion are to be found in the use of the words "Aryan" and "Celtic" as racial designations. In their correct sense both of these terms apply strictly to national characteristics, and to speak of the Aryan race or the Celtic race is, as one writer has said, just as absurd as to talk about a brachycephalic dictionary or a brunette grammar.

As soon as the era of race mingling set in, however, the distinction between race and nationality became of vital practical importance, because the two exhibit entirely different types of behavior in cases of group contact. And as soon as the age of intelligent social engineering dawned the importance became academic as well as practical, because no constructive social policy can possibly be worked out to govern intergroup relationships which does not take strict account of the difference between these two foundations of unity. One of the chief sources of fallacy in the figure of the melting pot lay in the failure to make this crucial distinction. It will be well, therefore, to examine in somewhat greater detail the nature of national traits and the method of their transmission.

As has been shown, race traits are due solely to inheritance. Race traits are group traits only because community of kinship has been harmonious with the processes of group formation and group maintenance. They are by no means inseparable from group affiliation. An individual takes his race with him wherever he goes and passes it on to his offspring wherever he may be. Two parents of a given race will produce a child of the same race no matter in what sort of a group they may be living at the time of the child's birth. And the child must keep that race until the day of his death no matter into what groups the vicissitudes of life may lead him.

The traits of nationality, on the other hand, are distinctly group realities. They arise solely out of the group relationship. They impress themselves on the individual, but by no means ineradicably. Race is inherited, nationality is acquired. Or, it may be said that race is biologically transmitted, and nationality is socially transmitted. For nationality is passed on from generation to generation just as truly as race, but in an entirely different way. The processes of social transmission are the processes of individual acquirement. As far as the individual is concerned, nationality is an acquired characteristic, and must follow the laws of acquired characteristics rather than of inherited traits.

Every individual is born with no nationality at all. He has no language, no dress, no moral code, no religion, no single one of the manifold accomplishments that compose human culture. He is just a little uncivilized animal, with the whole course of cultural evolution to go through with in the years that lie before him, just as in the prenatal period he went through the whole course of biological evolution from the single cell up. The great biogenetic law of recapitulation—"ontogeny repeats phylogeny," the development of the individual is a condensed repetition of the evolution of the species—holds good for the cultural development of the human individual after birth just as for his physical development before birth. But the cultural development is determined by the cultural medium, or mediums, in which his postnatal life is spent, while his physical development is determined by the kind of germ plasm that went into that original embryonic cell.

No national trait is inherited or is present at birth, though there may be some inherited aptitudes that correspond in a general way to certain types of nationality. Thus there is some evidence of slight physical differences in the organs of speech that prevent the members of certain races from completely mastering certain languages. It is also claimed (on rather inadequate grounds), that the Nordic race has a special aptitude for free institutions. There are probably certain inherent variations of temperament, disposition, or even intelligence which facilitate the development by certain racial groups of certain types of institutions. But all of these influences, whatsoever they may actually be, are of the most general sort, and there is the scantiest possible evidence of any inherited tendency to develop a specific national trait. . . .

There is accordingly no necessary connection between the nationality of parents and that of their children. The only reason why the two are ordinarily the same is that in the usual course of affairs children and parents live in the same social environment. The only sense in which children get their nationality from their parents is that the parents represent the environment to them in a peculiarly intimate and potent way. This is a steadily diminishing influence from the time of infancy—when the parents constitute the major part, if not virtually the whole, of the social environment of the child—to full maturity when the parental bond is reduced to a more or less negligible factor, according to the customs of the nationality itself. But let a child be removed from its parents immediately after birth and placed in the midst of a different nationality and it will inevitably acquire the full nationality of the group in which it is brought up. Take a new-born child of Scandinavian parents and place it in a native negro home in the jungles of Africa. At maturity it will have the blond hair, blue eyes, and fair skin (tanned, of course) of its Nordic ancestry, but its language, religion, moral code, habits of life, and whole outlook on the universe will be that of the primitive group of which its foster parents have been a part.

Since the national equipment of an individual consists of traits acquired from the social environment during his lifetime, it follows that it is subject to change as long as life lasts. But the acquisition of national traits takes place much more rapidly and easily during the impressionable, plastic years of infancy and early childhood than in the later periods of life. In general, the receptivity to national impressions diminishes steadily with increasing age. It is really astounding, when one stops to think of it, how much of the important business of life a child has learned by the time it reaches the end of its second year. Yet one never entirely ceases responding to the influence of his environment while he lives. There is always more of nationality than any one individual can fully absorb, and since, as will appear later, nationality is always a more or less dynamic factor, the traits of the individual are constantly called upon to respond to a varying environment. In the case of the ordinary individual who spends virtually his whole life in the midst of a single group environment the process is a harmonious and largely unconscious one. It is when a sudden change in environment takes place, as will be seen, that strain arises.

The channels through which the national group impresses its characteristics upon its individual members include practically every variety of human relationship. As has been observed, the earliest of these, and probably in the long run the most influential, is the family. One after another the church, the school, the playground, the recreation center, the lodge, the shop, the factory, the theater, the political rally, the union, all manner of associations and organizations bring the influence of group standards to bear upon the individual. Some of these institutions owe their existence in part to the necessity of group control over the social unit. Other institutions, the State *par excellence,* have been evolved by society directly for the purpose of securing conformity to group requirements. The development of national traits on the part of the individual through participation in these various relationships is neither voluntary nor conscious under ordinary conditions. But it is irresistible. One cannot possibly avoid receiving the imprint of his environment, nor can he modify it even in slight degree until he reaches the age of discrimination and reasoning, and by that time the basic traits of nationality are so deeply graven on his character that there is little scope left for the play of analysis and reason. . . .

A Nation in the Making

Up to 1882, these three sources—the United Kingdom, Germany, and the Scandinavian countries—contributed almost the entire bulk of the immigration to the United States. Minor contingents came from France and Switzerland, and of course there were scattered representatives from most of the countries of the world. From the racial point of view, it is easy to see, the effects upon the American population were of little significance. No new elements were brought in, and the relative proportions of the different basic stocks were probably little altered. . . .

In a general way, then, it may be said that the immigration problem in the United States was not a racial problem previous to the year 1882. The result of immigration was to rebuild on American soil out of the same basic elements the particular type of composite population which had furnished the original settlers, and which had maintained itself as the preponderant stock in the native population from the very beginning. It is consequently very doubtful if true racial antipathy played any appreciable part in the sentiment of the American people toward immigration during the first one hundred years of our national life. There was opposition and criticism in plenty, as is well known, but it rested almost entirely upon other than racial grounds. Possibly the fact that the Irish and the Scandinavians were more nearly of a single race than the average American may have occasioned some slight sense of racial alienation, but it can not have exerted more than an infinitesimal influence.

A New Menace

Beginning about 1882, however, a marked change in the situation began to develop. Certain new streams of immigration, which had hitherto trickled in almost unnoticed, began to swell to portentous proportions. Foremost among these were the currents from Italy, Austria-Hungary, and the Russian Empire and Finland. Streams smaller in proportion but of immense volume in the total came from various of the Balkan states, Portugal, Turkey, Greece, etc. Even after they began to increase these currents remained below the older ones for a number of years. Italy, which had never sent more than nine thousand before 1880, in that year raised its contribution to over 12,000, and in 1882 sent 32,159, a very considerable body of people, but quite trifling compared with the delegations from the United Kingdom and Germany. The movement from Austria-Hungary, previous to 1880, had reached about the same maximum as that from Italy, but in that year it rose to over 17,000 and two years later to over 29,000. The Russian Empire still lagged behind, sending only 16,918 in 1882.

It is not necessary for present purposes to make a detailed inquiry into the causes of the sudden expansion of these streams. The development of transportation facilties by land and water, the spread of popular education and geographical knowledge, the extending reputation of the United States as the land of promise, and the gradual development of a spirit of independence and initiative among the peasants of southern and eastern Europe all played their part. The important fact is that, having once received the impetus, these streams continued to grow until, in a very short time, they dominated the situation. As the "new immigration" increased the "old immigration" diminished, not only relatively but absolutely. The records set by the United Kingdom, Germany, and the Scandinavian countries were never equaled again. The definite turn of the balance came about the year 1896. From that time on until the outbreak of the Great War a larger and larger majority of the total flow was claimed by the new immigration. In 1914 the old immigration amounted to only 13.6 per cent of the entire number. It seems evident that forces were at work which, if they had not been interrupted by the

War, would in a few years have reduced the old immigration almost to zero.

The question of immediate interest is: What was the racial significance of this radical change in the sources of immigration? Were the immigrants of the past generation simply continuing to rebuild the American population along the original lines? Were they notably altering the proportions of the racial composite? Were they introducing some entirely new elements? The answer to these questions is to be found in the racial composition of the people of the countries of southern and eastern Europe, a most baffling field of investigation, to be sure.

The outstanding feature of the racial situation in these lands is the very small proportion of Nordic blood represented in their populations. This by itself means that immigration from these sources tends inevitably to reduce the Nordic proportion in the American population. In its place will be substituted primarily Mediterranean and Alpine elements. . . .

The product of the mating of different racial stocks really is a mixture. It may be compared to pouring together various chemically inert liquids—water, milk, wine, ink, etc. If the resulting mixture is thoroughly stirred, it will have the appearance of a smooth homogeneous liquid. But every separate molecule remains just what it was before the mixing took place; there is just as much water, just as much milk, just as much wine, just as much ink, as there was at the beginning. The analogy with race mixture is particularly close if some of the ingredients—like milk, for instance—are themselves mixtures, corresponding to mixed races.

It will be obvious at once that in this respect the analogy of the melting pot itself is not far amiss. The fusion that takes place within a crucible, assuming that there is no true chemical action, is not unlike the process of race mixture. The product is a molecular mosaic, just as the human body is a mosaic of separate racial traits. If the problem to which the figure of the melting pot was applied had been simply the question as to whether race mixture could and would take place in the United States as a result of indiscriminate immigration there would have been little to criticize. In fact, it was vastly more than that. The symbol of the melting pot was pitiably inadequate in the first place because, as we shall see later, the major part of the problem had nothing to do with race mixture, and, in the second place, because it confined itself exclusively to the *process*, and gave no heed to the *result*. And the result is the really important consideration.

A melting pot is not an end in itself. The purpose of a melting pot is to get heterogeneous substances into a form of unity and fluidity. But two great questions remain: What kind of a substance are you going to have when the fusion is complete? And what are you going to do with it?

Taking the latter of these queries first, it has been aptly observed that a melting pot implies a mold. The object in fusing the various ingredients is to get them into a plastic state so that they may be cast into a predetermined form which they will thereafter retain permanently. In this respect the analogy of the melting pot as applied to races in America obviously breaks down completely. The assumption is that the mixture itself is the final goal; there is nothing even remotely corresponding to a mold into which it is to be poured.

Much more important than this, however, is the question as to the character of the mixture itself. On this point, the champions of racial amalgamation for the most part beg the question. They seem to assume that if it can be proved that racial fusion will eventually be complete, that settles the matter. Nothing more need be said. They ignore the consideration as to whether the molten mass will be good for anything. True, certain sweeping statements are made to the effect that mixed races are superior to either of the originals, especially if the latter are not too far apart, and some efforts are made to bolster up this assertion by reference to various of the great civilizations of history. But these are mostly *ex cathedra* pronouncements, without a semblance of support by any factual evidence. It is, indeed, as already stated, a matter about which we know very little. The various cases of race mixture about which information is available are so complicated by social and environmental factors, often of a very unfavorable kind—as, for instance, in the case of the racial nondescripts in the seaports of the world—that it is practically impossible to isolate the results of purely racial factors. Consequently, it is easy to assert that the environmental factors are the ones responsible for the poor results, and that if these racial crosses had been given half a chance they would have been at least the equals of either of their parents.

Here, again, biology fortunately comes to our aid. The mixing of races among plants and animals has been carried on to a very vast extent, and many definite principles and rules have been worked out. Only the simplest and most fundamental need concern us here. First of all it should be recognized that many of the most beautiful, most useful, and generally finest types of plants and animals are crosses. The crossing of races is not necessarily disastrous. But these desirable crosses are either the result of long experimentation with various combinations or else of the union of carefully selected varieties chosen deliberately for certain traits which they possess and which promise to blend to advantage. No breeder would expect to improve his stock by random crossing with any variety that chanced to present itself. In other words, the desirable crosses are just as definite in their racial composition as the pure varieties.

More than this, the plant or animal breeder knows that the indiscriminate mixing of a large number of varieties can be expected to produce just one result—the mongrel. This is true even though the different varieties themselves may each be of a high type. The reason for this is clear. As remarked above, the germ plasm carried by every individual contains two classes of genes, first, those that are common to all the members of his species and give him the characteristic features of his species, and second, those that are peculiar to his own variety or race, and mark him off as a member of that particular kin-group. The varieties of the various species have been produced by specialization in the germ plasm. In wild plants and animals this specialization is produced by the general processes of natural selection; in domesticated creatures it is the result of the manipulations of the breeder, usually with a definite type or program in mind; and in man it is the outcome of the processes of race formation which have already been discussed. Accordingly, when a large number of different varieties are bred together the tendency is for the specialized genes to neutralize or cancel each other, and for the common general genes to support each other and intensify the corresponding qualities. The result to be looked for in the offspring is therefore a primitive, generalized type—often spoken of as a "reversion," "atavism," or "throwback."

There is every reason to believe that these rules hold good for man in his biological aspects. Many mixtures of human races have taken place, and some of them seem to have not only definite traits, but desirable traits according to certain widely accepted criteria. The combination of a large amount of Nordic with smaller proportions of Mediterranean and Alpine has certainly produced a type with outstanding characteristics; in the judgment of many persons (specifically those who are members of it) it is a type of peculiar excellence. This is the English type and it is the American type. It remained the prevailing type of the immigrants to America up till nearly the close of the nineteenth century. It is certainly a notable type, with a remarkable record of achievement in the past and promise of achievement for the future. Whether one likes the type or not, it is at least a known quantity. And it is a highly specialized type.

The change in the character of immigration which developed within the past generation and a half signalized the beginning of the process of mongrelization of this type. This process was not nearly so extreme in degree or rapid in rate as it would have been if we had not definitely excluded, by various means, the Chinese, Japanese, and Hindus as soon as their respective numbers began to reach serious proportions, and if the immigration of Negroes and Malays had not been negligible in proportions for reasons which need not delay us here. Nevertheless, the new arrivals were sufficiently different, not only in their racial proportions but in their basic elements, to threaten the existing type with annihilation. What the resulting product would have been at the end of two centuries can not be definitely determined, nor can it be positively asserted that it would have been inferior to the present type. The latter is largely a matter of taste. It is almost certain that it would have been a much less specialized type, resembling much more closely a more primitive stage of human evolution. If any one, contemplating this probability, is led to deplore the check to such a development he is of course fully entitled to his own views.

It should be emphasized that this process of mongrelization takes place regardless of whether or not the component elements are of a high type. If we must have a symbol for race mixture, much more accurate than the figure of the melting pot is the figure of the village pound. If one can imagine a pound from which no dog was ever rescued, and in which all the denizens were free to interbreed at will, and into which dogs of every variety were introduced continuously for many dog generations, he will have an excellent representation of the racial situation of a country which receives all races of immigrants indiscriminately. The population of the pound, after a few generations, would be composed, aside from the newcomers, exclusively of mongrels. And this would be true even though none but thoroughbreds—Airedales, Greyhounds, Chows, Pekinese, Cockers, Doberman-Pintschers, etc.—had been placed within its confines. Mongrelization implies no inferiority on the part of the original constituents. So in a human society the prediction of a mongrel population as the almost certain product of a free-for-all immigration policy carries no more slur against the foreign elements than against the natives. It simply means a loss of specialization on all sides.

Now whether this loss of specialization, or mongrelization, among human stocks is a thing to be desired or a thing to be shunned is a matter partly of knowledge, partly of judgment, partly of taste. There is certainly a good deal to be said for the mongrel. As a canine, he is tough, resourceful, and remarkably able to take care of himself. It may be that as a human he would display corresponding features. . . .

But few dog lovers regard the mongrel as the most admirable product of canine evolution, and few members of any of the more highly specialized human groups are likely to look with favor upon the submergence of the distinctive traits of their stock. . . . At any rate there is this to be said: Whatever the qualities of the races of to-day may be, good or bad, they are at least known. The qualities of a future composite race are not known. It is conceivable that they might be good. But it is also wholly possible that they might be very bad. It is a very widespread, and probably salutary, human trait that

> makes us rather bear those ills we have
> Than fly to others that we know not of.

Furthermore, in this respect it is never too late to mend. If the progress of future scientific research should establish the fact that indiscriminate race mixing is desirable, or that certain definite crosses can be depended upon to produce good results, it would be relatively easy by deliberate social policies to promote whatever combinations the evidence called for. But, on the other hand, if racial mixture is actually allowed to take place, and then the results are found to be undesirable, it is virtually impossible to correct the mistake. The false steps could not be retraced. It is as impossible to unmix races as to unscramble the proverbial egg. This whole matter of race mixture seems to be one where it is quite legitimate to apply the good old maxim, "In case of doubt, don't."

It is probably an evidence of the sound judgment of democracies, to which reference has already been made, that the people of the United States, by successive steps, have expressed their determination to keep the racial tone of the population about what it was at the time of the Declaration of Independence. Each time that the threat of dilution by a widely different race has appeared it has been met decisively. . . .

As far as we can look into the future, then, it appears that the race problem in the United States will be confined to the unification of the various elements already established here. Further additions represented by the immigration of the future will involve few complications of a truly racial character. With reference to the sections of the white race already included in the American population, there is little doubt that the process of unification by amalgamation will go on steadily and irresistibly, until at the end of a few generations racial differentiation will have been practically wiped out, and the population of the country will once more present a racially homogeneous aspect. And we may hope that, diverse as the present varieties may be, the proportions of the definitely esoteric elements are sufficiently small so that the degree of resulting mongrelization will not be enough to reduce seriously the racial effectiveness of the American people. . . .

The Duty of America

The discussion thus far has rested on the assumption that the importance of national unity is axiomatic. It has been taken for granted that any conditions which threaten the unity of the United States will, by general consent among Americans, be recognized as intolerable. This assumption probably comes close to the truth in the case of the great majority of Americans. But there is a notable body of public thought, all the more influential because it parades under the guise of liberalism, that questions the validity of this axiom. The question is raised whether the United States, in the light of international ethics, has any right to consider only its own national welfare, or whether we are not under a moral obligation to promote the prosperity and well-being of other groups and of their individual members, even at heavy sacrifice to ourselves.

In considering this doctrine we are once more confronted with an impressive illustration of the power of the label or symbol. The words "broad" and "liberal" on the one side, and "narrow" and "illiberal" on the other, have for so long been used to apply to certain positions in the immigration problem that they have become indissolubly connected with those positions. They have virtually become the property of one side in the immigration controversy. If the reader of these lines was told that a certain person held "liberal" views on the immigration question he would understand without hesitation that the person referred to was opposed to restriction, and in favor of keeping the door as wide open as possible. A person with "narrow" views, on the other hand, is assumed to be concerned solely with American interests in a rather selfish way.

This fact places an incalculable handicap on the advocates of restriction or rigid selection. The protagonist who is forced to enter the lists as the champion of an avowed "illiberal" cause has already more than half lost his battle. If he wins, it will be only in the face of stupendous odds. This does not mean in the least that the American people have carefully thought the matter through, and have concluded that a policy of restriction is really a narrow and illiberal policy. Such is not the nature of the label. It simply means that we all spontaneously and intuitively believe in liberality and that the advocates of the open door have succeeded in attaching that particular label to their program so effectively that the average hearer accepts the alliance without reflection.

In our present effort, therefore, to get beneath the label it will be helpful to ask, first of all, what is liberalism and what is a liberal policy and then to consider whether the policy of restriction or of the open door comes closest to the definition.

At first blush one might be tempted to say that liberalism consists in letting everybody do exactly as he pleases to the maximum extent. But on second thought this conception will be discarded, in the realization that such a doctrine more deserves the name "anarchism" than "liberalism." In its place the following may be suggested: Liberalism consists in a desire for the evenest possible distribution of benefits among the largest possible number of persons over the longest possible period of time, and a liberal policy is one that is calculated to produce this result. Such a policy may also fairly be called broad. It is opposed to all favoritism, special privilege, and concentration of advantages.

Now it is so obvious as to be almost a platitude that the residents of the United States enjoy special privileges. They are certainly more favorably situated than the people of any other great nation on earth with reference to their material well-being, and probably also with respect to their political independence, and various other social relationships. The basic stimulus to immigration lies in the desire of persons less fortunately situated to share in these advantages. A policy of restriction makes it impossible for them to do so. It reserves the enjoyment of these unique blessings to those who happen to be established in the country at any particular time, and to their descendants. Is not such a policy, then, on the very face of it, narrow and illiberal? As these words are being written the morning paper brings an announcement of a proposal made by a person who is described as the "organizer of the Liberal Immigration League" to the effect that in the future there shall be no limit to the number of immigrants, though a rigid selection and control is to be exercised.

If the United States is to be thought of as a gigantic pork barrel or plum pudding, and if only the present and the immediate future are to be considered, an excellent case can be made out for this doctrine. Here is an accumulation of good things which Fate has placed in the possession of one hundred and ten million people. The remaining sixteen hundred million of the earth's population would like their share. Very well! let them come and take it, and the smaller the portions into which it is divided the more exactly will the cause of liberalism be served.

It is to reveal the fallacy of just such an interpretation that so much space has been devoted to the exposition of the United States as a nation. The great question of liberalism is: What would be left of the American nation, and what effect would its fate have on the future destiny of mankind, if the natural desire of foreign individuals to share in American advantages were left unrestrained? It has already been suggested that the idea that all immigrants benefit by casting in their lot with the United States is not nearly so well founded on fact as we should like to believe. But for purposes of argument, let it be granted that all immigrants do improve their situation by coming to this country. Does their gain mean a general rise in the average well-being of mankind, not only in the present, but in the generations to come?

The answer to this question depends upon what happens to the United States as a result of their coming, and to the countries of Europe as a result of their leaving.

As far as the United States is concerned, the first and most direct effect of unrestricted immigration is a retardation, if not a definite lowering, of the standard of living of the common people. It is the search for a higher standard of living which, more than anything else, brings the immigrant here. The standard of the American is higher than his. He can raise his by coming. If in the process he lowers the standard of the American that is no concern of his. Nor would this lowering of the American standard, however repugnant to the sentiment of American patriotism, be inconsistent with the principle of liberalism if the final result was an improvement in the general average of comfort of all concerned, native and foreigner alike. If the total gain won by the foreigners more than offset the total loss suffered by the natives, the result would be a more even distribution of benefits wholly consistent with liberalism.

Such, however, is not the case. The nature of the competition between standards of living is such that the lower pulls down the upper much more than it elevates itself. Each successively lower standard that is allowed to enter the competition reduces the level just so much more. The truth has long been recognized by students of the problem, and forcibly expressed by General

Francis A. Walker, that the ultimate outcome of unrestricted immigration is a progressive deterioration of the standard until no "difference of *economic level* exists between our population and that of the most degraded communities abroad." Certainly the ideal of liberalism is not to be found in such a dénouement as this.

But what may be expected in the countries of source while this is taking place in the country of destination? Does not the departure of their surplus population so relieve the pressure at home as to produce a compensating improvement in their social and economic situation? The complete answer to this question involves a technical analysis too long and complicated to be introduced here. Suffice it to say that the almost unanimous conclusion of scientific students of the problem is that the kind of exodus represented by ordinary emigration produces no relief whatever in the pressure of population, and may even make it worse. To put it in concrete terms, we could draw off a million Chinamen a year from China for fifty years, or any other length of time, and at the end of the period there would be just as many Chinamen in China as if not one had emigrated. The same principle holds good for any overcrowded country. No such country can hope to find any permanent relief from its problems of over-population—whether they be unemployment, pauperism, disease, or anything else—by shipping its excess nationals to a less crowded region.

There can be only one conclusion. The eventual effect of an unrestricted immigration movement, governed only by the economic self-interest of the migrating individuals, must under modern conditions be a progressive depression of the standard of living of mankind as a whole. It is therefore contrary to the liberal spirit, and the label so vigorously exploited, and so confidently flaunted in the face of the American public, is found to have been falsely applied.

But there is more to the question than this. Other interests than the economic call for consideration.

It has been repeatedly stated that the consequence of nonassimilation is the destruction of nationality. This is the central truth of the whole problem of immigration and it cannot be overemphasized. An immigration movement that did not involve non-assimilation might be tolerated, though it might have other evil consequences which would condemn it. But an immigration movement that does involve nonassimilation—like the movement to the United States during the last fifty years at least—is a blow at the very heart of nationality and can not be endured if nationality is conceived to have any value whatsoever. The American nationality has already been compared to a plant. There is, indeed, a striking parallelism between a nation and a noble tree—for instance, one of our own incomparable redwoods—which may be followed a little further, not with any expectation or desire of popularizing a new symbol, but merely for the clarification that it affords.

A nation, like a tree, is a living vital thing. Growth is one of its conditions of life, and when it ceases to grow there is good reason to fear that it is about to decay and die. Every nation, like every tree, belongs to a certain general type, but it is also uniquely individual within that type. Its peculiar form is determined by various forces, some of which are internal and some external. No nation need fear the changes which come as the result of the operation of natural, wholesome internal forces, that is to say, the ideas and activities of its own true members. These forces may, in the course of time, produce a form and character wholly different from the original, just as the mature plant may have an entirely different aspect from the seedling. This is nothing to be dreaded or opposed. No change that represents the natural evoltution of internal forces need be dreaded. But there are other forces which originate without which threaten not only the form and character but also the vigor and perhaps the very life of the nation. Some of these are the forcible attacks of other nations, like the crowding of trees upon each other, or the unwholesome influence of alien ideas which may be compared with harsh and uncongenial winds which blow upon trees, dwarfing and distorting them.

Most dangerous of all however, are those foreign forces which, among trees, are represented by minute hostile organisms that make their way into the very tissue of the tree itself and feed upon its life substances, and among nations to alien individuals who are accepted as immigrants and by a process of "boring from within" (in something much more than a mere trade-union sense) sap the very vitality of their host. In so doing the immigrants may be merely following out their natural and defensible impulses without any hostility toward the receiving nation, any more than the parasites upon a tree may be considered to have any hostility to the tree. Nor can the immigrants, any more than the parasites, be expected to foresee that their activities will eventually destroy the very organism upon which they depend for their existence. The simple fact is that they are alien particles, not assimilated, and therefore wholly different from the foreign particles which the tree takes in the form of food, and transforms into cells of its own body.

Herein is found the full justification for a special application of the principles of freedom of speech to aliens differing widely from the interpretation in the case of citizens. This is particularly true with reference to attempts at free speech which take the character of criticisms of the form of government or the processes of the governing agencies. The citizen is presumed to be familiar with the genius and spirit of his own government, and to be sincerely devoted to it. No check should be put upon his criticisms, as long as they are honest and candid. The criticisms of its own citizens are the wholesome internal forces of change in any government, out of which new and more highly deevloped forms will emerge. But the criticisms and the attacks of the alien may be malicious, and are certain to be ignorant and ill-informed. The alien, just because he is an alien, is not in a position to comprehend the meaning of the various political and social phenomena which he observes about him, he is incapable of interpreting them in the light of their true significance and bearing on the entire scheme of government, and because he has a potential audience of millions equally alien he may do incalculable harm. False doctrines may be infinitely dangerous even though held by those who can not express them in votes.

It actually seems as if each nation developed an immunity to certain ideas, just as the trees in a given locality develop a practical immunity to the pests of their own vicinity. Our own Department of Agriculture is constantly on the alert to prevent the introduction of foreign parasites against which our native plants have no effective protection. Numerous cases are on record—one of the most spectacular being the chestnut trees of New England—where a type of plant which from time immemorial had been able to hold its own in its native balance of nature has been devastated if not exterminated by the sudden introduction of a parasite against which it had not developed a means of protection. So in a nation, ideas are constantly circulating which are inherently destructive, but against which the natives have developed an adequate protection so that they produce no serious harm. But the sudden entrance of new ideas or of foreign varieties of old ideas may find the country unprepared to counteract them. The safest way to guard against such a calamity is to reduce to a small figure the number of those newcomers by which such alien ideas may be introduced.

These considerations do not in any measure justify treating the alien as if he had no rights and were not entitled to express himself on any subject, as has sometimes been done by overzealous patriots under the stress of acute national hysteria. But they do justify the exercise of a wholly different type of control over the public utterances of aliens from that imposed upon citizens, and even more the exclusion of those who in the nature of the case are likely to indulge in un-American utterances because they are imbued with un-American ideas.

There are, it should be noted, a few foreigners whose attitude toward the United States is more positively destructive than that of those who simply can not understand America because they are not Americans. Among this number are those, very few altogether, who make it their business to launch direct attacks upon the fundamental form and institutions of the American government. To them the deportation acts may most appropriately be applied. But much more dangerous are those who insolently regard the United States as a mere economic catch basin, to which they have come to get out of it what they can, confessing no obligation to it, recognizing no claim on its part to the preservation of its own identity, displaying no intention to contribute to its development or to remain permanently as a part of it. One type of this group looks forward to a return to the native land as soon as America has been bled of all it has to offer. Another type looks upon America as a sort of no man's land, or every man's land, upon which they can develop a separate group existence along any lines that they see fit. For instance, we are told upon the best of authority that there has already developed in the United States a distinct Polish-American society, which is neither truly Polish nor truly American, but which has a vigorous and distinct character and existence of its own.

More dangerous, however, than any foreign elements, are certain individuals of native birth who in an excess of zeal for the foreigner, emanating, it may be presumed, from a misguided and sentimental though well-meaning reaction from the attitude of ethno-centric superiority so characteristic of many Americans, go to the extreme of denying any merit in American institutions, and ignoring any claim on the part of America to the perpetuation of its peculiar existence. They are ready to throw any and all distinctly American characteristics into the discard if only we can absorb the "dear foreigners" into our midst. They applaud any expression of national pride on the part of a foreigner as an evidence of sturdy and commendable patriotism, but condemn a similar expression on the part of an American as narrow bigotry. A representative of this type, apparently of native extraction, was talking at an Americanization meeting called by a prominent commercial organization in one of our great cities. Working herself up to a fine pitch of emotionalism she finally exclaimed, "The noblest and finest persons I ever knew in my life were newly arrived immigrants, and the meanest, the lowest, the most contemptible were descendants of the old New England stock!" This was the keynote of the meeting, and called forth a tumult of applause.

The central factor in the world organization of the present is nationalism. Strong, self-conscious nationalities are indispensable to the efficient ordering and peaceful promotion of international relations. Every well-developed nationality is a priceless product of social evolution. Each has its peculiar contribution to make to future progress. The destruction of any one would be an irreparable loss to mankind.

Among the nations of the world America stands out unique, and in many ways preëminent. Favored by Nature above all other nations in her physical endowment, favored by history in the character of her people and the type of her institutions, she has a rôle to play in the development of human affairs which no other nation can play. Foremost in this rôle is the development of true democracy. In America the stage is set more favorably than anywhere else for the great drama of the common man.

Here if anywhere the conditions are auspicious for the upward movement of the masses. If democracy fails in America, where shall we look for it to succeed? Any program or policy which interferes in the slightest degree with the prosecution of this great enterprise must be condemned as treason to our high destiny. Any yielding to a specious and superficial humanitarianism which threatens the material, political, and social standards of the average American must be branded as a violation of our trust. The highest service of America to mankind is to point the way, to demonstrate the possibilties, to lead onward to the goal of human happiness. Any force that tends to impair our capacity for leadership is a menace to mankind and a flagrant violation of the spirit of liberalism.

Unrestricted immigration was such a force. It was slowly, insidiously, irresistibly eating away the very heart of the United States. What was being melted in the great Melting Pot, losing all form and symmetry, all beauty and character, all nobility and usefulness, was the American nationality itself. Let the justification for checking this force for all time be voiced in the words of two distinguished foreigners. First, Rabbi Joel Blau: "The chief duty that a people owes both itself and the world is reverence for its own soul, the mystic centre of its being." Then, Gustave LeBon: "A preponderating influence of foreigners is a sure solvent of the existence of States. It takes away from a people its most precious possession—its soul."

18

The Outlawing of War
Frank B. Kellogg's "Address," November 11, 1928

American leadership during the 1920's, despite the U.S. Senate's repudiation of the League of Nations and the World Court, concluded that the maintenance of peace was a prerequisite for the continuance of American prosperity. Admittedly, difficulties blocked the way of the peacemakers; the treaty settlement after the war had not eliminated conflicting aims and ambitions of national states. Distrustful of the League's ability to prevent war among the major powers, officials on both sides of the Atlantic sought the means to bolster the determination to maintain the peace. The idea that the powers might make war illegal became a captivating one. Building on several precursors, Aristide Briand (1862-1932), six times prime minister of France and minister of foreign affairs, 1925-1930, and Secretary of State Frank B. Kellogg (1856-1937) worked out a simple formula that emerged as the Pact of Paris. The United States and France signed the document on August 27, 1928, and invited the rest of the world's nations to join them. Sixty-two governments including all of the great powers signed the pact condemning "recourse to war for the solution of international controversies," and renounced war "as an instrument of national policy." Secretary Kellogg won the Nobel Peace Prize in 1929 for his part in developing the pact. See Robert H. Ferrell's *Peace in Their Time: The Origins of the Kellogg-Briand Pact* (New Haven: Yale University Press, 1952) for a history of the peace pact. For an unconventional essay concerning twentieth-century American foreign policy one might consult °William A. Williams, *The Tragedy of American Diplomacy* (New York: Dell Publishing Company, 1961). More conventional is Herbert Feis's *The Diplomacy of the Dollar 1919-1932* (Baltimore: Johns Hopkins Press, 1950). Allan Nevins succinctly surveys the role of the United States in world affairs during the period in *The United States in a Chaotic World: A Chronicle of International Affairs, 1918-1933* (New Haven: Yale University Press, 1950). For the wider setting in which foreign policy was made and implemented consult °John D. Hicks, *Republican Ascendency, 1921-*

Frank B. Kellogg, *The Settlement of International Controversies by Pacific Means* (Washington: Government Printing Office, 1928).

403]

1933 (New York: Harper and Brothers, 1960). In reading this selection note (1) what Kellogg regarded as the best way to abolish war; (2) what additional measure he advocated; (3) what steps he took upon assuming office to extend peace-keeping machinery; (4) his estimate of world opinion respecting war; (5) what he thought was responsible for the ease with which the Paris Peace Pact was negotiated; (6) the wording of the pact; (7) what he thought would prevent an aggressor from going to war; and (8) how he defended the treaty against the charge that it was visionary and idealistic.

Mr. Chairman: IN THIS PERIOD OF GREAT PROGRESS in cordial understanding between nations, I am pleased to accept your invitation to discuss the steps taken by the United States, in collaboration with other nations, to advance amicable relations, to remove the causes of war, and to pledge the nations solemnly to renounce war as an instrument of their national policy and adopt instead the principle of the settlement of all disputes by pacific means. No more fitting time could be chosen for this peace movement than the tenth anniversary of the signing of the Armistice which brought to a close the greatest war, the most appalling catastrophe of all the ages.

The best way to abolish war as a means of settling international disputes is to extend the field of arbitration to cover all juridical questions, to negotiate treaties applying the principles of conciliation to all questions which do not come within the scope of arbitration, and to pledge all the nations of the world to condemn recourse to war, renounce it as an instrument of international policy, and declare themselves in favor of the settlement of all controversies by pacific means. Thus may the illegality of war be established in the world as a principle of international law.

There is one other means which can be taken by governmental authorities and also by private organizations like yours throughout the world, and that is to inculcate into the minds of the people a peaceful attitude, teaching them that war is not only a barbarous means of settling disputes but one which has brought upon the world the greatest affliction, suffering, and disaster. If the people are minded that there shall be no war, there will not be. Arbitration is the machinery by which peace may be maintained. It can not function effectively unless there is back of it a popular will for peace.

I can not go into detail concerning all the steps which have been taken to extend the principles of arbitration and conciliation as a part of the machinery for the maintenance of peace. In a general way, I can say that when I came into office I found that on account of the war many of our arbitration treaties and treaties of amity and commerce had lapsed and that many of the boards of conciliation under the Bryan treaties had become incomplete or vacant through death or resignation. These boards have been filled and there are now in force 19 of the original Bryan treaties, among the signatories being included many of the principal nations of the world. We have already negotiated five new treaties and are negotiating many more. We have negotiated with many countries a new arbitration treaty for the settlement of all juridical questions which is an advance over the old form of treaty. In Central and South America practically all of the countries have signed and ratified a general conciliation treaty to which the United States is a party. Under this treaty, in the event of failure to settle a dispute by diplomatic means or arbitration, the signatory nations agree to submit it to boards of conciliation for examination and report and not to go to war for a reasonable time pending such examination. Furthermore, pursuant to a resolution of the Pan American Conference held in Habana in January and February, 1928, the United States has called a conference on arbitration and conciliation of all the states parties to the Pan American Union to be held in Washington on December 10. Thus it will be seen that the United States and the nations of all Central and South America are taking steps to extend the principles of arbitration and conciliation.

I might, if I had the time, show you the progress of this principle in other nations. It is evident that there is a great forward movement all over the world and a growth of an enlightened sentiment for the settlement of international controversies by means other than the arbitrament of war. I might mention in this connection the Locarno treaties and many others negotiated in Europe as well as in Central and South America. Probably no part of the world has made such progress in arbitration as Central and South America, and certainly there is no part of the world where the sentiment for peace is stronger and, consequently, where there is less danger of the outbreak of war.

Arbitration and conciliation are appealing more and more to the imagination of the peoples of all nations. I deem this movement of surpassing importance in the advancement of world peace. When all nations come to the conclusion that their disputes can best be settled by diplomatic means and, when these fail, by arbitration or commissions of conciliation, the world will have made a great step forward. I realize that treaties of arbitration and conciliation have existed for many years and that in spite of them there occurred the greatest war of all history. But this should not be a cause of discouragement, because to-day world sentiment is stronger for such means of settling international disputes than ever before. I realize also that there are many political questions which can not be arbitrated, although they may be settled by conciliation. I know that national jealousies and ambitions and racial animosities often are the causes of war. These causes of conflict can be eliminated through education, through the development of tolerance, and through the creation of an effective desire for peace.

In addition to these means of insuring universal peace, I know of but one other step, and that is a treaty solemnly pledging all the nations of the earth to condemn recourse to war, to renounce it as an instrument of their national policy toward each other, and solemnly to declare that the settlement of international disputes, of whatever nature or of whatever origin they may be, shall never be sought except by pacific means. This leads me to the discussion of the multilateral antiwar treaty lately signed in Paris.

As you know, the original suggestion of this movement came from Monsieur Briand, Minister of Foreign Affairs of France, in a proposition to the United States to enter into a bilateral treaty with France to abjure war as a means of settling disputes between them. The American Government believed that this grand conception should be extended to all the nations of the world so that its declaration might become a part of international law and the foundation stone for a temple of everlasting peace. I need not discuss the details of this negotiation, which lasted more than a year. All notes exchanged between the nations upon this subject were published from time to time as they were sent by the various powers. It seemed clear that no treaty of such world-wide importance, so affecting the peoples of all nations, marking so great a forward step, could be taken without the support not only of the statesmen but of the press and the people of the world themselves, and, as you know, the multilateral antiwar treaty was negotiated in the blazing light of full publicity.

The annnouncement of the purpose to negotiate such a treaty was at first met by much skepticism, the expression of which soon ended because it was drowned in the voice of the people of all nations strongly supporting the movement. The consummation of the treaty was not the work of any single nation or of any individual. It is doubtful if such a treaty could have been negotiated between the ministers of the different governments in secret. I did not attempt it. Neither did Monsieur Briand. We could not have succeeded. And the reason for this is that the treaty is the expression of the hope of millions of people in the world to-day. It came from the visualized expression of the desolated battlefields, from ruined homes and broken men, and stirred the great beating heart of humanity. Is there any wonder that there should be in this modern and enlightened age a world-wide protest against the horrors of war? We are but 10 years removed from the greatest calamity of all time. No one can portray the desolation, death, or the misery and sorrow inflicted by that last conflict. As we look back over the ages on the gradual growth and advancement of our civilization is there any wonder that the people are now demanding some guarantee for peace?

In the negotiation of this treaty I had the hearty cooperation of the statesmen of other countries, of President Coolidge, of statesmen of all parties, and of publicists throughout the United States. It was not a political move. I consulted with Senators and Representatives and public men, the sanest and wisest of our time, and I can say without the slightest doubt that the treaty meets the matured judgment of the people of the United States.

It was an impressive sight when representatives of 15 nations gathered around the historic table in the French Foreign Office and solemnly pledged their governments before the world to renounce war as an instrumentality of their countries, agreeing to settle all international disputes by pacific means.

The treaty is a simple and plain declaration and agreement.

It is not cumbered with reservations and conditions stipulating when a nation might be justified in going to war. Such a treaty, if attempted, would fail because of the complexity of national aspirations and the wide difference of conditions. It contains but two articles, as follows:

ARTICLE 1. The High Contracting Parties solemnly declare in the names of their respective peoples that they condemn recourse to war for the solution of international controversies, and renounce it as an instrument of national policy in their relations with one another.

ARTICLE 2. The High Contracting Parties agree that the settlement or solution of all disputes or conflicts of whatever nature or of whatever origin they may be, which may arise among them, shall never be sought except by pacific means.

There are some matters which have been the subject of press comment which I desire to discuss. I have been asked why we did not attempt to negotiate the treaty with all the nations of the world and make them original signatories. The reasons are these: It was my opinion that to attempt to negotiate a treaty with over 60 nations would entail so much discussion and so prolong the negotiations as to make it difficult, if not impossible, to sign a treaty and obtain its ratification within a reasonable time. Furthermore, if any one country failed to ratify, the treaty would not go into effect, thereby postponing the matter for an indefinite period. It seemed to me best to select four of the large nations of Europe, the seat of the last war, where there was perhaps more danger of conflict than anywhere else, and Japan in the Far East, and to negotiate with them a treaty which would be open to adhesion by all the nations of the world. I felt sure, after very careful consideration, that a treaty satisfactory to those powers would be readily accepted by the others. There were two additions to the six original powers involved in the negotiation, the British Dominions and India and the additional powers parties to the Locarno treaties. The British Government, for example, stated that the proposed treaty from its very nature was not one which concerned His Majesty's Government in Great Britain alone but was one in which they could not undertake to participate otherwise than jointly and simultaneously with the Governments in the Dominions and the Government of India, and suggested that the United States invite those Governments to become original signatories. This was done and the Dominions and India promptly and readily accepted the treaty and signed at the same time as the British Government.

In the course of the discussion, France raised the question of whether the proposed treaty would in any way conflict with the obligations of the Locarno treaties, the League of Nations, or other treaties guaranteeing neutrality. My reply was that I did not understand the League of Nations to impose any obligation to go to war; that the question must ultimately be decided by each country for itself; that if there was any similar obligation in the Locarno treaties, the United States would agree that all of the powers parties to the Locarno treaties should become original signatories of the present treaty. Belgium, Poland, and Czechoslovakia therefore were brought in as original parties because they were the only signatories to the Locarno treaties outside of the nations included in the negotiations of the antiwar treaty. The following countries were parties to the Locarno treaties: Great Britain, France, Belgium, Germany, Italy, Czechoslovakia, and Poland. The treaty contained a clause undertaking not to go to war, and if there was a flagrant violation by one of the high contracting parties, each of the other parties undertook immediately to come to the help of the party against whom such violation or breach was directed. It, therefore, was simply a matter of law that if any of the parties to the Locarno treaties went to war in violation of that treaty and were at the same time parties to the multilateral treaty, they would violate this treaty also; and that it was a general principle of law that if one of the parties to a treaty should violate it, the others would be released, and would be entirely free and under no obligation to take any action unless they saw fit.

For these reasons the Locarno powers became original signatories, and all of the nations agreed that under these circumstances no modification of the present treaty was needed. It was my expectation that if the treaty was signed, it would be readily adhered to by many, if not all, of the other nations. My expectations have been more than fulfilled. Up to the present time 58 nations have either signed the treaty as original parties, or have adhered to it or have notified the Department of their intention to adhere to it. It is my belief that all the nations of the world will adhere to this treaty and make it one of the principles of their national policy. I believe that this is the first time in history when any treaty has received the approval of so many nations of the world.

There are no collateral reservations or amendments made to the treaty as finally agreed upon. During the negotiation of this treaty, as in the case of other treaties, questions were raised by various governments and discussed, and in many of my notes I explained the legal effect or construction of the treaty. There is nothing in any of these notes, or in my speeches sent to the signatory powers during the negotiations, which is inconsistent with, or changes the meaning of, the treaty as finally signed. Finally the countries were satisfied that no modification of the treaty was necessary to meet their views.

To illustrate: The question was raised as to whether this treaty prevented a country from defending itself in the event of attack. It seemed to me incomprehensible that any nation should believe that a country should be deprived of its legitimate right of self-defense. No nation would sign a treaty expressly or clearly implying an obligation denying it the right to defend itself if attacked by any other country. I stated that this was a right inherent in every sovereign state and that it alone is competent to decide whether circumstances require resort to war in self-defense. If it has a good case, the world will applaud it and not condemn it, but a nation must answer to the tribunal of public opinion as to whether its claim of the right of self-defense is an adequate justification for it to go to war.

In the discussion of the treaty I noticed in one or two instances a criticism that by recognizing the right of self-defense, the treaty had been greatly weakened—that if a nation should go to war claiming that it was acting in self-defense, the mere claim must be accepted by the peoples of the world and that, therefore, the multilateral treaty does not change the present juridical position. I can not agree with this criticism. As I have already stated, a nation claiming to act in self-defense must justify itself before the bar of world opinion as well as before the signatories of the treaty. For that reason I declined to place in the treaty a definition of aggressor or of self-defense because I believed that no comprehensive legalistic definition could be framed in advance. Such an attempt would have led to endless difficulty. For years statesmen interested in preventing war have tried to frame definitions of aggressor and the right of self-defense in an attempt to prevent conflicts between states. They have failed to accomplish this object. Furthermore, technical definitions are easily evaded by a nation which desires to go to war for selfish purposes. It, therefore, seemed best simply to make a broad declaration against war. This would make it more difficult rather than less difficult for an aggressor nation to prove its innocence. If there is a narrow, legalistic treaty definition as to the meaning of self-defense or of aggression—and such a definition would be very difficult if not impossible to make in advance—the nation making war might well find justification through a technicality far easier than if it had to face a broad political examination by other signatories of a simple antiwar treaty in the light of world opinion. The mere claim of self-defense is not going to justify a nation before the world. Furthermore, I do not believe that any tribunal can be set up to decide this question infallibly. To attempt to negotiate a treaty establishing such a tribunal would meet with endless difficulties and the opposition of many nations. I am certain that the United States and many countries would never have become parties to a treaty submitting for determination to a tribunal the question of the right of self-defense; certainly not if the decision of the tribunal was to be followed by the application of sanctions or by military action to punish the offending state. I know there are men who believe in the lofty ideal of a world tribunal or super-state to decide when a nation has violated its agreement not to go to war, or by force to maintain peace and to punish the offender, but I do not believe that all the independent nations have yet arrived at the advanced stage of thought which will permit such a tribunal to be established. Shall we postpone world agreements not to go to war until some indefinite time when the peoples of the world will have come to the conclusion that they can make a sovereign state subservient to an international tribunal of this kind? Shall we take no step at all until we can accomplish in one single act an entire revolution in the independence of sovereign nations? I have the greatest hope that in the advancement of our civilization all peoples will be trained in the thought and come to the belief that nations in their relations with each other should be governed by principles of law and that the decisions of arbitrators or judicial tribunals and the efforts of conciliation commissions should be relied upon in the settlement of international disputes rather than war. But this stage of human development must come by education, by experience, through treaties of arbitration and conciliation and solemn agreements not to resort to war. How many centuries have passed in the upward struggle of the human race to substitute government and law for force and internal conflicts in the adjustment of the rights of citizens as between each other? Is it too much to hope for the ultimate realization of this grand idea in the adjustment of international as well as personal relations, as a part of the great movement of world advancement? The last war certainly gave an impetus, and it is for this reason that I believe the time has come for united world denunciation of war.

Another question which has been raised in connection with the treaty was as to whether, if any country violated the treaty, the other parties would be released from any obligation as to the belligerent state. I have no doubt whatever of the general principle of law governing this question and therefore declined to place in the treaty a reservation to that effect. Recognition of this principle was, however, included in the preamble, which recites that the parties to the treaty are "Deeply sensible of their solemn duty to promote the welfare of mankind; persuaded that the time has come when a frank renunciation of war as an instrument of national policy should be made to the end that the peaceful and friendly relations now existing between their peoples may be perpetuated; convinced that all changes in their relations with one another should be sought only by pacific means and be the result of peaceful and orderly process and that any signatory power which shall hereafter seek to promote its national interests by resort to war should be denied the benefits furnished by this treaty."

What were the benefits to be furnished? An unconditional agreement not to go to war. This is the recognition of a general principle that if one nation violates the treaty, it is deprived of the benefits of this agreement and the other parties are therefore necessarily released from their obligations as to the belligerent state.

I have seen from time to time claims, on the one hand, that this treaty is weak because it does not provide the means for enforcing it either by military or other sanctions against the treaty-breaking state and, on the other hand, that through it the United States has become entangled in European affairs and, while under no express obligation, is under moral obligation to join other nations and enforce the treaty by military or other assistance. Neither of these positions is correct. I know that men will differ on the question of whether it is better to provide sanctions or military agreements to punish a violator of the treaty or military alliances to enforce it. But whatever the merits of this controversy may be, as I have already said, I do not believe the United States or many nations in the world would be willing to submit to any tribunal to decide the question of whether a nation had violated this treaty or irrevocably pledge themselves to military or other action to enforce it. My personal opinion is that such alliances have been futile in the past and will be in the future; that the carrying out of this treaty must rest on the solemn pledges and the honor of nations; that if by this treaty all the nations solemnly pronounce against war as an institution for settling international disputes, the world will have taken a forward step, created a public opinion, marshaled the great moral forces of the world for its observance, and entered into a sacred obligation which will make it far more difficult to plunge the world into another great conflict. In any event, it is not at all practical for the United States to enter into such an obligation.

It has also been said that the treaty entangles us in the affairs of Europe. I can not understand why such an argument should be made. It no more entangles us in the political affairs of foreign countries than any other treaties which we have made and if, through any such fear, the United States can not take any step toward the maintenance of world peace, it would be a sad commentary on our intelligence and patriotism. But, it is said, we are under moral obligations, though not under binding written obligations, to apply sanctions to punish a treaty-breaking state or to enforce its obligations. No one of the governments in any of the notes leading up to the signing of this treaty made any such claim, and there is not a word in the treaty or in the correspondence that intimates that there is such an obligation. I made it perfectly plain, whatever the other countries might think, that the United States could not join in any such undertaking. In the first speech I made on the subject, which was afterwards circulated to the nations, I said: "I can not state too emphatically that it (the United States) will not become a party to any agreement which directly or indirectly, expressly or by implication, is a military alliance. The United States can not obligate itself in advance to use its armed forces against any other nation of the world. It does not believe that the peace of the world or of Europe depends upon or can be assured by treaties of military alliance, the futility of which as guarantors is repeatedly demonstrated in the pages of history." I believe that for this same reason Great Britain and some of the other nations of Europe rejected the treaty of mutual assistance. Whether the Locarno treaties will be construed as agreements to apply sanctions, I can not say; but, whether they are or not, I do not believe that it is possible to enforce such a treaty. I know of no moral obligation to agree to apply sanctions or to punish a treaty-breaking state unless there is some promise to do so, and no one can claim that there is such a promise in this treaty. It is true that some of the press in Europe have indicated that the United States will now be under some moral obligation to do so, and these speculations have been echoed in the press of this country. But no government has made any such claim, and press speculations can certainly not be called a part of the treaty. There have been, of course, expressions of gratification on the part of European statesmen and journalists that the United States is again taking an interest in European affairs and is willing to aid in the furtherance and maintenance of peace. I, for one, believe the United States has always had a deep interest in the maintenance of peace all over the world. Why should not our Government and our people feel a deep interest in this question? In modern times no great war can occur without seriously affecting every nation. Of course the United States is anxious for the peace, prosperity, and happiness of the people of Europe as well as of the rest of the world. Because we did not approve of the Treaty of Versailles and the League of Nations in all respects, it has been assumed by some that we no longer take any interest in Europe and world affairs. I, for one, do not accept this as a just estimate of our national character and vision.

By some this grand conception of a world pledge for peace is considered visionary and idealistic. I do not think that all the statesmen of Europe and of the world who have solemnly pledged their nations against the institution of war can be called visionary idealists. Idealists they are, of course. Idealists have led the world in all great accomplishments for the advancement of government, for the dissemination of learning, and for the development of the arts and sciences which have marked the progress of this great growing age. To-day probably more than at any time in recorded history, there is a longing for peace—that we may not again go through the horrors and devastation of a world war. I am sure that the people of this country are willing to try this last and greatest step, the solemn pledge of peoples and of nations. I can not believe that such a declaration, entered into, not in the frenzy of public excitement but in the cool deliberation of peoples, can fail to have a world-wide moral effect. I believe that this treaty is approved by almost unanimous sentiment in the United States and in the world. Such approval means advancement in the ideals of government and of civilization. Of course, I know there are some who criticize it either as an attempt to accomplish too much or too little. Against these men I have no complaint. I have always been pleased to have the treaty discussed in all its phases with the greatest freedom, and I am willing to submit it to the matured judgment of all the world. I believe it is the bounden duty of the United States in every way possible, by its example, by treaties of arbitration and conciliation, and by solemn pledges against war to do what it can to advance peace and thus to bring about realization of the highest civilization. When that time comes the maintenance of world peace will rest largely in your hands—you men and women here in the great audience before me, the many millions who, though absent, are following this meeting by means of the radio, and our brothers and sisters in the other countries of the world. France and the United States pointed out to other nations a hopeful pathway to world peace. The other nations have gladly joined France and the United States and have agreed to follow that path with us. Whether or not we reach our common goal depends not so much upon governments as upon the peoples from whom their power flows. I believe in the people. I have confidence in mankind, and I am happy that I have been privileged to participate in the conclusion of a treaty which should make it easier for men and women to realize their long cherished ideal of peace on earth.

19

This Is the Dead Land This Is Cactus Land
T. S. Eliot's "The Hollow Men"

Thomas Stearns Eliot (1888-1965) was one of the most influential poets and critics of the post World War I era. Born in St. Louis, Missouri, he graduated from Harvard in 1910 and attended the Sorbonne and Oxford University. Eliot left the United States in 1914 and in 1927 he renounced his American citizenship and became a British subject. In common with many American expatriates who fled the "Babbitt warren," as the English philosopher C. E. M. Joad branded the United States, Eliot found Britain more congenial to the life of the spirit than the modern, sometimes sordid, materialistic culture emerging in the United States. A perfectionist, Eliot with expert craftsmanship fashioned his verse to suit the demands of his own high standards. He was a rationalist in the sense that he believed in the intellect in contrast to the emotions or to the unconscious drives which Freud had taught the world to honor. He was also a traditionalist who was convinced that the past had more to contribute to the life of the mind than the present. Literature had a rich life of its own; it should be mined, refined and fabricated into usable form by the poet for the illumination of the present. Eliot became the darling of the young literary rebels until the publication of *The Waste Land* in 1922. Eliot by 1922 was saying in effect, as Malcolm Cowley put it, "that the present is inferior to the past. The past was dignified; the present is barren of emotion." This judgment seemed not to correspond to the experience of his contemporaries. Moreover, as Eliot moved closer toward Anglo-Catholicism, made abundantly clear in his *Ash Wednesday* (1930), those who had emancipated themselves from religious ties and convictions concluded that he no longer spoke for them. A generation later following the debacle of the depression, a second world war, and the constant threat of nuclear incineration, we are readier to heed Eliot's warning of doom that awaits modern society unless it learns to accept "the permanent conditions upon which God allows us to live upon this planet." For an excellent introduction to the literature of the 1920's see °Frederick J. Hoffman's *The Twenties: American Writing in the Postwar Decade* (New York: The Viking Press,

T. S. Eliot, "The Hollow Men," *Collected Poems, 1909-1935* (New York: Harcourt, Brace and Company, 1936), pp. 99-105.

1955). The student will also find *Joseph Wood Krutch's *The Modern Temper: A Study and a Confession* (New York: Harcourt, Brace and Company, 1929) invaluable in his effort to recapture the spirit of the times. *Malcolm Cowley's *Exile's Return: A Literary Odyssey of the 1920's* (New York: The Viking Press, 1951) gives an intimate as well as a penetrating insight into the life of the literary rebels of the decade. No adequate biography of Eliot exists. Eliot's poetry, while highly expressive of certain qualities of life during the twenties, is of such a nature that it needs explication. A brief guide book is *Leonard Unger's *T. S. Eliot,* number 8 in the *University of Minnesota Pamphlets on American Writers* (Minneapolis: University of Minnesota Press, 1961). More detailed and quite useful is *Grover Smith's *T. S. Eliot's Poetry and Plays: A Study in Sources and Meaning* (Chicago: University of Chicago Press, 1956). In reading this poem note (1) the form and dominant mood of the poem; (2) what images and symbols Eliot used to convey a sense of alienation and isolation; (3) evidence of the impact of modern science upon thought regarding man's fate; (4) what ultimate destiny he envisioned for man; and (5) what hope of escape, retreat, or salvation Eliot offered.

Mistah Kurtz—he dead

A penny for the Old Guy

I

WE are the hollow men
We are the stuffed men
Leaning together
Headpiece filled with straw. Alas!
Our dried voices, when
We whisper together
Are quiet and meaningless
As wind in dry grass
Or rats' feet over broken glass
In our dry cellar

Shape without form, shade without colour,
Paralysed force, gesture without motion;

Those who have crossed
With direct eyes, to death's other Kingdom
Remember us—if at all—not as lost

Violent souls, but only
As the hollow men
The stuffed men.

II

Eyes I dare not meet in dreams
In death's dream kingdom
These do not appear:
There, the eyes are
Sunlight on a broken column
There, is a tree swinging
And voices are
In the wind's singing
More distant and more solemn
Than a fading star.

Let me be no nearer
In death's dream kingdom
Let me also wear
Such deliberate disguises
Rat's coat, crowskin, crossed staves
In a field
Behaving as the wind behaves
No nearer—

Not that final meeting
In the twilight kingdom

III

This is the dead land
This is cactus land
Here the stone images
Are raised, here they receive
The supplication of a dead man's hand
Under the twinkle of a fading star.

Is it like this
In death's other kingdom

Waking alone
At the hour when we are
Trembling with tenderness
Lips that would kiss
Form prayers to broken stone.

IV

The eyes are not here
There are no eyes here
In this valley of dying stars
In this hollow valley
This broken jaw of our lost kingdoms

In this last of meeting places
We grope together
And avoid speech
Gathered on this beach of the tumid river

Sightless, unless
The eyes reappear
As the perpetual star
Multifoliate rose
Of death's twilight kingdom
The hope only
Of empty men.

V

Here we go round the prickly pear
Prickly pear prickly pear
Here we go round the prickly pear
At five o'clock in the morning.

Between the idea
And the reality
Between the motion
And the act
Falls the Shadow

For Thine is the Kingdom

Between the conception
And the creation
Between the emotion
And the response
Falls the Shadow

Life is very long

Between the desire
And the spasm
Between the potency
And the existence
Between the essence
And the descent
Falls the Shadow

For Thine is the Kingdom

For Thine is
Life is
For Thine is the

This is the way the world ends
This is the way the world ends
This is the way the world ends
Not with a bang but a whimper.

20

A Retrospective Look at the Great Crash
Edwin Lefèvre's "The Little Fellow in Wall Street"

Edwin Lefèvre (1871-1943), author and journalist, wrote extensively on the subject of finance, its organization, and its cultural impact upon the country. Titles of his books include *Wall Street Stories* (1901); *The Golden Flood* (1905); *Reminiscences of a Stock Operator* (1923); and *The Making of a Stock Broker* (1925). Shortly after the big crash he wrote the article reprinted below. The Florida land boom of the mid-twenties initiated the speculative fever accompanying the flush times of the golden decade. Following the collapse of the Florida bubble, speculators looked to the stock market as a means of satisfying the get-rich-quick passions loosed by the endless vistas of prosperity opening to view. Expectations of great wealth to be made on the exchange stimulated countless thousands of middle class Americans to play the market. It is difficult to know how widespread the participation in the game was; one estimate places the number of traders at slightly over 1.5 million people of whom something less than one million were active speculators. Despite the relatively small proportion of the total population involved in buying and selling stocks, speculation as such had penetrated to the core of American culture. The crash in Wall Street in October of 1929 made that year a memorable one; scarcely a person in the country emerged from the holocaust unaffected by the crash and its aftermath. The best account of the panic of 1929 is °John Kenneth Galbraith's *The Great Crash, 1929* (Boston: Houghton Mifflin Company, 1955). °Frederick Lewis Allen's *Only Yesterday: An Informal History of the Nineteen Twenties* (New York: Harper and Brothers, 1931), despite some limitations, remains one of the liveliest and most engaging accounts of the fabulous twenties, one that ably catches the mood of the decade. °William E. Leuchtenburg's *The Perils of Prosperity, 1914-1932* (Chicago: University of Chicago Press, 1958) is an unusually perceptive study of the period broader in scope than the title or its inclusion in connection with this selection suggests. One might also consult Otis Pease's *The Responsibilities of American*

Edwin Lefèvre, "The Little Fellow in Wall Street," *The Saturday Evening Post,* January 4, 1930, pp. 6-7, 97, 100, 102, 105.

Advertising: Private Control and Public Influence, 1920-1940 (New Haven: Yale University Press, 1958). In reading the selection note (1) the author's description of the crowds in New York's financial district on October 24, 1929 and how he contrasted them with the workers inside the brokers' offices; (2) his explanation of why a panic occurred in the market; (3) his estimates of how many people lost money in the crash; (4) to what device he attributed the bull market; (5) what impact the bull market had upon everyday life; (6) his characterization of stock speculation: (7) the ways in which different people reacted to their losses; (8) his judgment concerning the relative success of the expert and the novice in the market; (9) to what extent he agreed with the observation that the crash was a rich man's panic; (10) what it was in his opinion that drew the rich, the poor and the middling into the market; and (11) how the panic of 1929 differed from earlier ones.

ON OCTOBER 24, 1929, MILLIONS OF AMERICANS recalled poignantly the hundreds of blithe prophecies that our feelings never again would be harrowed by absurd exhibitions of mob hysteria or mass emotionalism in the stock market. We were living in a new era. Everybody told you this, the week before, whether he was carrying ten shares or 10,000. The short cut to riches having been surveyed and mapped, the day of reckoning had been erased from the calendar by that modern efficiency which made panics obsolete.

On this fine fall day, New Yorkers on their way to Wall Street noticed, on nearly every square, places where the crowd had overflowed from the buildings and were blocking the sidewalks. Those were branch offices of stockbrokers. Scores were inside looking at the quotation board. The white-faced hundreds outside were trying to glimpse the translux. In any building where the branch office happened to be next to the main entrance, the nonspeculating tenants could not go in or out without help from janitors or porters; the white-faced men choked the way. They moved their bodies a few inches to let the tenant through, but their gaze remained fixed on the brokers' door. They were waiting for scraps of news to be relayed from person to person—surgeons' bulletins from the operating room, formerly known as quotations.

The patient was worse. Prices were still going down—fast! No bottom! The chances for the miracle that alone could save the white faces were growing slimmer and the faces growing whiter. But they stood there, hour after hour, unable to go away—dying men counting their own last pulse beats. Every one of the hundreds of branch offices in New York had its crowd. I paused by several of them that morning, and, on my word, not once did I hear a single victim tell his neighbor his tale of woe. This struck me as the unbelievable limit of suffering!

And when you arrived at Wall Street you found Broad Street packed more densely than in the old Liberty Loan drives when famous men spoke at noon from the Sub-Treasury steps. Those thousands just stood there, staring fascinatedly at the white façade of the New York Stock Exchange.

The monumental temple of the ticker had ceased to be the purveyor of unearned money, to become the altar where the dreams of millions of men about millions of dollars had gone up in smoke. The gaping thousands had read it in the newspapers. There were not so many tense faces as outside the uptown branches, for these men had not lost their all. Aware that the floors of all the offices in all the buildings within sight were strewn with the ashes of untaken paper profits, they naturally hoped that some of the late rich in those offices who still breathed would presently come out and be seen. So they blocked traffic and waited.

Inside, in not a single customers' room in all Wall Street could you have pushed your way through the hundreds who stood, hour after hour, in a space intended for dozens, their faces showing not so much suffering as a sort of horrified incredulity—the dazed unbelief of men who have been robbed of their all by their dearest and most trusted friend. The same quotation board that had been so generous during so many happy months was now sentencing its former beneficiaries to unthinkable tortures. And yet it really meant well! The tape was hours behind the market, and it was only when reports from the floor of the Stock Exchange came in, giving the actual prices, that the customers realized how kindly the ticker had acted—suspending sentence two hours! But the untickered truth meant much more than the end of hopes. It meant poverty, debt, a fresh start under heavier handicaps.

I visited a dozen offices and nowhere did I see the hysterical melodrama that people always expect in Wall Street at such times. Perhaps the customers were packed too tightly to permit emotional outbursts. But every now and then, when the telephoned reports showed how much worse things actually were on the floor, one man might gulp and another shake his head, answering his own unspoken question with a "No!" Here and there some would grin—the only kind of grin that men can negotiate in public at such a time—and you somehow felt that those were married men, prematurely minimizing the damage, rehearsing for that evening at home. Everywhere else in the offices was pandemonium; in the wire rooms and the outer offices and the cubby-holes where low-voiced colloquies were carried on.

No need to tell anyone what their purport was; everybody knew. Orders were coming in in torrents, to be received by clerks who had not slept in thirty hours. Some firms handled more than 1,000,000 shares in one day; one odd-lot house more than 3,000,000; and nearly all orders were to sell! Sell! Sell! By the tens and the hundreds and the thousands and the tens of thousands, in answer to the telegrams sent out the night before, calling for more margin. Millionaires, workingmen, clerks, merchants, doctors, lawyers, teachers, trolley conductors, actors, and even poets, saw flitting past their eyes, in a silence indescribably tragical, the fateful shadow figures of the translux that told the story of the panic, as befitted the day of the aeroplane when compared with the age of the horse and buggy. The same modern newspapers that during the bull market so often quoted the bull leaders' panegyrics about the new era, now duly front-paged the debacle that was never again to be; and some of them printed nearly one-tenth of the truth.

On that same day, in *The Saturday Evening Post,* issue of October twenty-sixth, you might have read, on page 117, these words of Professor Albert Einstein, indisputably one of the world's great men: "The ordinary human being does not live long enough to draw any substantial benefit from his own experience. . . . We can transmit to them neither our knowledge of life nor of mathematics. Each must learn its lesson anew."

Well, that is why we had a panic in the stock market, which

makes it proper to answer three questions: Who lost? Why? And how?

Before the panic had run half its course, a famous international banker said to me: "Everybody has lost money excepting liars and beggars. Liars don't tell the truth and beggars have no money to lose!"

The head of a bond house, who has developed a statistical turn of mind by reason of his investment business, heard this and permitted himself to assert that at last 5,000,000 people had lost money through trading in stocks in 1929. He admitted that his estimate was largely guesswork, but he swore he had been keeping a careful tab on the business that stock houses did in places where formerly he used to sell bonds. Later reports from his agents and other assistants made him feel that his first estimate had been too conservative. He told me:

"I shouldn't be at all surprised if 10,000,000 Americans lost money directly by the crash in the stock market. You must not forget that the bull market lasted more than six years, even though the public did not come in in hordes until 1928. Of course, there was plenty of justification for a bull market. There always is. But don't forget that this time we had factors that made it the greatest of all bull markets: Increased population, greater wealth, more widespread prosperity, and marvelous machinery for the distribution of bull tips on a scale unprecedented in the world's history. You know that stocks do not go up; they are put up. Incidentally, this observation, attributed to arouse men, was first made by the late Francis D. Carley. The best way to bull a stock is by advertising through the ticker. No ticker, no free quotations. No free quotations, no dreams. No dreams, no speculators. No speculators, no buyers. No buyers, no losers! This time the stock-market manipulators could reach practically everybody in the United States; and this time, also, the manipulators were not old market plungers but high-class bankers and financiers and industrial leaders of fine repute. It wasn't necessary to go to your broker's offices to get the gambling dope. You got it by radio in your own home, as well as by long-distance ticker, by telegraph, by telephone, by wireless, by daily newspapers, by statistical agencies and by neighbors.

"One of my recreations is antiquing. I regularly and optimistically motor through the Atlantic States and New England in the hope of finding bargains in the country shops. Last August, when the danger signals in the stock market were beginning to make themselves plain to an old bond man, I stopped at an antique shop in a small town in Southern New Jersey.

"I caught the owner as he was about to leave. The shop was on a main-traveled highway and a chap on the job would have kept open evenings. But the bull market long ago taught me that a profit, whether on paper or safe in bank, demoralizes all bulls.

" 'You close early,' I said.

" 'Yes, unless someone telephones they are on the way. Looking for anything in particular?'

" 'Glass,' I said.

" 'Haven't any that's any good. I haven't got around as much as usual, this year.'

" 'Don't let me keep you from going home,' I said politely.

" 'That's all right. I live upstairs, but I got to get to the drug store.'

" 'You don't look sick.'

" 'Oh, no. We just meet there every night at seven, to get the close.'

" 'What close?'

" 'The stock market,' he said. I understood then why he didn't have any glass. But all I asked was: 'Who else, beside you, goes?'

" 'Oh,' he answered, 'the gang! Everybody!'

"I am no Sherlock Holmes, but I knew those Jerseymen, representing the best element in the village, met not merely to get the closing prices, which they could have at home from their own radios, but to talk about the market. You know that nine out of ten people who talk about the market really talk about their profits. They crave applause for their cleverness. That is why the profit gets away from them. In this late bull market the long time that the average trader had those paper profits to enjoy was one of the reasons for the huge losses. People became accustomed to being long of stocks. They would have felt uncomfortable without the need to look at the financial page the first thing in the morning and the last at night.

"A rather intelligent commercial traveler who covers a wide territory told me: 'I firmly believe that there isn't a town of 10,000 inhabitants or over in the United States, North, South,

East and West, that hasn't at least one night club. In the past year and a half I have been in a hundred or more of them, and I'll swear that nine-tenths of the people I saw there were having the time of their lives spending their uncashed stock-market profits. It struck me that these people had acquired the worst habits of the idle rich, without the riches.'

"Well," continued the bond man, "it is too early to tell how being busted will affect people who have been living in a fool's golden paradise for eighteen months. My son told me the popular Wall Street word of late was 'multi.' When somebody wanted to say that a man had a great deal of money, they referred to him as a 'multi.' There are not so many multimillionaires now."

Never before did so many people make so much money, or spend it so lavishly, as during the late bull market. Prolonged prosperity makes the new-rich seek new ways of spending; and spending for new luxuries gives to money a pleasure-giving power that it did not have in the less affluent days. But as expenses rise, there develops the need of increasing the income to keep pace with the new living standard.

From hardship to comfort, the gap is a million miles wide. From comfort to luxury, the step is only four inches long. Ask any man who has made easy money.

Stock speculation always has seemed the cleanest way of making easy money. It is legalized gambling masquerading as a legitimate business. It possesses insidious attractions. It tickles the vanity of the speculator to feel that it is his superior judgment, clear vision and financial courage that win the money for him. That is why stock speculators refuse to regard their operations as attempts to get something for nothing. They know that nobody gets that. Speculating, to them, is getting something for something. To cash in is to win the Victoria Cross of finance, the reward of valor. When a man risks greatly, the reward should be commensurate, and so on. Old stuff a hundred years ago, and still going strong.

On one of those awful days when it looked as if the crash would engulf everybody I noticed that a man next to me in the customers' room of a large brokerage house smiled as they dropped meteorlike.

"Short of 'em?" I asked my neighbor.

I had never seen him before, but it was not a rude question to ask an utter stranger. On the contrary, on an occasion like this it was one of the greatest compliments—a diplomatic way of implying that he was the wisest man in that room.

"No," he answered cheerfully. "I wish I were. The reason I smiled was that I was thinking of my wife."

"Here is a model husband," thought I; "one who minds mamma." How wonderful is their intuition!

"Ah, yes," I said; "and she is going to tell you 'I told you so' tonight, and you are going to admit cheerfully that she was right, eh?"

"Not by a damsite," he said quickly. "For nearly two years she has been making my life miserable, telling me how her brother-in-law made so much in Radio; and her friend's husband made $27,000 in Steel; and Tom took enough out of one deal that he's retired from business; and how Joe bought two swell cars for his wife, who had never looked for better than a secondhand flivver; and why in heck couldn't I do the same? All the wives of all my friends were going about, giving disgusting exhibitions of *joie de vivre* and money burning. Of course, if I had the nerve of a louse, she'd have the motor. I was a hopeless pill, and worse. . . . Are you married? You know the line, then. Well, sir, last night I ate my dinner in comfort—you know, in silence. Tonight I expect to be told that I am not so dumb as I look. Tomorrow, when she gets the reports of the casualties in our set, I will be restored to the esteem in which I was held before the bull market."

"And how were you able to keep out of the market?"

"Well, we've always been hard workers in my family. We were all brought up to be what they call plodders. I figure that if I can quit when I am fifty, I'll have a good time during what ought to be one-third of my life—the third when it feels good not to have to hustle. So I just bide my time and buy bonds and preferred stocks and a few common stocks that look good, and have a future that I can see. I don't want a stock that I'll have to wait fifty years for dividends. And, then, I listen to warnings. Here is a piece I clipped from *The Saturday Evening Post* last winter." He took out a long clipping, and while I modestly blushed, he read from an article written in 1928, substantially as follows:

Sold-out bulls would be an element of strength, were it not for the well-known fact that the desire to buy disappears when the market begins to break. When everybody is selling, the bottom looks miles away. . . . The public is bound to lose its money; and the greater the boom, the greater the wallop. . . . When a stock rises 300 points, and it breaks, the collapse must carry it beyond the limits of what was once considered a salutary readjustment of values. I have no hesitation in asserting my belief that the bigger the margin, the greater the loss, when the slump comes. Warn your customers about the real *coup de grâce*—in 1929.

A customers' man in the same office, a little later, told me of the different ways in which people take a licking:

"A little chap had been trading here with moderate success for several months; then somebody gave him a red-hot one on one of the new flotations, and he plunged. A few weeks later the slump came. He was pretty well margined—we saw to that—but the break was so much worse than anybody expected, that we had to call for more margins. The little trader responded promptly with a check for a little less than we asked him. I thought he was being normally businesslike by holding out on his broker, but he assured me: 'That is every cent I've got in the bank.'

" 'Hasn't your wife got a bank account?'

" 'No,' he said. 'She's the old-fashioned kind. Everything is still in my name.'

"On the second break the little fellow's stock was one of the leaders of the drop. It looked as if nobody wanted it at any price. I asked him if he didn't want to let it go. He looked at me and remarked:

" 'I don't know as much about Wall Street as I thought I did, but I know that the time to sell is not when nobody wants to buy. I guess I'll hold on.'

" 'Then you will have to put up more margin.'

" 'I told you I gave you every cent I had in the world already.'

" 'Don't you own the house where you live?'

" 'I don't live in a house. I exist in a flat, and I pay rent—too much rent, if you ask me.'

" 'You must have some assets of some kind. Don't you own your shop?'

" 'Sure.'

" 'Well, we don't want to sell you out. Put up anything you've got.'

"He looked at me for a moment. Presently he smiled, held out his hand, shook mine warmly and, in a congratulating voice, said: 'Mister, you got a fur business!'

"There was another case. I wish it hadn't happened in this office. On that fatal Tuesday when the market broke wide open, this chap saw me coming toward him, and he said: 'Don't ask me. I haven't anything to give you. Everything I had in the world is gone!'"

"He tried to smile, and it was tough, for he was a pleasant chap with a lovely wife and a couple of kids. I know that his one desire had been to make money for them.

"He shook hands with me and said: 'Let the stock go! I only hope it won't show you fellows a loss, because I don't think I'd be able to pay you, ever'—and he walked out of the office. The next morning somebody from his home called up to tell us that the poor devil had committed suicide. He left a note in which he begged his wife's pardon for doing what he did. His brother, who also has an account here, told me about it. No, he couldn't blame us, because he heard me beg his brother more than once to take his profit. He was nearly $7000 ahead of the game at one time, at that—more than twice his original stake—but like most of those chaps, he had fixed his mind on a certain sum. It beats the Dutch how many people think that it is just as easy to make $1,000,000 with fifty shares as with 50,000. They don't think that there is any limit to a rise. That chap couldn't stand the gaff. The same day that cleaned him out also wiped out the little trader. After he got his report, what do you think he said?"

" 'Twenty-seven years ago I started business in a basement,' he said. 'I had nothing but health. Now I got to start business with nothing but health. For twenty-seven years I eat and drink and I make money and save money and lose money. And all the time I was saving money I really was a sucker. I could have spent it having a good time.'

" 'You've still got your fur business,' I reminded him.

" 'I tell you the truth; it ain't worth the mortgage you fellows took on it. Who the devil is going to buy furs this year?' Then he brightened up and said: 'But I'll run it for this firm on a salary! Ask the boss if he wants me to!' "

"Are you going to let him?" I asked out of curiosity.

"Oh, no. We'll take the loss and let him keep the business. He may pay us sometime. Do you know how much this firm has lost through impaired margins as well as through errors and mistakes due to the hellish rush? More than $500,000 to date. You hear a great deal about brokers' profits. On October twenty-ninth we did more than 1,000,000 shares, but we don't know yet how much we really made in commissions, because the machine broke down. I can't tell you how many orders we received, executed, and then reported to the customer. Later, we could not find who bought the stock from us. Lost in the shuffle! We found ourselves technically short of stocks that had rallied, and we had to cover at a loss. The number and character of mistakes that could not be avoided are beyond computing. Nobody can make plain to outsiders the strain under which everybody in Wall Street worked for weeks. For instance, take the day the official records showed sales transactions of more than 16,000,000 shares. You know, odd lots do not appear on the tape. Also, in the terrific excitement of such trading, a large percentage of the sales are not given out to the official reporters. It is safe to say that the actual transactions that day were nearer 25,000,000 shares than 16,000,000. That means commissions for buying and selling —in other words, commissions on 50,000,000 shares in one day. On paper the Stock Exchange houses made many millions in commissions, but it will be months before any of us will know what the panic cost us. The telegraph operators handling our out-of-town business went without sleep for thirty and thirty-five hours, time and again. Trays with sandwiches and coffee were passed around every two hours. None of our clerks went home at all during the worst. My brother didn't sleep a wink in twenty-seven hours. He had been working eighteen hours a day for weeks, and he was only one of hundreds of clerks. Girls at the adding machines and typewriters fainted at their work. In one odd-lot house thirty-four keeled over in one afternoon from sheer exhaustion. In another, nineteen had to be sent home.

"Our worst trouble was answering customers who asked for reports on their orders. With the tape hours behind the market, nobody knew where he stood. I know we didn't at times. Neither did the banks. A chap from a broker's office downstairs told me that a clergyman telephoned for a report, and the broker told

him: 'I'm sorry, but we will not be able to give you a report for
some time. It may be this evening, or it may not be until tomorrow sometime. We will telegraph you. You have no idea what
we are up against. The specialists simply refuse to listen, leave
alone answer questions. . . . You ask me what I think you ought
to do? I'll tell you the only thing you can do: Wait—wait and
pray!'

"That story may not be true, but I can tell you this: If that
man is praying, he is not praying for the broker."

For at least two years, wherever one went one met people
who told of their stock-market winnings. At dinner tables, at
bridge, on golf links, on trolley cars, in country post offices, in
barber shops, in factories and shops of all kinds. If I went into a
hospital, within five minutes after hearing that the patient I
called to see was inconsiderately getting well, I learned that the
nurses, the internes, the doorkeeper, the elevator man, the other
patients, and every doctor on the staff, were making fortunes.
A few had cashed in. The rest were all waiting for a stake big
enough to retire on, and all told me how moderate they were!
It was the same thing in hotels, in clubs, in your friends' offices,
even in the vestry rooms of churches.

The ticker's advertising was successful beyond expectations.
Never before had such sensational advances been scored by so
many stocks, and, naturally, never such fortunes made overnight
by so many people. It taxes belief to hear reputable bankers
and brokers tell about this or that man, unknown to fame, who,
starting with $100,000 or at the most, $500,000, had run his stake
up to twenty or thirty millions of dollars. A man came down
from the north with a little less than $1,000,000, and began to
trade with such success that within three months he had to hire
an office and three clerks. Before the end came he had nineteen
brokers' telephones, and kept them busy. One of his most intimate friends told me that this man made fully $30,000,000 within
eight months. All gone now—every cent! A very well-known
broker, whose exploits in a market favorite, time and again,
were picturesquely exploited by the papers, made $21,000,000
for his customers in one year. The fact that even before
the sad November days the $21,000,000 plus had become about
$6,000,000 minus did not detract from the advertising value of

the winnings during the bull market, when such advertising did the most good.

One of the best known of the great bull operators, who did as much as any one man to boost stocks in 1927 and 1928, was not exaggerating when he admitted that his profits were in excess of $100,000,000 before the end of 1928. How he lost most of that $100,000,000 will be told later. Another man, whose name is a household word to newspaper readers, was philanthropically eased of his burden in March, when a syndicate took over from him 300,000 shares of one stock alone. I am told that the average loss on his line was about thirty dollars a share. The syndicate paid him very much less than the market and sold much of this stock at a profit in the following few months, but in the hectic fall days when everybody was selling and nobody bought, some large blocks of these stocks were dumped on the market with disastrous results. A man who ought to know, told me it was the syndicate, selling, at huge losses, the stock they had taken over from the plunger and had been unable to sell. They were too late. There you have an able business man guilty of as big a sucker play as the veriest tyro, and a syndicate headed by two of the best-known security experts in Wall Street doing the same thing—that is, misjudging the time—which is another way of saying, failing to read stock-market conditions accurately. If such men do such things and lose twenty or thirty millions of dollars, what chance does Joe Smith have in the game?

About two months before the first October break, in the office of one of the very largest stock-brokerage concerns in the country, the head of the firm remarked: "It is a wonder to me that you do not write up the marvelous career of W. H. Roberts." That, of course, was not the name. "What would you say if I told you that this man Roberts has made in this bull market between $500,000,000 and $1,000,000,000? He is the head of many public-utilities corporations and the largest holder in all of them. His career reads like a romance. He is really a remarkable man, and even if his life did not abound in dramatic incidents— which, as a matter of fact, it does—no man can make $1,000,000,000 and not have a story to tell that people will listen to."

It sounded promising, but as I was about to leave, a mutual

friend who was present—one of the shrewdest judges of the stock market in Wall Street—told me: "I am glad I was here to hear Jack's words. Some months ago, you wrote about running past the signal. To my mind, this talk is the reddest light of all. I am now a bear!" This was in late August. Less than two months later, the shares of the companies controlled by the billionaire were selling for 20 per cent, or less, of what they sold for when I was advised to interview him.

Another public-utilities man, whose name was synonymous with dazzling sucecss in his promotions as well as in his individual stock-market deals, was actually reported to have placed the value of his estate at $880,000,000. . . . Don't laugh. Those figures were repeated soberly by men who should have known what they were talking about.

During the first stages of the panic, this great magnate's stocks suffered so severely that in the private office of the president of one of the largest banks in the United States a vice president remarked to his chief: "What about that $880,000,000 fortune of Hendricks?"

"Well," said the bank president, always willing to help a suffering fellow mortal, "there's no sense in taking away the man's whole fortune. Just remove one zero from it. He'll never miss it."

It was in one of the later crashes that Hendricks' stocks broke in a way that made people fear the worst. All manner of rumors circulated about the solvency of one or another syndicate that Hendricks had headed. You heard that the big bankers had advanced him $50,000,000 to tide him over. Another rumor was that his properties had been taken over by a syndicate of altruistic capitalists to be liquidated in an orderly and leisurely manner. Indeed, the gossip reached a point where it had to be officially denied.

SCENE: Same office in same bank.
PRESENT: The same president and vice president.
VICE PRESIDENT (nervously): What about this Hendricks talk?
PRESIDENT (benignantly): Take off another zero!

The original estimate had been $880,000,000. The president took off two zeros. The panic took off more than that in the case of thousands.

Nearly everybody in Wall Street insists that it really was a rich man's panic, and that the greatest losses were sustained by the very men who had been the biggest winners during the bull market. Of course, it was a blue-chip game that the American people sat down to in 1928 and 1929. Literally scores of brokers numbered among their customers scores of unknown and unsung men who, in an earlier day, would have been world-famous plungers. One day a broker friend and I amused ourselves trying to figure the winnings of these unknowns. My friend called up the heads of a dozen firms, and within half an hour we had obtained figures that showed that less than a hundred men had made more than $1,000,000,000 in the bull market—on paper, of course—and we didn't include the super-promoters.

After the panic, it was asserted that very few of these very rich men had cashed in. A watchful providence kept them from becoming still richer by making them think of the income tax or by believing that the hour for selling had not struck. It is easy to hear what you wish to hear. Wisdom whispers, but greed thunders, and the $1,000,000 winners had no better ears than the little chap who, with twenty shares of Wireless, hoped to make enough to pay for a house in the suburbs—not a very large house, you understand, and only a shell of a garage. The big ten did not escape any more than the little million. When the day came, they shared the same grave. A sucker play is a sucker play in summer or in winter, for high stakes or for pennies. The suckers may differ in many particulars, but the sucker play is never anything else than the sucker play. It cost the public probably $2,000,000,000 to assimilate this axiom.

The case of the individual plungers of great wealth is not so amazing as that of no end of business men who enjoyed a reputation for shrewdness and ability as heads of manufacturing enterprises or of mercantile concerns. Here were men long familiar with financial, industrial and commercial methods, as the prosperity of their companies amply proved. Nevertheless, they personally lost more in one week than they made in two years of boom. They overstayed their market like any lamb, their unearned millions proving as inflammable as the pikers' paper profits. There is no appreciable difference between the brand of hoggishness of the multi and the greed of the twenty-share man.

While the panic was on, you could not go into the main office of any corporation whose shares had been actively traded in without becoming aware that the ticker had played the dickens in that office. From the keeper at the gate to the president in conference, everybody showed the strain.

Never before in the history of stock speculation in these United States did so many executives of corporations not only encourage but even advise their subordinates to buy all the stock they could carry. The same fever burned in the souls of all. The honored heads of departments and their underlings alike spent half their time reading the financial pages or talking about their market operations.

Men high in the employ of great corporations have lost or will lose their jobs, just as they lost their fortunes. But of course it is the losses of the humbler employes that are often most distressing.

I met one of the high officials of a widely known concern. He volunteered the information that he had lost every penny he had in the world. From his looks, it was the only thing he had thought of in many sleepless nights.

"What did you have?" I asked.

"My own stock, of course. Would you think such a thing could happen?"

"Oh, well," I said. "You know the old adage: A big enough bankroll and inside information will break anybody. It has always been so. A pool, was it?"

"No; we were not in it in our office, excepting Cramer, the president. But of course we knew all about the pool in Celian & MacDermott's office. They are the house that Earl Seiwell trades through, and he was doing the work. Of course, we chaps in the office knew how much the company was earning, what the prospects were, and between that and what we heard of Seiwell's success in running other pools, we felt certain our stock would go skyhigh. Mr. Cramer, our president, was in touch with the pool managers, so we all loaded up without a qualm.

"You know what the stock did—went up more than 100 points —and still the top seemed as far away as ever. Then it stopped going up, because it was too high-priced to trade in with any comfort, so it was split four to one. Seiwell thought it would be a good notion to merge with North Central Products. From what had happened with other split-ups and mergers, we were sure our stock would be good for another 100.

"One day Mr. Cramer, the president, came into my office as cheerful as could be, and said: 'You chaps needn't be afraid of buying it at these prices.'

" 'It takes a heap of margin,' I said. And he came back at me: 'Listen, rash hero; if that stock should go back to 150, you will find that the company is prepared to take every share of the capital stock at that figure. Remember that and figure your margin accordingly.'

"Of course a good many of us owned stock that we bought at the beginning of the boom, but now we all took on much more at the high level, knowing the stock was pegged at 150. The word went around the office, and I imagine every employe bought. If they had no money of their own, they borrowed it. It was perfectly safe. Weren't all the wise higher-ups doing the same thing?

"Everything was lovely—for a while. But when the slump came and the paper profits began to melt away, we were very unhappy. Still, we knew it couldn't go below 150. On the second slump we discovered that it could. We wondered why nobody seemed to want it at 150. Before it touched 125, all the little chaps were wiped out. When it broke 100 it broke me. I was one of the last. I am not only busted but in debt. Many of our help have lost the savings of a lifetime beyond all possibility of recovery; and I have to see their faces every day! I don't know whether it was inside information or not that busted me, but I have discovered that a firm may be successful promoters and make millions, and yet not know any more about the stock market than I do."

I didn't volunteer any opinions about that firm. I was thinking of the faces he had to see every day.

The vice president of one of the largest utilities corporations, the stock of which showed highly sensational advances all through the boom, told me after the third slump: "I was abroad on a big job for several months. Of course I knew that our stock had gone up beyond all rime or reason. I used to travel between Central Europe and Paris or London, and every time I went to either city I ran across compatriots who developed an amazing affection for me. More than once I wished that my wife were there to see what a husband she had, until I discovered that every one of these admirers invariably ended by asking me how much higher my stock was going. Naturally, I think well of our property, but I cannot forget that I've never had any dividends except from the preferred stock. I held my common because it cost me less than five dollars a share and I could afford to be patient. But if I couldn't very well advise people to buy it at the prevailing prices, neither could I tell them to sell out. So, after some floundering, I finally settled upon an answer. It was something like this: 'Of course you understand that I am an engineer and not a stock speculator. The stock is doing what you should expect of a stock in a bull market. As for telling you whether to hold on or buy more or sell out, I long ago reached the conviction that I am not a stock-market prophet. I am no man to get a tip from. I wish I were, for your sake.' That left them disgruntled, but not murderous."

"When I got back to New York, I found everybody in our office was loaded up. They had quintupled or decupled their original holdings. Every vice president, every head of department, every clerk, male and female—in short, every employe— had pleasing paper profits. They told me all about it. Not only was this true of our office but of the building as well. The elevator men, the barbers, the bootblack, the engineers, the porters, the news-stand man and the help in the drug store were long of our stock. Being in the same building with our company made them insiders, in the estimation of their admiring friends. I gather that hundreds of people got these inside buying tips from the building, and they in turn passed it on, so that thousands were properly advised from our office, and the real inside dope was that we were earning less than two dollars a share on the stock and the price was more than 200. Everybody knew it, but nobody cared about earnings. Their concern was with a further rise.

"Well, I am no philanthropist and I did not feel called upon to come out with an interview telling the public our stock was too high. Officials who did that were accused of being short. In all bull markets, what people buy are quotations, not securities. They are betting, not investing. However, I did my best to make our own people get out. Some of us sold out long before the top was reached; but the under-employes didn't. You see, a profit of fifty points on 1000 shares looks pretty good, but a profit of 100 points on ten shares does not seem so big to the clerk that has just heard how her boss cleaned up $250,000 in that same stock. Knowing that he had never been in the millionaire class, she could not see now why she might not do at least one-tenth as well. Ten to one was the proportion of his salary to hers. Logic is logic. It was logical to hold on."

"Well, many of my own subordinates sold out, but others didn't. Then came the panic. In their anxiety to stave off a worse crash, newspapers and bankers, business men and political leaders all over the United States emitted optimism through a megaphone. Every loud-speaker in the land told the public that the worst was over—always just before a fresh break.

"I can tell you that I don't want to go through again what I did in November. Girls that I had known for years—hard-working, respectable women; many of them middle-aged, and older—came out of the panic flat broke; some of them in debt; all of them wrecks. Do you know where I have just come from? From a visit to my secretary, who told me that she had sold when she hadn't. She is in a hospital uptown, suffering from a nervous breakdown. We are paying the bills and she gets her salary, but I doubt if she'll ever get over the blow.

"I was talking to the doctor at the hospital. He told me that there were thousands of cases of nervous collapse among men and women who lost everything in the stock market—not only well-to-do people but school-teachers, bookkeepers, wage earners of all degrees.

"The day of the panic I happened to get into a Subway car full of Jewish women. They were rocking from side to side, moaning, red-eyed, wan, sickly—stock-market losers on their way to the Wailing Place in Williamsburg. I asked the doctor who was looking after my secretary whether many of his patients had been hit by the panic.

"'All of them!' he said. 'That is, all that I have seen in the past two weeks. One of them is a man of sixty who retired from business six years ago. He lives in Westchester County, has a nice home, two fine girls and a lovely wife. They lived comfortably on the income from his investments. I don't know whose fault it was, but he decided to increase his principal; so, instead of putting up his stocks as margin with his brokers, he borrowed $150,000 on them from the local bank, because he got the money cheaper there than in Wall Street. He used the cash as margin.

Well, he was sold out. Now he cannot pay off the bank, and the interest of the $150,000 takes $9000 from his income, so that he and his family cannot live on what they get from their investments. He is a pretty old man to go back to work, and I don't know what they are going to do.'

"You know, we have thousands of stockholders, for we were among the pioneers in the stockholder-customer plan. We are getting reports from our superintendents in various towns and cities all over the United States. Everybody lost money! Probably everybody had some to lose, but I tell you it is going to make a big difference in the lives and careers of thousands of boys and girls. In our own office I know of seven men whose sons will not go to college next year as a result of the panic. The first vice president of our company—a widower—has a daughter in a girls' boarding school in Connecticut. It is a rather fashionable school and the girls all come from well-to-do families. My friend's daughter, ever since her mother died, has been writing daily to her father, knowing how lonesome he was. He read me the letter that she wrote him on October twenty-ninth: 'Nothing happened today except that all day long girls were busy with long-distance calls, telephoning home to find out whether they would be able to finish school or whether they must curtail their expenses or cancel orders for fur coats and other expensive articles.' Think of what the panic has done to the careers of thousands of the next generation. I do not like to think of the responsibility of certain men and cliques.

"Then, take the case of the people who raised money in various ways to stave off losses which they eventually had to take. Of course, to some extent, this was due to the fact that in this panic there was not one terrific smash, but a series of panics, a succession of liquidating movements with alternations of hope and despair, which was like dying by slow inches. Millionaires followed pikers. Then syndicates and great plungers, and then the surviving little fellow let go. Bear markets have lasted months and years, but a panic on such a scale, of that violence and duration, was never known before. That is why the mortality was so great.

"People survived the first slump, and the second, only to go under on the third and fourth. But it gave them all time to raise money through pawning of jewels, or borrowing on insurance policies, or mortgaging homes—methods that should never have been resorted to. It would have been far better for the panic to have been sharp and sudden, so that there would not have been time in which to negotiate such loans. In nine out of ten cases they meant greater losses."

It struck me as remarkable at the time that so little notice was taken by the daily newspapers of the extent to which losing speculators made use of their life-insurance policies for margin purposes. All the companies in New York reported that never in their history had they experienced anything that remotely resembled the rush in late October and early November, by holders wishing to cash in or to borrow on their policies. The applications ran into the tens of thousands, and practically every applicant wanted the money for margin purposes.

Similar reports came from all the country. Friends in Vermont and Indiana, in Massachusetts and Illinois, in New Jersey and on the Pacific Coast, have either told me or written to me that in the insurance offices in their cities crowds of men clamored for more money to give to brokers who were clamoring for more margin. One agent told me that he thought more than 100,000 policyholders throughout the country had been forced to fall back on that last resort of the considerate father and loving husband, and used their policies to bolster up their Wall Street accounts.

Much of the money thus obtained was lost in the crash. But, of course, more than the mere money loss is involved. It means the loss of that comfort that a right-thinking man feels when he provides for his family.

That was one way in which the new-style panic of 1929 did much damage to the morale of millions. Giving up a life-insurance policy is one degree worse than taking money out of a savings bank for the brokers' benefit. After all, a savings-bank deposit is merely your particular reserve fund for use in dire need. When letters and telegrams calling for more margins come, the need seems dire.

I went into a stationery shop the other day to buy the paper on which I am writing this article. The proprietor was an old friend, a good-natured, philosophical sort of chap who shared some of my literary prejudices, or said he did. We had been friendly for years. He didn't look very well that morning, and I asked him what the trouble was.

"You ought to know." He spoke in such an accusing voice that I said:

"I don't know what you've got, but I'm sure I didn't give it to you. What's the matter?"

"What's the matter with everybody these days?" he retorted impatiently.

"You mean the market?"

"What else? Talk to any man and what do you get?"

"You mean you feel the effect of the panic on your business already?"

"No, I mean I'm busted!"

"What? Again?" And I recalled how, in the deflation slump of 1921, he was picked so clean that we both feared he must lose his business.

He sighed and nodded.

"Yes. I'll tell you what you can do: Write a piece about the biggest fool in the world. I'll give you my photograph."

"But I remember distinctly your telling me that they wouldn't catch you again."

"Yes! Yes!" he said angrily. "That was the whole trouble. Three years ago I knew this was a bull market. I told everybody this would be the biggest ever. No easy money for me any more, because I had learned my lesson. But I told them what stock to buy. Those who bought when I told them to are all rich."

"Are they?"

"Well, they were up to this week. I don't know now how they are; but anyhow, I didn't buy any stocks myself. Instead of remembering that 1921 was an exception, I only remembered that I had lost everything, first in 1907, because who knew that Northern Pacific was going to be cornered? And later, because we had to deflate. And then I remembered, too, that I had to work hard for fifteen years and save every penny, before I had enough money to lose in another bull market. So I said to myself: 'You are not as young as you were. If you lose what little you've got now, it is good-by forever!' Every time people told me how much money they were making on my tips, I remembered how Larry Livingston said nobody could beat the stock market; and if he, with all his money and all his knowledge, went broke more than once, what chance did I have? So I kept out of the market and stocks kept going up. I passed up some wonderful tips. Now, there was Consolidated Wireless that I got from a customer——"

"I know!" I said. "And finally what did you do?"

"Do? I fell for the old bull. Got in. At first I made money, but for months I held stocks at a loss, waiting for a rally. I didn't know enough to get out with a small loss. No, sir, I held on. I put in $8700 cash. It all went. That's the third time I've lost everything I owned in the world!"

"Well," I said asininely, trying to comfort him, "you certainly have plenty of company."

"Say, listen! I ain't the kind that finds comfort because my neighbor has a toothache. That don't cure my neuritis. I'd be all right if it wasn't for my customers. They come in here and I see on their faces what they are going to tell me. But before they can open their mouths I say, 'No, please! Nobody lost any more than I did in that panic. Nobody can lose more than everything they've got. And that's what I lost!' But they all go away mad because I beat them to the tale of woe. But I don't want to think about my trouble, and if I talk about it I couldn't forget it, could I?"

"No, of course not. . . . Did many of your customers get caught?"

"Say, if there is one chap on my newspaper route that didn't lose money, I would like to hire him to stand in this shop with a sign on his chest: I DIDN'T LOSE ANYTHING IN THE STOCK MARKET. People would come around from all over to see that bird. But there is no excuse for me. The third time!"

He looked at me meditatively for a moment, nodded slowly and said: "Three strikes and out!"

He walked back to the rear of his shop, and when his back was to me he blew his nose so loudly that I am sure his brokers downtown could have heard him.

As I left the shop I remembered what a brilliant operator once told me. He had a picturesque and at times highly successful career as a tipster and as a promoter of worthless mining stocks and divers get-rich-quick schemes. He is now enjoying Uncle Sam's hospitality at a Federal hostelry where he will remain a few years, but in his prosperous bucketeering days he told me:

"Listen! You ask me where all the suckers come from and how long they last. Well, they come from everywhere and they last a darn sight longer than people think. These here brokers all tell you that their business is hazardous because people might get into them on slumps, and that, anyhow, when the customers go broke, the firm has to hustle to find a new crop. They say it's worse than the subscription business of a children's magazine where the life of the average subscription is only about three years.

"Say, those birds don't know their own business. They call themselves stockbrokers, but they are really saps. I don't consider I've lost a customer just because I've taken all his money away from him. Hell, no! I've had to scold many of my smart salesmen for talking so rough to a customer who was cleaned out, that it was a cinch that he would never come back to the place.

"'But that bozo is done for keeps,' they say. 'He ain't got nothing left. He's deader than Christopher Columbus.' And then I'd have to show them wise Willies where they were all wrong. I'd tell them: 'I've been in this business longer than any of you, and anybody who kills a sucker after you've cleaned him out is a fool. My experience is that a sucker always comes back three times. Don't ever forget that! He is good for three pluckings. Don't let me catch any of you acting as if you thought the first time would be the last.'"

The story of my friend, the stationery-shop proprietor, corroborated the assertion of the old bucketeer. There seem to have been a great many stationers in the market!

21

The Responsibilities of Power
Harry F. Ward's "Progress or Decadence?"

Harry F. Ward (1873-   ), London-born and American-educated, was ordained as a minister by the Methodist Episcopal Church. From 1918 until his retirement in 1941, Ward held an appointment as Professor of Christian Ethics at Union Theological Seminary in New York City. At the time he prepared this essay he was also the General Secretary of the unofficial Methodist Federation of Social Service and the author of such books as *The Labor Movement* (1917); *The Gospel for a Working World* (1918); *The New Social Order* (1919); and *Our Economic Morality* (1929). A crusader for the social gospel, Ward remained in the vanguard of those who were impatient to see the Kingdom of God established on earth. An iconoclast at heart, and deeply committed to his religious and social convictions, Ward did not hesitate freely to criticize and censure conditions which he believed inimical to the advancement of a Christian social common-wealth. Ward lost some of his following after the depression, when he moved farther to the left in his analyses and prescriptions. In this essay, however, one finds a species of critical analysis more or less typical of those intellectuals who became disenchanted with what James Truslow Adams called "our business civilization." In addition to the book from which this essay was taken there were a number of other symposia and studies appearing during and after the golden era that undertook to chart the motion and direction of American culture. Among the more substantial of these was Charles A. Beard (ed.), *Whither Mankind: A Panorama of Modern Civilization* (New York: Longmans, Green and Company, 1928). Appearing a little later was Harold E. Stearns (ed.), *America Now: An Inquiry into Civilization in the United States by Thirty-six Americans* (New York: The Literary Guild of America, Inc., 1938). Waldo Frank's *The Rediscovery of America: An Introduction to a Philosophy of American Life* (New York: Charles Scribner's Sons, 1929) might be consulted. Less speculative is The President's Research Committee on Social Trends,

---

Harry F. Ward, "Progress or Decadence?" in Kirby Page (ed.), *Reecnt Gains in American Civilization* (New York: Harcourt, Brace and Company, 1928), pp. 279-303.

Recent Social Trends in the United States . . . cited earlier. A summary of British estimates of American culture during the decade of the twenties is contained in George H. Knoles's *The Jazz Age Revisited: British Criticism of American Civilization During the 1920's* (Stanford: Stanford University Press, 1955). In reading this selection note (1) evidences of Ward's point of view; (2) what he thought were unique features in the American heritage; (3) how, in his judgment, these were faring in the United States; (4) what he thought had happened to civil rights in America—and why; (5) what effects he thought these developments would have upon the possibility of progress; (6) the distinction he made between a class culture and a universal culture; (7) what alternatives he envisioned for the United States *vis-à-vis* its neighbors; (8) the paradox which he saw emerging which had to be overcome to avoid disaster; (10) what prescription he offered as a solution; and (11) how he answered the question posed in the title of his essay.

WHEN THIS SYMPOSIUM WAS FIRST ANNOUNCED I said to the editor that the title had established a world record by begging three questions in five words—first that there was anything which could properly be called civilization; second that these United States had a title to the term America; third that there were any gains in the life of this country since the war. To this I added my grave doubts about a procedure which looks for something people want to find instead of going to see what is there. For good measure I threw in my very strong objection to any undertaking which seemed either designed or likely to fortify our comfortable, middle-class religionists in the false security which emanates from the idea of automatic progress that left them so unprepared and helpless when the World War hit them. That shelter must be ruthlessly destroyed before such people will set to work to make the future. So that I should now be asked to review the whole situation is some evidence of the temper in which this venture is being conducted.

I am informed that this series was not planned to give any aid or comfort to Pollyanna Rotarians, that the writers were told to describe what they saw, not merely the promising spots in the scene. Hence the title is one of the customary sacrifices to the great god Publicity. It really should have had a question mark after it. I understand that I am to put in the question mark.

Clearly these reviewers of our contemporary life in this country have reported to us some advances; but they give the impression of having had heavy going, especially at vital points. The best they can do for us is to recount some surface improvements without setting them against the underlying situation or, in the crucial matters of war, race, industry and religion to express faith that principles are being accepted, situations faced, attitudes changed. Just what is the worth of technical improvements in education and government in the face of the extent to which business enterprise, consciously and unconsciously, manages to control them and determine their objectives? The challenge of the Goose Step and of Teapot Dome with all its ramifications is yet to be faced by the people of this nation. Will the few who have accepted the ethics of Jesus in the matter of race relationships avail any more as the black people join the issue on economic and cultural equality than did those of the same sort in the slavery fight? What is the possibility of peacefully democratizing economic procedure and socializing industry by way of gigantic trusts whose predatory claws have been trimmed and who have found some humanitarian feeling, when these dividend-collecting organizations increase a luxury leisure class and diminish accordingly the means of development for the working section of the population? If religion must either function as a savior in the practical affairs of mankind or be sloughed off with other useless encumbrances, where are the signs that an ethical religion is actually developing among us? Where was it when the humanitarian conscience of Europe was shocked by the callousness with which we tortured to death two Italian workers?

These and other questions which our writers have raised, in the nature of the case, they could not answer. That was not merely because the period they were looking at was too short for an estimate of the balance of social forces. Nor was it simply that they were dealing with the aftermath of a war, which always throws the evil of life to the surface and leaves it lying there for a while to poison the air. The answers to the real questions they faced were to be found, if at all, at the points where the field which each one covered impinged upon the fields of all the others. Even a general survey is not likely to tell us whether

or not life is moving ahead in these United States if it merely
tries to add and subtract particular events or situations in the
effort to determine where lies the balance of gain or loss. How,
for instance, is our offer to Europe to write engagements to
abandon war as an instrument of national policy to be assessed
when at the same time we are dropping bombs on villages in
Nicaragua? Are identical or antagonistic forces dictating these
dissimilar events? Or do they represent the contradictory impulses of immaturity? In either case is it yet clear which indicates our future course, or is that left to the historian of another
day to tell?

Because life in this country is still adolescent, with all the
crudities, the warring tendencies, the illusions of that stage, the
best that can be done in the attempt to measure and evaluate its
recent activities and attitudes is an estimate of trends. And for
these there are some standards. When we apply the word
civilization to our collective behavior we challenge comparison
with that kind of life in other times and places which in common
usage is described by that term. That judgment comes with most
authority from those not of our nation or race, particularly from
those scholars of the Orient who have been trained in the cultures of both East and West and have seen the best and the
worst of life in both hemispheres. To their words we had better
listen with humility.

But we have also standards of our own. Young as we are we
yet have a past. It is marked off by the World War, which
changed not only our relations with the rest of the world but
also the course of our own development. In that past the term
American stood for some other things besides machines and
money-making. And it stood for those other things first, anywhere in the world. America was different from Europe in their
minds as well as ours. And the difference was not the fusion of
the conglomerate in the melting pot. For that was Europe, with
its barriers down, modifying itself. America meant more than
that, to itself as well as to the Old World. It meant freedom and
it meant equality. Europe had come to know that these were not
only the perennial ideals of man but his desperate needs. Here,
with many others of another sort, came those who sought these
high goods, prepared to pay the price. Here, with the richest
continent of the globe to exploit, men could and did move a little

nearer to these ideals. For a time the Declaration of Independence, to whose principles so many of its beneficiaries are now recreant, meant something. And those principles are not ours to appropriate or to mutilate. They belong to mankind and it was the whole continent here, South as well as North, that gave the more adventurous of Europe a chance to move again in their development. The test of life here then, with its advantages of great natural wealth and a small population, is whether it now moves toward or away from freedom and equality. The achievement of these values in larger measure than was possible under the limitations of Europe was to be the distinctive characteristic of American culture. Here is where we were going to be different from the Old World.

How goes it then with freedom and equality in these United States at the present time? The answer to this question does not lie in the experience of most of the educated middle class. They are free to say and do most of the things they want to say or do. They feel themselves the equal of anybody and most of them are in command of the means of self-development. In order to see the state of freedom in its simplest and also most illusory form— freedom of opportunity—we must get to the viewpoint of the people who see what culture we have from outside and below. It is those who have not yet arrived who can tell us how free and equal is the chance to develop life in these United States, that is, they could if they could talk. I wonder what the gains that have been written about in this series mean to them; especially if they happen to live in a textile center, a steel or coal company-owned town, on a tenant or mortgaged farm, or even in that apotheosis of our development—an automobile city; and more especially if they have a desire to achieve some genuine culture for themselves or for their children. This possibility, on even terms with others, they have been promised by the American philosophy of equality. Is it not advertised to the ends of the earth as the great achievement of the democratic way of life on which we possess the patent? How does our knowledge of producing and developing better babies—the basic test of any civilization—extend to them? What proportion of their children will go to high school or college? How will that proportion compare with the record of those who came to this land of free natural resources earlier? And with those of other economic

strata today? This is the test of whether or not a democratic
civilization is developing. Does it spread its culture to the bottom
of its population? Is it penetrating to those who are least efficient economically? Or is it static, resting on a certain income
level? This is the test and meaning of statistics of income and
ownership. If we can estimate the amount of culture and the
desire for it among the lowest economic strata of the population
we shall get reality into the dispute over the amount and meaning of the recent rise in real wages for sections of city workers
and of the fall in real income for large sections of farmers.

It is indisputable that cultural equality and economic equality
are interdependent. The former can only be realized as the latter
is approximated. Hence the significance of the recent concentration of income and ownership in this nation. It means a stratified
class culture. It means that the United States is beginning to
repeat that particular aspect of European life of which it has
been stridently critical, and is losing that equalitarian tone which
was distinctive of its democracy. It cannot be denied that to an
increasing section of the workers on the soil and in the city the
door to the cultural life for their children is shut and barred.
Those who survive the influence upon their tastes and standards
of the press and the radio, if they are also physically strong
enough to withstand the fatigue of monotonous, high-speed
labor, may some of them still earn their way through college.
But more of them will go as beneficiaries of endowments. Likewise those who prefer less stereotyped education will avail themselves of libraries, museums and lectures by the grace of charity.
It is the same with religion. That, too, is dispensed as alms, not
only to the unfortunate and inefficient but also to those who are
where they are, as against the prosperous, simply because they
or their parents came too late to share in the initial exploitation
of the unparalleled natural resources of this continent. The control of these resources, and of the trade and investment they
made possible, by the successful, under the original American
doctrine of freedom of opportunity, is the stern economic fact
which determines the future of that doctrine.

To know how far it has been abandoned, it is necessary to
estimate that intangible thing—public opinion. But there can be
little doubt about the public temper since the war. The official
hypothesis of the country, almost unanimously repeated by the

press, is that the more money we let the successful money-makers acquire the better off we will all be. That is, the more inequality we have in economic control the more equality in all things else. Apparently this paradoxical dogma has been accepted with acquiescence by most of the people. At least they are supposed to be satisfied with the radios, cars, silk hosiery they are supposed to be owning. But if all of this should turn out to be something more than the illusions of a fool's paradise what does it mean in essence? If the greater part of the population of this free man's country is from now on to get more goods and culture only by grace of the captains of industry and finance, exactly as the underlying citizens of Germany got some of these things before the war by grace of Bismarck and the Kaiser as God-appointed trustees of the new Teutonic capitalism, is not this clearly the reversal of the distinctive American process?

Heretofore it has been our boast that a man could get what he needed of the true values of life by his own effort, joined co-operatively with the efforts of others who were equally free and equally certain of being dependent upon their own initiative and of being assured the just results of its exercise. But now most of us are to be recipients of the overflowing productivity of those who have a genius for the making and care of money. Out of their magnanimity, and the intelligence of their self-interest, they will provide for the rest of us. It looks as though not the idle rich but the honest poor were from now on to be parasites. In any event, so far as it is accepted, to the degree that it is embodied in policy and law, this doctrine is the absolute denial of our original proclamation of equality of opportunity, the complete destruction of its practice. This is no sudden turn. The World War with its financial aftermath, made vocal the fact that we had been treading a new way of life ever since our free land, timber and minerals, came to an end. If this is the permanent trend, there can be no question but that it means decadence. If the children of those who once set up a new standard of freedom and equality, in terms of culture as well as politics, can be satisfied with the present equivalent of bread and circuses as a substitute for the control of their own development, it means that corruption has reached the heart of the democratic experiment and is not merely an excrescence on its skin.

That the situation has this ominous possibility is made clearer when we look at the state of freedom. There definite facts speak louder than in the matter of equality of cultural opportunity. The similarity in external appearance, the ease with which income and occupational differences are crossed in conversation, which so impress Europeans habituated to a world of status inherited from feudalism, carries with it no corresponding equality in control of government or of the means of livelihood. A discriminating visitor from across the sea recently remarked that our social attitudes were more, our institutions less, democratic than those of his country. It is increasingly difficult for the ordinary run of citizen to make himself effective in the machinery of politics. The net result of the company union schemes that have propagated themselves so abundantly since the war is to strengthen the control of industry by a paternalistic, financial oligarchy and so to make more difficult and costly a real sharing of power.

If there be doubt about this, there is certainly no question concerning what has been happening to those who seek to change our political and economic institutions in the direction of the original American ideals of freedom and equality. For them there are blacklists, injunctions, the fists, clubs and horses' hoofs of the police. If these prove insufficient, then there are frame-ups, long jail sentences, and in extremity, the electric chair. When the workers in our mines, mills and factories, true to the American tradition, try to push open the door of opportunity which they see closing against their children, they find behind that door all the powers of the government.

Since the War most of our states have passed laws which can be, and in some cases are, administered so as to prevent any advocacy of basic change in our political or economic institutions. These laws and this use of them have now been twice upheld by the Supreme Court, with a small dissenting minority. Since the war it has become the habitual practice of local officials in a number of industrial centers arbitrarily to forbid the exercise of the historic rights of free speech and then further brutally to break up peaceful assemblage for public protest against this and other administrative abuses. Again, the courts, instead of rebuking such unconstitutional tyranny, have given jail sentences to the defenders of our traditional freedom. It is true that a recent decision in New Jersey has put a stop to the use of the law regarding unlawful assembly to prevent peaceful protest against wrongs and emphatically affirms the necessity of the most liberal interpretation of the historic civil liberties. But in other industrial states the opposite practice and law continue. The denial of free speech is therefore now entrenched in legal precedent. The courts have torn up and thrown away the Bill of Rights and rewritten the Constitution. Jefferson and Lincoln are now only historic names. Their principles are enshrined for lip worship; they are no longer effective to charm away the demon of tyranny. In place of our supposed constitutional rights we have judge-made law, evolved by former corporation lawyers, whose aim and habit throughout their professional career has been not the preservation of freedom but the protection of property. Inevitably when these conflict they decide for the lesser value.

This loss of civil liberties is one of the two most significant and revealing trends in our recent public life. It cannot be dismissed as a temporary holdover of the supposedly necessary suppression of wartime. The war, through the Espionage Act, gave the legal precedent for later expansions of repression, but this, like the other determining development of recent history—our growing imperialism—is the result of a long continued concentration of ownership and income, accelerated by the enormous increase of financial wealth which the war brought in its train. The inevitable concomitant of this economic fact is that the propertied class should use the state wherever possible to prevent change in the property system and that the state should then use coercion, if necessary, to prevent advocacy of change. Here is the chief reason why liberty is now mutilated and sometimes killed in this land of the free. That is why Fascism has become the practice of some of those who denounce its rejection of democracy, that is why there are American citizens who will in private declare their belief that it is necessary for the salvation of this country.

The meaning of our recent and growing repression of historic civil liberties cannot be assessed by balancing against it any increase of comfort that has come to certain sections of the people. Judging from the apathy with which this destruction of a vital tradition has been viewed by the public, the police and the courts have behind them sufficient support to register a change in ideals. The desire for freedom of a revolutionary, pioneer stock in a land of opportunity is not that of a wealthy, capitalistic nation, rapidly becoming class-stratified. The ultimate significance of this lies in the future. If it registers a permanent change in the mind-set of this nation then the possibility of progress by way of the democratic process is ruled out, and only the way of conflict is left. The continuance of the use of coercion by the democratic state to prevent certain types of discussion of the distribution of economic power means that coercion will be used in the effort to secure and prevent that distribution.

To avert that contingency, already it is necessary to reverse two Supreme Court decisions and the decisions of several courts of last resort in several states. Most of the force of government and most of the power of law is now most of the time behind property rights, regardless of the results to freedom or social progress. This means that the weight of the American government is thrown a good deal of the time against the struggle of the masses for freedom and equality, to which purpose the government was once dedicated. If this tendency is not reversed it means that the democratic state has lost its function. It was to make possible social change without recourse to force and violence. In so far as it is now preventing discussion of change it is now making inevitable the use of force and violence to secure change. Indeed in many instances of current record it is itself the first to use the force and violence which it was supposed to make unnecessary. Thus does capitalistic society add to its distribution of bread and circuses in place of the rights of a free citizenship the use of another Pretorian Guard in the vain attempt to maintain power which has outlived its usefulness.

If this trend cannot be reversed before its gets too late, if education and religion can do no more to prevent this country from drifting into the class war than they did to keep it from being pulled into the World War, then the meaning of recent improvements in either our comforts or our institutions, will be to make the next advance in human life more costly than it would have been without them, because they increase both the destructiveness and the bitterness of the conflict. They mean more things to defend or to capture. Russia and China can pass into a cooperative economic order by way of civil warfare with less cost than Germany, Great Britain or the United States. Yet at present with us the economic world, with the state behind it, is definitely turning toward that catastrophe. The Sacco-Vanzetti tragedy cracked for a moment the crust of our sodden, guzzling complacency and showed those who have eyes to see the molten lava beneath. Education and religion are theoretically against the conflict method as a means to progress. What they are worth is now to be proved. Is there any evidence in the last decade that they have checked a trend which goes clearly against their basic purpose and which if it continues will nullify any other gains they may have made?

The inexorable fate of a class culture is to contribute to more of the people whatever gains it has wrought out in its course only through a conquest of power by the rising class. The only way it can avoid this fate is by becoming a universal culture, that is, by ceasing to be. If we want to know whether what we have here is merely another class culture which in time must go the way of its predecessors of the old world, we shall once more have to get the viewpoint of those who see us from without. It is at the point of our impact upon other peoples that the nature of our way of life is revealed. Civilization in an inter-communicating, inter-dependent world is henceforth universal and the measure of the culture of any particular people is those elements in their life which the other peoples recognize to have common worth.

A class culture is inevitably nationalistic and imperialistic. It asserts the same privileges against other nations abroad that it holds against other classes at home. It is either patronizing or aggressive, condescending or cruel, supercilious or blatant. In short, it is typically one hundred per cent American; it is America First; it is the supremacy of the White Nordic Protestant, or of the intelligent who have tested the intelligence of the others and signed the certificate of their own. But a manner of living that is entitled today to the name civilization must be part and parcel of the whole life and struggle of mankind. It must both draw from and pour into the common pool of resources for the development of the common life of man. It must be not only willing but anxious to universalize its gains, to share its experience and resources with all other peoples and in like manner to receive from them. Because we now live and move on the world stage we can no longer measure one sectional life against another under the term civilizations. They are but cultures, still predominantly local perhaps, but not exclusively so. Therefore the life of any people must now be measured by what it contributes to the rest of the life of man. No way of life that draws tribute from others, that waxes strong at the cost of making others weak, can henceforth be regarded as civilized, no matter what the state of its machinery, art, literature or religion. Imperialism is as barbarous now that the sun of world brotherhood is rising as was the plundering of the Goths when the sun of imperial Rome was setting.

What then is the significance of the fact that by the smaller nations to the south of us we are increasingly regarded as a menace? To an ever-growing number of their people we are a great, predatory power, encroaching upon their freedom with our control and shaping their destiny in ways alien to their desire. This empire of trade and investment that desires no more territory yet must have its tribute. The demand for profit and interest is as inexorable as the requisition of the Roman tax-gatherer. We seek and get advantage, not the mutual pooling of effort and sharing of the increment resulting therefrom. Benevolent we may be as long as our paternalism is not resisted, but we still regard the resources of this continent, both natural and human, as our occasion for profit; and if our praiseworthy intentions are resisted, we can and do kill the rebels as relentlessly as Rome or Britain. On this basis what relations can develop between the peoples of this continent that are worthy of the name civilization? How can a world of mutual effort and sharing be built on investment for profit? The basic facts of economic exploitation and economic inequality will have the same effect in international relations that they have produced in this country in the contacts between the races. Desire it as we may, a warless, fraternal world remains as unrealized as the freedom and citizenship of the Negro so long as one people continues to use another for its economic advantage without an equivalent return. On that basis, all we can have is a class, a national, a racial culture with all the passion and strife that they breed.

This is still more evident when we look at our manner of life from the viewpoint of those on the other side of the world. Then we get a fuller estimate of the nature and worth of this particular development that we vaingloriously call Western civilization, of whose essential features we are the chief exemplars and exponents. The wise men of the East are far enough away to see the whole of our life and not too far away to escape its impact. Moreover, plenty of them have been here to see and learn for themselves what manner of people we are, and to comprehend that which we call education and wisdom. To some of them we are still barbarians, destroying both nature and the past by the use of science for the sake of immediate satisfactions. To others, of more detachment, we are still essentially children playing ignorantly with dangerous toys, eager for motion and careless concerning its direction, more interested in becoming than in being, enjoying the means of life but not willing to wrestle with life itself, absorbed in particular problems but apathetic to human destiny.

To those who make this appraisal of us we are not yet a civilization but only the possibility of one. To realize this possibility we must acquire humility enough to learn from older peoples and grace enough to share with the rest of the world our capacities and the capital made possible by our exceptionally favorable environment. Yet it is against this course that we have recently been moving. Our recent development of investment imperialism and crass nationalism go in the opposite direction. They bring segregation and conflict, not fusion and cooperation. Moreover, the distinctive elements of early American life, its passion for freedom and equality, which have universal value and appeal, and which therefore are the qualities that fit us to take part in the development of a universal civilization, are precisely the qualities we have recently been losing. Without them what are we in the end but another imperialism which must give way to a civilization yet to be established on a different basis from profit?

There is another test which our own wisdom as well as that of the East is beginning to put to our manner of life. The essential characteristic of that manner of living which in the past has in common usage been called civilization, whether it was in China, Greece or Medieval Europe, is unity. Life was within the compass of a scheme; it had unity. Its relationships were ordered; there was a universal sense of status and obligation. But this is exactly what is lacking in the Western world, and most of all in these United States. And over its absence we even exult. The

transition from the obligation of status to freedom of contract is
hailed as a great step forward. Is not the road to the top always
open for the most able? Let every one look out for himself and
the common weal will automatically be taken care of! Let individual selfishness go its own way, within the limits of the
criminal law, and social harmony will come without thought or
effort, especially if we put the most potent curses on every proposal to improve life by ordered effort. The actual outcome of
course is mostly chaos and conflict. We have not yet begun to
make our civilization. We live in a disordered world, in a time
and place too full of antagonisms.

The essence of harmony in those days and scenes where men
achieved some unity of life was in the conjunction between the
cultural and the economic aspects of living. In Greece the aristocracy of the intellect and the labor of the slaves were
interwoven; in China the family determined both ethics and economics; in the high days of Medieval Europe feudalism gave
everybody his place and duty in the common life for which they all
lived. Today there is not only no plan, system or order over vast
areas of our economic life save the control set up by organized
greed, but our cultural life and our economic activities are proceeding by contrary principles. Democracy is the slogan of our
culture, autocracy the dominant principle in our industrialism
which comes increasingly within the grip of a financial oligarchy.
The ethics of our professed religion is to love our neighbor as
ourselves; the law of business enterprise is to make a profit out
of him. Our political philosophy is rooted in freedom and
equality, our industrial practice tends irresistibly toward monopoly and concentration of power. It is this basic conflict between our culture and our economic activities that tears our life
asunder and leaves it broken and disordered. And this disorder
again is at odds with the machine, which demands a technique
of coordination. The condition of civilization for a machine age is
social planning and social control. This will bring not only order
where there is now chaos but spiritual unity where there is now
warfare and anarchy. And since the power machine both makes
possible and requires a world civilization this planning and control
must be on a world scale.

Here is our test. If our economic philosophy and arrangements
make for class culture and conflict they make also for nationalism

and imperialism. In that case any gains which may be registered in a paper program against war, in the spread of education or the socialization of religion are deficient in reality and will not show permanence. If these gains are to endure and continue, the economic forces must be brought into harmony with them, which means they have to be transformed from planless, divisive activities into ordered, integrating pursuits.

What evidence is there that in the last decade or two the people of the United States have addressed themselves to this basic problem of modern life? Everywhere, from child labor to electric power, the scant forces that seek the civilization which the machine makes possible are holding the trenches against the continuous assaults of greed and ignorance. Never was the philosophy of profit-seeking as the way to the Promised Land so vocal or so dominant in our public life. Never was our government so controlled by successful business enterprise nor our press so given over to money-making. When were the people so indifferent to their freedom? The days since the World War are, like those that followed our civil strife, the dark days of our record. In them we have been moving away from our early ideals and away from those by which alone a free and ordered, a just and fraternal world can be fashioned. A sophisticated, imperialist United States is more dangerous to the rest of mankind than one that was ignorant and isolated. It is too early yet to know whether these recent tendencies represent the real drift of the American current or are only a side eddy. If they continue there is history enough to read their meaning—they spell decadence once again. If this country is to contribute anything more toward progress it is necessary for it to apply its bent for invention to the discovering and developing of the forms of economic organization which will enable its original principles to be realized throughout its population and its genuine friendliness toward other nations to become a practical reality.